Peace Education
SECOND EDITION

Peace Education

SECOND EDITION

by Ian M. Harris
and Mary Lee Morrison

Foreword by Timothy Reagan

McFarland & Company, Inc., Publishers
Jefferson, North Carolina, and London

Library of Congress Cataloguing-in-Publication Data

Harris, Ian M., 1943–
    Peace education—2nd ed. / by Ian M. Harris and Mary Lee Morrison.
    p.   cm.
    Includes bibliographical references and index.

    ISBN 0-7864-1487-1 (softcover : 50# alkaline paper) ∞

    1. Peace—Study and teaching.   I. Morrison, Mary Lee.   II. Title.
JZ1237.H37   2003
303.6'6—dc21   2002152687

British Library cataloguing data are available

©2003 Ian M. Harris and Mary Lee Morrison. All rights reserved

No part of this book may be reproduced or transmitted in any form or by any means, electronic or mechanical, including photocopying or recording, or by any information storage and retrieval system, without permission in writing from the publisher.

Front cover artwork by Sarah Sanders

Manufactured in the United States of America

McFarland & Company, Inc., Publishers
  Box 611, Jefferson, North Carolina 28640
    www.mcfarlandpub.com

Acknowledgments

The authors would like to express special thanks for those people who have made the writing and publication of this book possible. Particular thanks go to our spouses, Sara Spence and William Upholt, whose deep commitment to social justice has been inspirational. We thank also Timothy Reagan for agreeing to write the foreword. Thanks go to our children for teaching us, in their own ways, how to be peacemakers: Paul Spellman, Jessie Washburne-Harris and Gretchen and Boyce Upholt. We particularly would like to acknowledge the contributions given us for this manuscript by Aline Stomfay-Stitz, Åke Bjerstedt and Helen Raisz.

Without the courage and conviction of those thousands of individuals involved in peace movements throughout the world, this book would not have been possible. We are indebted to these people for the hope they have provided us. We also would like to recognize the support we have each received from our Quaker spiritual communities, adding to our awareness of the role of nonviolence and love in the affairs of human beings.

Ian Harris would like to thank the students he has taught in peace education classes at the University of Wisconsin-Milwaukee since 1993. They have dared to open themselves up to exploring the frightful issues of violence in their lives and have supported his quest for peace and justice. Mary Lee Morrison would like to thank all of the young people and adults with whom she has taught and collaborated, elementary age through college, and the dedicated teachers, administrators and community and church leaders who have made a commitment to educating for peace and have been an inspiration to her.

The various peace organizations with which the authors have been associated have provided both an activist and an academic framework for their efforts in peace education. Colleagues within these organizations have inspired us by helping to legitimize this growing field. These include the International Peace Research Association and its Peace Education Commission, The Peace and Justice Studies Association (formerly the Consortium on Peace Research, Education and Development and the Peace Studies Association), The Society for the Study of Peace, Conflict and Violence, the Peace Psychology Division 48 of the American Psychological Association, The New England Peace Studies Association, the Fellowship of Reconciliation, the American Friends Service Committee, and the Peace Education Special Interest Group of the American Educational Research Association.

In the year 2001 as Dr. Harris was preparing to teach his course on "Peace Education," he was told by his publishers at McFarland that the original version of the book was on the verge of going out of print. He was asked if he would be interested in putting out a new edition. He was pleased because since the original publication there have been many new developments in peace education. Pressed for time, he contacted Dr. Mary Lee Morrison and asked her to co-author this second edition. Dr. Morrison herself enjoyed collaborating on this important work.

Table of Contents

Acknowledgments   v
Foreword by Timothy Reagan   1
Introduction   3

1. What Is Peace Education?   9
2. Religious and Historical Concepts of War, Peace and Peace Education   37
3. The Practice of Peace Education—What Does It Look Like? Types of Peace Education   65
4. Peace Education as Empowerment Education   84
5. Getting Started: First Steps in Educating for Peace   97
6. Essential Concepts for the Teaching of Peace   116
7. Foundations for Educating for Peace: Families and Issues in Child and Adult Development   145
8. Sensitive Issues in Peace Education   164
9. Schools as Cultures of War: Overcoming Obstacles   191
10. Moving Forward with Peace Pedagogy: The Basics for Teaching Peace   207
11. Conclusion: Visions for a More Hopeful and Interdependent World   227

Appendix: Syllabus for a Course in Peace Studies   243
Notes   251
Bibliography and Resource Guide   271
Index   293

Foreword

Baruch Spinoza's observation that "Peace is not an absence of war"[1] has become something of a rhetorical commonplace, and yet it is an important point that requires both reflection and commitment. Peace education in all its forms is, at the most basic level, concerned with the creation of a better world. It shares this goal with education more broadly conceived, of course, but has a special and profound focus. If the purpose of education is, as the authors of *Peace Education* suggest, "to reveal and tap into those energies that make possible the full human enjoyment of a meaningful and productive existence," then peace education must be not only an important part of that process, but a necessary prerequisite for it. As Leland Miles, the President Emeritus of the International Association of University Presidents, once noted, "Peace is not a discipline, but a problem, in fact, the *ultimate* problem. And all academic fields ... can help provide solutions to that problem."[2] Along similar lines, every aspect of education can and should be utilized to promote peace and understanding, as this book makes clear.

The authors of this second edition of *Peace Education* deserve our thanks for their hard work in producing a valuable and timely text that addresses many of the central issues surrounding contemporary peace education, particularly in the U.S. context. They deserve far more than this, though, as well: their efforts challenge us, as parents, educators, and citizens, to take seriously the need to strive for making peace a reality in our own families, communities, and world.

Bahá'u'lláh, the founder of the Bahá'í faith, asserted that "It is not for him to pride himself who loveth his own country, but rather for him who loveth the whole world. The earth is but one country, and mankind its citizens."[3] While such sentiments would seem to be contradicted by the ongoing violence in many parts of the world reported to us on a daily basis, they are at the same time increasingly being recognized as fundamentally true by more and more people throughout the world—and thus, as worthy of all of our efforts to promote not simple peace, but justice. Returning to Spinoza, peace is not the absence of war—rather, "it is a virtue, a state of mind, a disposition for benevolence, confidence, justice." Peace is our future, and peace education is a key means toward reaching that future.

Timothy Reagan
The University of Connecticut

Notes

1. Baruch Spinoza, *Theological-political treatise* (1670).
2. Leland Miles, "Forword," *Language and peace*, eds. Christina Schäffner and Anita Wenden (p. viii). Amsterdam: Hardwood Academic Publishers, 1995.
3. Bahá'u'lláh, *Gleanings from the writings of Bahá'u'lláh* (CXVII, p. 250). Wilmette, IL: Bahá'í Publishing Trust, 1976.

Introduction

Some years ago, an art professor at a large Midwest university asked his students to draw pictures depicting peace. His students were bewildered by this request. Many thought for a while, but had a hard time imagining peaceful images. After a while a few students drew pictures of rainbows, doves, or other natural scenes. These students had a hard time responding to this simple request because the concepts associated with peace are not prevalent in our contemporary culture. On the contrary, images of violence, destruction, and death often dominate.

In 1910 William James, the distinguished American philosopher, wrote "The Moral Equivalent of War," an essay stating that educators and leaders should wage a campaign against the militaristic thinking that was perverting civilization. Such a campaign would galvanize popular opinion, capturing the imagination of citizens heretofore influenced by war, often associated with heroism, bravery, and glory.

The struggle for peace, if it is to be successful, must also provoke courage, must be understood as a heroic task, and must recruit thousands if not millions of converts willing to renounce violent means to settle disputes. Educators have an important role to play in this struggle because they help to influence the important values and beliefs of their students.

Since the nineteenth century, social reformers have looked to schools, churches and community groups to provide the basic foundations for changes in society. Those opposed to the horrors of war have held out hope that education might help create a more peaceful society by raising young people to have an aversion to violence, an international awareness, a desire to settle disputes in nonviolent ways, an ability to resolve social conflicts peacefully, and an understanding of the calamity of war.

Most recently, fear of war has grown because nuclear weapons threaten the very existence of human civilization. War has "come home" to citizens of the United States, as a result of the attacks on the World Trade Center and the Pentagon on September 11, 2001. Forty years after the development of the first atomic weapons, masses of citizens around the world are coming to grips with their horrifying consequences. The very nature of war has dramatically changed over the course of the twentieth century. No longer seen as purely conflicts between autonomous nation-states, much of modern warfare exists *within* countries and regions and guerrilla warfare and terrorist attacks portend more of the same for the immediate and long-term future.

Much needs to be learned and taught about the complex forces promoting violence and ways to create a more hopeful and interdependent world. Peace education is becoming a more widely heralded field, including national and local organizations providing conferences, courses, curricula, public events, and seminars that enhance public awareness about the problems of war and peace. School districts are adopting resolutions requiring teachers to address the issues around violence and war. The number of schools adopting conflict resolution and peer mediation programs has dramatically increased. Churches are conducting forums, workshops, retreats, and study groups to inform their congregations about the consequences of current military strategy. Colleges are teaching courses and funding research institutes that concentrate on war, peace, and conflict. Scholars are publishing research on the problems associated with violence. Concerned citizens are conducting community education forums to draw attention to policies that promote war. A large peace movement with millions of members in countries throughout the world is demanding the abolition of war and the resolution of conflicts by peaceful means. Organizations, by using educational means to promote knowledge about peace and how to achieve it, are discovering the richness of the pedagogy and practices concerned with creating a more hopeful world.

Peace education involves students and educators in a commitment to create a more just and peaceful world order. This type of education (adaptable to all ages and all sorts of settings) provides citizens with information about current policies, sharpens their ability to analyze current states of affairs, encourages commitment to various spheres of individual concern and endeavor—politics, public affairs, trade union activities, social and cultural life—and strives to promote the free will necessary to make personal choices about public policy. Students of peace education study current defense policies so that they might either support or challenge them. Peace educators point current and future citizens towards practical steps they might take to resolve conflicts in their own lives, as well as to become more effective actors in political systems. Although schools provide an ideal forum for dealing with the issues of violence, these public institutions are not the only arena for programs dealing with peace and war. Because adults, in addition to young people, need to be informed about these critical issues, church groups, neighborhood organizations, civic clubs, and volunteer associations are becoming actively involved in peace education. Such community groups also provide programs addressing conflict and peace issues for young people.

Peace education enhances the purpose of education, which is to reveal and tap into those energies that make possible the full human enjoyment of a meaningful and productive existence. Educators try to create the grounding for a healthy growth and development in children and adults. The nature of human consciousness, as Camus wrote, requires a belief in the future. Thus, as modern nations produce weapons systems that can annihilate human existence, this may portend the altering of the structure of human consciousness, which will in turn affect pedagogical relationships between teachers and students. Students who don't believe in the future may give up in school. The gravity of not dealing with issues around war and peace may make many educational activities meaningless.

Teachers at all levels can contribute both by helping their students understand and deal creatively with the consequences of violent human behavior and by teaching them how to be peacemakers. Securing peace will require knowledge, changing attitudes, new ways of behaving, skills for managing conflict, and political change.

This book, *Peace Education*, introduces a relatively new area of educational reform. It has been written for a broad audience that includes school teachers and personnel, university professors, scholars, church and community leaders, and peace movement activists. Many different types of people are currently concerned with peace, and the issues of violence that spark their interest cover many different realms, from domestic abuse to international terrorism. Such diversity requires a book with many different foci. We have attempted to address these in useful ways.

This second edition of *Peace Education*, in addition to including the contributions of a second author, Mary Lee Morrison, provides readers with revisions in content and the reorganization of some chapters. The world has dramatically changed since the original publication in 1988. The very notion of what we mean by peace has been deeply affected by the events of September 11, 2001. Included in this new edition are contributions of feminist theorists to our understanding of peacemaking. There is also a section on the role of the family in educating for peace. Additional discussions of nonviolence appear in the material in several chapters. The final chapter on creating visions and hope is new as well.

It is important to mention that the focus of the book is, in large degree, oriented to peace educators in the United States. Delimiting has occurred for mainly two reasons: both authors have practiced and taught mainly within the United States, and to cover international peace education would greatly increase the scope and length of the book. This is not to say, however, that those working across global cultures cannot find useful information herein. This is our hope.

Chapter 1 gives an overview of the concepts of peace and of peace education. Peace education is both a philosophy and a process, involving skills and understanding. Various strategies for achieving peace are discussed as well as assumptions and goals.

Chapter 2 discusses some religious and historical conceptions of war, peace and peace education. The idea of peace is rooted in all of the world's religions. In addition, there have been rich contributions to the literature of peace and its pedagogy from both European and American educators and philosophers. A brief history of peace education is included.

Chapter 3 discusses the various types of peace education. The role of human rights and of the United Nations is included as well as a description of peace education in adult settings. A comparison of peace education with the discipline of peace studies is included.

Chapter 4 raises issues relating to empowerment and social change. Along with empowerment comes the questioning of societal norms. The notion of schools as enforcers of the "status quo," and agents of oppressive structures is addressed. Peace education can help both individuals and larger constituencies deal with the fears involved in social change. To be effective, this must be done within the context of community.

Chapter 5 describes ways to begin to implement peace education in schools, colleges, churches and community settings. Two key themes are finding good resources and connecting with like-minded educators.

Chapter 6 clarifies key concepts and topics relevant to the teaching of peace. Issues touched on are the defense establishment, world order and the United Nations, the role of nongovernmental organizations (NGOs), and creative conflict resolution and cross-cultural dialoguing. There is discussion of various theories of the root causes of violence, and a large section on nonviolence and its role in education and the movement toward restorative justice and international truth commissions.

Chapter 7 examines important factors in human growth and development, both biological and cultural, relating to students' and adults' motivations to work for peace and social change. There is discussion of the role of the family. Feminists have contributed to related pedagogical thinking, advocating the role of nurturance and care in educational settings.

Peace education is essentially moral education. Educators' roles in helping with this process of growth and development are crucial.

Chapter 8 discusses some sensitive issues, of which it is helpful for peace educators to be aware. Some topics included are: propaganda versus information, the controversial nature of language, the long-term nature of peace education, emotions, and differing attitudes and values and the effects of media violence on children and adults and its implications for peace educators. Included also is a discussion of the evaluation of peace education.

Chapter 9 evaluates various barriers facing those who teach peace in classrooms and in communities. These include psychological, cultural, political, and educational (structural).

Chapter 10 explores the "how of peace education"—optimal pedagogy and practices. Classroom practices are interrelated with the ideas of cooperative learning and democratic community building.

Chapter 11—the final chapter—explores the important links between hopeful visions of a future world and the concepts of peace education. The literature of futures studies is helpful as a way of integrating the important work involved in imaging and then putting visions "into practice." A holistic view of a sustainable planet is necessary for there to be true peace and justice.

Finally, at the back of the book are a list of helpful peace education resources, a bibliography, an appendix (the syllabus for the peace education course taught by Ian Harris), and an index.

We conclude this introduction with an excerpt from a 1992 poem by Quaker economist and poet Kenneth Boulding:

For the Learning of Peace

Now, when the world so desperately needs peace
We all need endlessly to learn and teach
And teach and learn, as far as we can reach
To make cruel war decline, and peace increase
For peace, with all blessings in its train
Comes from unused potential in our brain

Ian Harris
The University of Wisconsin–Milwaukee

Mary Lee Morrison
Pax Educare–The Connecticut Center for Peace Education

CHAPTER 1

What Is Peace Education?

> *Since wars begin in the minds of men, it is in the minds of men that the defenses of peace must be constructed.*
> —Preamble of the Constitution of the United Nations Educational, Scientific and Cultural Organization (UNESCO)

Peace education is currently considered to be both a philosophy and a process involving skills, including listening, reflection, problem-solving, cooperation and conflict resolution.[1] The process involves empowering people with the skills, attitudes and knowledge to create a safe world and build a sustainable environment. The philosophy teaches nonviolence, love, compassion and reverence for all life. Peace education confronts indirectly the forms of violence that dominate society by teaching about its causes and providing knowledge of alternatives. Peace education also seeks to transform the present human condition by, as noted educator Betty Reardon states, "changing social structures and patterns of thought that have created it."[2] Peace education is taught in many different settings, from nursery school to college and beyond. Community groups teach peace education to adults and to children.

Violence in our world may be seen in its various forms from domestic abuse to militarism, which has been defined as "the result of a process whereby military values, ideology and patterns of behavior achieve a dominating influence over the political, social, economic and foreign affairs of the state."[3] Militarism comes from values, opinions and social organizations which support war and violence as legitimate ways to manage human affairs. Military traditions—salutes, orders, parades, war movies, paramilitary societies, and other militaristic rituals are deeply rooted in minds throughout the world and contribute a global predicament where nuclear warheads imperil human civilization, where arms races gobble up precious resources, and where political elites use military means to protect their privileges.

Peace education aims to create in the human consciousness a similar, if not greater, commitment to the ways of peace. Just as a doctor learns in medical school how to minister to the sick, students in peace education classes learn how to solve problems caused by violence:

> Social violence and warfare can be described as a form of pathology, a disease. Few people would be satisfied with simply treating the symptoms of a severely debilitating or life-threatening disease. Yet, we continue to respond to most forms of violence by preparing for the continued incidence of social violence and the repeated outbreak of warfare, rather than by trying to eliminate their causes.[4]

Peace education tries to inoculate students against the evil effects of violence by teaching them skills to manage their conflicts nonviolently and by motivating them to choose peace when faced with conflict. Societies spend money and resources training doctors to heal the ill. Why should not they also educate their citizens to conduct affairs nonviolently?

Educators have helped to contribute to advances that have created a global village of our planet. Now it is time for schools and communities to use their crafts to create what Dr. Martin Luther King called beloved communities. In a postmodern era young people faced with street crimes, domestic violence, ethnic hatred and environmental destruction are bombarded every day with a plethora of negative and violent images that make life difficult, confusing, and frightening. Fear of violence is changing the behavior of American youth.[5] The sources of violence are many. Poor people struggling to survive in structurally violent societies that deny them economic and social security rely on a violent underground economy for sustenance. State systems squander precious resources on a militaristic approach to problem solving, investing in police forces and armed forces, rather than quality education and social justice. Families and schools use authoritarian tactics to resolve disputes, teaching young people to use force when faced with conflict. Cultural images of violence capture the imaginations of children.

It seems that one of the reasons there is so much violence in the postmodern world is that people neither understand nor appreciate the power of nonviolence. Education about nonviolence can help counter a culture of violence that reverberates in the media, entertainment industry, politics, national policy, schools, community, and the family. By the time children become citizens, if they have neither learned how to resolve conflicts nonviolently nor how to treat living things in a peaceful manner, they may become violent adults, further promoting dysfunctional social behaviors.

School personnel—teachers, guidance counselors, administrators, and psychologists—can help counteract an ignorance about nonviolence that exists at all levels of society by teaching alternatives to violence. At a time when there is widespread conflict and victimization throughout the world, when neighborhoods and schools are experiencing outbursts of violence, and when there is increasing evidence of racial intolerance and social injustice, educators are turning to peace education strategies to deal with rising levels of violence[6] in schools and to build a culture of peace.[7]

Peace educators approach problems of violence at three different levels.[8] These are peacekeeping, peacemaking and peacebuilding. At the peacekeeping level, educators use violence prevention activities to create an orderly learning climate in schools. These get-tough policies in schools mirror peace-through-strength policies followed widely throughout the United States where governments invest billions of dollars in defense and prisons to provide security for citizens. At the peacemaking level, conflict resolution has become one of the fastest growing school reforms. School personnel are teaching dispute resolution techniques so that students can learn to manage their own conflicts constructively. In spite of a widespread interest in violence prevention and conflict resolution in schools,[9] there has been little or no discussion either in educational journals or in debates in professional education societies about peace building in schools.[10] Peace theory postulates that the goal of peace education should not be just to stop the violence, but rather to create in children's minds a desire to learn how nonviolence can provide the basis for a just and sustainable future.[11] Children who learn about nonviolence can promote positive peace, which is proactive and seeks to avoid violence and conflict, as opposed to peacekeeping and peacemaking which react to violent situations trying to stop them.

What Do We Mean When We Talk About Peace?

Before proceeding directly into a discussion of peace education, it is important to develop an understanding of the concept of peace. Peace and peace education are intricately linked, yet the latter seems to naturally assume the existence of, or at least the conceptual visioning of, the former. The concept of peace has changed throughout recorded history as different groups and individuals have struggled to realize a harmonious state of existence. In the contemporary world understandings of peace vary from country to country and within different cultural contexts. Many people think of peace as tranquility or the absence of war. Peace is a positive concept that implies much more than the absence of war.[12] As a necessary condition for human survival, it implies that human beings resolve conflicts without using force, and it represents an ideal that humans have long striven to achieve.

As peace researchers have pointed out, peace has both a negative and a positive connotation. In its negative meaning, "peace" implies stopping some form of violence, but "peace" also has positive connotations, involving following standards of justice, living in balance with nature, and providing meaningful participation to citizens in their government. People use various strategies to pursue peace. Some rely on the use of force to stop aggression. Others rely on nonviolent communication skills to manage conflicts without the use of force. The pursuit of peace involves a worldly outlook that links local struggles to global aspects and vice versa. "Peace" has been defined by Joel Kovel as a state of existence where:

> Neither the overt violence of war nor the covert violence of unjust systems is used as an instrument for extending the interests of a particular nation or group. It is a world where basic human needs are met, and in which justice can be obtained and conflict resolved through nonviolent processes and human and material resources are shared for the benefit of all people.[13]

"Peace," a concept that motivates the imagination, connotes more than "no violence." It implies human beings working together to resolve conflicts, respect standards of justice, satisfy basic needs, and honor human rights. Peace involves a respect for life and for the dignity of each human being without discrimination or prejudice.

While the absence of war can be understood as peace, and the absence of peace is often war, peace and war are not correlatives. A state not at war may not be peaceful. Its citizens may reside in neighborhoods with high crime rates or live in families where they are beaten. They may exist in conditions where they are oppressed economically, starved or in miserable health. Violence can imply more than a direct, physical confrontation. It is expressed not only on battlefields but also through circumstances that limit life, civil rights, health, personal freedom, and self-fulfillment. This type of violence, referred to as *structural violence*, occurs when wealth and power exploit or oppress others, and standards of justice are not upheld. It is created by the deprivation of basic human needs and creates suffering for individuals throughout the world. Structural violence implies that those situations where an individual's survival is threatened are not peaceful.

Paul Smoker and Linda Groff have described several different types of peace.[14] They vary according to the kind of violence they address. In the international system, peace is not just the absence of war, but it also represents a balance of forces. As mentioned above, peace also can appear in civic society, when a country is not at war, and there is no structural violence at the macro level. At the micro level peace implies managing interpersonal relations without violence. It means sharing material resources to put an end to exclusion, injustice, and political and economic oppression. In addition there are holistic systems of peace that focus on unity and diversity. Intercultural peace exists when different religious and ethnic groups live together harmoniously. Living peacefully involves defending freedom of expression and cultural diversity, as well as using democratic principles to create a sense of solidarity that comes through the creation of inclusive communities. This type of peace provides alternatives to the violent images often found in popular media. A sixth type of peace concerns the way human beings relate to the Earth and is achieved when human beings live sustainably on this planet. The final form of peace has to do with inner peace that is achieved through the psyche. There are philosophers and religious leaders, such as the Dalai Lama and Thich Nhat Hanh, both from the Buddhist Tradition, who maintain that "inner peace" and "outer peace" are interrelated. Those who hope to work for peace in the world must themselves be striving for a sense of inner harmony.

Since societies will always have hostilities, disagreements, and arguments, the pursuit of peace does not strive for an idealized state of human existence with no aggression or conflict. It strives, rather, for the means to resolve disagreements without resorting to warfare or physical force, and for justice where human beings are treated with the dignity afforded them by their human rights. Peace has an individual context which implies peace of mind and the absence of fear. For an individual to live peacefully he or she must be able to satisfy basic needs and resolve conflicts within friendships, workplaces, families, and communities in a way that promotes the well-being of all.

Peace is concerned with different forms of violence and operates at many different levels of human existence. Traditionally, concern about peace relates to nations and their ability to settle disagreements without resorting to war, providing security for citizens. Wars between nations require peace strategies that are international in scope. Most countries (with the exception of Costa Rica and Iceland) have military forces that they maintain to protect their boundaries. Societies provide peace for their citizens by developing a collective security with laws that govern human behavior. At this global level peace implies that governments respect the sovereignty of nations and will use methods other than force to manage conflicts.

At the national level peace implies law and order, self-control, a respect for others, and the guarantee of human rights. At the cultural level artists create peaceful images to counteract some of the violent images propagated through the mass media and entertainment industries. At the institutional level administrators use organizational development techniques to resolve conflicts. At the interpersonal level individuals can learn how to arbitrate conflicts and negotiate agreements. At the psychic level peace implies a certain calm and spiritual connectedness to other forms of life.

The creation of peace is one of the great unsolved human problems. Since the advent of organized societies, human beings have prayed for, dreamed about, and worked to achieve peace. In recent years human warlike propensities have reached new heights. The creation of the atomic bomb, the development of biological and chemical warfare, and the manufacture of high tech weaponry have elevated the dangers of war to a point where the future can no longer be taken for granted. Since the attacks on the American World Trade Center of September 11, 2001, the very definition of war is undergoing dramatic revision. The scientific modes of thinking developed in Europe in the eighteenth century have created an industrial society that has brought the human race to a point where it can no longer rely on militaristic ways to resolve differences but must adopt nonviolent solutions to problems. As Albert Einstein said fifty years ago,

> We stand, therefore, at the parting of the ways. Whether we find the way of peace or continue along the road of brute force, so unworthy of our civilization, depends on ourselves. On the one side the freedom of the individual and the security of society beckon to us; on the other, slavery for the individual and the annihilation of our civilization threaten us. Our fate will be according to our deserts.[15]

People learn violent behavior from parents, friends, teachers, cultural norms, social institutions, and the mass media. Violent images promoted in the culture instill the belief that aggression must be regulated through violent means. This need not be true. Indeed, Margaret Mead and other anthropologists have discovered supportive, caring cultures that practice nonviolence. For example, the Inuits, commonly known as Eskimos, do not fight among themselves but rather channel aggressive impulses to overcome the harsh vicissitudes of an Arctic existence. If some cultures exist peacefully, why not all of them?

To a large extent cultural norms and messages determine behavior in a given society. If individuals receive messages that describe social reality as violent, they will be fearful. If people believe that the only way to preserve their lives, liberties, and properties is through physical violence, they will construct and live in armed encampments. Even within the midst of this violent milieu, the ways of peace have successfully altered aggressive behavior.

Mahatma Gandhi's nonviolent principles liberated India from one of the world's greatest empires. United States citizens, organizing for peace in the nineteen sixties and seventies, contributed to the end of America's involvement in the Vietnam war. Neighborhood block clubs where individuals organize against crime have been shown to decrease urban vandalism. In the United States Dr. Martin Luther King, Jr., and other civil rights leaders, dedicated to the principles of nonviolence, helped minority people gain dignity and civil rights. In the nineteen fifties and nineteen sixties citizen protests against atmospheric testing of nuclear weapons led to a partial test ban treaty. In 1986 the Philippine people used nonviolent tactics to depose Ferdinand Marcos. In 1989 peace protests in countries in Eastern Europe led to the collapse of the Soviet Union.

In order to eliminate war and violence humans must understand, desire, and struggle to achieve peace. If and when the desire for peace becomes strongly rooted in human consciousness, people will strive for it, demanding new social structures that reduce risks of violence. Peace education provides not only a way to promote such a desire for peace within the human mind but also knowledge about peacemaking skills so that human beings learn alternative nonviolent ways of dealing with each other.

Strategies for Peace

Although most people desire peace, there exists within human communities considerable disagreement about how to achieve it. It is helpful to distinguish between several strategies for achieving peace, each with its own aims. As previously noted, one way of distinguishing the various strategies is to divide them into three categories: peacekeeping, peacemaking and peacebuilding. *Peacekeeping*'s aim is to respond to violence and stop it from escalating. On a micro level this might mean schools employing security guards to break up fights. On a more macro level, it implies the use of military force to quell violence in the world, an example being the use of force to respond to the terrorist attacks of September 11. Dur-

	ASSUMPTIONS ABOUT HUMAN NATURE	TACTICS	PROBLEMS WITH STRATEGY
Peace Through Strength	Humans are violent. World is competitive.	Arms, balance of power, force, deterrence.	Cost, danger, retribution.
Peace Through Justice	Human beings have basic needs.	Organize to meet needs; remove institutions not responsive to human needs; preserve rights.	Contradictory claims lead to controversy and violence.
Peace Through Transformation (Pacifism)	Human beings are capable of love that can overcome feelings of hatred.	Transform individual behavior and beliefs, withdraw allegiance to violent institutions.	No broad following; creates vulnerability.
Peace Through Politics (Institution building)	Humans are rational; conflicts can be managed without violence by appealing to common interest.	Create institutions, laws, treaties, etc. to negotiate conflicts.	Private agendas block solutions; disagreements cause conflicts.
Peace Through Sustainability	Humans are both spiritually and materially connected to all others and to the natural world; there can be enough material and emotional-spiritual security for all.	Work toward nonviolence in all relationships, with the human and natural world; education is both holistic and biocentric.	Technological progress depends partly upon the destruction of the environment; short-term economic gains often obscure long-term goals of sustainability.
Peace Education	Human beings capable of changing violent behaviors and beliefs.	Teach alternatives to violence; explain consequences of violence.	Long-term solutions difficult to evaluate.

Table 1. Strategies for Peace

ing war a strategy for peace may be militaristic where leaders use peace through policies to stop contestants who are fighting. Once the fighting has stopped, *peacemaking* strategies can be used to get the parties together to try to work out their differences. Peacemaking has as its aims the teaching of skills to resolve conflicts without the use of force. In order to prevent conflict, *peacebuilding* strategies are used to create a culture of peace that does not celebrate violence, but rather promotes nonviolence as a way to avoid the horror of war.

These different approaches to peace are not mutually exclusive. In fact, some believe they can complement each other to help overcome the complex sources of violence found in the modern world. In times when a country is not waging a war, a strategy for peace might involve constructing elaborate defenses against perceived enemies, or a literacy campaign to relieve the oppression of citizens unable to satisfy basic needs.

What particular approach to peace a given society uses depends upon the inclinations, experiences, and desires of those in power or upon well organized grass-roots movements. In addition to the above mentioned group of three strategies for peace, an additional way of categorizing involves the following, as seen in the paradigm below: These are: (1) peace through strength, (2) pacifism, (3) peace with justice, (4) institution building, (5) peace through sustainability, and (6) peace education. These different strategies are not mutually exclusive, rather they all come into interplay in addressing the complex problems of violence found in the modern world and may, in some sense, be rather arbitrary in their grouping.

Peace education here is noted as a strategy. However, it is important to think of it as, metaphorically, a light "covering," reaching among and between all of the other strategies. Educators can teach about all the different strategies in their settings. Peace educators need to become familiar with these different approaches so they can present their strengths and weaknesses to students who may, in turn, decide for themselves the best ways to achieve peace. These particular approaches to peace are illustrated in Table 1 and described in the ensuing text.

Peace Through Strength

The concept of "peace through strength" is credited to the Roman Empire: *si vis parem, para bellum* (if you desire peace, prepare for war). In modern terms peace through strength requires massive armaments, and it is often discussed in terms of balance of power. Under this approach to peace a state, an individual, or group of individuals is dissuaded from going to war because the opposition is so well armed that a state, individual, or group of individuals cannot be sure that it (they) will win. A balance of power depends upon approximate equality of military force. If one country has military superiority over another, the weaker nation may feel threatened. A balance of power occurs when a country has no military superiority over another.

Deterrence and peace through strength currently dominate the thinking of most governments that devote large portions of their budgets to maintaining armed forces. These expenses are justified because the thinking is that a well-prepared military is seen as necessary to provide security in a dangerous world. The use of collective force is justified as an unavoidable use of force to quell dissent and establish peace. Peace through strength, the current policy endorsed by those in power in many of the nations of the world, is credited by many for deterring a war during the Cold War between the two superpowers, the United States and the Soviet Union.

Because most nations of the world approach the problem of conflict with a militaristic strategy to destroy or wipe out other humans (enemies) who are seen as the sources of conflict, peace has a controversial history. Military regimes go to war in order to provide peace for their citizens. At the same time, this helps to secure the privileges of those who hold structural power within a given society. These strategies are being played out in a tragic manner in the State of Israel, where the Israeli government is using force to suppress Palestinian opposition, but the "blowback" from these militaristic approaches to providing security is producing terrorists who are further aggravating an unsettled situation. Some critics of the "War on Terrorism" believe that the invasion of Afghanistan, following on the September 11 attacks in New York and Washington, D.C., with its concomitant killing of innocent Afghan civilians and with what some regard as the United States' refusal to understand the root causes of terrorism, may, in the long run, produce an increase in the amount of terrorist attacks against U.S. citizens around the world.

There are several strong arguments against peace through strength. First is its tremendous cost. Economists have done numerous studies that indicate that an increase in military expenditure is inversely correlated with the growth of a "civilian economy."[16] Money spent on defense comes from social services, so that an increase in military spending often means a lowered standard of living and services for many citizens. This approach to peace presents severe difficulties for countries in the underdeveloped world, where scarce resources are directed away from human needs toward human destruction. The total amount of money spent on arms each year in the world is fast approaching one trillion dollars—a huge sum of money that diverts resources from solving many of the problems which cause wars in the first place. An American taxpayer can now expect to pay nearly fifty percent of his or her federal tax bill to support current and past military spending.

A second problem with peace through strength is that this approach relies on technological solutions to social problems, as researchers and defense experts spend time and money developing sophisticated weapon systems. The conflicts that cause wars are human, and their resolution requires the energy, talents, and creativity of human beings, not relying on machines, but rather on trusting human instincts to bridge and resolve the issues inherent in conflict. More sophisticated weaponry creates a situation where civilization could be annihilated through some technical error. The irony of peace through strength is that the invention of modern weapons has created a destabilizing world climate where many citizens feel insecure because of the tremendous threats posed by weapons of mass destruction that have been created to enhance their security. And on September 11, 2001, the world watched in horror when a few men armed with box cutters managed to destroy the World Trade Center in New York City. In this "post-modern moment" on that day, the most sophisticated fighting force ever assembled on this planet was unable to protect the citizens of the United States, as the world watched suicide bombers employing U.S. airplanes to carry out their plans.

A third problem concerns the use of these weapons that can kill millions of people, severely altering the earth's ecosystem. This scenario has been detailed by scientists who describe it as "nuclear winter," where the use of nuclear, chemical and biological weapons relied upon by deterrence theory could destroy human civilization.[17] Concern about this threat has stimulated large peace movements in industrialized societies and has created a desire on the part of many people to live in a world that no longer relies on war to solve its problems.

PEACE THROUGH JUSTICE

Peace through justice implies that peace may be attained by eliminating social oppression and economic exploitation. Peace through justice is concerned with the elimination of poverty, disease, starvation, human misery, and with the preservation of human rights. People who promote peace through justice take an active stand against structural violence by publicly demonstrating to rally public opinion, and by discrediting the violence of those they oppose.

Peace through justice addresses the tremendous suffering and misery that exist in the world. As important as it may seem to diplomats and political scientists to promote arms control agreements, forty-one thousand people a day starve to death in this world. In the twentieth century, the overwhelming majority of victims of war have been women and children. Millions suffer from disease, lack of sanitary conditions, racial injustice, inadequate health care, and malnutrition. People living under such conditions suffer or even face death because they cannot meet basic survival needs. Addressing these needs is a way to eradicate violence on this planet.

Championing justice can be controversial. In a postmodern world there are no universal standards of justice. The banner of peace through justice is carried by many "combatants," each claiming that its side stands for justice while the opposition stands for tyranny and oppression. Appeals to justice result in competing claims which have no easy resolution. In combating oppression, cries for justice challenge the authority and legitimacy of governing elites. Because peace through justice identifies with oppressed people, it is practiced outside the realm of traditional politics, for the most part. Traditional politics represents the attempts of elites to consolidate their power. The independent peace movement, for example, is repressed in Serbia, as the radical Catholic Worker movement in the United States is treated with suspicion. Peace through justice, championed by a liberation theology that has grown up in South and Central America, points toward an emancipatory theology that can threaten power elites. Thus, peace through justice is highly political, often involving personal risk.

Pacifism (Peace Through Transformation)

In contrast to peace through strength, which relies upon force to subdue hostilities, the pacifist road to peace implies the total absence of violence, though not necessarily the avoidance of confrontation per se. "Nonviolence is the human force," according to theologian Walter Wink.[18] Violence is confronted, not by violence in return, but by, in Gandhi's words, "truth force." Pacifism exudes a confidence in the infinite possibilities of the human spirit.

Pacifists turn the other cheek and do not strike out, even if attacked. The term "turn the other cheek" comes from the teachings of Jesus in the Christian Bible. Nonviolent theorists postulate that Jesus' admonition to turn the other cheek implies not a passive resistance to evil, but instead a radical "turning on its head" of the cultural norms of the ancient Judeo-Roman world. Jesus, by confronting openly the cultural taboos of his society at that time, and at the same time advocating love of God and love of neighbor, was inviting controversy by refusing to abide by the ancient traditions of class and gender separation. Jesus was a radical for his time.[19]

Pacifists have a profound respect for life and a moral aversion to war. Pacifism comes from the Latin "pacem," peace, and "facere" to make. Literally it means "to make peace." Thus, pacifism should not be equated with being passive. Pacifism is often equated with "active nonviolence." Pacifists reject violence in all its forms—physical, sexual, psychological, economical, and social—and employ nonviolent conflict resolution strategies to deal with human aggression. Pacifism depends upon love of fellow human beings and has strong roots in most spiritual traditions, typified by Jesus' teaching to "love your enemies." Active nonviolence seeks to break the cycles of violence, creating more human alternatives and inviting personal and political transformation.

Pacifism depends upon human connectedness and human interaction. Inherent within it is the notion of human repentance, the acknowledgment of violence within ourselves and others. On an international scale this approach to peace suggests that if all nations disarm, there will be no wars.[20]

Pacifism has a moral and spiritual strength. Pacifists have, throughout history, taken stands against armaments. Buddhists renounce the use of violence as a part of a spirituality that finds all forms of life sacred. Early Christians opposed conscription in the Roman army. Quakers in England in the seventeenth century resisted Cromwell's forced conscription throughout the British countryside. By using civil disobedience tactics, pacifists have succeeded in mobilizing support for alternatives to physical force and violence. There is a small but growing movement of individuals who, for conscience reasons, refuse to pay a portion or all of their federal tax dollars to support war. Although in most societies pacifists represent a very small minority, they have in determined ways provided a moral force against the wholesale use of violence endorsed by nation states.

Pacifism has had a glorious history in the twentieth century.[21] Largely based on the nonviolent efforts of Mahatma Gandhi to dispel the British from India, nonviolent resistance has been taken up by people throughout the planet to oppose tyranny. Examples include the aforementioned civil rights efforts of Dr. Martin Luther King, Jr., the nonviolent overthrow of the Marcos regime in the Philippines in 1988 and the collapse of the Soviet Union in 1989. Walter Wink notes,

> In 1989–90 alone, thirteen nations underwent nonviolent revolutions, all of them successful but one (China), and all of them nonviolent on the

part of revolutionaries except one (Romania, and there it was largely the secret police fighting the army, with the public maintaining nonviolent demonstrations throughout). Those nonviolent struggles affected 1.7 billion people—one-third of the population of the world. If we add all the nonviolent efforts of this century, we get the astonishing figure of 3.3 billion people—over half of the human race! No one can ever say that nonviolence doesn't work. But it is true that we don't always know how to make it work.[22]

Nonviolent struggle withdraws support from rulers and mobilizes people to take action against despotism. In this way, pacifism as a strategy, at both the macro level of a society and at the micro level of human interaction, provides a paradigm that, among other things, uses communication to resolve differences in nonviolent ways.

Human societies are so structured that pacifist policies create insecurities. People who live in violent or potentially violent areas believe that they need to arm in order to protect themselves. People in urban areas in the United States expect that their police will rid the streets of criminals. There is a widespread perception that if a particular nation were to disarm, it could be vulnerable to attack from armed states that desire its resources. Hence the belief is that a pacifist strategy allows nations with strong militaries to dominate the world. Human social institutions and nation states are so constructed that there is a widespread fear that to adopt a pacifist stand creates vulnerability.

INSTITUTION BUILDING (PEACE THROUGH POLITICS)

The development of effective international institutions aims to avoid war by creating legal and political alternatives for resolving international conflicts. The whole judicial system with courts, lawyers, punishment, and standards of justice attempts to provide fair procedures for maintaining order in civil society. Known as "peace through politics," which emphasizes working through political channels, this method for achieving peace is best typified by the United Nations, whose charter enumerates measures for the prevention of war and removal of threats to peace. The primary purpose of the United Nations Educational, Scientific, and Cultural Organization (UNESCO), an organization of the United Nations, is

> to contribute to peace and security by promoting collaboration among the nations through education, science and culture in order to further universal respect for justice, for the rule of law and for the human rights and fundamental freedoms which are affirmed for the peoples of the

world, without distinction of race, sex, language or religion, by the Charter of the United Nations.[23]

The United Nations and UNESCO declared the year 2000 and the decade 2001–2010 the Year and Decade for a Culture of Peace and Nonviolence for the Children of the World. This was an initiative begun earlier by all of the living Nobel peace laureates. The purpose of the designation is to promote activities which, according to a 1989 UNESCO monograph, are consistent with the "values, attitudes, and modes of behavior based on nonviolence and respect for the fundamental rights and freedom of all people."[24] UNESCO's initiative includes the following precepts:

- power as defined as active nonviolence
- people being mobilized to build understanding, not to defeat a common enemy
- democratic processes to replace vertical and hierarchical power structures and authority
- free flow of information replacing secrecy
- male dominated cultures replacing by power sharing among women, men and children
- feminine cultures as centers of peacebuilding (including connectedness, power sharing) replacing traditional structures glorifying war and the preparations for war
- exploitation of the environment, closely associated with warfare, replaced by cooperative sustainability

Imbedded in the UNESCO program for a Culture of Peace is the recognition of the increasing role of citizens' groups, or nongovernmental organizations (NGOs), which are energizing the United Nations system. These organizations, many of which have formal ties with the UN and its agencies, have as their goals the betterment of humankind and, in many cases, the alleviation of the root causes of war.

Another example of a kind of institution that promotes peace between nations is the International Law of the Sea. Arms control treaties also fall under the heading of institution building. Such organizations use political processes, laws, and traditions to provide alternatives to armed conflict.

Another example of an institution that promotes peace is the United States Institute of Peace, an independent, nonpartisan federal institution created and funded by Congress to strengthen the nation's capacity to promote the peaceful resolution of domestic and international conflict. Established in 1984, the Institute meets its congressional mandate through an array of programs, including grants, fellowships, conferences and workshops, library services, publications, and other educational activities. The objectives of the Institute are to support research on different aspects of peacekeeping, peacemaking, and peacebuilding, to train international affairs professionals in conflict management and resolution techniques, mediation, and negotiating skills, and to raise the level of public awareness about international conflicts and peacemaking efforts through grants, scholarships, publications, electronic outreach, and conferences. Of late, the Institute has been supporting programs teaching the skills of peacebuilding to young people in schools and elsewhere.

Developing institutions to resolve disagreements represents the rational solution to resolving conflicts between groups of human beings. Diplomats and heads of states negotiate and bargain to reduce hostilities on a global scale. They also look to international law to settle disputes. Advocates of this position hope to create institutions to which appeals may be made in seeking to resolve disputes. This strategy is limited, however, by the same pressures that cause disputes to rise in the first place. Countries go to war because they disagree strongly with the actions of another country and use military means to gain advantage. War is a gamble, and they hope to win. These same countries may not be interested in resolving their disputes through arbitration. They may fight to impose their will and the power of elites within those societies may be reinforced. Arbitration and diplomatic resolution of conflicts are at times invoked if a military strategy has become stalled, but seldom are they the first avenues that nations use to resolve their differences. Another problem of peace through politics is the question of sanctions—what exactly can be done to punish a country that violates international treaties and obligations? If there are no effective nonmilitary means to punish aggressive states, there may be no way to enforce international agreements, thus weakening peace through institution building. In the twentieth century the international community has looked to sanctions as a way to avoid war, but in countries like Cuba and Iraq these sanctions have solidified the power of dictators and created suffering for the masses of people who have been disenfranchised. In Serbia, on the other hand, sanctions, coupled with nonviolent street demonstrations, deposed a vicious president, Slobadon Milosevic, in 2000.

Peace Through Sustainability

Environmental destruction presents an extreme challenge to human beings, who depend upon the natural world for sustenance. As J. Alfred Prufrock said in a poem by T.S. Eliot, "That is the way the world ends;

not in a bang but in a whimper." Ecological violence is a key concept for peace education. However, peace educators in their rush to address the complex forms of violence manifested in human communities have often overlooked the dramatic effects of human violence upon the Earth, its ecosystems, and the various species that inhabit it. Peace educators hope to get humans to think of the Earth less as a resource for profit and more as a home that needs to be carefully maintained.

Peacebuilding in its broadest sense is based upon a commitment to nonviolence in relation to both the human and natural world. Environmental educators attempt to develop an ecological world outlook that is both holistic and biocentric, emphasizing the interconnectedness of all beings. The challenge is to learn to share limited resources equitably, and to live within the limits of environmental sustainability. This will become increasingly important in the 21st century as human populations increase in numbers and in expectations of a better life.

The problems with this approach are that humans must consume natural products, and, as they become more technologically developed, their capacity to destroy the environment expands with the wealth generating mechanisms they depend upon for their well-being, such as the use of fossil fuels. Although environmentalists have argued for a "green" technology, it is hard to imagine industrial giants converting to such practices because of the amount of money that is invested in technologies that exploit the environment for maximum profit. Furthermore, as more and more people around the world clamor for access to advanced technologies, there will be even greater pressure on the environment. An example is the generation of gases that are eliminating ozone from the atmosphere and hence warming the planet. The "path to progress" depends upon destruction of the environment. Poor people in richly forested areas, like the Amazon, are eager to sell their trees in order to earn money and improve their living conditions. The short-term gains that humans experience from environmental destruction blind them to the long-term consequences of overusing natural resources. The task for peace educators is, among other things, to foster a view that negates the short-term and focuses on longevity. (Further discussion of ecology and sustainability is contained in Chapter 11 in a discussion of visions for a more hopeful world.)

Peace Education

Our last approach, peace education, refers to teaching about peace — what it is, why it doesn't exist, and how to achieve it. As previously noted, it is both a philosophy and is inclusive of skills and processes. Peace educators use their educational skills to teach about peaceful conditions and the process of creating them. One main goal of peace education is to provide images of peace, so that when people are faced with conflict, they will choose to be peaceful. Students can learn that alternatives to violence do exist. Peace education names problems of violence and then provides nonviolent alternatives to address those problems. Peace educators point out the problems of violence that exist in society and then instruct their pupils about strategies that can be used to address those problems, hence empowering them to redress the circumstances that lead to violence. Peace educators teach negotiation, reconciliation, nonviolent struggle, the use of treaties, and armed struggle. They also teach about different peace strategies and help their students to evaluate what are the best strategies to use in particular circumstances.

One assumption behind peace education is that if citizens have more information about the dangers of violence and war, they will abjure the ways of violence. This assumption was tested in California by members of Physicians for Social Responsibility in the San Francisco area who distributed a two part questionnaire at a series of fifty-seven separate educational events. [25] The first part, distributed prior to presentations on the medical effects of nuclear war, asked among other questions "are there causes worth fighting a nuclear war for?" Ten percent of the one thousand three hundred fifty-five people who completed the survey responded "yes" to this item. After the presentation half of the people who originally said they thought there were causes worth fighting a nuclear war for changed their minds and answered "false" to this item. Although this study represents only a brief attitude change, it indicates that education can be an effective strategy in developing an aversion to war.

However, peace education involves much more than a focus on the fearful consequences of violence and war. Peace education, as a strategy for lasting peace on the macro level, relies on educating enough people within a given population to establish widespread support for peaceful policies. Everett Rogers, a professor at Stanford University, showed in his studies how an idea or innovation spreads throughout society. [26] The six stages of adoption that he has defined are attention, interest, evaluation, trial, adoption, and confirmation. Individuals have to first become aware of a new idea, for example, through media exposure. Interest is developed, and a favorable or unfavorable attitude forms. The pros and cons of the idea are compared and the idea is tried out. A decision is then made to adopt or reject the idea. Finally, the individual seeks confirmation for a particular decision concerning this idea. The rate of adoption is influenced by the degree to which the new idea is perceived as offering an advantage

1. What Is Peace Education?

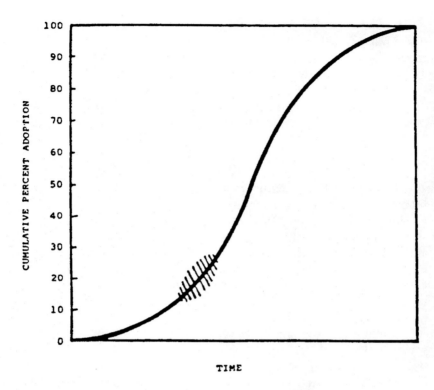

Table 2. S-Shaped Cumulative Curve for Adopter Distribution.

over the presently held idea and the degree to which the new idea is compatible with an individual's present beliefs. This research is most applicable to peace education when it discusses how a new idea, such as a freeze in production of nuclear weapons, becomes adopted by a society. His research has shown that the adoption of a new idea follows an s-shaped curve as illustrated in Table 2.[27]

This s-shaped curve of adoption rises slowly at first when there are few people who adopt a new idea. It then accelerates to a maximum until half of the individuals in a society accept that idea. The curve increases at a slower rate as remaining individuals finally adopt the idea. The shaded area marks the time period during which the adoption process takes off. As Rogers points out, after a new idea is adopted by twenty percent of the population, it is virtually unstoppable. An important goal of peace education is, then, to have twenty percent of the population of any given country renounce the use of force to settle conflicts and seek nonviolent solutions. This theory implies that a concern for peace would seep through society and become a norm guiding human conduct. This approach to peace was typified by President Dwight D. Eisenhower, one of the great modern warriors, in a comment he made in a radio interview with Prime Minister Harold MacMillan on August 31, 1959:

> The people in the long run are going to do more to promote peace than our government. Indeed, I think that people want peace so much that one of these days governments had better get out of their way and let them have it.

Peace education attempts to transform society by creating a peaceful consciousness that condemns violent behavior. Parents can use nonviolent techniques to raise their children. Teachers can teach peacemaking skills to their students. Professors can teach about the problems of war and peace. Neighbors can advocate for recycling programs. Citizens can pressure their governments to adopt nonviolent policies towards other countries. And concerned residents can construct community education programs about specific peace issues as they attempt to educate the broader public about the value of peace policies.

A major disadvantage of peace education is that it offers a long term solution to immediate threats. For peace education to be effective, it must transform ways of thinking that have been developed over the millennia of human history. At best peace education represents an indirect solution to the problems of violence. As a strategy it depends upon millions of students being educated who must in turn work to change violent behavior.

A teacher who teaches the topics of peace education has no guarantee that his or her students will either embrace peace or work to reduce violence. Research is needed into how and why peace education programs work. Anecdotal evidence is often the only source for this. Institutions of higher education are introducing research studies showing the effectiveness of teaching processes and skills. More is needed. Education influences culture slowly.

A teacher does not ultimately control what a pupil learns. Teachers lay the groundwork for learning, often using their skills and knowledge to transmit messages to their pupils, who may ultimately develop behaviors and attitudes that shape cultural norms. Peace activists believe that the creation of peace requires more than education. It also demands action, and there is no guarantee that students who are learning about peace in an educational setting will become activists who advocate for peaceful strategies.

Some Additional Assumptions About Peace Education

The word "education" comes from the Latin word "educare," to draw or lead out. Peace education draws from people their instincts to live peacefully with others and emphasizes peaceful values upon which society should be based. Peace education attempts to help people understand the root causes of violent events in their lives.

Traditionally, peace education has focused on the causes of war, sometimes called organized violence over territories.[28] More recently, the domain of peace education has expanded to include the study of domestic and interpersonal violence and environmental destruction. During the twentieth century there has been a growth in concern about horrific forms of violence, like ecocide, genocide, technological warfare, ethnic hatred, racism, sexual abuse, domestic violence, and a corresponding growth in the field of peace education. Educators, from day care to adult, can hone their professional skills to warn their fellow citizens about imminent dangers and advise them about paths to peace. Peace education may be seen to rest on two main assumptions: that conflict and violence are all around us and that there are means to address and transform this.

Peace education assumes that conflict is ubiquitous. It is not to be avoided, but addressed in ways that promote understanding and transformation. In fact sociologists have pointed out that conflicts are a necessary ingredient in social change.[29] Some theorists, such as Dahrendorf,[30] believe that conflict resolution is a myth because social conflicts are inherent in the very nature of social organization and structure. Peace is not then the absence of conflict but entails learning how to live with conflict in a constructive manner. The role of peace educators is to point out both the value and risks of conflict. Conflicts unattended can become conflagrations, as happened in Rwanda in 1994, whereas conflicts that are managed nonviolently can be the source of growth as positive change, as in the case of Gandhi's salt march in India in 1948. However, it is important to point out that Gandhi's campaign did not eliminate violence from the Indian subcontinent, which today is wracked with extreme religious, economic, ethnic, and nationalistic forms of conflict. The concept of peace and the educational strategies used to educate people toward peace vary according to the form of violence, addressed within specific peace education endeavors.

In a world which often looks bleak, full of genocide, environmental destruction, multiple holocausts, unemployment, terrorism, and continuing poverty, the achievement of peace is not something that is easily visualized, but rather it provides a goal for human endeavors, somewhat like the concept of infinity that provides a framework for calculus. Yet visualize and imagine peace educators must. Peace educators, among other things, show how conflicts can be managed for competing parties, such that they can continue to co-exist.

A European peace educator has defined peace education as "The initiation of learning processes aiming at the actualization and rational resolution of conflicts regarding man as subject of action."[31] According to this definition peace education gives pupils skills to become active peacemakers. A Japanese peace educator states that peace education is concerned with peaceless situations.[32] These include struggles for power and resources, ethnic conflicts in local communities, child abuse, and wars. In this way students in peace education classes study institutions that create violence as well as the values that give credibility to those structures. American peace educator Betty Reardon defines peace education as "learning intended to prepare the learners to contribute toward the achievement of peace."[33] She goes on to state that peace education "might be education for authentic security,"[34] where a need for security motivates humans to form communities and nations. Because individuals disagree about how to achieve security, there are many different paths to peace.

Peace educators teach about the various ways to provide security so that students may select which paths to follow. They instruct about the sources of conflicts and the best ways to resolve them. Peace education has a moral thrust; through education, human beings work together to create a better social order. The study of peace attempts to nourish those energies and impulses that make possible a meaningful and life enhancing existence. Betty Goezt Lall notes:

> The advantage of peace education and peace research is that it enables us to keep criticizing the structure and using brains and imaginations on alternatives, so that when the opportunities come—and they do come—we can use them.[35]

Peace educators address the violent nature of society, and ask, Must it be this way? Aren't there nonviolent ways that human beings can solve their conflicts? How do we get to these other ways? Just as war has its adherents and its schools, peace can be taught and promoted so that it becomes active in the minds of citizens and world leaders.

Throughout history many educational efforts have supported and promoted war. Thorton B. Munoz writes:

> It is obvious that a warfare curriculum for human beings has been developed and refined over the entire course of man's history. Its

teachings have been part of man's education in almost all societies in each succeeding generation.[36]

Traditional education glorifies established political power which uses brute force to oppress people and legitimize its authority. History books praise military heroes and ignore the contributions of peacemakers. Violence is carried on by governments oppressing weaker nations and exhibited in homes where physical assault handles conflict, disobedience, anger, and frustration. Traditional education does not question forms of structural violence that condemn people to substandard levels of existence, nor does it challenge environmental exploitation. Traditional education reproduces violent cultures. Children too often learn in school to respect the military and to support those structures which contribute to violence, like violent forms of popular entertainment. Peace education questions the structures of violence that dominate everyday life and tries to create a peaceful disposition to counteract the omnipotent values of militarism.

Some Goals of Peace Education

Educational activity is purposeful. Teachers try, through instructional activities, to achieve certain goals that help structure and evaluate the learning process. As Douglas Sloan has pointed out, peace education has short- and long-term goals. Peace educators must respond to the immediate situations that threaten "life" in their classrooms and in the world. The longer term goals are to create in human consciousness the permanent structures that desire peaceful existence and hence transform human values to promote nonviolence.

A good illustration of the relationship between these short- and long-term goals of peace education has been provided by a Romanian peace educator, Adrian Nastase. Quoting the French philosopher Pascal, Nastase observes that human beings are "running carelessly towards a precipice after having put something in front of us to hinder us from seeing it." Drawing from this analogy, he suggests that the goals of peace education are to discover "the precipice" and to understand the irrational state of the present world, realizing that the development of technology contains the tremendous contradictions of both improving the human condition and threatening its destruction.[37] Peace education alerts people to the danger of their own destructive fantasies and demonstrates the obstacles that keep us from focusing on our suicidal behavior. Once this awareness has been achieved, peace education develops alternatives that could become the basis for gradually braking and finally stopping this mad rush toward the "precipice." As H.G. Wells points out: human beings are embarked upon "a race between education and catastrophe."[38]

Whether working to achieve immediate or long range objectives, peace education may be said to contain at least ten main goals: (1) to appreciate the richness of the concept of peace, (2) to address fears, (3) to provide information about security, (4) to understand war behavior, (5) to develop intercultural understanding, (6) to provide a "futures" orientation, (7) to teach peace as a process, (8) to promote a concept of peace accompanied by social justice, (9) to stimulate a respect for life, and (10) to manage conflicts nonviolently. These goals include both the philosophy of educating for peace and the skills and processes that are involved.

Peace education is a broad field that includes many different academic disciplines. Peace education is taught in many settings, from day care centers to universities and in more informal educational centers such as community organizations. There are many topics included within the purview of educating for peace. These ten goals as outlined may be seen as providing a framework for planning educational activities for the various learning objectives involved in educating for peace.

(1) Peace education provides in students' minds a dynamic vision of peace to counteract the violent images that dominate culture. Examples of this come from arts and literature as well as history—the film *Gandhi*, the novels *War and Peace* and *Fail Safe*, and religious texts. Drawing upon history provides examples of how peace has stimulated human imagination throughout different historical epochs. Every major religion values peace. Peace educators teach about past, present and proposed future efforts to achieve peace and justice. Art can be an important part of that effort, allowing students to express their wishes for peace.

(2) Peace educators address people's fears. Children are abused at home. Citizens fear being attacked on streets. The events of September 11 have spawned deep fears of additional terrorist attacks. Biochemical warfare poses threats. Violence permeates schools. Increases in teenage suicide have been linked to despair about the future. People upset about violent situations often have strong emotions. Citizens grieve about violence and fear conflict. Because powerful emotions about violent experiences can interfere with pedagogical efforts, peace educators enter the affective domain to become aware of the tensions and problems created by living in a violent world. Addressing student concerns about violence can relieve anxiety in young people and help them focus on their school lessons. In this way peace education has the potential to improve academic achievement in schools.

(3) Citizens of all countries need information about how best to achieve security. The notion of collective security implies that nations build weapons and create armies, navies, and air forces because they provide protection from attack. Citizens need to know what goes into these systems, the implications of developing and depending upon them, and their cost. A citizenry ignorant of what these weapons represent cannot make informed decisions about them. Peace educators need to teach about the causes, nature, and consequences of the arms race. At the same time that each nation develops a war apparatus, often referred to as "the national security state," to defend itself, many nations shroud their security operations in secrecy. Peace education demystifies the public structures created to provide national security, so that citizens may make enlightened choices about the best security systems for their circumstances. Leaving these decisions in the hands of the military guarantees the perpetuation of militaristic policies. Peace educators discuss the modern ramifications of peace through strength and encourage students to draw their own conclusions about how best to provide security. New paradigms for security are addressed, focusing on the structural needs of humankind and on the skills of listening and conflict resolution.

(4) Students in peace education classes study the major causes of violence and war. Throughout recorded history there have been many instances of violent, armed conflict, but anthropologists have located on this planet at least 47 relatively peaceful societies.[39] A review of the literature of cultures that have achieved peace reveals a statement by Thomas Gregor:

> First, there are no cultures that wholly eliminate the possibility of interpersonal violence. Second, a good number of societies, especially those at the simplest socioeconomic level, appear to have successfully avoided organized violence, that is war. This is a significant accomplishment.[40]

There are those who believe that "cultures of peace" have existed and do still, often hidden within larger cultures espousing the values that contribute to violence and war.[41] Within these cultures, the skills of listening and the promotion of the value of care for others is seen as paramount, contributing to the formation of community.

Is aggression a natural part of human nature or is it learned through socialization? Individuals such as Alexander the Great, Napoleon, and Hitler have played a strong role in promoting wars, but some believe that we all have destructive fantasies. Why do some resort to violence while others do not? Peace educators provide their students with an understanding of how different individuals, cultures and political systems satisfy or frustrate human needs. It is not enough to assume that wars and warlike behavior are created by a few "others." Education must shed light on these important differences.

(5) Since wars occur as a result of conflicts between different groupings of human individuals, peace education promotes respect for different cultures and helps students appreciate the diversity of the human community. Intercultural understanding provides an important aspect of any peace education endeavor. In order to appreciate the perilousness of human existence, students learn about the interrelatedness of human beings on this planet. Survival depends upon cooperation.

(6) Peace education, by providing students with a "futures" orientation, strives to recreate society as it should be. In a violent world, children can often become enmeshed in despair. Future studies attempts to provide young people with positive images of the future and give them reason to hope.[42] Students and teachers in peace studies classes imagine what the future will be like and then discuss what can be done to achieve peace. Peace education includes futures courses that provide different possibilities for life on this planet to stimulate students to think about less violent ways of managing human behavior.

(7) As important as it is to emphasize knowledge, peace education also teaches skills. To move the world away from violence will require change. How can we bring peace to the world if we can't even create it in our own personal lives? Peace education focuses on strategies to achieve both individual and societal change. Peacemaking is a process that must be taught if human beings are to alter their violent behavior. Mahatma Gandhi meditated daily to place himself in a peaceful frame of mind so that he could deal with the turmoil around him. People wishing to achieve peace understand that peace is a process that transforms their own lives as they start personifying their visions of the future. In peace education classes students examine how their daily actions and beliefs contribute to the perpetuation of injustice and the development of war. They learn strategies to deal with aggressive behaviors and concrete skills that will help them become effective peacemakers.

(8) Because the struggle for peace embraces justice, peace education students learn about the problems of human rights and justice. They should understand that the absence of war does not necessarily bring peace or harmony. With this emphasis, peace studies programs do not focus only on national security issues but also include the study of social justice, human rights, development, feminism, racism, nonviolence, and strategies for social change. Jaime Diaz writes:

> To facilitate education for justice and peace, one must, above all, believe: believe that justice and peace are possible, believe that each and every one of us can do something to bring justice and peace into being.[43]

Teachers must, themselves, become aware of the problems brought about by oppression and use this knowledge to empower others to struggle against institutions that are dominant and coercive.

(9) The achievement of peace represents a humanizing process whereby individuals overcome their violent tendencies. Peace education teaches a respect for all forms of life. Peace education students need to develop positive self images, a sense of responsibility for self and others, a capacity to trust others and a caring for the well-being of the natural world. Peace education contributes to the social growth of all children if it helps them develop characteristics essential for the attainment of peace—a sense of dignity and self-worth, a confidence to question their values, communication skills, an ethical awareness, and an empathy for others:

> To prevent future upheavals human beings must be lifted from their selfish natural state to the social and finally to the moral state. Education must help the people regain their sense of moral independence and inner security. This training should be extended to all children, and should be rooted in love.[44]

Peace educators teach caring and empathy, not just a rational understanding of the problems faced by others. This caring applies not just to other human beings but also to the planet with an appreciation of the ecological balances that support life. Students must experience the sound of the earth crying, the pain of people who suffer in war, and the agony of people repressed by militarism. In this way peace education emphasizes the sacredness of life.

(10) The ultimate goal of peace education is to manage conflicts nonviolently. The world is consumed with violent behavior. Street crime, war, domestic quarrels, ethnic conflicts and poverty result in millions of people having to live in violent conditions where they have little or no security and struggle to survive. Peace educators teach about how conflicts get started, their perspectives, and the effects of violent solutions to conflict, and alternatives to violent behavior. Peace education students learn how to resolve disputes nonviolently and learn about different strategies for peace at both the macro and micro level. Until violence is curtailed, human beings will not be able to achieve their full potential. Peace educators need to help their students challenge stereotypes about "the other," and learn to empathize with the plight of diverse human beings. Awareness of the

role of the United Nations and other world systems is crucial to understanding what institutions human beings can create to bridge different cultures and guarantee survival on "spaceship earth." Peace educators focus on how human groups and institutions manage conflicts and overcome obstacles that inhibit human welfare.

To achieve these goals is necessary, but not easy. The task is heroic, can be energizing, and is crucial, according to those who believe the survival of our planet depends upon it.

Educators can teach about the nature of violence and develop in their classes strong visions of peace that motivate people to seek nonviolent ways to manage their conflicts. In order to create a less violent world, human beings must delegitimize the basic premises underlying the current global order and reassess fundamental assumptions regarding human motivations, essential values, and ultimate goals. This is a difficult task that many teachers avoid in their rush to have their students reach standardized goals of academic achievement. Without paying attention to these large scale concerns that loom over every classroom, teachers are in danger of promoting curricula that are hopelessly inadequate to the task of empowering youth to build a better future.

Teachers and educators can play an important role in students' lives when they provide them with a sophisticated understanding of the sources of conflict in this postmodern world and train them in the peacemaking skills that will help them manage conflicts in their lives. They can liberate students from the old ways of thinking that rely on the inevitability of human aggression. They need to ask their students, what kind of world do we really want, and help them to achieve a vision that will motivate a fundamental change in the way humans conduct their affairs.

CHAPTER 2

Religious and Historical Concepts of War, Peace and Peace Education

Without a vision, the people perish.
Book of Proverbs

This chapter will trace the evolution of concepts of war, peace and peace education from their historical origins in world religions, through their development in Europe, to their modern manifestations in the United States. Peace education begins with the study of how the concept "peace" has motivated our consciousness. These positive images are at the very core of peace education.

The study of peace reveals historical attempts both to stop violence and to create a utopian world where humans can realize the best aspects of their nature. Further discussion on utopias and futures studies is contained in Chapter 11. The cessation of a particular form of violence, referred to as negative peace, connotes a focus on a narrow form of violence, e.g., stopping a war, for example, in places like Kosovo and the Middle East. This does not address broader issues of interpersonal, gender, and environmental violence. Most peacekeeping strategies depend upon the use of force to contain violence. As important a contribution as it is, the cessation of violence does not supply a positive vision to motivate people to act peacefully. Negative peace depends for its enforcement on punishment and threats of violence that are meant to deter.

As mentioned in the previous chapter, peace education contributes to the longer term peacebuilding strategy of providing people with positive images of peace that will motivate their conduct in ways that build what Dr. Martin Luther King called "the beloved community." Positive peace implies more than the absence of war. It provides a vision of individuals and human societies actively attempting to resolve their disputes nonviolently. The achievement of positive peace demands a commitment to economic well being, social justice, democratic participation, ecological balance, global citizenship and the full protection of human rights:

> There are two ways of thinking of peace—negative peace and positive peace. The first is an absence of war and overt violence; the second implies a deep change in the structure of society, so as to remove the causes of war. In order to achieve even negative peace, education must make people aware of the nature of the arms race, and the likely effects of nuclear war. To bring about positive peace, education will be about understanding the nature of conflict, studying the causes and consequences of violence, and developing an awareness of the rights and responsibilities of individuals [statement by the National Union of Teachers, London, 1984].[1]

Dreams and visions help to provide motivation for tasks that must be done. Peace education can help stimulate positive visions of human behavior. Dreaming and creating visions are a part of everyday life. When people imagine, they express a cherished wish for how they would like to live and how they would like the world to be. Various scriptures revered within the world's religions contain many references to utopian ideas of human existence, and great thinkers like Mahatma Gandhi have been called visionary for their ability to create nonviolent images that attract the imaginations of millions of people.

Peace educators promote peace as an important goal for human societies. In contrast to standard history texts that emphasize war, peace educators need to explain to their students what images have motivated humans to strive for peace. As Elise Boulding has pointed out, "utopian visioning and utopian experiments persist through time as an expression of the human longing for peaceable lifeways."[2] Visions help people achieve their dreams for a peaceful world by clarifying concepts of peace and choosing strategies to achieve it. Peace is the presence of sustenance and security accompanied by justice and mercy. It is the love of the Earth, and the flowering of human creativity. Such a positive vision sustains human beings through hard times and points to future directions for human striving.

World Religions and the Concept of Peace

All of the great religions of the world—Judaism, Hinduism, Buddhism, Christianity, Taoism, and Islam—have considered peace an important part of their mission. In nurturing the spiritual aspects of human beings, these traditional religions have established peace as necessary, but not sufficient, for the procurement of the divine kingdom on earth. Organized religions promote their own visions of peace. Within the Christian tradition, the three historic peace churches, the Brethren, the Mennonites and the Quakers have at their core the spiritual work of building peace.

Elise Boulding notes that in every major world religion there have been two strands, called the "Holy War Doctrine" and the doctrine of "Holy Peace."[3] Examples such as the Christian Crusades and the Islamic Holy Jihad have been glorified by some as major accomplishments of civilization. In many parts of the world such as in Northern Ireland, where Protestants and Catholics have been fighting for many years, the initial struggle was for land. In this case the Protestant Oliver Cromwell gave the land of Catholic peasants to his Protestant troops. Thus issues of religion can become conflated with others that are at the root of conflicts. In the Middle East a contest between Israelis and Palestinians over land and territory has become a "religious" war, as zealots and religious fanatics from both sides seek the destruction of their enemies who have other religious beliefs (and claims for the same land). That the great religions have contributed as much to war as to peace might be seen as indicative of certain ironic and contradictory aspects of human nature.

Anthropological research has uncovered evidence that indicates that the earliest human societies did not have a separate class of people who were warriors, and hence they did not practice war as much as did later and more advanced societies.[4] Recent evidence suggests that human beings have experienced war for only the past 10,000 years and lived without war for the previous one million.

> Remember that people have been around for at least several million years with the same "nature" (i.e., the same pool of genes), and that it is only in the last four thousand years of this span that states, and the inevitable companion, warfare, got going.[5]

Once human settlements were formed into cities, they developed elaborate chains of command and hierarchies to mobilize citizens to wage aggressive acts of war against other peoples. Early recorded histories of these settlements contain fables of war and conquest. Many primitive tribes with polytheistic religions worshipped gods of war and sacrificed to the gods to help them achieve victory in battle. Early people constructed religious systems based upon their views of nature. These early hunters and gatherers in primitive societies personified natural elements in their religious and spiritual activities.

In the Greek pantheon, Ares, the God of War, was one of the most powerful deities. War was an intricate part of early Greek society as portrayed in *The Iliad*, which Simon Weil characterized as a poem of force.[6] This heroic tale, in relating the story of the great war between the Greeks and Trojans, portrayed the greatest crisis of that time, the destruction of a city. Likewise, early Scandinavian myths contained humorous references to war. The Yoruba tribe in Africa had a god of war, and the early legends of the Yoruba are also replete with tales of tribes engaging in war, and praying for victory. John Ferguson writes:

> War has throughout human history been an integral part of the life of most societies; as such it has been regarded as a religious activity, to be surrounded with prayer, ritual, sacrifice and purification. Polytheistic societies have often, though not always, believed in a special God of war who has to be honored and propitiated. Gods (or goddesses) of peace as such are less widely found, but naturally the powers to preside over agriculture and domestics life are powers who make for peace.[7]

In many primitive societies gods were cast in the image of men with superhuman military skills. Courageous in defeating their enemies, their prowess in battle gave them a larger than life significance.

In spite of the importance of war in tribal societies, aggression, violence, and warlike behavior have not always prevailed among humans. Anthropologists have discovered, researched, and written about human societies religiously organized for peace.[8] Many matriarchal societies have historically exhibited an affirmation of life and a lack of extreme violence against other humans. In one such tribe, the Arapesh in New Guinea, aggressive behavior received strong social disapproval. Gentleness was the norm. There were no religious or magical sanctions for warfare. Anyone roused to kill was the object of pity, not of admiration or vengeance.

The Hebrew Bible contains many references to both war and peace. Judaism stresses belief in one God, Yahweh, called the Prince of Peace. The Ten Commandments—codes from Yahweh that contained principles for organizing society—are central to the Old Testament. References to peace in the Old Testament are limited, however. The book of Isaiah contains the famous quote about beating swords into plowshares, but other books are full of battle stories about the tribulations of wars which were necessary to preserve the Jewish state. David, who was referred to as the prince of peace, gained his fame by leading the Jews in war.

However, the Hebrew Bible does contain the concept of "Shalom," the modern Hebrew word for peace. Life is sacred, and violence is to be avoided because it begets violence:

> Allah invites to the Abode of Peace whom He pleases and guides them to the straight path. Those who perform good deeds will reap rewards in abundance and their faces will not be covered by gloom or humiliation, for they will reside in the gardens of Paradise forever.[9]

The Hebrew Bible enjoins people to avoid war and destruction because of the tragedies they cause. It also emphasizes mercy. The Ten Commandments themselves prohibit the taking of human life. In Judaism war is justified if it fills some greater end, but people are encouraged to transform situations of hatred and show kindness to their fellow human beings.

The concept "Shalom" is a rich concept, deeply embedded in Jewish culture. "Be of the disciples of [The High Priest] Aaron: love peace, pursue peace, and make peace between people."[10] Shalom means living according to God's commandments, and sharing in the responsibility to care for each other. It is not private peace, but rather comes from the social and public order from living together and loving one's neighbor as oneself. It implies wholeness, prosperity, welfare, happiness, and security.[11] In this way peace is tied into the collective life and well-being of a community. The notion of shalom still occupies a powerful place in Jewish tradition. A song for peace, containing a plea, climaxes Jewish liturgy and Judaism uses a universal greeting, "Peace be with you."

Buddhism is based upon nonviolent principles. Buddha was a wealthy prince who renounced his material possessions and social obligations to pursue a spiritual quest. Ultimately Buddha himself became a symbol of peace. Peace is both a means and an end in Buddhism. As a means it implies a principle by which one should organize one's life, living peacefully and non-violently. As an end, the ultimate goal of Buddhism is to achieve peace and tranquility through wisdom and meditation. War and conflicts are the external manifestations of greed, hatred, ill will, violence, and ignorance. Devout Buddhists who pursue the path to peace renounce property, do not kill, practice love, refuse to kill for meat, remain celibate, free themselves from enmity, and try to overcome hostilities.[12] Buddha was concerned with poverty and saw that its hardships were an impediment to peace. He talked about the need for education and public health to help eradicate human misery. Buddhism strives both to enter into and to deliver human beings from suffering. War, understood as a disaster because of the calamities it wrought, is to be overcome by developing a strong inner morality and commitment to peaceful living. Buddha became a symbol of peace, because he condemned crime and greed and called on kings not to wage war. His religion and thought hold compassion for the sufferings of common people.

Taoism is based on similar principles. Aggression is forbidden. Weapons are seen as an instrument of evil. Lao-Tzu opposed ambition, political power, and worldly authority. He saw governments as a necessary evil. Taoism seeks unity through an ardent love in universal brotherhood, preaching disarmament, and a belief in the fundamental goodness of human nature. "Everything in the world longs for peace. Why then should there be some who address themselves so earnestly to governing empires?"[13] The follower of Taoism has a reverence for life, believes it is wrong to kill living things, and has a scorn for worldly striving after riches and wealth.

In order to understand the contribution of Hindu philosophy to the concept of peace, it is necessary to discuss both ancient and modern developments in the Hindu religion. The ancient concept of peace in Hinduism is spelled out in *The Upanishads* and in the *Bhagavad Gita*, sacred Hindu texts developed several centuries B.C. The modern concept of nonviolence has been formulated by Mahatma Gandhi. The term "Hinduism" represents many religions and an amalgam of beliefs from different times and from different prophets. For example, Buddhist principles of nonviolence were eventually adopted by Hindus, but these principles weren't in the original holy texts.

The *Bhagavad Gita* justifies war, but only under certain conditions, in fulfilling one's dharma, duty of mission in life. Hinduism provides a body of spiritual insights into the nature of truth. Spiritual peace leads to the "truth" of the human spirit. Hate is the opposite of the peace of mind that enables human beings to perceive the truth. God is the innermost truth in all human beings:

> Each human being has the innate divine nature, the Atman, to achieve peace within, and project that peace outside in the form of charity, tolerance, and fellow feeling. Peacelessness and tension are the characteristics of man as the ego, man at the sensate level. Hinduism—in fact, every world religion—seeks to take man above this level and lead him to the experience of the peace of God. The Atman is described by the Upanishads as peace.[14]

A Hindu respects all beings because each carries within him or her the Atman, or spirit of truth and peace. Wars may be looked at as manifestations of internal human turmoil, and the religious Hindu tries to discipline the forces of egoism, selfishness, lust and greed which cause wars. To the extent that a human being realizes the inner call and spirit, he or she will be free from the tendency to wage war.

Followers of Hinduism may be seen as either "householders" or "renouncers." The householders live in this world. They have families, businesses, and conduct affairs in their communities. The renouncers strive for spiritual truth. They are the great teachers and saints. Mahatma Gandhi's life might be seen as combining these two paths. A man of the spirit who sought truth through love and the principles of nonviolence, he took inspiration from Thoreau, Ruskin, and Tolstoy, and applied ideal principles to the world of householders. He lived simply, wearing woven cloth of the ashrams within which he lived. He believed that the truth force existed in the world of householders and could be realized by practicing nonviolence. Gandhi was a man of action who did not believe in renouncing the world around him. Yet he spent much time in prayer, fasting and contemplation. Gandhi believed that Hindus must practice this truth force. He derived this belief from the *Bhagavad Gita*, which teaches that not harming other creatures is a virtue similar to truthfulness and honesty.

Christianity also has deep pacifist roots. In the Old Testament there are many predictions that the Messiah would be a great warrior. Instead Jesus Christ practiced nonviolence and preached love for enemies. In the Sermon on the Mount Jesus said that peacemakers are blessed. He refused to defend himself with violence and proposed that Christians should turn the other cheek when confronted with violence. Christ himself was called the prince of peace. During the first three centuries the Church rigorously defended these principles, withdrew from conscription, and resisted the Roman Empire in pacifist ways. After Constantine came to power in the 4th century A.D. and converted to Christianity, these pacifist principles were altered. During the Middle Ages, St. Augustine, Aquinas, and other theologians adopted theories to justify war and set forth conditions under which Christians could participate in war. This was the beginning of the "just war" theory.

Under the "just war" theory it is always immoral to start a war. Diplomatic means should be used to resolve conflicts and fend off aggression. If these nonviolent means fail, and one nation unjustly attacks another, the victim nation has, as a last resort, the right and duty to use violent means to defend itself within certain moral limits. The military response to any attack may not exceed the limits of legitimate self defense. The wholesale slaughter of civilians in large population centers remains immoral, according to the theory.

In modern times Pope John XXIII delivered an encyclical in 1963 denouncing modern notions of war, demanding a reduction in the arms race, and declaring all war evil in the atomic age:

> Men are becoming more and more convinced that disputes which arise between states should not be resolved by recourse to arms, but rather by negotiation.[15]

In 1984 the National Conference of Bishops issued a pastoral letter that said that the threat of nuclear war is a central concern of the universal church, and called for extensive dialogue among churches on this issue. Many Protestant sects also called on their membership to think through the threat to humanity caused by modern weapons. As previously mentioned, three Christian sects retain a strict adherence to pacifist principles, the Mennonites, the Brethren, and the Quakers.

The great prophet Mohammed was both a political and religious leader. Islam does not recognize distinctions between politics and religion. The religious is political, the political, religious. Mohammed preached giving alms to the poor and sharing wealth. He and his followers strove to create one community under Allah. The central purpose of Islam is the promotion of peace and fellowship in the world and the development of understanding among different races, religions, and tribes. The universal greeting of Islam is "Peace be with you."

Islam, particularly after the World Trade Center and the Pentagon attacks of September 11, 2001, has often been associated with Jihad, or holy warfare. Islamic theologians dispute this. After the attacks, Muslim leaders around the world began to speak out against the terrorist attacks and publicized the importance of the pursuit of peace as the basis of Islamic belief. Jihad means striving in the way of Allah. The Jihad implies that Allah (God) is to be followed in all aspects of life and entails an active striving to follow God's will. The major Jihad, however, is within each person as the individual struggles against greed, exploitation, violence, and the denial of justice. Islam attempts to provide the Kingdom of God on earth, concerned with the welfare of all, and run according to the principles of the Koran or the holy book.

The last religion mentioned in this chapter is Baha'i (or, Bahā'ī). The faith, founded in the nineteenth century, is also a God-centered religion that has a deep belief in the "brotherhood of man." Baha'is consider themselves as the latest group in the historical progression of God's ongoing revelations, beginning with Judaism and progressing through Hinduism, Zoroastrianism, Buddhism, Christianity, and Islam. They worship all the major prophets in an attempt to unify humankind into one spiritual community:

> The Baha'i faith ... starts from the conversion and responsibility of the individual convert is called on to see himself as a citizen of the world. Baha'u'llah said in a conversation: "Let not a man glory in this that he loves his country; let him rather glory in this, that he loves kind...." The primary practical task laid on his followers by Baha'u'llah was the unification of mankind.[16]

In this religion peace comes from harmony within a family, a house, a country, and the world. Peace comes from within individuals and affects the larger social order. The Baha'i faith values peace among nations very highly, and it attempts to contribute to a peaceful world community based on individual behavior.

Contributions to Peace Education and to the Concept of Peace from Europe and America

Historically, certain Europeans may be seen to have contributed to the development of the modern concept of peace in western civilization. These include Desiderius Erasmus, Comenius, Immanuel Kant, Leo Tolstoy, Maria Montessori, Herbert Read, Teilhard de Chardin, Danilo Dolci, and Johan Galtung. Of these Maria Montessori was the only professional educator. The others looked at education as a means to instill in the human spirit a desire for peace.

Erasmus is an important figure, because he strongly criticized the just war theory that had caused so much bloodshed during medieval times. Ordained a priest in 1492, Erasmus rebelled against the church. He spent most of his life in England, and wrote two pamphlets, *Complaint of Peace* and *Antipolemus*, both of which place him within the pacifist tradition. He argued strongly that there could be no just war, that war by its very nature represented the total depravity of human nature:

> Peace is the mother and nurse of all good things. War suddenly and at once overthrow, destroyeth, and utterly for doeth everything that is pleasant and fair, and bringeth in among men a monster of all mischievous things.[17]

To Erasmus wars proceeded from internal greed, ambition, "wantonness of unbridled power, or from some other mental distemper."[18] He was particularly critical of the church, which glorified war in Christ's name. Christ's example is one of mildness and gentleness. Erasmus urged the pope, bishops, cardinals, abbots, and pastors to eschew the worldly matters of the state and to return to the original pacifist teachings of Christ. He believed that if wars were to be declared, they should be done so by the full and unanimous consent of the whole people who pay the price of war, not just by the heads of governments. The work of Erasmus points out the tensions that existed at that time, and continue to exist, within traditional Christianity, between those who justify war as a means to peace and those who renounce all war.

European peace education traces its roots to the famous pedagogue from Czechoslovakia, Comenius. In 1667 he asked for information on the educational issues relating to a treaty between England and the Netherlands.

Immanuel Kant, one of the greatest philosophers of all time, turned his energies, toward the latter part of his life, to the question of how to achieve peace. He wrote a pamphlet called *Perpetual Peace* (1795) which stated that war represents the natural state of human societies, while at the same time peace as an institution must become integral to all societies:

> A state of peace among men who live side by side is not the natural state, which is rather to be described as a state of war: that is to say, although there is not perhaps always actual open hostility, yet there is a constant threatening that an outbreak may occur. Thus the state of peace has to be established.[19]

The pamphlet contained articles suggesting the eschewing of war, domination, intimidation, and an arms build-up. Living in an autocratic state—Prussia—Kant also argued for a democratic government, saying, "The civil constitution of each state shall be republican."[20] In order to establish peace among nations, he suggested international laws that would become the framework for adjudicating disputes between different countries. Kant's genius was to assert that peace would not happen easily among nations, but it is something people and nations must work to achieve. He did not believe in one international government ruled by reason or force, but rather a free association of nations which would support international law so that citizens could live in peace and harmony. He saw that human beings would both make progress and would regress in terms of achieving peace, but that the best road to follow was to submit voluntarily to the rule of law.

Nonviolence is one form of the expression of love. Pestalozzi, the nineteenth century Swiss educator, promoted educational methods based upon a loving relationship between teacher and student.[21]

Leo Tolstoy figures as one of the major contributors of the twentieth century toward our understanding of peace. After completing his two great novels, *War and Peace* and *Anna Karenina*, Tolstoy underwent, at age fifty-seven, a spiritual transformation in which he turned against organized religion (in his case it was Christianity) and attacked the social violence he saw as being perpetrated by the Russian government. His pacifist position is seen as developing in the writing of two of his books *Christianity and Pacifism* (1892) and *The Kingdom of God is Within You* (1894). Tolstoy corresponded with Mahatma Gandhi, and his "Letter to a Hindu," written in 1908, was widely circulated in India and had a profound impact upon the nonviolent struggle against British colonialism.

In *The Kingdom of God is Within You* Tolstoy lambasted the notion of patriotism which he characterized as an affront to Christian ethics. He believed that patriotism provided a justification for war. As W.B. Gallie writes:

> The great mass of men, as he [Tolstoy] repeats again and again, are hypnotized into war, by their governments in the first instance, but alas, and even more remarkably by each other. By nailing the lie of patriotism, we can begin to rescue men from their hypnotized condition, and to save them, not so much from each other, as from themselves.[22]

Tolstoy attacked the existing social status quo, stating that war was a means used by the upper classes to dominate, economically and socially. The greatest crime that governments perpetrated, according to Tolstoy, was to appeal to Christian teaching to justify wars. Christian teaching not only opposed war, but also murder, and all forms of violence. Governments that appealed to Christian scripture perverted that teaching. Because Tolstoy saw that people were being oppressed all around him, he called on Christians to oppose this. Though not an organizer in the sense of Gandhi, Tolstoy believed that "love is the only means of saving people from those disasters which they undergo."[23] For him, peace and spiritual transformation were inseparable.

One of the great contributions of Tolstoy is his belief that governments themselves, independent of the wars they wage, are destructive to the cause of peace, in that they oppress people, and he called for resistance to that oppression. The wealthy people of his time benefited from the established government that helped keep millions of serfs in bondage. Tolstoy saw that such conditions were themselves the source of tremendous violence and suffering, and called upon the use of love as a spiritual force to unite against tyranny. Opposed to violence of all sorts, Tolstoy hoped the power of love could conquer the evil of institutions. Often referred to as the father of the modern peace movement, Tolstoy urged opposition through nonviolent means to the oppressive power that supports war.

Maria Montessori was an Italian physician and peace educator whose ideas initially had a much greater impact in Europe, beginning in the early part of this century, than they did in the United States. Montessori established a framework for peace education. Montessori's work can be seen as laying the groundwork for much of the philosophy and theory of educating for peace in the latter half of the century. Montessori's work with children began with Italian street youth. She later developed extensive theoretical work on child development. Montessori was deeply influenced by her Christian faith and her philosophy reflects this. As well, she was influenced by the new field of psychoanalysis developing at that time. Montessori believed strongly in the inherent creativity and spirituality of every child. According to her, children can and should be teachers of the adults around them.

Montessori emphasized the need for adults to teach children how to resolve conflicts nonviolently and to keep children from being fascinated by war: writing in a Fascist state, at the beginning of what would become the Second World War, this great Italian educator, invoking the teachings of Jesus, declared that a child provides a guide for adults to the Kingdom of Heaven. Montessori believed that adults must become more like children if they are to achieve "heaven on earth." Children are trusting and open. Children have a love for others that provides the basis for peaceful coexistence on this planet. Montessori believed that educators must develop the spiritual side of themselves and prepare children for a way of life that will support peace:

> Society at present does not adequately prepare man for civic life; there is no "moral organization" of the masses. Human beings are brought up to regard themselves as isolated individuals who must satisfy their immediate needs by competing with other individuals. A powerful campaign or organization would be required to enable men to understand and structure social phenomenon, to prepare and pursue collective ends, and thus to bring about orderly social progress.[24]

Montessori wrote that "establishing a lasting peace is the work of education; all politics can do is keep us out of war."[25] She believed that science attempted to understand the physical world, but scientists knew little of the inner workings of the human spirit. Educators should fill children with a faith in the greatness and grandeur of the human spirit. Whereas modern technology might make it possible to master the objective world, the educator's task is to free the human spirit to develop a sense of humanity that will worship life and lead to peaceful coexistence. The spiritual life of human beings, properly nourished, will help create a better world where harmony reigns.

Maria Montessori was suspicious of authoritarian pedagogues and authoritarian families, which, she felt, contributed to the people in Europe (specifically in Spain with Franco, in Germany with Hitler, and in her native Italy with Mussolini) accepting fascist rule. In her classroom the teacher was not an authoritarian figure. Rather, as she wrote, students should be free to select their learning activities (within carefully prescribed choices). She felt that giving children the right to make their own decisions about what to learn in school would train them to think independently, so that they would not be so easily swayed by demagogues.

Herbert Read, an English art critic, lectured widely after the Second World War on the topic of peace education. A collection of his essays entitled *Education for Peace* (1949) argued that moral education contributes to the development of a sense of the human spirit and a reverence for life. Information about the world and maps and lectures about different cultures won't provide, by itself, the moral fiber that provides a basis for human coexistence. The moral person commands him or herself. The peaceful person controls him or herself and respects other people. Schools can give children this disposition toward peace. Art teaches respect for order, balance, symmetry, rhythm, and harmony. In education teachers should seek to avoid hate by positive means, teaching in ways that promote the good of the social order. Moral behavior does not require rational calculations, but rather a disposition to act kindly toward each other. Like Maria Montessori, Read felt that children were naturally moral, and thus peaceful, and that educators had to nourish and refine these tendencies.

Read applied these educational concepts to the social sphere. He believed that schools foster unhealthy competitive relationships among children. Teachers, school boards, and principals all play a role in perpetrating this unequal social structure. Read underscored the importance of meaningful work. People who are bored with nothing to do end up creating mischief. According to Read, the Nazi party in Germany recruited from the streets young unemployed hooligans who had no gainful employment. "The difficulty is not to maintain oneself, but to create a society in which the self can expand and find its fulfillment."[26] Read was not just interested in education helping to create pacifist human beings, but he also wanted education to be part of the creation of a better world. Education should seek to unite human beings, not classify and divide them, according to Read. Art education can provide an emotional catharsis for students that will channel violent impulses and help people to concretize their dreams of peace.

Another person writing during period of the Second World War was Teilhard de Chardin, a French theologian who spent much time studying evolution. Because he was a Catholic friar and his writings on evolution were controversial, his superiors ordered him not to publish. His books were printed posthumously in the 1950s. De Chardin saw the human species as an "animal phylum" that had spread throughout the world into different branches, with human consciousness developing as a "spiral" of this spread, moving toward greater unity. The ultimate end of human consciousness was the "omega point," where all differences among human beings would be settled and human consciousness unified. Love provided the energy that propelled human consciousness forward towards this unity.[27]

De Chardin has been one of the key contributors to futurist thinking (further discussion on futures studies is contained in Chapter 11). Futurists proclaim that human societies have evolved from tribal communities, to city states, to sovereign nations, to federations of different states like the Soviet Union, the United States, and India, to the European community, and the next step is a vision of a global society. The advent of television, satellite technologies, and the Internet have concretized the vision put forth by de Chardin of the unity of human consciousness. As this consciousness builds towards a critical mass, it seeks new solutions to global problems, attempting to foster a world community, and discarding the old military means for solving problems. Such a vision, hastened by the development of nuclear weapons, unifies all creatures and makes war unacceptable because it threatens the destruction of the whole human race.

Danilo Dolci, educated as an architect, became a leading figure in the struggle to use nonviolent means to achieve social justice. He moved to Sicily in 1952 and died in 1999. While in Sicily he helped to establish a "people's college," an educational center for primary school children, a variety of centers for conflict resolution, and also developed social survey that drew attention to the extreme poverty in Sicily. Working with the poor and uneducated, he set up study groups that have provided a model for adult education, using group discussion methods to create "a dialogue through which each individual develops the ability to openly use the group situation to the best advantage."[28] Although his work was mostly in community development, Dolci used an educational style in which the teacher or educator takes on the role of midwife and helps "give birth" to ideas. Dolci's educational methods provided a model for helping people to understand the violent nature of their circumstances. It helped his pupils to become more active in promoting projects which improved their lives. His educational groups exposed the conditions under which people lived at that time and he taught villagers to use nonviolent means to gain their ends. As a result of this work, in Sicily there have been many public improvements and jobs created. One significant recent accomplishment has been the construction of a dam on the Iato River which provides irrigation for over a dozen villages in western Sicily.

> The only solution is to organize democratic groups and coordinate them so well that they successfully pressure politicians. The bosses may appear invulnerable, but the politicians need votes, and the businessmen need sales. They all fear public education.[29]

Like Gandhi, Dolci was a man of action. He felt that the struggle for peace and justice needed more than love and Christian nonviolent strategies. His contribution to peace education was to get people working collectively to develop a more sophisticated consciousness and to seek concrete solutions to problems caused by violence.

Outside of Europe, in the 1970s a Brazilian educator, Paulo Freire, developed an educational methodology to help peasants to understand more fully the sources of their own oppression. He posited that humans need to understand how to overcome the sources of their own oppression in order to be free. Although not known as a peace educator per se, Freire celebrated the human capacity for love that can help humans achieve freedom in a just and democratic society. He saw that the right kind of education can liberate people from structural violence.

Johan Galtung, a Norwegian born in 1930, continues to promote peace education and peace research. He was trained as a mathematician and sociologist and was a professor of peace research at the University of Oslo. A founder in 1968 of the International Peace Institute (PRIO), in Oslo, Norway, he has become a leading figure in peace research and scholarship. His earlier writings promoted the concept of structural violence— where poverty, discrimination and oppression, underdevelopment, and illiteracy are understood to contribute to the violent state of the world. Addressing these issues has helped to promote exchanges in ideas, programs and strategies between those interested in peace education and those interested in development education. The aim is to provide awareness in "First World" countries about how problems of underdevelopment in the Third World contribute to violence.

Galtung has also emphasized that peace education must be taught peacefully. He has criticized violence in the classroom and has argued that peace education itself must use methods and techniques that model peace, including allowing students to participate fully in running the class, affirming differences and skills that students bring to peace education, and engaging in open ended dialogue about the problems of war and peace. He and other European peace educators have emphasized that peace education will not be effective relying on traditional educational methods—where expert teachers, by imposing their opinions on students, do not give students any concrete experience with democracy. Peace education must provide, through its methods, new ways to teach and learn that model the kind of world toward which peace educators strive.

Galtung, the original director of PRIO in Norway, now serves as a consultant to educators and researchers in the Third World, helping them work on issues of literacy and peace education. He has written numerous books, articles and a five volume collection, *Essays in Peace Research*.[30] Some of his books include *Peace by Peaceful Means*[31] and *Searching for Peace*.[32] He helped found two of the leading peace research journals, *Bulletin of Peace Proposals* and *Journal of Peace Research*, both of which are published by PRIO. His serious dedication to peace scholarships has helped make peace research a respected academic discipline.

The Concept of Peace in the American Experience

Throughout American history, peace has been a concern, and people have organized to achieve it. It is important that American peace educators gain an understanding of the historical dimensions of peace in the U.S. Peace education, per se, has its roots in the social reform movement of the latter half of the nineteenth century and is largely a result of the rise of the women's movement in the twentieth century.[33] The distinctions between peace and peace education are sometimes arbitrary. This section of the chapter will focus on the evolving conceptual dimensions in America of peace and education for peace. Both Johan Galtung and Elise Boulding have noted that in reality there are "fuzzy distinctions" between peace research, education and peace activism. Good researchers are also educators and activists, and so forth. Yet peace education has its own conceptual dimensions as well.

First is a historical overview of the peace movement in the U.S. Following this is a discussion of the major themes and a more in-depth look at historical trends in peace and peace education in the United States. Specific contributions and programs are mentioned.

The peace movement in the U.S. has its roots in the early days of American settlement, and is signified by the pacifists such as the Quakers, Mennonites and Brethren settling in this country, practicing their form of Christianity which followed the nonviolent teachings of Jesus. The Quakers and other groups also set up their own schools, in order that the education of their young people be "guarded," that is removed from the "ways of the world." Quaker education influenced the slow and gradual ascension of the public school movement in the nineteenth century within the United States, and thus may be said to have indirectly contributed to the growth of peace education. Quaker schools to this day have active programs educating for peace.

Out of the ashes of the first World War came the founding of several organizations in the U.S. devoted to peace. These included the Fellowship of Reconciliation, an interfaith religious organization devoted to working for peace and justice. A.J. Muste was its long term executive director. Also founded at this time, by Jane Addams and other leading feminist reformers, was the Women's International League for Peace and Freedom. Several noted American feminists, also at that time working for women's suffrage, attended the founding meeting of the WILPF, held in the Hague in 1915. Woodrow Wilson is recorded as saying about the formulations for peace developed at that Congress that they were "by far the best formulation which up to the moment has been put up by anybody."[34] The American Friends Service Committee was founded by the Quakers in 1917 as an organization devoted to providing war relief and alternatives to military service for young conscientious objectors. In 1947 the AFSC won the Nobel Peace Prize. Such organizations and others like them have formed the backbone of civic society from the beginning of this century.

The most recent period of the peace movement began in the 1960s, when large numbers of people began questioning the United States' involvement in Vietnam. During the 1970s there came an increasing concern among peace activists over the growth and development of nuclear weapons. At the same time, the feminist movement was challenging male-dominated views of the nature of war and aggression. Feminist peace scholars such as Elise Boulding, Betty Reardon and Norwegian Birgit Brock-Utne were questioning the emphasis placed within the peace movement on the arms race, the exclusion of issues relating to structural violence.[35]

In the mid twentieth century, the first of the programs in the U.S. devoted to an academic understanding of peace were founded. The first of these was the Lentz Institute in St. Louis, the oldest continually operating peace research center in the U.S., founded in 1945. Others followed: the Center for Research on Conflict Resolution at the University of Michigan in 1959, founded in part by economist and systems thinker Kenneth Boulding the International Peace Research Association (IPRA) in 1965, founded in part by both Kenneth and Elise Boulding, as an international linking agency with many other U.S. peace academics counted among its founders. COPRED, the Consortium on Peace Research, Education and Development, often called the American section of IPRA, was founded in 1970 in Boulder, Colorado. The latter half of the century found a dramatic increase in the number of programs on college campuses devoted to the study and practice of peace. The first college peace studies program was founded in 1948 at Manchester College, a Brethren college in Indiana. At the end of the twentieth century, after the collapse of the Berlin Wall in the late 1980s, and partly under the influence of the women's movement that has highlighted the severity of domestic violence, peace activists have begun to study and work for violence reduction in homes and in communities, including civil crime, sexual assault, youth violence, and media violence, as well as to show linkages between this and global violence.

At the beginning of the Twenty-First century U.S. attention is focusing on the threat of terrorism, as the disenfranchised of the world, unable to wage war against a state, perform individual acts of extreme violence to impact upon the lives of those living in "enemy countries." Fear of bioterrorism, chemical war, and nuclear sabotage is complementing a deep concern about the health of the environment that is developing as forests die, the ozone layer depletes, temperatures rise, and water becomes scarce. A further concern is globalization, where large multinational corporations are accumulating power and wealth that transcend national boundaries.

The history of the United States contains a struggle between those who desire peace and those who wage wars. Clearly, the militarists' force has dominated this struggle, so much so that American history texts describe in depth the heroic acts of warriors and make few references to the noble efforts of those who have worked for peace. The Boston Tea Party itself, an American benchmark", may be considered a peaceful act of civil disobedience. Rarely is it discussed as such, usually rather as an introduction to the study of the Revolutionary War.

Many of the solid contributions toward peace made by Americans have remained uncelebrated. Quaker settlements in Pennsylvania were well known for their respectful relations with Indians, and from their early days as settlers, the Society of Friends (as the Quakers refer to themselves) used nonviolent means to settle disputes that arose between themselves and the native people. Indeed, William Penn's founding of the colony of Pennsylvania was to be an experiment in living out the Peaceable Kingdom. One Quaker, John Woolman, wrote in his journal in 1774 that all wars come from a desire for profit. "First to plunder them; then to protect them."[36] Largely due Woolman's writing about slavery, many Quakers voluntarily freed their slaves before the Revolutionary War. Later Quakers led in the abolitionist movement. In the days of the early colonies many Quakers were persecuted for their refusal to bear arms.

Benjamin Banneker, the black astronomer, suggested to President George Washington that he establish a federal peace office. Dr. Benjamin Rush, a distinguished Philadelphia physician, recommended in 1798 that a Secretary of Peace be established to propagandize for the abolition of war. Although a loyal patriot during the Revolutionary War, Benjamin Franklin declared afterwards "that there has never been, nor ever will be, any such things as a good war or a bad peace."[37] In his later life Franklin became convinced that all wars are folly, and that in the interest of common sense and for the brotherhood of people, efforts must be taken to prevent war. One of these efforts eventually ended in the movement to establish free and universal public education. Thomas Paine had a vision of an alliance of nations in which all disputes would be referred to arbitration, in which aggressors were to be penalized. In *The Federalist Papers*, Alexander Hamilton, James Madison, and John Jay wrote that a strong federal union would prevent the outbreak of war and lay the foundation for peace.

New England clergy led the resistance to the War of 1812. Opposition to this war gave rise to the Anglo-American agreement of 1817, which was the first arms limitation agreement in history. The period following that war led to a great deal of concern for humanitarian causes, including women's rights, the emancipation of slaves, and the abolition of capital punishment. It was during this period that several peace societies were founded. The American Peace Society (1826) had chapters in all major cities on the East Coast, and became a leading proponent for peace. In 1837 the New York Peace Society called for a congress of nations, and many leading Americans participated in peace congresses held in Brussels in 1848, Paris in 1849, and Frankfurt in 1850. The leaders of this movement argued that war was anachronistic—a remnant of the social jungle out of which civilization had evolved.

At this time many Americans opposed U.S. involvement in the Mexican-American War, the foremost opponent being Henry David Thoreau, who was jailed for his refusal to pay taxes to support that war. His pamphlet, *Civil Disobedience*,[38] explained his opposition to war taxes. In this essay Thoreau appealed to conscience. People opposed to the unjust actions of their government should do more than just talk about these injustices. They should follow the dictates of their conscience and break those laws which they perceive to be unjust. In such cases it is important to take a stand, not because taking such a stand will overthrow the government, but rather because acts of civil disobedience educate others about injustice. Thoreau argued that governments get their authority from the allegiance of their citizens. Citizens opposed to an unjust government can make an individual decision based on the Preamble to the Declaration of Independence, which states that all people have the right of revolution, to overthrow tyranny and withdraw their allegiance from that government.

After the Civil War, advocating for peace in the United States became more popular. Based on repulsion to the horrors of the war, peace activists believed they could persuade government rulers of the justice of their cause. Leaders of the peace movement in 1898 called for an international arbitration conference in the Hague. These activists were strongly opposed to what they considered President McKinley's and the United States's imperialist designs in the Caribbean and the Pacific. At the beginning of the twentieth century wealthy people who established private foundations to support peace causes helped solidify support among the middle classes for the peace movement. In 1901 Alfred Nobel established the Nobel Peace Prize.[39] Andrew Carnegie established the Carnegie Endowment for International Peace in 1912, at which time there were 63 different societies in the United States advocating for peace.

The growing era of war in Europe stimulated the involvement of many leading churches in peace work in the 19-teens. William Jennings Bryan, democratic candidate for President, was a Christian pacifist who had opposed the Spanish-American War and visited Tolstoy in 1903. President Woodrow Wilson was a member of the American Peace Society, and his interest in this issue motivated him to work hard for the League of Nations after the First World War.

In 1906 the American Peace Society appointed a committee to investigate the contents and spirit of school textbooks in relation to war, peace, nationalism, and internationalism. In its report this group indicated that between 1843 and 1845 some forty percent of the content of American history books was devoted to war. That was reduced to 27 percent between 1890 and 1904.[40] Educators responded to this groundswell of interest in peace by forming in 1907 the American School Peace League that established, with the support of the National Education Association, state chapters that promoted peace in schools. Teachers in this organization advocated for citizen education, international relations, and peace education. Under the leadership of Fanny Fern Andrews, the League was conceived of as a way to organize teachers into an active campaign to prevent a world war.[41] She first proposed the establishment of an International Bureau of Education, under the framework of the League of Nations, at a Paris peace conference in 1919. Finally in 1929 such an organization was established in Geneva, Switzerland. Today the International Bureau of Education continues to support peace education activities around the world.[42]

After the First World War interest in peace increased in the United States among some scholars. During the years between the two world wars many people feared the terror of war. These years saw the beginning of the attempts by the League of Nations to resolve international conflicts. Much effort was directed towards international education in the hope that understanding of different cultures would lead to peaceful coexistence on this planet.

Yet due to the rise of the influence of communism and the "Red Scare," during the 1930s there was less talk of peace per se. A theme still echoing into the Twenty-First century, peace to a certain extent was and is considered unpatriotic. There was also growing anti–German sentiment and animosity toward foreigners in general in the 1930s. The American School Peace League had by this time been renamed the American School Citizenship League. Using the term "peace" for work in schools became highly politically sensitive.

John Dewey, American progressive educator, also took up the cause of peace. Although roundly denounced by many peace advocates for supporting United States involvement in World War One, he maintained that military training should not take place in schools. His support for progressive education led him to a position where education for democracy required the training of creative and free thinking individuals. According to Dewey, there was an intricate connection between children's minds (whose purpose toward which education should be directed), experience and the pursuit of peace. Biographer Charles Hawlett writes:

> His own misgivings with regard to the crusade to "make the world safe for democracy" [World War I] added to his conviction therefore that it was high time for the schools to become agents of peace instead of vehicles for hyper-patriotism and ultranationalism.[43]

For Dewey, democracy was the embodiment of social and moral growth in human beings. In order to prepare people for citizenship in a democracy, schools had to teach cooperation and understanding. Any form of externally imposed strict discipline ran counter to his views on progressive education. Education, he argued:

> has to avoid all dogmatism in instruction, for such a course gradually but surely created the impression that everything is already settled and nothing remains to be found out.[44]

Dewey believed that militarism in all its forms must be opposed by educators who desire to create free-thinking individuals.

A leading figure of the peace movement between the First and Second World Wars was A. J. Muste, who, as previously mentioned, in the 1940s was the executive director of the Fellowship of Reconciliation. In the 1950s and 1960s he helped leaders from CORE (the Congress of Racial Equality) organize freedom rides and other nonviolent protest tactics to help black people acquire civil rights. An ordained minister who helped organize the textile mill strike of 1919 in Lawrence, Massachusetts, he resigned in 1936 from active participation in the United States Communist Party to adopt a religious pacifist position. He stated that it was the Christian duty of pacifists to practice civil disobedience against militarism:

> Non-conformity, Holy Disobedience, becomes a virtue and indeed a necessary and indispensable measure of spiritual self preservation, in a day when the impulse to confirm, to acquiesce, to go along, is the instrument which is used to subject men to totalitarian rule and involve them in permanent war.[45]

In this same essay Muste discussed the failure of the Germans to oppose Nazism and urged people to speak out and take a stand against injustice. Such stands provide others with the courage to act upon their convictions.

The Second World War brought new horrors to the human imagination. Saturation bombing and the development of the atomic bomb meant that civilian populations were no longer spared the terror of war. Albert Einstein, whose scientific discoveries made possible the splitting of the atom, urged President Franklin Delano Roosevelt to desist in making the A-bomb on humanitarian grounds. Roosevelt proceeded with the top-secret Manhattan Project and in August of 1945 the first atomic bomb was dropped on Hiroshima. Karl Jaspers, a German philosopher, called this the new fact that fundamentally altered human existence. Albert Einstein said that the splitting of the atom changed everything but human thinking.

Soon after World War II there arose concerns about the threat of nuclear war and a renewed effort to teach about the consequences of the arms race. The idea of educating for global citizenship continued to be popular, the consequences being an increase in student exchange programs and the development of world order model projects.[46] The 1950s were also a low point in the history of the development of new programs for educating for peace, as McCarthyism took its toll on dissenters in the U.S. In 1958 the National Defense Education Act passed, greatly increasing federal aid to education in the areas of science, math, engineering and foreign languages. This followed on the heels of the 1957 launching of Sputnik by the Soviets and American's fear that we were "falling behind" technologically. Because of this and the continued Red Scare, the output of peace education material greatly diminished during this time.[47]

The Cold War, which followed the Second World War, used anti–Communist hysteria to justify further weapons build-up to the point where today the military budget and the defense establishment dominate United States' policies. In the 1950s a few scientists and citizens became alarmed by the prospect of nuclear weaponry. A group of mothers protested atmospheric testing of nuclear weapons and "went out on strike" in the early 1960s, calling themselves the Women's Strike for Peace. President Kennedy loudly praised their work on behalf of children in the world when he signed the atmospheric test ban treaty in 1962. If it had not been for the courageous work of these women, some of whom had never before been activists, millions of people throughout this planet might have been poisoned by radioactive fallout.

The greatest nonviolent hero to many in the United States in the twentieth century is the late Dr. Martin Luther King, Jr. A Baptist minister, King gained worldwide prominence when he and others organized the nonviolent bus boycott among Blacks in Montgomery, Alabama. Deeply influenced by Mahatma Gandhi, he took a trip to India:

> As I delved deeper into the philosophy of Gandhi my skepticism concerning the power of love gradually diminished, and I came to see for the first time that the Christian doctrine of love operating through the Gandhian method of nonviolence was one of the most potent weapons available to oppressed people in their struggle for freedom.[48]

Although Dr. King made his name known throughout the world for his opposition to racial injustice, he also spoke out very strongly against United States involvement in Vietnam and militarism:

> War, I felt, horrible as it is, might be preferable to surrender to a totalitarian system. But more and more I have come to the conclusion

that the potential destructiveness of modern weapons of war totally rules out the possibility of war ever serving again as a negative good. If we assume that mankind has a right to survive then we must find an alternative to war and destruction. In a day when sputniks dash through outer space and guided ballistic missiles are carving highways of death through the stratosphere, nobody can win a war. The choice today is no longer between violence and nonviolence. It is either nonviolence or nonexistence....[49]

King understood that laws can regulate behavior, but morality cannot be legislated. An orientation towards justice and peace can only come through education that changes inner attitudes away from complacency about suffering to anger towards injustice. Education has a key role to play in developing a world perspective, so that children and adults see that they have similarities with people from other cultures, nations, and races. Martin Luther King, Jr. saw an urgency to teach about nonviolence:

> The alternative to disarmament, the alternative to a greater suspension of nuclear tests, the alternative to strengthening the United Nations and thereby disarming the whole world may well be civilization plunged into the abyss of annihilation, or our earthly habitat would be transformed into an inferno that even the mind of Dante could not imagine.[50]

Dr. King believed in the power of dissent to establish a creative tension that challenges the violence of the status quo and awakens feelings of compassion for the victims of violence. He would often use public demonstrations, like the Montgomery bus boycott, to bring problems out into the open where they would be subject to public scrutiny and debate. King saw that violence begets more violence and makes brotherhood impossible. The only way out of cycles of violence is through nonviolence.

Dr. King was killed in 1968. With his death the peace movement that was building to oppose the Vietnamese War lost some of its concern for racial and social justice. Dr. King's addition to the peace movement had linked together the desire for peace with the desire for racial and economic justice, fusing these causes together into a strong nonviolent movement for social change.

In 1974 the Quaker Project on Community Conflict in New York city published *The Friendly Classroom for a Small Planet*, a curriculum for teachers of young children who wanted to enable students to develop a sense of self-worth, build community and acquire the skills of creative conflict resolution. Since that time, the curriculum has gone through 25 editions and has been translated into seven different languages. It is being used extensively in schools in El Salvador, as well as in other countries.

The preface from the first edition sums up its philosophy and states the goals of many modern peace education programs in primary schools:

> Our particular program has three main goals in the classroom: 1. to promote growth toward a community in which children are capable and desirous of open communication; 2. to help children gain insights into the nature of human feelings and share their own feelings; and 3. to explore with children the unique personal ways in which they can respond to problems and begin to prevent or solve conflicts.[51]

One example of a major U.S. initiative for peace in the late twentieth century is the establishment of the U.S. Institute for Peace. George Washington said in 1783, "There can be little doubt but the Congress will recommend a proper peace establishment for the United States."[52] In 1978 the Senate amended an education bill to provide for a commission to study proposals for a National Academy of Peace and Conflict Resolution, and subsequently authorized funds to hold public hearings that were conducted in twelve major cities where more than 300 witnesses produced 7,000 pages of testimony. Noted peace researcher and educator Elise Boulding had been nominated by President Carter to this commission. The commission decided to establish in the nation's capital an institute that would serve as a clearinghouse for peace research and peace education. The agency was created in 1986. This institute has an international focus on the causes of war and promotes education and research on the effectiveness of various peace strategies.

The second wave of the feminist movement of the 1970s saw an increase in emphasis to connect the root causes of war (injustice) to both domestic and international violence. Feminists brought to the public an awareness of the breadth of suffering caused by violence in many forms, including child abuse and neglect and domestic abuse. These topics had heretofore been ignored by peace educators. As the century came to a close, schools continued to take on more of the role of socially serving their students, while at the same time there was growing concern about the culture of violence within our educational institutions. Peace education programs have diversified to include domestic violence, the teaching of mediation skills, an emphasis on ecology, and have reflected the growing realization of the interconnectedness of the planet.

In the 1980s three books were published by American peace educators, representing the evolution of peace education from its earlier emphasis on the prevention of war to the more recent concerns around nuclear annihilation, feminist concerns about the effects of militarization and structural violence on all humans, but in particular women and children, and the growing role of nongovernmental and grass-roots organizations working for peace. These books are: *Comprehensive Peace Education* by Betty Reardon, *Building a Global Civic Culture* by Elise Boulding, and *Peace Education* by Ian Harris, the first edition of the current book.[53] Reardon argued that the core values of schooling should be care, concern and commitment, and the key concepts of peace education should be planetary stewardship, global citizenship, and humane relationships. Reardon's work echoed the work of educational thinkers such as philosophers as Nell Noddings and Jane Roland Martin, who emphasize the important role of nurturing that teachers and community-oriented classrooms can play in the development of healthy children (further information in these theorists is found in Chapter 3). Boulding's work offered theoretical underpinnings for the rapid proliferation of nongovernmental or "people's associations" and the role they are continuing to play in educating for global citizenship. Harris pointed out that the key ingredients of any peace pedagogy include cooperative learning, democratic community, moral sensitivity and critical thinking. Having taught in the inner city, he was concerned about the effects of various forms of civil violence upon classroom endeavors.

At the beginning of the 1990s peace educators became more concerned about civil, domestic, and ethnic forms of violence, as the term "cultural violence" began to be recognized as describing some aspects of our own society as well as others suffering the wounds of community intra-national strife. Beginning in the 1990s and continuing into the new century, schools are returning to the teaching of morals, hearkening back to earlier in the century and the work of Dewey. The 1990s also saw a huge increase in the number of formal conflict resolution programs seen in schools, from elementary through high school.[54] These programs teach nonviolent communication skills to children in the hope that they will be able to avoid violent confrontations with their peers. Violence prevention techniques are also taught to help youth resist various forms of violence that exist in our contemporary society. These include: violence against women, gang violence, sexual abuse and suicide. Modern peace educators are also concerned about images of cultural violence dominating the media and popular entertainment. (Further information about nonviolence in schools is found in Chapter 3.)

Conclusion

This chapter has addressed various religious and historic contributions to the development and expansion of our understanding of the concepts "peace" and "peace education." These contributions, though naming the "famous," reflect the hopes and dreams of millions of unnamed ordinary citizens who want peace and who have striven to achieve it, but do not become historic figures. The ideas and accomplishments of the more well known peace heroes mentioned in this chapter rest upon the shoulders of those citizen-activists whose dedication has created movements that have built a climate which allows peace to flourish.

The modern concept of peace contains many of the time-honored historic notions: respect for life, commitment to nonviolence, concern for social justice, manifestations of love for other creatures, desire for international law and order and the promotion of universal human rights. People throughout the world carry with them different visions of peace. Some draw from the historical and religious traditions mentioned in this chapter. Some dream of relationships without conflict, a society where hunger and starvation have been eliminated, a planet where people love their neighbors and live sustainably without destroying precious natural resources, and a world devoid of war. The challenge of peace, then, is to move beyond fear and hatred of others to a state of reconciliation where mutual respect and trust flourish and where deep instincts and desires for peace may be realized. Visions of "Spaceship Earth" suggest that human beings should become unified in their love for each other and for their planet before technological weaponry might possibly destroy human civilization.

The modern peace movement is extremely diverse, including feminists concerned with sexual assault, environmentalists concerned about global warming, and anti-trade protesters concerned about the New World Order. Peace educators respond to the concerns raised by these issues when they teach about the various problems of violence that exist on this planet and tell their students about nonviolent alternative strategies to address these problems. The history of peace provided here offers many positive visions, including how human beings have actively intervened to resolve conflicts nonviolently and are working to eliminate both physical and structural violence by eradicating social injustice and the causes of war. These visions, as suggested by some of the world's great religious thinkers, and by educational philosophers and peace educators, motivate people to work to for peace. This task will continue to demand the utmost of human creativity and energy.

Visions of peace have helped to motivate educators around the world to take risks and to use their professional skills to help make the world a less violent place. Peace education now being promoted by dedicated professionals and grassroots citizens takes different forms according to the cultural visions that motivate people in different parts of the world. Teachers share common goals to bring about peace, but use different names for their activities, various methods, and widely diverse programs to share their visions of peace with students.

CHAPTER 3

The Practice of Peace Education— What Does It Look Like? Types of Peace Education

> *We should ask what our schools, colleges, and universities have been doing to advance worldwide human survival and dignity. To what extent and in what ways have they sought to prepare our students to meet the twin challenge of peril and change that looms so large in front of each and every one of us?*
>
> Burns H. Weston

The actual practice of peace education varies throughout the world. What is presented in the name of peace education depends upon varying notions of security and peace, differing religious traditions, cultural values, and linguistic concepts. In each country peace educators initiate programs based on the political realities of their nations, emphasizing concepts valued by widely diverse cultures. Within all of these programs exists the commonality of teaching about the root causes of conflict as well as alternatives to violence. This chapter will provide a brief summary of how peace has been and is being taught. The final section will discuss the role of the church and adult education. This presentation is not exhaustive but highlights major trends, with the hope of illustrating the tremendous diversity of peace education.

Why Peace Education?

"Peace education" is preferred as a generic term because it includes concepts implied in many different educational approaches. All of these different approaches complement each other and contribute to the rich diversity of the emerging academic discipline, irenology, from the Greek word for peace, "irene." Different world cultures have contributed greatly to this emerging and broadly based discipline. From the South has come an emphasis on human rights and social justice. Japan has contributed an understanding of the horrors of a nuclear war, and the northern industrial societies have added their understanding of the psychological effects of violence. Peace education encompasses the root causes of war, the destruction of the environment, the national security state, international relations, human rights, and global cultures.

Peace education, as an overall paradigm, is closely connected, as we have discussed, with the concept of peace. Carl Jung refers to peace as an archetype that exists within the collective unconscious. As a major component of the world's religions, the search for peace rests on the assumption of the positive evolution of world order and innate goodness of the human spirit.

Current names for peace education, as it is being practiced throughout the world, include such diverse terms as "human rights education," "environmental education," "international education," "conflict resolution education," and "development education." All of these different approaches include education about the problems of violence, though in some approaches this is more implicit than in others. Peace education is the pedagogical effort to build a better world, including the teaching of the skills and techniques of conflict management—skills that aren't traditionally taught in such fields as international studies or world order studies. Peace education may be viewed as the educational activities that aim to help humans to achieve peace. Thus peace education, as has been discussed, includes both the philosophical and the practical. This chapter will provide a discussion of these different approaches to peace education. Included is a section on the importance of the United Nations to peace education. Also included is a section on peace education for adults, in churches and community settings.

Human Rights Education

Human rights education addresses injustices brought about by political repression, human suffering, misery, civil strife, and prejudice.[1] This kind of peace education has a literal and broad interpretation. Peace educators are guided by the Universal Declaration of Human Rights that provides a statement of values to be pursued in order to achieve economic, social, and political justice. Various statements of human rights derive from concepts of natural law, a higher set of laws that are universally applicable and supersede governmental laws. Narrowly construed, the study of human rights is the study of treaties, United Nations institutions, and domestic and international courts. People being persecuted by their governments for political beliefs often appeal to provisions of international law to gain support for their cause. Abuse of rights, and the struggle to eliminate that abuse, lies at the heart of many violent conflicts. Human rights institutions have begun to address rights against discrimination based upon gender, disability, and sexual orientation.

Elise Boulding[2] points out how nongovernmental organizations help protect the rights of people being oppressed by states and help build communities of solidarity through various peace movements. Peace educators can teach about these struggles in remote parts of the world as well as getting students to focus or the rights of minority groups within their own communities. Adam Curle[3] discusses how international nongovernmental organizations can intercede in the midst of violent conflict to support the rights of oppressed peoples. The study of human rights abuses in places like China, Myanmar, and Rwanda helps students develop an international perspective on the problems of violence.

On the local scene human rights education may be broadly construed in ways that honor the basic dignity of all people. This aspect of peace education includes multicultural understanding aimed at reducing stereotypes and hostilities between groups. In the words of noted peace educator Betty Reardon, "cross-cultural ignorance and the hostilities it helps maintain and exacerbate argue strongly for multicultural education as an essential element of education for peace."[4] In peace camps in the Middle East with Israeli and Palestinian children, and other places where people are attempting to transform ethnic, religious and racial hatred, this kind of education attempts to eliminate deep cultural biases and intergroup hate by challenging stereotypes, breaking down enemy images and changing perceptions of and ways of relating.

These approaches to peace education are concerned with the tendency to label others as enemies and to oppose or fight them. Here conflict is identity based, where people hate others who belong to groups different than theirs, perceived as the enemy. Peace educators in these contexts attempt to replace enemy images with an understanding of common heritage, and to help break through a process of numbing and denial about atrocities committed in seemingly intractable conflicts. A project called Compassionate Listening allows groups of committed people, Jews, Muslims and those of other faiths, opportunities to dialogue and hear stories of those who have suffered deeply on both sides of the Israeli-Palestinian conflict. The idea is that hearing stories can promote compassionate identification, even with those who may see the world in very different ways. Educators promote compassion for the suffering of many in the hopes of reducing ethnic and religious hatred and bringing members of conflicting groups together in a dialogic communication process that searches for common understandings. The key is to accept the other and respect the inherent humanity that resides within all. Self-imposed psychological boundaries must be broken down. The goal is an understanding of differences and an adoption of a disposition to care for others who belong to different social-religious, ethnic or national groups.

Environmental Education

Traditional peace educators, concerned about threats of war, have often ignored the environmental aspects connected with peacemaking. With the rise of global warming, rapid species extinction, and the adverse effects of pollution, educators are realizing that it is not sufficient just to talk about military security, as in protecting the citizens of a country from a foreign threat, but it is also necessary to promote a concept of peace based upon ecological security, where humans are protected and nourished by natural processes.

C. A. Bowers[5] has raised a devastating critique of Western notions of progress, which assume that the natural environment is an infinite resource that humans can use to their enjoyment without regarding the consequences of environmental despoliation. Scientific growth based upon rational modes of problem solving has created a planet that is despoiled and is losing many of its creatures to extinction. Instead of anthropocentric cultures, with autonomous individuals at the center of the universe, teachers concerned with environmental issues promote a survival culture that acknowledges the important values of traditional (native) cultures. They provide an awareness of the continuities of the past, rather than an unquestioning belief in new ideas, products etc., that promotes a view of change as progressive. Many technological advances are destructive to the natural world. Peace educators see that many different forms of knowledge (folk knowledge, and the like) have value.

Peace educators concerned about environmental destruction teach about appropriate technology and sustainable development. They emphasize the role of treaties, like the Law of the Sea Treaty or the Kyoto Accord, that attempt to preserve environmental resources. David Orr[6] has pointed out how schools need to teach ecological awareness and care so that a peace literate person is aware of the planet's plight, its social and ecological problems, and has a commitment to do something about them.

The goal of environmental education is to promote sustainable development that has been defined as:

> A process of social change in which policies and practices are established to meet human needs, both material (physical necessities) and nonmaterial (e.g., access to a clean environment, political and spiritual freedom, meaningful work, and good health). Social change, within this context, must not occur at the expense of the resource base upon which societies are dependent.[7]

The study of the environment lends to holistic thinking about how natural and human systems interrelate. Such studies should contribute to an ecological world outlook that contains basic ecological knowledge, develops strong personal convictions about protecting natural resources, and provides dynamic experiences conserving natural resources. Peace educators also emphasize preserving the habitat in which students are located, explaining the importance of bio-regionalism. People within a particular region, like the Middle East, learn how to draw upon the strengths of that region, rather than counting on advanced industrial conglomerates to conduct commerce. (A more extended discussion of ecology, the environment and sustainability and their relationship to visioning for the future is found in Chapter 11.)

International Education

Derek Heater[8] has pointed out how important it is for peace studies students to understand the international interstate system that so often leads to war. Global peace educators provide an understanding of how nation states construct security for their citizens. This type of peace education, also known as world order studies[9] or education for world citizenship, includes helping students understand the positive and negative aspects of globalization, which has led to the erosion of the power of national governments. There are three types of globalization: economic (particularly transnational corporations and the creation of a consumer-dominated global middle class), public order (governments working together on common problems such as health and environmental problems) and popular (the campaigns by grass roots organizations such as Amnesty International, Greenpeace, Medecins sans Frontieres, and other NGOs and GROs (grass roots organizations). The reality is that globalization is taking place and cannot be reversed. The growing interconnectedness of the world's citizens offers exciting potential for peacebuilding. The question peace educators should be asking is how we can bring together all of the parties to make sure that globalization works.

International education is a diverse field. Some researchers within this field look towards the creation of a federal world state with laws and courts that can adjudicate conflicts between nations, so that they don't go to war to settle their disagreements.[10] Others look to alternative ways to structure the global economy, so that debt does not further impoverish developing nations struggling with difficult conditions of structural violence.[11] Peace educators involved in global peace education efforts look toward the establishment of global institutions to provide collective security. The 1979 UNESCO Statement of Purposes for Worldwide Educational Policy states the goals:

> [to include] an international dimension at all levels of education: understanding and respect for all peoples, their cultures, values, and ways of life; furthermore awareness of the interdependence between peoples and nations' abilities to communicate across cultures; and last, but not least to enable the individual to acquire a critical understanding of problems at the national and international level.[12]

Teachers following these guidelines try to stimulate in their students' minds a global identity and awareness of problems around the planet. They hope that their students will think of themselves as compassionate global citizens who identify with people throughout the world struggling for peace. This educational approach to reducing tensions between states originated in the period between the First and Second World Wars. At that time peace educators tried to prepare students for world citizenship by providing information about different cultures, political arrangements, religions, and values—hoping to produce an aware citizenry that would eschew the use of violence to settle international differences.[13] This approach also continued into the Cold War era, as, for example, student exchange programs were promoted as a way of allowing young people access to a more global view of the world. A proponent of this approach, the British philosopher Bertrand Russell said in the nineteen thirties, "Education could easily, if man chose, produce a sense of solidarity of the human race, and of the importance of international cooperation.[14] Education for world citizenship or education for international understanding exists in many different countries. It teaches about cultural traditions and tries to promote cooperation among people.

The international costs of maintaining armies promotes a militaristic culture that subtracts from resources available for education and development, alternative means of providing security. In the 1970s some European peace educators promoted disarmament education,[15] which emphasized the tremendous cost of the arms race and the disparity between the developed and the underdeveloped nations of the world. The following definition of disarmament was provided in the Final Report and Document of the World Congress on Disarmament Education:

> For the purpose of disarmament education, disarmament may be understood as any form of action aimed at limiting, controlling and reducing arms, including unilateral disarmament initiatives and, ultimately general and complete disarmament under effective international control.[16]

Based upon the principles of the United Nations Charter, disarmament education attempts to provide an awareness of the consequences of vast armaments upon human communities. It teaches about the costs of the arms race, educates about arms control efforts, and provides an awareness of the production and use of weapons.

Often, in international affairs, international peacekeeping forces are used, as in Cyprus, to quell disturbances and impose order upon unruly citizens. Kofi Annan, the Secretary-General of the United Nations at the time of this writing, has urged international leaders to more strongly consider endorsing such a peacekeeping force as the first phase of the War on Terrorism winds down in Afghanistan. Leaders in many parts of the world facing such turmoil are looking for regional solutions, involving the help of more stable nation-states, the United States and NATO to help settle their own social instability. In peace education classes teachers evaluate the value of peace-through-strength approaches to resolving conflicts where governments devote considerable resources to armed forces to protect national interests and provide security for citizens. This approach to peace relies upon force to stop violence or to promote national interests. International peace educators teach how laws and institutions, like the United Nations, can and have helped avoid the terrors of war.

At the end of the millennium wars were increasingly shifting from interstate to intrastate conflicts, with the vast majority of killing occurring between ethnic groups rivaling for control of contested areas. The overwhelming majority of victims of this kind of conflict are civilians. In these conflicts issues of human rights become intertwined with governmental policies based upon peace through strength. Questions such as the following are raised: Are the rights of minorities being protected by political leaders who use military force to quell social unrest? How can multilateral peace agreements be reached that would avoid the necessity of armed intervention and help to resolve the claims of multiple parties involved in a conflict?

International relations is considered a type of peace education, although there has been a distinction made in academic circles between international studies that focuses on the existing world order, and those aspects of international studies that point out alternative ways to achieve peace. In many colleges and universities international relations prepares students for careers in various international settings. Rather than focusing on attaining peace, these courses highlight existing political realities and social systems. Whereas international relations programs include security studies to provide an understanding of defense systems and how various countries approach collective security, peace education programs tend to study alternatives to existing defense policies. International studies can provide important insights into how different cultures approach issues of security, and international relations can help students develop a broader global consciousness.

Conflict Resolution Education

Recent concern about escalating levels of civil violence has stimulated a variety of peace education programs loosely falling under the category of conflict resolution education. This approach to peace education helps individuals understand conflict dynamics and empowers them to use communication skills to build and manage peaceful relationships. The focus is on the skills and processes that make peace. Also emphasized are interpersonal relations and the processes that help disputing parties resolve their differences. Many schools in the United States have some sort of peer mediator program. Conflict resolution educators teach children basic skills such as anger management, impulse control, emotional awareness, empathy development, assertiveness, and problem solving skills. Research studies conducted on conflict resolution education in the United States show that it has a positive impact on school climate. Studies have reported a decrease in aggressiveness, violence, dropout rates, student suspensions, and victimized behavior.[17] Conflict resolution education results include improved academic performance, increased cooperation, and positive attitudes toward school.[18]

Conflict resolution educators teach alternative dispute resolution techniques to help students develop skills that will enable them to manage their conflicts nonviolently. A recent variation of this approach to peace education is violence prevention education. Peace educators interested in violence prevention aim for their students to understand that anger is a normal emotion that can be handled positively. To counter hostile behaviors learned in the broader culture, peace educators teach anger management techniques to help students avoid fights in school and angry disputes in their immediate lives. Cultural images of violence in the mass media are both disturbing and intriguing to young people, many of whom live in homes that are violent. Violent behavior patterns are learned in families that practice corporal punishment and in which domestic disputes are handled with physical conflict. Violence prevention programs do not assume that conflict is not a normal part of human interaction. Rather, peace educators using these programs teach their students how to assert themselves to avoid becoming bullies or victims. Students are first taught the beginning skills of reacting to conflict nonviolently. A prime generator of these programs, Deborah Prothrow-Stith, describes them in the following way:

> The point of the violence prevention course is to provide these young people with alternatives to fighting. The first three lessons of the ten-session curriculum provide adolescents with information about violence and homicide.[19]

Teaching students to be peacemakers involves creating a cooperative climate that encourages disputants to reach mutually acceptable compromises and to not dominate each other. Children need formal training in anger management, decision making, social problem solving, peer negotiation, conflict management, valuing diversity, social resistance skills, active listening, and effective communication. Conflict resolution education provides students with peacemaking skills which they can use to manage their interpersonal conflicts. The emphasis in this type of peace education is upon creating a safe school. It concerns the aspects of violence that school personnel feel they have some control over, e.g., the behavior of their pupils. Although the majority of conflict resolution education programs take place within school settings, the movement is growing and is being used increasingly in community organization settings, with both children and with adults.

At the beginning of the new millennium conflict resolution education is one of the fastest growing school reforms in the United States. Conflict resolution educators provide basic communications skills necessary for survival in a postmodern world. Lantieri and Patti[20] have developed an approach to school violence to urging teachers to "wage peace in the schools." (Their program, with the name Resolving Conflict Creatively Program, is known by its acronym RCCP.) Many conflict resolution programs are adding in bias awareness and multi-cultural education components. Educators are also promoting the teaching of affective skills so that children will be more cooperative.[21]

As the twentieth century has come to an end, it appears that conflict resolution education, which, at the beginning of the last decade of the century was fast becoming an educational movement, is now considered an essential part of the curriculum of many schools. It is also increasingly being used in other community settings. Student mediation is now used widely to settle disputes which otherwise might tie up the time and energy of school personnel. The term "conflict transformation" may be a more apt term as we enter a new millennium. The goal is not to eliminate conflict, but to understand its potential for growth and transformation, both for individuals and also for communities. There has been an increase in interest in the concept of restorative justice, that is, for parties involved in conflict to move beyond a superficial airing of grievances, to a process of healing and reconciliation. (Chapter 6 contains a more extensive discussion of the movement for Restorative Justice.)

Development Education

The term "development" is used broadly to connote human development within a broader community and societal sphere. Peace educators use development studies to provide their students with insights into the various aspects of structural violence, focusing on social institutions with their hierarchies and propensities for dominance and oppression. Students in peace education classes learn about the plight of the poor and construct developmental strategies to address problems of structural violence. The goal is to build peaceful communities by promoting an active democratic citizenry interested in an equitable sharing of the world's resources. This form of peace education teaches peacebuilding strategies that use nonviolence to improve human communities.

Peace educators question dominant patterns that have preoccupied the developed world for the past millennium which, in turn, has led to gross inequities in the distribution of the world's resources. They decry the poverty and misery produced by the advanced, capitalist economic order where an elite minority benefits from the suffering of a vast majority of people on this planet. They see that the path to peace comes from getting people mobilized into movements to protect human rights and the environment. Inspired by Dr. Martin Luther King, Jr., Mohandas Gandhi, and thousands of other activists who have used nonviolence to resolve major conflicts during the twentieth century, they seek a long-term solution to the underlying social conditions that give rise to violence.

Development educators are concerned about the rise of corporate capitalism and its impact upon human communities. Rather than promoting top-down strategies imposed by corporate elites, peace educators promote the involvement by oppressed people in planning, implementing, and controlling development programs. One goal is to see resources controlled equitably. Peace educators try to develop in their students a critical consciousness that challenges injustice and undemocratic policy-making structures promoted by large transnational corporations that have a development agenda based upon maximizing profit, destructive of human and natural communities. Peace educators promote a vision of positive peace that motivates people to struggle against injustice. This approach to peace education rests upon concepts of social justice.

In many countries of the south (the terms "north" and "south" denote the differences between the industrialized world and those countries considered developing or Third World), educators concerned about the problems of underdevelopment, starvation, poverty, illiteracy, and the lack of human rights refer to their efforts to make students aware of these problems of violence as development education. Educators provide an awareness of the political and economic conditions that promote poverty and encourage people to participate in decisions that will transform their social realities. Development education has been linked to a call for a new economic order, brought forth from developing countries, seeking understanding that the existing economic order, marked by extreme inequalities between the north and the south, does not auger well for world peace and international cooperation. It seeks an international understanding of the crises that exist in countries of the south and works for global solutions of the problems of underdevelopment.

The Role of the United Nations in Peace Education

At the end of the twentieth century under the leadership of the United Nations, there have been several strong appeals to make the teaching of peace and peace strategies more explicit in schools. In November 1995 the 186 member states of the 28th General Conference of UNESCO stated that the major challenge at the close of the 20th century is the transition from a culture of war and violence to a culture of peace. In November 1998 the United Nations General Assembly adopted resolutions declaring the year 2000 the International Year for the Culture of Peace and the years 2001–2010 to be the "International Decade for a Culture of Peace and Nonviolence for the Children of the World." From that mandate UNESCO has developed eight areas of action necessary for the transition from a culture of war to a culture of peace[22] (see Chapter 1 for a more complete discussion of the Culture of Peace). The first of these is a "Culture of Peace through Education." A manifesto written by the winners of the Nobel Peace Prize and published in Le Monde on July 2, 1997, states that the only way to fight violence with nonviolence is through education.

During the First World War many peace activists directed their energies towards the creation of the League of Nations, an organization designed to arbitrate conflicts and avert war. Limited in scope in resolving conflicts between nations (many of which the League was not able to successfully mediate), the League of Nations became a rallying point in many countries for peace education. In England the League of Nations Union promoted Education for International Understanding and Education for World Citizenship. These hopes for an international agency to resolve conflicts were transferred to the United Nations, created after World War II, with a broader focus to provide a center for worldwide dialogue, awareness, and problem solving.

The founding of the United Nations provided an impetus for an international effort to teach about the problems associated with war, violence, injustice, illiteracy, poverty, and other sources of human conflict. In keeping with the principles of the United Nations charter that promoted international cooperation and peace, the United Nations Educational, Social, and Cultural Organization (UNESCO) in 1953 sponsored an Associated School Project to study disarmament, the international economic order and human rights in schools throughout the world. The six main objectives of this project were:

(i) to improve the capacity of secondary school teachers to teach about world problems;
(ii) to increase young people's awareness of world problems;
(iii) to provide young people with skills which will eventually be useful in solving such problems;
(iv) to develop more effective teaching methods and materials to improve the teaching of three specific world problems (disarmament, the New International World Order, and human rights);
(v) to shed new light on how these three issues can effectively be studied in different countries; and
(vi) to understand better the complexity of world problems and facilitate finding solutions to them as a result of knowing other people's views and opinions regarding them.[23]

The Associated School Project has been carried out in many countries of the world, such as Australia, Finland, the former West Germany, Greece, Italy, Japan, England, Norway, Spain, Sweden, Switzerland, United Kingdom, USA, Bulgaria, the former East Germany, Hungary, USSR, India, and Argentina. From this initiative national commissions in these countries have been asked to develop special programs to increase knowledge of world problems, to promote international understanding through the study of different cultures, and to foster concern for human rights. These national commissions have helped endorse peace studies and programs in education for international understanding, and they have legitimized similar educational activities throughout the world.

In 1974 UNESCO recommended a generic approach to the study of world problems, appropriately named "education for international understanding, co-operation and peace and education relating to human rights and fundamental freedoms."[24] UNESCO's endorsement of educational efforts designed to provide an understanding of world problems has promoted, at the national level, educational projects focused on such areas as multicultural education, human rights education, world studies, and development studies. This recommendation also emphasized the study of such issues as human environment, food supply, and an increasing world population, so that citizens throughout the world might appreciate the magnitude of these global problems.

In 1978 the United Nations approved a Special Session on Disarmament, the World Congress on Disarmament Education, which was held in Paris in June 1980. The final document reflected the United Nations' recognition of education for peace as basic to the achievement of disarmament:

> Education is considered as an essential instrument for two main reasons: Firstly, educational systems can offer effective teaching on world problems to young people everywhere, thus fostering ideas that will lead to a better society; secondly, the school itself provides a solid framework for concrete action, both curricular and extra-curricular, which may promote greater international cooperation.[25]

At this conference a United Nations World Disarmament Campaign was launched. The document produced by this special session focused on disarmament education, saying, among other things,

> It aims at teaching how to think about disarmament rather than what to think about it. It should therefore be problem centered so as to develop the analytical and critical capacity to examine and evaluate practical steps toward the reduction of arms and the elimination of war as an acceptable international practice. Disarmament education should be based upon the values of international understanding, tolerance of ideological and cultural diversity, and commitment to social justice and human solidarity.[26]

As a result of these activities, scholars throughout the world have researched alternative security systems that can provide the basis for the abolition of war. Educators, politicians, and concerned citizens have been able to appeal to these statements as a rationale for introducing peace and world order studies in schools. The United Nations Department of Disarmament affairs provides fact sheets on disarmament issues. It publishes *The Disarmament Yearbook* and the journal *Disarmament*. Other useful publications are the *Disarmament Campaign Newsletter* and the UNESCO *Courier*, both available from United Nations headquarters in New York.

Peace Education for Adults

Peace education takes place in many more settings than just in formal schools. In communities throughout the world, organizations, churches, and elected officials have participated in forums designed to make adults more aware of war and peace. As educators, in a different sense than formally trained teachers, these adult leaders hope to educate people throughout the world about the folly of using weapons and arms to settle disputes. "The colossal growth of the popular peace movement in recent years has been, in many respects, a very significant adult education movement."[27] In response to various demands supported by peace movements throughout the world, peace activists have been turning to education to support their causes. The form and content of these adult programs varies in different parts of the world.

Churches have generated many educational guides and resources that are available to community groups, parishes, peace organizations, and others that wish to educate their membership about the threat of war and how to build peace. The role of religions in promoting peace education is not limited solely to adult education. In the Netherlands and in Australia, church supported schools have taken the initiative in introducing peace education at the elementary and secondary level. Other church sponsored schools throughout the world promote concepts of peace and justice not often found in traditional schools run by the state. As mentioned before, in Latin America priests and bishops have played a key role in thousands of base communities, which are communities of prayer and gospel sharing that provide mutual aid and often are geared towards changing society. These base communities promote a liberation theology which states that human redemption can occur, in part, by organizing to correct or overturn the conditions that cause that suffering.

In industrialized countries various churches support peace and justice centers which provide tapes, books, films, discussion groups, and places for meetings, as well as other resources for education and action. The American Friends Service Committee has ten such regional centers in the United States. Within the Catholic church some of these centers provide a place for meditation and study. The style and emphasis in these centers vary from diocese to diocese in different parts of the world. Some of them provide meals for the homeless and a retreat space where educators may reflect upon their peace education activities. These centers allow people working for peace to meet with others and to "recharge their batteries" for the sustained struggle to bring justice to the world.

These peace efforts within churches and various adult communities challenge traditional educational practices. Whereas traditional education promotes peace through strength and a belief in the national security apparatus, peace activists and peace educators are questioning both the security strategies of those in power and traditional educational goals and methods. Likewise, the traditional role of the church is being challenged by liberation ministries. Spurred by fears of modern forms of violence, educators throughout the world are questioning traditional notions of security that come from being armed, and are creating a new type of education that empowers people by asking them what kind of society they want to inhabit. The practice of these new forms of education often originates in informal educational systems, in church parishes and adult education settings, but also has impact upon the formal educational systems. As peace movements gather strength, educators in formal systems are placed in an existential dilemma. Do they want their efforts to continue to support the status quo, or are they willing to use their skills and professional status to help create a new social order that promotes an understanding of how to achieve peace?

Is There a Difference Between Peace Education and Peace Studies?

There are important distinctions between peace studies and peace education. Peace studies, the study of peace processes, began as a formal discipline in colleges and universities after the Second World War. Peace studies seeks "to analyze human conflicts in order to find the most peaceful (negatively peaceful) ways to turn unjust relationships into more just (positively peaceful) [ones].[28] It often has a geopolitical focus. Thus peace studies per se may be said to have a narrower focus than the broader field of peace education. Peace studies may be seen as both one kind of peace education (i.e., that practiced in settings of higher education) and also "the study of peace" as a concept.

In a literal sense peace education refers to teachers teaching about peace—what it is, why it may not exist, and how to achieve it. "Teachers," as the term is used here, does not refer uniquely to a professional educator. A peace educator may be a community activist trying to inform members of her community about nonviolent strategies. Peace educators explain the roots of violence and teach alternatives to violence. The concepts of peace used in peace education vary according to the form of violence addressed and the cultural context of the educational setting.

Peace studies tends to focus on the causes of war and alternatives to war; whereas peace education is more generic, attempting to draw out of people their natural inclinations to live in peace. Peace researchers identify processes that promote peace; whereas peace educators, educating people about those processes, use teaching skills to build a peace culture. Peace studies faculty, housed in political science or international relations university departments, study the causes of wars and ethnic conflicts, seeking ways to avoid and prevent them. Peace educators, on the other hand, are interested in all different aspects of violence from the interpersonal to the geopolitical. Peace education aims to achieve peace by providing awareness about different peace strategies, including peacekeeping (or peace through strength), peacemaking (or peace through communication,) and peacebuilding (or peace through a commitment to nonviolence).

Peace educators try to get students to think of themselves as concerned global citizens willing to transcend national and ethnic differences in order to promote peace. They hope through the study of security systems to teach how to construct laws and institutions, like the United Nations, that will help humans avoid the terror of war.

Peace education is not "pacifism education." The goal is not to make students and citizens quiet, complacent, and content. Peace educators try to point out the problems of violence that exist in society and then instruct their pupils about strategies that can be used to address those problems, hence empowering them to redress the circumstances that lead to violence. Mahatma Gandhi used insights he gained from a commitment to nonviolence to overthrow what was at that time the greatest force on earth (the British Empire). Community organizers and Dr. King's use of nonviolence in the Civil Rights struggle are examples of the legacy peace educators draw upon in teaching youth how to strive nonviolently for their dreams.

Recently in the United States a debate has emerged regarding the most appropriate way to promote peace education activities. Some educators working with public school systems prefer to call it "conflict resolution," while most college and university teachers call their efforts peace education, as evidenced by the term "peace and conflict studies," the name of peace studies programs in many universities and colleges in the United States. "Peace education" is seen as being too controversial, because it suggests a utopian, unrealistic visions of how human societies are organized. The term "peace" has again become highly politicized. Yet there continue to be those who call for more teaching of the skills of peace within our schools and community settings.

Peace education, to a large extent, owes its birth to the peace movement and social change movements that have brought the problems of war and peace into the public limelight. There seems to be both an indirect and an inverse relationship between the growth of peace movements and the growth of peace education. Indirectly, heightened concern about the threats of war and the problems of violence have put pressure on educational institutions to respond to these problems. An example is the rise of requests for programs teaching conflict resolution and mediation following the carnage at the high school in Littleton, Colorado, near Denver in 1999.[29] At times, peace education seems inversely related to the perception of peace. Such a relationship was demonstrated in Northern Ireland where when peace movements were seen to fail, leaders in various communities concerned about the level of violence in Northern Ireland suggested education for mutual understanding as a means to teach new ways of behavior to deal with traditions of conflict that had grown up in that country.

Peace education, action and research, as previously mentioned, are intricately related. The researchers attempt to understand, to describe, classify, and analyze the strategies and programs of the peace activists while the educators communicate research findings derived from experts. Researchers attempt to answer the question, "What do we need to know in order to create a peaceful world?"[30] They focus on the problems of violence, creating an understanding of how the use of force violates both basic human needs and rights. In teaching about these problems peace educators rely on the findings of peace researchers. Betty Reardon has called education the "interface" between peace research and peace action.[31]

In teaching about the problems of war and the challenges of peace, educators in colleges and universities also need to teach students how to conduct peace research, because if it is of high quality it enhances efforts to legitimize peace education activities in schools and universities. A peace educator who is also a peace researcher can provide students with up-to-date findings about the problems of violence and strategies for peace. Peace researchers rely on peace educators to communicate their findings. If scholars simply talk to themselves, the value of their efforts becomes minimal. In highlighting the problems produced by a commitment to nonviolence, these researchers often suggest solutions that will have a practical use for average citizens. In this way peace researchers need peace education to promote changes in public consciousness about the problems unearthed in scholarly research. As Mario Borrelli has pointed out:

> Peace education, therefore, while separate from peace research, dialogues with it so that the results of peace research can be transmitted easily to the community, making use of all the techniques and conceptual tools available through other disciplines (particularly anthropology, sociology, and psychology).[32]

Peace activists use research tools to understand how world problems can, at the micro level, contribute to local instances of violence. Peace research can also help evaluate the effectiveness of peace action.

Important questions remain about the practice of peace education throughout the modern world. Many countries which support peace education also use schools to train their youth for the military. They may say they want peace, but they continue to rely on peace through strength by preparing for war. The relationships between peace education and the various peace movements seems crucial. This is an area for further research and discussion. Educators need a strong and active peace movement to raise concerns within the public sphere. Without the support of a vigorous peace movement and well planned action steps, many of the efforts of researchers and educators might well stay hidden.

CHAPTER 4

Peace Education as Empowerment Education

Peace education has to that extent to be an empowering process—whether in a classroom or in the community; those who press for peace education have the responsibility of showing that ordinary people, children or adults, can do something effective about the problems that are raised—that they are problems created by human beings and can now be solved by them.

Nigel Young

This chapter addresses issues relating to empowerment and social change. Peace education contributes to the health of modern societies by teaching students about alternatives to violence and empowering them to contribute to the public debate about how to achieve security. Theodor Ebwert writes that "the task of peace education is to strengthen confidence in democracy and its capacity of solving problems."[1] Peace education adheres to democratic traditions, traditions which have relied upon schools to train people to shape society on the basis of accumulated wisdom. An informed public provides the basis of democracy. The strength of an open society rests upon citizens who think independently, who are free to talk, to meet, to think, to seek truth, to be different, to try something new, and to make the best of their lives according to their ideals. In a dynamic society, debate and controversy are signs of health.

Peace education requires people to question the use of force in human affairs and provides options to create a less violent world, employing educational strategies to develop a peace consciousness that will help to construct a world that does not rely on violence to resolve human conflict.

"Empower" in this sense implies enabling people to develop their own capacities to become effective citizens and change agents.

This raises a key question: Is peace education *about* peace, or is it education *for* peace? Peace education incorporates both. Peace education teaches about peace because many citizens need more knowledge about the problems associated with militarism and violence. Peace education also involves educating for social justice and social change, where teachers and students explore together solutions to violent social realities. The capacity for peace education to involve people in creating a more peaceful world can be illustrated by the following diagram:

DECREASING OF ACTING	INCREASING OF ACTING
apathy–seclusion–cynicism–ignorance	awareness–consciousness–engagement–ability
DECREASING POWER	INCREASING POWER

Peace education attempts to move people towards the right on this continuum, away from a condition of seclusion and despair to a condition of active involvement with others. The stage of 'ability' at the farthest right on the scale implies that people have a positive self image as socially responsible actors and have the knowledge of how to bring about changes in the world. For example, because of the secrecy surrounding the defense establishment, many citizens in the United States feel that they can't change government policies promoting war. In the face of this powerlessness, peace education strives to empower people by providing them with knowledge about strategies that can be used to build peace.

Using schools to address social problems comes from an academic tradition established by John Dewey in the early part of the twentieth century. In their laboratory school in Chicago the Deweys sought to develop in children "a habit of considering problems,"[2] an approach that encourages schools, colleges, and universities to allow students to shape informed opinions about the crucial dilemmas of their time. Under this orientation teachers encourage students to examine key social problems. Most specifically in peace education, this involves coming to grips with the causes and effects of violence upon the social order. According to Dewey, education aims to help people understand their environment so that they can control it rather than being controlled by it. In Dewey's classroom model learners select, organize, and direct their social experiences:

> Education is that reconstruction or reorganization of experience which adds to the meaning of experience and which increases ability to direct the course of subsequent experience.[3]

Dewey believed that education can reconstruct society by imbuing individuals with a capacity for reflective thinking so they can help to build a more equitable social order.

In considering social problems, students must intelligently organize their own experiences. Action without thinking is as unhealthy as is thinking without action. Students who express concern about a social problem such as violence often desire to improve their own lives and the communities they inhabit. This desire provides an important motivation for learning that can be supplemented by the gathering of relevant facts, the formulation of a plan of action, execution of the plan, and evaluation—all components of the scientific method which can lead to intelligent action.

This approach to education, developed during the 1930s as a part of the movement of progressive education, has been labeled "reconstructionism" by educational historians. This approach views the school as a chief means for building a new social order. George Counts typified reconstructionism in his book, *Dare the School Build a new Social Order?*[4] where he stated that unhealthy societies threaten individual survival and that something could be done to change the nature of social reality, and that education provides the means to build a better society.

A similar educational tradition has been carried forth into modern times by Jurgen Habermas[5] and other thinkers of the Frankfurt School. The search for meaning comes from critically questioning the dominant ideologies that support social reality. This approach to education attempts to free the learner to adopt new modes of belief and operation. Similar to reconstructionism, this critical pedagogy turns to education to question how social forces impact upon the beliefs and ideals that motivate individuals. The ability to think critically can empower people to come up with their own concepts of social justice and gives them the conceptual tools (understanding of social reality, familiarity with political systems, knowledge of alternatives, etc.) they need to act upon those concepts.

Historically in the United States many different educational efforts have been advanced to empower people to work through their own positions of oppression and to help create better lives for themselves. Examples of this include workers' educational centers sponsored by labor unions, citizenship schools established during the civil rights movement to prepare people for literacy tests so they could vote, and settlement schools, such as Hull House begun by Jane Addams, which provided immigrants with basic skills to keep and find work.[6] An outstanding example of this type of education is in Tennessee at the Highlander School, established during the 1930s. Early in its history Highlander worked with the Congress of Industrial Organizations (CIO) to help workers organize unions in the South. In the nineteen fifties the staff at Highlander helped to train civil rights workers who, in turn, provided literacy education for adults in rural Southern communities. Currently Highlander is working with Appalachian people on ways to create jobs in poor areas of the South. In discussing the educational principles that motivate Highlander's work, one of the staff members wrote, "Highlander had to learn not to convert, but to bring forth; education not only had to serve the people, but, more importantly, had to be of the people."[7] This principle requires educators to discover people's needs and to build with students educational programs that will address those needs.

THE VIOLENCE INHERENT IN TRADITIONAL AMERICAN EDUCATION

Traditional education is sometimes criticized for reinforcing the status quo. Corinne Kumor-D'souza writes:

> Education has fundamental connections with the idea of human emancipation, through it is constantly in danger of being captured for other interests. In a society disfigured by class exploitation, sexual and racial oppression, and in chronic danger of war and environmental destruction, the only education worth its name is one that forms people capable of taking part in their own liberation. The business of school is not propaganda. It is equipping people with the knowledge and skills and concepts relevant to remaking a dangerous and disordered world. In the most basic sense, the process of education and the process of liberation are the same. They are aspects of the painful growth of the human species' collective wisdom and self-control. At the beginning of the 1980s it is plain that the forces opposed to that growth here and on the world scale are not only powerful but have become increasingly militant. In such circumstances, education becomes a risky enterprise. Teachers too have to decide whose side they are on![8]

A recent analysis of schools in advanced industrial societies has led to the conclusion that education helps perpetuate some of the social inequities that can lead to war. Reproduction theory[9] argues that societies are economically, socially, and politically stratified, and that schools reproduce that stratification. Schools, rather than ameliorating the class divisions which cause structural violence, replicate and reinforce those divisions. Some revisionist historians have debunked as myth that public schools provide opportunities for upward mobility and argue that schools allow a few people, mostly children of the upper and middle classes, to gain the rewards offered by society, while the vast majority of children experience failure which leads to lives of poverty, misery, and substandard achievements.[10] Reproduction theory does not lay the blame for this on teachers, adult educators, school boards, curriculum developers, and state education departments to reproduce the inequality and structural violence that exist in society. Nor does it postulate a mechanistic, one-way determinism. Reproduction theory does posit that teachers, students, adult educators, and families can and do have effects upon young people, but at any given point in history, their efforts may be limited or shaped by broader social forces and that public education is linked to these forces.

Children learn violence in school as well as at home. Much of textbook history emphasizes the achievements of our country by violent means. Young people also learn violent behavior from the media. It is estimated that the average child in the United States between the age of five and eighteen watches fifteen thousand hours of television, thirty percent more time than is spent in school.[11] For peace educators this points to the necessity of counteracting the dominant violent messages that permeate society. Educators must work toward creating a peaceful learning environment that will encourage their students to work for peace.

In the 1960s a great deal of attention was focused on the shortcomings of American schools.[12] Many critics at that time sought to "humanize" the schools through such reforms as open classrooms, using principles of Montessori education, individually guided instruction, credit-noncredit evaluations instead of grades, alternative schools, and open admissions policies. Critical theorists such as Michael Apple believe, in spite of a continuing pattern of reforms in some areas, public schools continue patterns of social oppression.[13] The "hidden curriculum" is not what is taught, but is the way things are taught and messages learned about life in general, in addition to the formal school curriculum. It is the "atmosphere" of schools which contributes to this hidden curriculum.

Schools are structured hierarchically. For example, most school districts have their policies set by a school board and are led by administrators (superintendents who are "over" the principals). The hierarchy moves down to department heads within schools, then teachers, and finally, teacher-aids. Students are seen by critics as being at the bottom of this hierarchy. The amount of power over others is proportional to the place held within this hierarchy. In such an environment students learn obedience and are punished if they disagree with those in authority. Students may learn that they are powerless to change things. Fred Newmann writes:

> The process of instruction, regardless of subject area, usually places students in the passive role of receiving knowledge. For much of their

school life they are supposed to absorb materials by attending to presentations of teachers; by using textbooks and other media; by answering orally and in writing questions posed by teachers or texts; and by observing other classmates' responses to those questions. In short, the student must usually assume an unassertive, inactive, almost docile role, allowing the environment to impinge upon oneself, rather than taking initiative to influence it.[14]

Having been taught not to question authority, students may accept passively what teachers say. Students are taught to respect the limits set by authority figures and to pay attention to the clock. In this way schools may reproduce conditions in the larger society, some of which are conducive to the creation of an obedient work force that produces the economic goods that provide the basis for social wealth.

In addition to the hierarchy of the classroom, including the teaching of obedience to authority, critics view the competitive atmosphere seen in many public schools as unhealthy. The social relations established in the classroom become a microcosm for the larger society—with its divisions into "winners and losers." Grades are often given on a curve, so that some students excel, some are mediocre, and others fail. Such distinctions brand some students with marks of failure, while others are rewarded with success. Students may be taught to be aggressive in order to get ahead. Students may learn early that there aren't enough rewards to go around. This kind of competitive classroom environment neither encourages cooperation, nor teaches pupils the skills of working together. School achievement is seen as an individual accomplishment, and academic excellence is understood as individual brilliance, not collective enterprise. It should be said that, in response to some research showing the deleterious effects of competition upon learning, some university teacher training programs are incorporating the teaching of cooperative learning within their curricula. Some schools are beginning to understand the importance of teaching these skills to young people.

Speaking about the ways schools help create structural violence in society, Colin Greer has written:

> It was the schools as "the balance wheel of the social machinery" which triumphed—the balance being the imposition of controls for social stability in favor of the moneyed and powerful, and not the substance behind egalitarian rhetoric.[15]

Critics of the American educational system believe that it perpetuates the societal myth that if a person does not "succeed" in life, it is their own fault, a myth begun in the overly competitive climate of the public schools.[16] Svi Shapiro writes:

> The condition of growing disempowerment and domination afflicting millions of Americans in the closing decades of this century is rooted in the particular forms of domination and exploitation to be found in the economic, political, and cultural "instances" of the social formation. Education helps to provide the ideological "glue" sustaining this formation, providing the legitimateness, rationalizations, and distorted consciousnesses necessary to support the forms of domination and oppression which permeate the society.[17]

Public schools are charged with providing students preparation for mature citizenship and participation in the wider society, but in the United States fifty percent of the high school students enrolled in urban systems drop out of school and, thus, because of the increasing demands for educational credentials, find it difficult to become effective members of the community. The reinforcement of structural violence in schools may, in fact, be related to instances of community and societal violence. Schools may further disempower students through punishment. In the most extreme cases, corporal punishment is used, although many countries have outlawed it in public schools.

In addition to the way schools are administered and curricula established, the actual material taught in classes often glorifies war. History is presented as a succession of wars, and students are taught to revere the accomplishments of great warriors. The way to settle disagreements is seen as going to war, not to negotiate. A detailed examination of history books, according to noted educational critic Henry Giroux, reveals that they are dominated by themes such as:

> (1) an over-valuing of social harmony, social compromise and political consensus, with very little said about social struggle; (2) an intense nationalism and chauvinism; (3) an almost total exclusion of labor history; and (4) a number of myths regarding the nature of political, economic, and social life.[18]

Nonviolent strategies to resist violent governments have a long and glorious history, but often these struggles do not show up in history books. This has been well documented by Gene Sharp[19] and others. These need to be taught if students are to learn alternative ways of resolving conflict.

History seems too often to focus on the activities of the powerful, wealthy and elite and on the accomplishments of military leaders, ignoring the lives and contributions of ordinary citizens. "Our educational system is committed to a scale of values which confers immortality on egomaniacs and punishes the thoughtful with oblivion."[20] Power may be seen as a superior attribute but often ignored is a corollary of power, the oppression of the many. Peace education must promote the view that the voices of the powerless must become part of the public debate. Ultimately, in order for there to be peace, the powerful themselves must be converted by pressure from 'below.' Millions of courageous people in many parts of the world have attempted this,[21] but their stories are often excluded from history books.

Perhaps most destructive, as some view it, to the creation of peace is the promotion of national ideologies. Every country uses its schools to present a positive image, sometimes distorting reality. For example, little mention is made in the history books of the peaceful traditions of Native Americans, or the massive anti-war movement that existed in the United States prior to the First World War. Following the events of September 11, 2001, one school in author Mary Lee Morrison's town in Connecticut baked a huge cake and decorated it to resemble an American flag. Interestingly, at least one Quaker school eschewed flying the American flag during the fall of 2001, but instead chose to fly a flag depicting the globe.

Traditional education has emphasized the specialization of knowledge. Complex problems are couched by professors and other educated leaders as being beyond the grasp of ordinary citizens. It is not too complex to de-emphasize the elitist nature of defense policy decisions and simplify national security debates so that average citizens may contribute to the dialogue about the policies their taxes support.

How Peace Education Empowers

Educational endeavors ideally point to new ways of teaching and learning. Peace educators advocate educational training and skills to create a culture of peace. Mayumba Wa Nkongola writes:

> As today's elite, educators have become party to the problem and they have widened the gap between themselves and the rest of the members of their respective societies. The conflicts stemming from this gap make war everyday news while peace, for which we pray a lot, becomes an impossible dream.[22]

If education is to play a vital role in bringing peace to the world, it must cease as a vehicle that enables the privileged to strengthen their power and must help those without power learn how to become powerful. In this way peace education must reach down to the masses of people and build upon their hopes for more fulfilling lives, liberating them. Empowerment education frees the intellect to allow individuals to question even the most basic assumptions about the meaning of life and about social arrangements. As Magnas Haavelsrud and Robin Richardson note:

> The task of the school and education cannot be simply to "see" and theorize about these things. The school must try, whenever practicable, to do something about them. We need a different kind of education orientation with its implied applicative emphasis.[23]

The students who graduate from high schools, colleges, and universities who are prepared to work for peace must have a realistic understanding of their world and need to know how to exercise their rights of citizenship. They should be well trained in critical thinking, be committed to non-violence, and learn to be effective working in groups. They should be taught how to shape the course of their own lives. Empowerment education allows students to construct their own meanings and prepares them to be effective citizens in democratic states. Christian Bay writes:

> If experiments in real democracy are possible anywhere in our social order, they are possible in our academic communities, for in most of these communities the levels of articulation are relatively high and the levels of desperation relatively low.[24]

Empowerment education imbues people with the hope to learn and to trust their own capabilities. The key to this type of education is in the *process*. Peace educators use affirmation exercises to help students trust their own competence and set up classrooms that are modeled on democratic principles, so that students may learn how to articulate their concerns in safe group settings. In this model the teacher serves more as a kind of "midwife," helping the students give birth to their own ideas and inclinations.[25] Learning is based on mutual dialogue where teachers and students participate as equals. Teachers may have more information than students, but together they are seeking the answers to such thorny questions as "why are humans violent? "why do nations go to war?" Students of peace education need to learn communication skills so that they may participate in discussions exploring the hard dilemmas around war and peace.

One of the first steps in empowering people is to capture their imaginations.[26] Overcoming a feeling of powerlessness is often a question of motivation, then becomes one of vision. Because people must believe that by working for peace they can, in fact, achieve it, peace education tries to get students to see themselves as causal agents capable of contributing to the effort to bring peace to the world. By learning how peacemakers have practiced nonviolence, students' imaginations may be inspired by visions of a peaceful world, where ordinary citizens can realize their dreams. Part of capturing people's imaginations involves first confronting fear and then moving beyond it. Violence can be scary. People may not acknowledge these fears. They are often deeply embedded within the human psyche.

In the empowerment process, personal change begins to occur when people acknowledge their deep feelings about violence and the perilous nature of the world. Accepting feelings of fear and vulnerability as normal human reactions frees people to share those feelings with others and explore common links that provide the basis for joining together to address these problems. People make connections with others based on fear for their own survival and that of others, and concern for the future. Many see the relationships between the violence in everyday life—physical assault, rape, battering, child abuse—and the violence that occurs throughout the world, in communities and within and between nations.

A belief in the infinite worth of every human being and a fostering of a sense of delight in the world around us can help peace educators counter and move beyond their anxieties. Fostering a sense of hope, in the face of what can at times seem overwhelming "madness," is important. This may involve, for both teachers and students, times of retreat, spiritual support and the nurturance of peers who also are working for peace.

Students of peace education need to be informed about public issues, so that as responsible citizens, they may participate in politics. Peace education needs to sharpen people's abilities to make moral judgments and to think clearly about world affairs. Addressing the problems of war and peace can heighten intellectual abilities by encouraging pupils to study some of the most pressing problems facing the human species.

In many schools civic education passes down accepted wisdom about government in uncritical ways, teaching students how great and democratic their governments are without examining the role of force and the denial of freedom that may underlie some governmental policies. Empowerment education should move beyond traditional presentations of 'civics' to allow students to understand the informal channels of influence—money, social affiliations, political debts, etc.—that support war policies. Citizens who will be able to change the deep patterns of militarism that characterize modern states need to understand the dynamics of power close to their lives. Learning abstractly about the seats of power in remote capitals doesn't provide the knowledge of how to influence public policy.

Richard Remy has suggested that standard citizenship competencies include acquiring and using information, assessing involvement, forming decisions, making judgments, communicating, cooperating, and promoting interests.[27] In peace education classes students assess their own involvement in political situations, issues, decisions, and policies, developing their own ethical and moral standards. Students learn how to communicate their ideas to other citizens, decision makers, and local and national leaders and how to work with bureaucratically organized institutions.

Leadership training is another aspect of empowerment education. Peace educators need to know how to serve as facilitators of small groups, how to reach consensual decisions, how to manage organizations, how to respond to conflict, how to work on problems collaboratively, how to develop open and experimental attitudes in groups, and how to motivate others. Educators should be able to train students in group participation; in planning, conducting, and critiquing learning activities; and in sharing leadership. In order for people to be empowered they need to facilitate their own growth as well as the growth of others.

The final stage in empowerment education involves people taking action. As traditional education leads to knowledge, empowerment education should lead to both knowledge *and* action. As John Dewey stated, a person's development is related to his or her ability to influence the environment.[28] Other studies have indicated that an individual learns how to be effective by working on real problems. A sense of competence comes from the ability to affect reality.[29] James Coleman found that a sense of environmental competence, that is, a sense of control over one's environment and one's future, has a stronger relationship to school achievement than all other "school" factors that influence achievement.[30] Allowing people to express their concerns about the threat of war supports their psychological health, mental growth, and personality development. Mere reflection will not change the state of affairs that makes the world such a dangerous place.

All in all, empowerment education models the type of education used in community development.[31] This brings people together at a local level to work on commonly perceived problems. The work of Dolci (see Chapter 2) provides a prototype for this kind of activity, which encourages self-improvement through the study, planning, and action of concerned citizens. As a process of social action, community development tries to involve a wide variety of people in decision making and problem solving of issues that face a whole community. As an antidote to citizen apathy and irresponsibility, community development draws citizens into cooperative activities to focus on problems that directly touch their lives and helps them assume responsibility for managing their affairs.

4. Peace Education as Empowerment Education

As an educational process, community development teaches the skills of problem identification, data collection and analysis, decision making, planning, the carrying out of appropriate action, and evaluating the results of that action. Empowerment education can use these processes to teach students the social skills of working in collective settings. Under this model the community becomes a "laboratory of democracy," providing experience and practice in self-government, permitting citizens to learn democracy through direct participation.

Empowerment education rests heavily on the assumption that group settings are places which allow citizens to construct their own meaning of reality. Each individual interprets reality in a unique way. Working in a small community or group setting allows participants to share concerns and to move in the direction of questioning the role of violence in people's daily lives. Groups of people working together to promote nonviolence have traditionally been called "affinity groups,"[32] which are primarily "truth-seeking groups." In writing about affinity groups, one author has said:

> What is prefigurative here is the sense of being empowered, which arises as people begin to shake off their apathy and make the connection between the realities of everyday life—which they feel keenly enough, but in a limited way—and those of the nuclear order—which is felt insufficiently but places their whole future at stake.[33]

Affinity groups can be especially important for teachers who want to introduce peace topics into traditional school settings, either by themselves forming their own or using the model in organizing their classrooms. These types of groups, by providing support for the study of violence and peace, foster civic courage, as students and teachers alike challenge popularly held views about contemporary peacekeeping strategies. Questioning the dominant social order and challenging values about violence and militarism can be frightening and painful. Being in an affinity group where people trust each other allows contact with others who share concerns, so that together members can define a common reality and search for alternatives. With this type of support people may begin to perceive themselves as powerful, as they practice peace in a group where others value their contributions. In this way peace education enables individuals to translate their personal doubts and fears into social issues, gaining political understanding and the collective strength to resist the oppression of the wider "war apparatus."

Author Ian M. Harris has also found that group support plays a key role in helping people become peacemakers. For the past four years he has conducted a follow-up study of students in peace education classes at the university level. The preliminary results of this research indicate that people do change their attitudes about war and violence as a result of a class, but unfortunately most students don't become involved in political efforts to make the world more peaceful. They continue their lives after the class in much the same way as they did before. Whether they become actively involved in the peace movement depends very much upon the type of peer group with which they associate. Those graduates who have had friends involved in peace activities tend much more to become involved in working for peace than other students who don't have regular contacts with people promoting peace.

Ervin Lazlo, a leading futurist who works with the United Nations, posits a three-stage transition towards a less violent world[34] (further information on futures is contained in Chapter 11). These are: to build consensus, to change lifestyles and to participate. Peace education obviously has a lot to contribute toward building a consensus about how to reduce violence in this world. Peace educators, by educating about the problems of violence, try to raise consciousnesses about problems that come from the use of force and to help form notions of what can be done about those problems. Although educators themselves do not tell students what to think or imagine, they need to encourage students to develop their own images of a less violent, more wholesome future.

The author's research shows that students in peace education classes do change their attitudes and beliefs about violence and even change their lifestyles in more peaceful directions, but they don't necessarily participate in political activities to challenge public policies. Have the reconstructionists been too optimistic about the role of education in changing the world? It is up to educators to help foster an attitude of the importance of civic participation, and of the necessity of resisting social injustice when it is encountered. It seems that only with the support of peers will most individuals attempt to change the nature of political reality.

CHAPTER 5

Getting Started: First Steps in Educating for Peace

Education is the fundamental method of social progress and reform.
                                                John Dewey

This chapter discusses some ideas on how to begin to act on the desire to educate toward peace. Two key themes highlighted are: the importance of finding good resources upon which to build a course, curriculum or program, and connecting with like-minded educators for mutual sharing and support. (A list of resources and a bibliography are at the back of the book.)

An individual may "wake up" one day feeling a desire to do something to make the world safer and more just. Responding to these issues requires courage, skill, and a great deal of knowledge, not only about the topics of war, peace, conflict and social justice, but also how to initiate new courses, workshops, and programs, and how to locate research that helps to demonstrate that social change can occur. Exactly what a person does depends to a large extent upon where that person is located. The adage to "bloom where one is planted" is apt here. If a person is isolated and unaware of the various activities of peace and justice groups in the community, he or she can begin with a study of the problems of war and peace or change his or her lifestyle to adopt a more peaceful way of living. In addition, that person may discuss his or her concerns about conflict and security with fellow workers, or initiate discussions about violence in various other settings—veterans organizations, neighborhood groups, fraternal orders, churches, or social clubs—choosing to conduct adult education programs in those settings. If that individual does not belong to such a group or does belong and feels that those organizations are not receptive to these ideas, he or she may choose to gather together a few friends into an affinity group to learn more about how violence affects their lives and to formulate actions to express their concerns. If that person is a community educator, he or she may start planning public educational events on war and peace topics. For a teacher, an appropriate action would be to learn more about how peace and conflict studies can be included in classroom activities and to begin sharing concerns about violence with other professionals and students. If that person is a college teacher or trainer, he or she may start introducing peace and justice concepts into teacher education classes. This chapter will focus on getting started in peace education in two kinds of settings: nonformal education settings such as community agencies and churches, and formal school settings—elementary and secondary schools, universities, and colleges.

Peace Education in Community Settings

People alone can feel isolated and powerless in relation to their concerns about conflict in their lives. This isolation can be alleviated by joining a peace group. Many such organizations publish newsletters to inform the broader public about war and peace issues and sponsor public events—talks, forums, and speaker series—that provide information about security issues.

Community education about the problems of war, peace, and conflict in nonformal settings involves more than teaching. Adult educators should be successful organizers if they are to reach wide audiences. They need to listen carefully to the people they are trying to educate and understand the cultural traditions of the community in which they are working. Peace education programs need to respond to people's interests, not to a predetermined agenda that may be irrelevant to that community. Getting peace education events started involves at least seven different stages: coming together, needs assessment, setting goals, planning events, developing publicity, implementing events, and evaluating peace education activities.[1]

During the initial formation of a group, members get to know each other and develop a sense of trust that provides the basis for commitment to the group. Before dividing up tasks and planning an event, group members need to identify the different gifts and interests of those in the group. They should decide on a facilitator who will have responsibility to make sure the group meets its goals and stays on task. (This responsibility can be rotated.) Early on, a group can develop a sense of cohesion by becoming a planning group.

The second stage involves a needs assessment where educators try to understand the needs of the people they hope to educate. Noted peace educator Betty Reardon writes:

> First, determine whether the needs, assumptions, assertions, and values which you have clarified and articulated in the statement of purpose are shared by others in your community.[2]

This assessment of need for peace education can be done through a variety of survey techniques. A sample conducted over the telephone or through a mailed questionnaire can help determine educational needs. Because the return rate from mailed questionnaires is so low, it might be best to personally interview people at public places, such as peace gatherings or public forums, to gather data that can help to determine the content and form of a peace education program.

In the third stage the group sets goals for itself and decides what it hopes to accomplish with a specific peace education program. These goals should reflect the findings of the needs assessment and include a statement about what the outcome might be of a particular program.

During the fourth stage the group decides how to implement its program. This stage of the planning process involves deciding how the program will be conducted. Its particular nature should fit the cultural traditions of the community being served. Peace education programs may vary from a single event with a speaker or a film, to a day-long conference, to a whole week of activities focused on peace and national security issues. During this stage the group can develop a flow chart with a timetable that clearly delineates what has to be done, by what time it has to be accomplished, and who has responsibility for different aspects of the program. A budget should be developed with a fundraising schedule, to raise money to pay for the costs associated with educational events. These funds may pay for travel costs of guest speakers, honoraria, rental of films and slide shows, and publicity costs. Specific fundraising events can be a means of distributing information, as well as providing revenue.

The fifth stage centers around publicity. Peace educators want to reach new audiences to provide them with information about peace and national security issues. Most people now receive their news through the media. Therefore, a peace education planning group needs to devise a strategy to gain coverage this way. Minimally such a strategy would involve the delivering of press releases to all major media—print and electronic—that would provide a brief summary of the event: who is going to be featured, where and when it will be held, and the name of a contact. At its best, the media coverage will extend to the event itself with coverage on prime-time television and articles in leading newspapers. Any effective peace education group will, over time, develop a list of media contacts, people whom they entrust to provide coverage of peace education activities. An important aspect of publicity is reaching out to other groups who have mailing lists including people with similar interests. Such groups include political organizations, labor unions, professional networks, church groups, minority and ethnic organizations, and women's organizations. Posting events on the internet is another way of creating publicity, using web sites and "list serves."

The sixth stage of beginning a peace education program is the implementation of the event itself. Care should be taken to make sure that people will be comfortable, that there will be time for audience participation, and that the event keeps to its stated time. The organizers of the event should designate individuals to work with the press should its representatives have questions. The group can also provide a sign-up sheet and invite people in attendance to join the group or become more active in future events. Peace education in these kinds of settings involves organizing—trying to get people involved in an issue so they will want to pursue it further. With a successful event the group will meet its expenses, have more members, and more public interest in peace issues.

The final stage is an evaluation of the educational program. The entire process constitutes a significant occasion for learning. Participants may gain a deeper understanding of themselves and their participation in the group by seeking answers to the following questions: How were assignments carried out? What went well? What failed and why? How could this event be done more effectively? This evaluation process can allow the group to set new goals for itself and to provide support to its members for the risks they have taken and the care they have given to planning educational events. As a learning group, members should examine carefully what has been done and discuss in greater depth the content of the educational activities. Was the audience interested? How could they reach more people? Was the presentation appropriate?

Community education is an important part of all peace organizations. Most individuals concerned about violence and justice issues want to communicate their concerns to others. Following the process described above may help generate support and allow concerns to reach a wider audience. Peace education asks much of those who participate. Building contacts takes time. Raising funds can be difficult. Sometimes the best way to communicate with a broader audience is to publish a newsletter, which requires further funds for printing and mailing. However, a successfully executed program can result in new constituencies, enhanced learning and a renewed sense of energy for further work on the part of those who participate.

Peace Education Within Churches or Synagogues

Religious organizations can be valuable resources for peace education activities.[3] Inherent in most churches and organized religious denominations is a social mission to support and work for peace and social justice. Churches and synagogues have at least three levels at which educational activities might be planned. At the most superficial level, a church might be a place where a peace event occurs. In order to do this, a peace education group should approach the local minister, rabbi or congregation leader to get his or her support. If that person expresses reluctance, peace educators might identify parishioners and ask them to approach the head of the church.

It is important to understand the structure of churches and synagogues in order to approach one about a peace education program. Many parishes have directors of religious education whose tasks include developing educational programs. Most churches or synagogues have "Sunday schools" for children that are appropriate places to introduce peace and social justice concerns. A peace educator might offer a workshop for the Sunday school teachers, acquainting them with key topics, as well as teaching methods for introducing peace and justice issues into their classes. Another approach would be to offer to lead a study group to provide broader education to church members. An international organization called Pax Christi does exactly that within Catholic churches. Many religious groups have access to resources and bibliographic materials within the larger structure of their organizations. Peace educators can tap into these as well as contributing additional resources.

Getting Started in (Formal) School Settings

Teachers all over the world are "waking up" to the threats war and violence pose to our contemporary life. Teachers at all levels—from those working with young children in day care centers to university professors graduating Ph.D. candidates in peace studies—are finding ways to incorporate peace and conflict studies into their courses. Some teachers are writing their own curricula. Others are taking advantage of the growing number of programs and projects addressing war, peace and social justice issues (see Appendices).

It takes some courage to introduce peace education into school settings. For many teachers their daily routines and class lesson plans are already so full that they don't see how they could possibly introduce anything new. They don't want to take on something as controversial as peace that would "rock the boat." In spite of this, however, many creative teachers are introducing peace studies into their classes. Some do this by introducing new ideas into already existing curricula. Others use resources and devise entire programs designed to teach the skills of peacebuilding.

Critics of the American educational system complain that the traditional curricula has little relevance for some students' lives. John Dewey noted that one of the weightiest problems of education was the isolation of the curriculum from life experiences.[4] Alfred North Whitehead also called upon educators "to eradicate the fatal disconnection of subjects which kills the vitality of our modern curriculum," and advocated the study of "life in all its manifestations."[5] Because so many students face the fear of violence in their lives, the introduction of peace materials can provide deep relevance to their ongoing learning.

Become Informed

Teachers can begin to become informed about the complex nature of war, peace, and conflict by studying the vast amounts of material available, in print, in the media and on the internet, and calling upon community experts. Teacher training programs need to introduce these concepts into their curricula, as presently the teacher education programs stress, in large part, the academic and technical skills necessary for classroom work, to the exclusion of relevant material on peace and peacemaking.

Teachers at the elementary level generally receive broad academic training, while those at the secondary level usually major in a specific academic discipline. In the former, this broad education is supplemented in schools of education by two years of methods training and preparation for teaching. Secondary teacher education training usually includes a broad liberal arts requirement and an area of specialization in a field like mathematics before students take their teaching preparation courses. The only place where teachers in such traditional curricula might be introduced to peace and justice concepts would be in the liberal arts—philosophy, psychology, sociology, history, international relations, or political science, where they might study the nature of the international order and societal violence. Therefore, many teachers are ignorant of the academic areas of peace studies and often must pursue a process of self-education to learn more. Teachers can and do sometimes form study groups to discuss some of the current literature and research on peace and conflict. This is generally outside their normal curricula, however.

Teachers desiring to learn more about peace studies have access to excellent resources. Nearly every country that has an existing peace movement has at least one professional teachers' organization promoting peace education. A prototype for such an organization is the Council for Education in World Citizenship in England. Formed in 1939 as an outgrowth of the education committee of the League of Nations Union, this organization has promoted the study of foreign languages and cultures in schools, has initiated 'pen-friends' exchanges among pupils in different countries, and has sponsored exchanges of students between countries. In addition, the Council has provided information for teachers through newsletters, conferences, lectures, and debates on topics of world order, and has prepared a variety of audiovisual and printed materials for classroom use.[6] In Japan in the 1970s teachers helped to found the Hiroshima Institute for Peace Education which sponsors national symposia on atom-bomb education and has published a variety of materials for classroom teachers. Internationally, UNESCO has published classroom materials that promote international understanding. More recently in the United States, Educators for Social Responsibility (ESR), in Cambridge, Massachusetts, has been designing and delivering in-services for teachers and community leaders on conflict resolution education. Their original aim was to disseminate education on nuclear war. During the 1980s, ESR greatly expanded its mission to educators. ESR has available numerous publications for classroom teachers (see Resource List for further information).

Many of these organizations publish newsletters that provide teachers with up-to-date material on peace and peace education. Others publish journals, in print and online, that contain an in-depth analyses of the problems of war and peace. Through these organizations teachers can acquire the knowledge and skills necessary to orient their activities toward the attainment of a less violent world.

Although the above-mentioned organizations may be most useful because they have a specific focus on peace education, traditional teachers' organizations can also play a role in promoting peace education. Two organizations, the World Council for Curriculum Instruction and the

Association for Supervision and Curriculum Development, have already published peace and global educational resources for teachers. In the United States the two largest professional teacher unions, the National Educational Association (NEA) and the American Federation of Teachers (AFT), have actively promoted education for world citizenship, and the NEA has produced a curriculum for nuclear-age education called *Choices*.

Concerned educators can insure that annual teacher and administrative conferences sponsor workshops and forums on peace and justice topics. Members within these organizations can establish committees to address peace education and develop teaching materials. . The American Association of Educational Research has a very active peace education Special Interest Group (SIG) and each year at the annual conference sponsors a symposium and several related workshops. Traditional teacher organizations can develop and encourage exchanges among teachers interested in peace education at the local, national, and global level. Members within these organizations can assert the right of teachers to teach about political and social issues and can help sensitize professional educators to the urgency of the task of educating for peace. Some of these professional organizations may even choose to become more active politically by supporting political candidates committed to de-escalating the arms race or by advocating government budgets that take funds from the military and divert them to education.

BUILDING A NETWORK

The key to getting started in peace education is to develop a network of like-minded people who share concerns about war, peace and conflict. Many teachers who feel isolated with their concerns for peace welcome the opportunity to talk with others about how to incorporate peace and justice in their classrooms. A good way to start such a network is through a social activity such as a potluck or a luncheon meeting outside of the formal school setting. Informal word of mouth can be used to identify other school personnel who may be interested in peace studies. Faculty might use these networks to share classroom activities and to create curricula. Parents and community members interested in peace might be invited to such a gathering. Parent-teacher groups can be a vehicle for the introduction of programs and might also offer funding for curricula. Parents of students can also be used as additional teaching sources. Author Morrison got her start in peace education by volunteering to introduce conflict resolution and mediation programs into her children's elementary school in West Hartford, Connecticut. Working with the fourth grade teacher, she began with one class and eventually wrote and implemented a mediation curriculum and trained several groups of fourth and fifth graders, with the active support of the principal, before turning the program over to other parents and a teacher as her children moved on to middle school.

Peace educators often form regional networking groups. One such example is the Five-College Consortium in Massachusetts—Amherst, Smith, the University of Massachusetts, Mount Holyoke, and Hampshire College—which has hired an expert on global security issues. This group sponsors programs and activities, reaching out to New England and beyond. The philosophy behind this consortium is that there is "strength in numbers." Peace education is often marginalized on college campuses. Resources are often hard to come by. Networking and connecting makes sense, both for fiscal and other reasons. Because faculty who want to promote peace education often find themselves beset by hostile colleagues, these networks can provide emotional support for peace educators volunteering time to promote activities that aren't valued by traditional educational institutions.

INFUSING PEACE EDUCATION INTO EXISTING COURSES

Peace education can be introduced into a classroom as a program in and of itself. Peace education can also be part of the ongoing curricula in a classroom, with concepts being introduced as they seem to fit.

Teachers have relative autonomy in their classrooms. They may have to teach preset curricula, but they can often alter this to introduce new topics, to develop new approaches, or even to initiate new programs. Infusing peace and justice concepts into existing courses seems to be the easiest way to promote peace education within schools, colleges, and universities. An example of this "infusion method" was the funding by the U.S. federal government during the 1970s for the introduction of teaching material on the environment. As with peace studies, environmental studies was seen as an inchoate field, not yet worthy of a separate discipline, and environmental topics were taught in traditional sciences such as biology, geology, chemistry, and physics. With an infusion approach, teachers introduce concepts dealing with war, peace, and violence into existing courses. Infusion might be the preferred method for teachers to get started with peace education at the elementary and secondary level, where there is already prescribed curricula, and if there is little or no room for extra courses. Infusion does not require teachers to develop entirely new courses and hence may not be as time consuming as introducing a whole separate curriculum. Infusion also does not require getting permission from department heads or school administrators. This approach also works well in higher education. There is no one discipline that determines the academic content of peace studies. Scholars and teachers from many different fields can find ways to investigate the problems of violence in their courses.

PEACE AND JUSTICE WITHIN THE EXISTING CURRICULUM

Educators who want to introduce peace and justice topics into their classes may have to redesign their curricula somewhat, adding some new elements. Following this model, an individual teacher should assess the course or curriculum to see where peace and justice topics might be introduced. One question, is do the students' backgrounds, needs, and interests mesh with the curriculum? From that assessment a statement of objectives can be made. What are the goals for peace students in this class? Once a set of objectives has been defined, a teacher decides the next steps toward realizing those objectives.

Every teacher can infuse peace and justice concepts by using his or her imagination to tailor the content to a particular group of students. Table 1 presents a brief guide for teachers. These are examples, which can be adjusted according to the age and abilities of the students. Table 1 is not meant to be exhaustive, but rather to convey some sense of how broad the concepts of peace and justice are and to illustrate how teachers might use their creative talents to infuse these topics into existing courses.

On the college and university level, concepts of peace and justice can become components of courses taught in fields as diverse as atmospheric science (the effects of radiation upon the stratosphere) to law (the study of international law and its ability to ease world tensions).[7] The concepts associated with peace and justice, in some sense, are at the core of a liberal arts curricula, including an appreciation of liberty and justice. Liberal education attempts to give students an understanding of their traditions and teach them what they need to know in order to exercise their responsibilities as citizens. The study of war and peace allows students to examine the basic assumptions of experts and policy makers and to develop their own conclusions about complicated public policy issues. Introducing these topics into college classes helps give students an understanding of at least one of the crucial challenges of modern life: how to survive in a postmodern world that appears committed to the use of advanced technological forms of weaponry and rife with various forms of conflict.

MATHEMATICS	World problems involving cost of defense budgets and local impact. How many people would be killed by a 10-megaton bomb dropped in this area? How many by a 20-kiloton bomb?
TYPING CLASSES	Instead of typing abstract paragraphs, type articles related to peace. Send letters to elected representatives expressing concerns about violence in the community.
ART	Create school displays on violence and peace themes—posters and murals. Do specific projects to highlight the necessity of peace to human community.
DRAMA	Act and produce plays that have war or peace themes. Make films about violence in students' lives. Critique action films.
HOME ECONOMICS (Clothing and Food)	Prepare and discuss foods from different countries. Compare clothing from various countries. Prepare a meal that would represent unequal distribution of world's resources.
MUSIC	Analyze contemporary music and videos: How do they present violence and peace? Study the works of numerous musicians who have written songs with peace themes.
BIOLOGY	Study the earth as a spaceship, the effects of radiation upon ecosystems, the interrelatedness of living things, and ecology.
CHEMISTRY	Study atomic particles, fission, and fusion. How is the biochemistry of organisms affected by radiation?
PHYSICS	Emphasize relativity and the physics of nuclear weapons, the generation of power and electricity, and alternative energy sources and pollution.
ENGLISH	Study violence in television shows and commercials. Read essays and novels on war and peace. Write on topics centered around the role of violence in daily life.
HISTORY	Study the role of peacemakers and peace movements, places in the past and present where nonviolence has occurred. What have ordinary people done to bring about social change?
POLITICS AND ECONOMICS	Analyze the impact of the defense budget on different communities, resource distribution throughout the world, international organizations, and the activities of peace groups on politics.
ATHLETICS	Practice new games and cooperative exercises that de-emphasize competition.

Table 1. Infusing Peace and Justice Concepts into School Curricula

Once an educator has examined his or her existing courses to see where peace and justice topics may be used and has determined exactly what to introduce, he or she needs to develop an instructional strategy to infuse peace and justice concepts into courses. Such a strategy will attempt to adjust the content to the abilities, needs, and interests of students. Some peace educators have asked their students to help plan a peace events for the classroom. Working with the teacher to plan curriculum gives students a sense of ownership to enable them to take steps to create a more peaceful world. Because different students have different learning styles, the instructor must choose appropriate lessons. Peace educators have many resources from which to draw in selecting these experiences. Lessons may include small-group exercises, readings, essays, student projects, films, guest lectures, and more, depending upon the age and needs of the students. Students are given material and draw their own conclusions, part of a problem-solving approach to learning. Panels and forums offering a wide variety of opinions about the problems associated with conflict and violence can present students with different points of view on these complex issues. People from the community may also be able to provide important resources for teachers who may, at times, feel inadequate to addressing the complexity of some of these issues.

Teachers must evaluate the efficacy of their curricula for their students. Evaluation requires three distinct stages. The first, preassessment, determines what it is students know prior to being introduced to the peace concepts. This preassessment should take place before actual instruction, as it can help the teacher determine different students' levels of awareness about peace and justice issues. The second stage is the formative evaluation, which takes place during instruction itself where teachers try to assess how students are proceeding with a particular lesson. These evaluations are usually informal, with teachers asking questions of students or observing how students react to the subject matter. The final stage is the summative evaluation, which takes place at the end of a course or unit. Here teachers may want to ask students what went well in the class or how it could be improved. At this point teachers try to determine both generally and more specifically what students have learned. An important question for teachers to ask is, "what next?" After students have been introduced to peace and justice topics and have been allowed to examine these issues, they might have some important suggestions about what they would next like to study.

Evaluation helps the teacher assess what students have learned and whether the curriculum design was effective. With data from these assessments, peace educators can work to further redesign their curricula. As an expert in the field of curriculum development has put it:

What is implied in all of this is that curriculum planning is a continuous process and that as materials and procedures are developed, they are tried out, their results are appraised, their inadequacies identified, suggested improvements indicated; there is replanning, redevelopment and then reappraisal and in this kind of continuing cycle, it is possible for the curriculum and instructional program to be continually improved over the years. In this way we may hope to have an increasingly more effective educational program rather than depending so much upon hit and miss judgement as a basis for curriculum development.[8]

Teaching about war and peace requires a constant examination of thought patterns and behaviors, as well as an analysis of current events and a re-examination of curriculum. Peace and conflict issues impact people in many complex and subtle ways. Teachers need to continue to examine their classroom activities to ascertain how best to help students understand the impact of these issues upon their lives.

In addition to specific classroom activities, peace and justice issues may be infused into general school life in a variety of creative ways. Libraries can feature these topics in special displays. Bulletin boards in individual classrooms and corridors can highlight war and peace themes. Assembly programs can present information about war and foreign policy. Special holidays such as United Nations Day or Martin Luther King's birthday can be celebrated with guest speakers. Certain schools have declared peace weeks where teachers and students in all classes focus attention on peace.

Infusion works best when the whole faculty of a school or an institution is involved. Community involvement underscores the importance of the topic of peace itself and allows students to receive a more comprehensive approach to the subject. Such integration challenges students to reflect more deeply than if a single teacher or classroom pursues issues relating to peace. The emphasis in infusing peace and justice concepts into traditional school activities should be to get students to think about the important war and peace dilemmas that face our civilization on a community and wider national and international level. Students can acquire skills and understanding that can become the basis for responding to these issues as informed adults. Essentially, infusion helps sensitize students to the different issues included under the heading "peace and conflict studies." The more frequently they have these topics brought to their attention, the greater their understanding. Students can become aware that peace itself is an "everyday topic."

Developing Separate Courses and Programs

As convenient as an infusion technique may be for teaching about peace and conflict, it has one main disadvantage. This method risks presenting an overly simplistic view of extremely complex topics. Unless an instructor is willing to explain in great detail the complex aspects of international relations and human behaviors that lead to violence, students may come away from classes where these topics have been introduced with shallow notions of how they might be solved. A more thorough approach would be to introduce whole courses and programs dealing with the topics of violence and peace, where students and instructors can examine in-depth the nature of violence and the promise of peace. This approach is most applicable in formal school settings at the university and college level, although some high schools might choose to offer courses in international relations that would highlight how the behavior of nations contributes to the threat of war. Similarly, teachers in elementary or secondary schools may choose to develop whole peace curricula that they hope will be adopted by teachers throughout a school system. Such curricula might involve the teaching of the skills of conflict resolution and point up the similarities, for instance, of the approach to mediation practiced by individuals in conflict and nations attempting to negotiate treaties, such as Israel and Palestine in the Middle East.

In proposing new courses, programs, or even departments, peace educators find themselves involved in educational change. William Schubert writes:

> The central point for those who want to initiate curriculum improvement is that changing attitudes toward acceptance of proposals is not merely a rational process. To be sure, sound rational argument can help a great deal, but it is a political process, too.[9]

The introduction of new courses can shift teachers away from classroom considerations into a more political realm, where the need for advocating for social change becomes more apparent. Literature on bringing about change in social organizations suggests a process known as action planning.[10] Through this process an activist identifies changes he or she would like to see and then describes the forces in his or her institution that will help bring about this change and the barriers involved. Successful change strategies require negating the barriers and increasing the supportive forces so that proposals win acceptance from key individuals within social organizations.

Peace educators will have to become acquainted with "the lay of the land." Who are the important people who have final say over curriculum revision? In order to work through the complex labyrinths of educational institutions, peace educators need to form a leadership group that can identify what barriers exist in a given organization, can help with the difficult tasks of preparing proposals, and can get approval for those proposals.

Teachers need to feel a sense of ownership of new curricula, and they are, in fact, the best people to develop new materials in their classrooms. Teachers can assess whether or not a particular implementation will benefit students and determine costs in terms of time, energy, and anxiety in changing their routines to adopt peace and justice concepts. Curriculum improvement occurs best as a cooperative approach, as opposed to a top-down approach. Those who wish to change existing school practices need to involve as many stakeholders as possible in the process of change. Margaret Lindsey writes: "If decisions are to have meaning for the individual teacher and to provide direction for his work, he [she] must be personally involved in making them."[11] Curriculum implementation is a process that takes place over time. Teachers working together in a cooperative effort to revise school curricula receive important experiences in peacemaking as they work together to achieve mutually agreed-upon goals.

Research from the field of curriculum development shows other factors that help to facilitate teacher innovation.[12] Foremost among these is the use of an outside consultant to provide new ideas and to help teachers develop new skills. Consultants can come from local peace organizations, as well as from colleges and universities that have peace studies programs. Teachers often have to become their own consultants by reading and experimenting with different approaches to peace education: "Learning the new educational practice, therefore, is not a simple matter of absorbing the written transmission of information," writes Lippert.[13] Teachers need the support of a peer group to encourage them and give helpful feedback about new suggestions for peace lessons.

Teacher Training

An important part of peace education involves training teachers. In an ideal world truly concerned about the well-being of its citizens, all teachers would be trained peacemakers. Their teacher preparation courses would provide them with knowledge of the existential dilemmas around the peace and conflict that face humanity, skills to deal with violence and violent issues in the classroom, and an awareness of how to structure classes in ways that prepare young people to become peacemakers. In the current world, however, very few teacher education programs are preparing teachers with the requisite skills and knowledge to teach peace education.[14]

Educators receive professional preparation in three different ways. Their preservice education, normally called undergraduate teacher education, consists of three areas: general education, professional courses, and student teaching. Once they have become teachers, school districts provide in-service education, which attempts to keep teachers abreast of current developments. In addition, most teachers earn graduate credits and advanced degrees. A successful strategy to prepare peace educators would address all three of these areas of teacher training.

In a teacher training program with the goal of preparing peace educators, prospective teachers would be introduced to the concepts in all aspects of their undergraduate education. In the general education component where teachers acquire knowledge of subject matter, they would study the history of war and peace, learn about the psychology and sociology of violence, take courses in conflict resolution and human communications, and be introduced to the study of international relations. Such a comprehensive approach in the general education part of their training would provide them the knowledge they need to discuss in-depth the complex topics of peace education in their classes. In the professional education (methods) component of their teacher training program, prospective teachers would learn how to set up peaceful classes that promote problem-solving and critical-thinking skills. In their student teaching experiences they would work with supervisors and cooperating teachers to learn how to establish a peaceful classroom based on nonviolent principles. Teachers themselves, as part of their preservice training, need to learn how to resolve conflicts so that they can model peaceful behavior in their classrooms. Such a comprehensive approach for preparing peace educators would produce teachers who are prepared to teach about the role of violence in the social order and the use of nonviolent techniques to establish peaceful classrooms.

Robin Richardson, associated with the World Studies Project in London, has suggested a model for workshops and seminars in peace education.[15] The first stage builds a trusting climate by establishing the knowledge base of the participants, helping them recognize their own "ignorance" and facilitating group interaction in a safe climate. The second stage involves inquiry into the subject matter. The final stage is a synthesis stage, where participants embark on collaborative planning, generalize from their own experiences, and develop action proposals to implement in their classes.

A different model of in-service education for teachers uses a summer workshop. Various universities offer summer workshops that usually last for about a week and expose participants to a wide variety of experts. For example, the International Institute for Peace Education, co-sponsored by the Teachers College Peace Education Program at Columbia University, regularly offers to teachers summer institutes which take place in different parts of the world. These workshops allow participants to examine practical ways to approach peace-related topics in classroom settings.

Currently, some graduate schools of education provide courses in global perspectives that provide the following goals:

> (1) valuing diversity while acknowledging commonalities in all human beings, (2) making decisions and understanding the consequences of individual and collective behavior, (3) effecting value judgements among alternative solutions to world problems and (4) exercising influence competently through participation.[16]

Such courses help students develop an awareness of different cultures and an understanding of the interrelatedness of all people. In addition to providing information about problems associated with violence, these courses promote the skills associated with critical thinking and communication, important in learning negotiation and mediation, both inter-personally and on a more global scale. Also basic to these courses is the questioning of assumptions underlying foreign policy decisions.

Graduate courses in peace education can allow teachers to discuss their experiences relating to individual, social, and international peace and encourage peacemaking in their classes. These courses help teachers identify the topics of peace education, understand the key issues involved, and confront the various obstacles to peace that make their work so difficult. Teachers can acquire important skills in part by asking the questions, "what do we know about peace and how do our teaching activities convey the message of the importance of nonviolent resolution of conflict?" To answer these questions, teachers can share with each other ideas that work. Practicing teachers can generate suggestions that will help their classrooms become more peaceful.

The Controversies

So far, this chapter has described how peace educators at different levels can get started with peace education. Although many peace educators feel a sense of urgency, they need to pause and consider how making peace can be both possible and probable within their particular institutional or community settings. At the same time, educators need to be aware of the controversial nature of peace and of peace education. (A more extensive discussion of various obstacles is discussed in Chapter 9.)

Many peace educators make the mistake of thinking that people are eager to embrace peace. To be sure, human beings desire peace, but there exists considerable controversy about how to achieve it and what, exactly, is peace. Some believe that peace through strength is the only strategy that will "work" to stop violence and wars. On a continuum toward those who embrace positive peace, this negative notion of peace is one that is espoused by those who believe in a strong national defense. On a more local level, school districts that employ security personnel whose role it is to stop violence also use peace through strength. Some policy makers who believe in peace-through-strength strategies promoted by governments throughout the world have opposed peace education. These proponents feel that peace education, by offering alternatives to existing security policies, will threaten the hegemony of national leaders to continue military policies. On another level, millions of people throughout the world earn their livelihood by working for the armed forces or working for companies that provide for the armed forces. If armaments were drastically reduced, these people might lose their jobs.

When author Harris first taught a course in peace education, leaders of the business community in Milwaukee sent a letter to the Chancellor of the University of Wisconsin–Milwaukee with these words:

> It is clearly evident from the outline and from the text used that it's [the course on peace education] not a scholarly objective presentation of academic subject matter. It is rather a "how to" course designed to produce anti-defense activists and protestors on the streets of Milwaukee.

In response, the head of the Academic Program and Curriculum Committee said that this course had been approved by the appropriate faculty review bodies and that other major universities offered a variety of courses "from Greek Philosophy to Military Science and from Bio-Chemistry to Peace Education." Partly because of long-held traditions of academic freedom, and to the gratitude of the author, this course was supported by administrators and faculty from throughout the university.

Similarly, when a teacher from a middle school in the suburbs who was active in the Wisconsin chapter of Educators for Social Responsibility (WESR) wrote an article for the local newspaper praising peace education, another business leader in Milwaukee ridiculed these efforts in a opinion column titled "Activist Posing as Teacher Seeks to Give the Peace Away." He preferred the acronym WENI to the acronym WESR. WENI, he said, stands for Wisconsin Educators for National Irresponsibility and attacked peace education for promoting pacifism and disarmament which, he believed, would abandon the United States to the rapacious forces of the Soviet Union. (This was during the height of the Cold War.)

In 1984 the director of Teachers for Peace in London received a phone call from a reporter from the *Daily Mail*, asking about the activities of her organization. The next day the newspaper featured a center section entitled "Communist Teachers Spreading Peace in British Schools." The article mentioned where she resided, and she subsequently received bomb threats. In Australia there have been strong attacks from the "new right" on peace studies programs in that country. In the United States, the October 1986 edition of *Commentary* directly attacked the Peace Studies program at Tufts University.

As frightening as these attacks may seem, peace studies programs continue to grow and thrive. In fact, such negative publicity at times has brought out "closet supporters." In some cases, peace educators face risks to their jobs, as at Tufts University, where the director of the Peace Studies program did not get academic tenure. But in other cases, hostile attacks have elicited support for peace studies programs. But it must be remembered that peace education is and will be controversial. Sobering is the realization that such great peacemakers as Dr. Martin Luther King Jr., Mahatma Gandhi, and Jesus Christ have all died violent deaths.

Peace educators need to stand firm in their conviction that the public in a democratic society has a right to hear all different sides of controversial issues. They must be prepared to meet such attacks and attempt to transform them. Finding common ground with others on issues can be important. Good listening skills are essential. Educators can meet with parents who question why peace education is being introduced into school curricula. Using appropriate institutional "channels" may take time, but in the long run may prove to be beneficial. Peace educators need to prepare arguments that spell out the advantages to be gained by studying about the problems associated with violence. And they need to just "begin."

As much as educators believe what they are doing is right, others may see things differently. By publicly communicating the urgency associated with educating for peace, teachers themselves become models for social change. Education for peace is essentially education for compassion and empathy—for oneself, for others and for the earth. As simple as this sounds, peace educators need to be aware that their efforts may, to some, be challenging and threatening. This need not stop them.

CHAPTER 6

Essential Concepts for the Teaching of Peace

I am certain that after the dust of centuries has passed over our cities, we, too, will be remembered not for our victories or defeats in battle or in politics, but for our contribution to the human spirit.
                                                John F. Kennedy

The material in this chapter will help clarify key concepts and topics relevant to the teaching of peace. In the last chapter we discussed ways of getting started with peace education. This chapter takes the previous discussion a bit further by illuminating and clarifying topics helpful in building a base of knowledge for educating for peace. Most likely the material covered here will be most helpful for peace educators who work with high school and college students and adults, although those who work with younger students may find some of the material relevant. Since many books have been written on each of these topics, it is not possible in such a brief overview to offer a thorough analysis of their complexity here. They will be presented in such a way as to provide the reader with an introduction to key ideas and concepts of a peace studies program. Further resources are listed in the resource guide and bibliography.

An educator interested in teaching about peace issues needs, first of all, to become familiar with the wide variety of information available. There is much "out there" both in print and on the Internet. The study of war and peace can include literature, music and art, as well as a detailed historic examination of the causes of war and the search for peace. It can include topics as varied as conflict resolution, national security systems, international relations, and human aggression. And again, peace education itself is both a *philosophy* and a *process*. Not only is it important to impart information, but a realization of the power of nonviolence and a wish to promote social change is based upon *attitudes* and *inner transformative* work as well.

Key concepts outlined in this chapter will include: (1) an understanding of some of the roots of violent behavior, (2) the defense establishment and the transformation of military resources to peacekeeping resources (3) world order and the understanding of the role of the United Nations, (4) a familiarity with NGOs (nongovernmental organizations) and GROs (grass-roots organizations) and their role in peacebuilding, (5) creative conflict resolution and cross-cultural dialogues (6) truth and reconciliation and the movement for restorative justice and (7) an understanding of nonviolence. All of these topics address issues relating to both the individual and to society, in terms of behaviors and the potential for transformation. It is important to begin this discussion with an understanding of the causes of violence. After that it is possible to present different strategies to redress different types of violence. As mentioned previously in this book, peace through strength is the most widely adopted strategy to deal with conflict.

An Understanding of Some of the Root Causes of Violence

Numerous theories abound about why humans are aggressive and how violence and wars begin. It is safe to say that historically there has not been consensus on these. Yet some understanding of these issues is important for peace educators. Aggression has been defined by one scientist as "behavior whose goal is the injury of some person or object."[1] Underlying this are "wants and needs": a person, community, nation, etc. has something that another wants. This could be candy, in the case of children, women (in the case of Greek tragedies) and territory, power and influence, in the case of countries or ethnic groups.

Three different types of theories have been advanced to account for individual aggressive behavior. The first set of theories says that aggression is rooted in human nature. Associated with Konrad Lorenz,[2] this theory states that human beings have a predisposition to aggressive behavior programmed in the human genetic code. Some scientists have even argued that men, because of their Y-chromosomes, are by nature violent. This theory postulates that violence comes from high levels of testosterone.[3] Sigmund Freud wrote about violence being a part of human nature.[4] Violent behavior expresses urges that exist deep within the human psyche.

The second set of theories about violence views individual human aggression as the result of hostility brought about by frustration. Human beings are goal-oriented. As long as they make progress toward achieving their goals, individuals do not become frustrated and angry—two emotions that can lead to violence. Frustration builds up to a point where it gets released in aggressive behavior.

The third set of theories concerning individual aggression and violence emphasizes the role of social conditioning in aggressive behavior.[5] According to this approach, human beings acquire violent behaviors by observing friends, family members, and images in the media. Violence is essentially based on modeled behavior. Inherent in this is the association of violent behavior with rewards.

Psychologist David Adams has done extensive work, testing out whether humans are innately aggressive.[6] After years of research, Adams has concluded that there is little concrete evidence that humans are intrinsically violent by virtue of our genes. Rather, we are taught war-like behavior by our culture, which includes some of the elements discussed above. Adams was part of a 1986 initiative, a signatory report signed by twenty of the world's leading social scientists, called the Seville Statement on Violence (signed in Seville, Spain) which categorically rejects the notion that warfare is inevitable, and states that "misuse of scientific theories and data to justify violence and war is not new, but has been made since the advent of modern science."[7] The statement goes on to note that "the fact that warfare has changed so radically over time indicates that it is a product of culture. Its biological connection is primarily through language."[8]

Recent work by psychologist David Barash[9] seems to contradict some of the precepts inherent in the work of Adams and in the Seville Statement. It is Barash's contention that in virtually all human cultures of the world, the ratio of male to female perpetration of violence indicates a vastly higher rate of aggression among males. Barash concludes that there are evolutionary and biological reasons for these much higher rates, connected with competition for procreation. "The power of reproduction explains why males are often so eager to dominate, occasionally carrying their eagerness to extremes."[10] Barash also points out that men have overwhelmingly higher rates of drug use and other serious crimes. He makes the case that despite this biological-evolutionary evidence, or perhaps because of it, humans must do all that is possible to ameliorate conditions

6. Essential Concepts for the Teaching of Peace

over which we do have control. Thus it is important for those who desire to educate for peace to understand the important implication in the findings that war and aggression are not inevitable. The focus can be on the possibilities of peaceful behaviors imbedded within our cultural learning.

Human beings can become frustrated because of violence done personally to them. When a person has been violated, he or she may develop an inner pool of anger that is often the origin of violent behavior.[11] In its most extreme case people who suffer from post-traumatic stress disorders can suffer from distorted views of self and others that damage systems of attachment and meaning that link an individual to his or her community. A traumatic aversive event can destroy a victim's fundamental trust assumptions and contribute to a paranoid view where the world is seen as full of enemies that are out to destroy. Under this viewpoint, a strong military is seen as necessary in order to protect against perceived enemies.

Wars, both between nations and intra-state, may be seen to be caused by differing economic systems, religious and ethnic differences, political ideologies, and the desire to assert authority. War is glamorized. An article in *Esquire* magazine some years ago stated that "war is, for men, at some level the closest thing to what childbirth is for women: The initiation into the power of life and death."[12] The danger inherent in war as seen as an enduring part of the human psyche and glorified as a noble enterprise is that humans will continue to support large outlays for military security, resources which take away from the deep human needs on our planet.

Societies reinforce violent behavior in individuals through the collective power of a group, state or nation to celebrate its war heroes. Social groups reinforce war-like behavior in complex ways that transcend some of the psychological explanations of violence. According to Andrew Schmookler, the author of *The Parable of the Tribes*,[13] humans organize themselves into social groups, some of which have resources that other groups want. They rob and plunder weaker groups. Human communities per se are engaged in a vicious cycle of violence, needing to arm in order to protect themselves against marauders. If they all choose the way of peace, they may live in peace. However, as soon as one of the social groups develops offensive weapons, the others have to arm in order to protect themselves. In this way, group tensions and competition for resources contributes to warfare. States contribute to heightening social aggression by devaluing others to generate feelings of superiority. Schmookler's arguments point strongly to the important role peace education can play in helping social groups choose the way of peace. Peace through justice strategies that address problems of poverty, misery, starvation, and various barriers that keep human beings from reaching their full potential attempt to alleviate some of these structural causes of violence.

The Defense Establishment

A primary goal of peace educators must be to challenge students to think through what is a reasonable national defense and what constitutes national security. Many critics of the arms race say the build up of nuclear arms, justified as a contribution to national security has, in fact, made the world less secure. In order to be literate about defense policies, students need to understand the full cost of defense budgets, including the amount of the gross national product of the world's countries that is allocated for defense. American students in particular need to be aware of the role of the United States as a huge supplier of arms to many smaller nations.

In 1959, in his final speech to the nation as President, Dwight Eisenhower warned about a growing military industrial complex:

> There is no way in which a country can satisfy the craving for absolute security—but it can easily bankrupt itself, morally and economically, in attempting to reach that illusionary goal through arms alone. The military establishment, not productive of itself, necessarily must feed on the energy, productivity, and brainpower of the country, and if it takes too much, our total strength declines.[14]

The total expenditures on defense are growing to the point where in 1985 the nations of the world spent over one trillion dollars on wars, weaponry, and defense planning. This trend is increasing. Citizens of many countries, ignorant about these expenditures, know little about where their tax money goes, nor do many understand the economic ramifications of bloated defense budgets. Increasingly world order is being stifled by what Helen Caldicott calls the "iron triangle"[15]—the network of private contractors, defense experts, and government officials—all of whom profit from this military-industrial complex. Much of the profit goes to companies in the United States. Poor countries in the Third World borrow money to buy modern weapons. Increasing amounts of scant resources go to pay back loans rather than provide food and other basic necessities for people. At the same time that so much money is being spent on weaponry, at least forty-one thousand people a day, mostly children, are dying from starvation.

During the 1980s, U.S. President Ronald Reagan began a trend by raising the defense budget from $140 billion in 1980 to $300 billion in 1983. In the next three years he proposed spending $1.6 trillion on defense, a sum equivalent to all the money spent on defense between the years 1946 and 1980. This amounts to spending $91,000 an hour for every hour going back to Christ's birth. This enormous sum of money, as Seymour Melman has pointed out in *The Permanent War Economy*,[16] means that money is not invested in industry and social services in ways that could help sustain a healthy economy. Following the World Trade Center attacks in 2001, President George Bush was able to dramatically increase the defense budget of the U.S., including obtaining public support for the "Star Wars" anti-missile defense system, this with practically no Congressional dissent, even as it was clear that no sophisticated weapons system could have prevented the attacks in New York and in Washington.

Students need to learn about the horror of nuclear weapons, the physics and chemistry of how they work, their effects upon the ecosystem, and the history of their production. Recent studies have indicated that the use of nuclear weapons could create a phenomenon referred to as "nuclear winter," where so much damage would be done to the atmosphere and so much dust created that the whole ecosphere could be seriously altered; this, in turn, would drastically affect life on this planet.[17] This teaching needs to be done in such a way that students are able to discuss their fears, but also feel empowered that they may be able to influence public policy to reduce the world's reliance on nuclear weapons. Educators must be able to help them move beyond a feeling of helplessness.

Peace education students can learn of the history of arms control negotiations. Current arms policy rests on deterrence theory, which necessitates that superpowers have sufficient capability to "wipe out" the other side should there ever be a first strike. Many world leaders, sensing the danger of new weapons systems and the cost of their production, have attempted to prod the countries possessing nuclear weapons to sign arms control agreements that would halt or even reverse the arms race. The desire to reduce these stockpiles is so great that in many European nations "peace education" is referred to as disarmament education. Many educational leaders in these countries are convinced that the path to peace must come through a disarmament process whereby the huge arsenals that now threaten human existence are reduced and ultimately eliminated.

Along with the study of disarmament and nuclear issues, students can learn of the increasing role of peacekeeping by the world's armies and the use of the "Blue Helmeted" troops associated with the United Nations. During the War in Afghanistan, U.S. and other troops were used to help in the distribution of food and aid done by international NGOs and by

United Nations agencies. This "blurring of boundaries" between the role of a soldier as a warrior and as a helper is an interesting phenomenon. UN Peacekeepers in Rwanda during the civil war in the mid–1990s found their "hands tied" to be able to stop the terrible violence, as they were required to not intervene in their role as international observers. These historical events, with their philosophical underpinnings, are important for students to ponder.

World Order and the United Nations

Increasingly, wars are now seen as being not between nation-states, but *intra-state*. Often called civil wars, many of these conflicts are in developing parts of the world and have their root causes, as previously mentioned, in historical events and processes put in place many years before. Policies set in motion by Belgium, for example, which colonized Africa, are partially to blame for the conflicts that erupted in the 1990s in the Congo, Burundi and in Rwanda. It remains to be seen at this writing what the impact will be on global terrorism following the events of September 11 in the U.S. and in American's response, a response which many in other nations believe to be a unilateral one on the part of Americans. At this writing, it appears that, particularly some European and Middle-Eastern governments are critical of the policies of the administration of George Bush, for his and other policy makers' lack of understanding of the importance of cooperating with other nations in the "War on Terrorism." Peace scholars and activists have spoken out for the need to use the international processes that are already in place (The United Nations and its agencies, for instance) to address not only the need for justice for the victims of the attacks, but also to understand more fully the root causes of terrorism.

All of this points to the importance of students understanding more fully the role of "world order" in building peace. The United Nations was begun in the aftermath of World War II. The nature of war has changed dramatically since then. A trend was begun in that war, and continues, that the overwhelming number of victims of war are now civilians, mostly women and children. Students must understand both the strength of organizations promoting world order and also the limitations of, for instance, the United Nations in building world peace. Students must have an understanding of the many agencies associated with the United Nations and their roles in promoting world security as defined as freedom from hunger, a place to live and freedom from violence.

World studies, often referred to as education for international understanding, includes the teaching of current trends towards a more global world. An important part of education about the international order is developing a vision of the world in which human needs are met, respect for cultural differences flourish, and where justice thrives, resources are distributed equally, and starvation does not exist. Glossop writes:

> War, huge military expenditures, waste of resources, pollution, diseases, and national disasters are the enemies of the human race against which all people can direct aggressive tendencies.[18]

Peace educators interested in world order promote a view of the importance of "global citizenry." This view promotes "planetary consciousness" and a loyalty that extends beyond the boundaries of an individual town or nation, to one that embraces the world as a community. A question educators may pose is "what role does loyalty to a cause, a country or a neighborhood play in promoting or inhibiting cooperation in human communities?" One approach advocated by Global Education Associates promotes *Gaia consciousness,* an awareness of the intricacies of the planet earth and a commitment to respect basic ecological requirements of the earth. Elise Boulding uses the term "species identity" to indicate the common humanity of all people on earth.[19] This concept of a global civic culture involves a shared identity with all other human beings.

The world faces more problems associated with violence than the threat of war, and peace education should provide students with an awareness of the serious problems that confront all global citizens. The planet is crowded and getting more so. Three quarters of the world's population live in social misery. The ratio of the Gross National Product per individual in the northern industrial societies is ten times that of those who live in the Third World, and is increasing. Pressure on the ecosystem has reached the point where at least one species a week is becoming extinct. Totalitarian governments are repressing political freedom. Human and natural resources are being wasted. These global problems are at the root cause of structural violence and need to be addressed if the world is to move towards a more peaceful state where human beings may achieve their full potential.

There have been several prominent movements to promote the establishment of world order. Probably the most important world organization promoting peace is the United Nations, which grew out of attempts to establish a League of Nations after the First World War. The League of Nations ended in 1940 partly because it was not able successfully to resolve conflicts such as the Japanese invasion of Manchuria (1933), the Italian invasion of Ethiopia (1936) and the Soviet Union's attack of Finland (1939). The United Nations was founded in 1943 based on the principles of the Atlantic Charter which were reinforced by the United States, Great Britain, the Soviet Union, and China (1943). In 1945, at Yalta, the "big powers" agreed on the essential structure of the United Nations, which held its first session in London in 1946 and moved to its permanent headquarters in New York in 1952. Originally founded with fifty members, the United Nations now is composed of 190 nation-states, East Timor being the latest entry. The UN has promoted various treaties to resolve conflicts over territory, has helped in the transition of many countries in the world from colonies to independent nation states, has provided a democratic forum for the resolution of the world's problems, and has used peacekeeping forces in various troubled spots around the world. The United Nations preamble begins with a reference "to save succeeding generations from the scourge of war." Chapter I on "Purpose and Principles" states as its first purpose "to maintain international peace and security." Peace operations of the United Nations range from civilian missions with lightly armed personnel to the use of armed troops in major world conflicts.[20] In a number of notable instances the United Nations has lived up to these goals by preventing or ending armed conflicts in such places as Cyprus, the Golan Heights, the former Belgian Congo, and South West Africa. In other conflicts, however, combatants have bypassed by United Nations and its peacekeeping functions (an example is the use of NATO forces in the conflicts in the Balkans in the mid and late 1990s).

Elise Boulding, peace scholar and educator, has written that the events that happen at the United Nations center in New York are a relatively minor part of all of the UN activities. There are working bodies all over the world, in Geneva, Rome, Vienna, Washington, D.C., Nairobi and the political centers of many other countries. Boulding goes on to note:

> Areas in which UN experts do a great deal of work are economic and social development at the local and regional levels, dispute settlement, and special assistance programs to particularly deprived populations including women, children, and refugees. In each of these areas the successes are far more numerous than the failures, but it is the failures which are publicized. [The UN] deals with the whole range of problems faced by the human community (and does so on a budget of one billion dollars, compared to the world military budget of eight hundred billion dollars [the article from which the quote is taken is dated 1987; budgets in both categories have substantially increased]. As new needs are identified, the UN develops programs to deal with them.[21]

6. Essential Concepts for the Teaching of Peace

One branch of the United Nations, the United Nations Educational, Scientific, and Cultural Organization (UNESCO), has made important contributions to peace by increasing international cooperation in education (especially literacy programs), scientific research, and exchange of culturally important projects. From the very beginning UNESCO has focused some of its energies on the tensions and underlying issues that cause war. Though some of its focus has been on disarmament education, during the last twenty years or so, partly as a result of women peace researchers speaking out, there has been more emphasis on the social causes underlying violence and the war system. UNESCO has helped to stimulate interest in the social sciences, peace research, and education. It has examined textbooks and promoted curricula to develop an understanding of international order. UNESCO has worked with the International Peace Research Association (IPRA) to sponsor conferences and publications that highlight information exchanges among different countries about the problems of war and peace.

In 1992 UNESCO's Executive Board moved to request a program for a Culture of Peace as a contribution to the UN peacekeeping efforts.[22] David Adams, chair of UNESCO's task force on a Culture of Peace, writes:

> As the concept matured, the culture of peace began to be understood as a profound shift from the dominant civilization traits associated with war and violence to a new culture of peace and nonviolence. The culture of war and violence—power as violence, hierarchical authority, the necessity of an enemy, male domination, secrecy, exploitation and sharpening of inequalities—had both come from and contributed to the institution of war and to the very foundation of the nation-state and other institutions derived from it. The alternatives to this culture are already being developed at many points in society: power as dialogue, democratic participation in decision making, universal tolerance and solidarity, equality of women, free flow of information, and development seen as a participative process.[23]

Eventually, UNESCO led the initiative for the General Assembly to declare the Year 2000 as the International Year for a Culture of Peace. The theme was taken up by all of the living Nobel Peace laureates and adopted with enthusiasm by many NGOs. Finally, in November of 1998, the UN General Assembly approved a request from the Economic and Security Council, based on the request from the Nobel laureates, to proclaim the decade 2001–2010 as the Decade for a Culture of Peace and Nonviolence for the Children of the World. A 2000 UN General Assembly report from the Secretary-General reiterates the notion that children should be at the center of the Decade. This report goes on to note: "Priority should be given to education, including the teaching of the practice of peace and nonviolence to children."[24] The report indicates that education for peace needs to go on in both formal and informal settings, including the family and the in the media. Both governments and civil society should be involved. Needed by all participants is "reflection upon their own current values, attitudes and practices with respect to peaceful conflict resolution, in recognition of their impact as role models for young people."[25]

In addition to the work of the United Nations and its associate bodies, other international attempts to the resolve world conflicts include the World Court, various treaties such as the Law of the Sea Treaty, and a wide variety of international organizations as diversified as the International Red Cross and the World Council for Curriculum and Instruction. (These kinds of organizations are discussed more in depth below under NGOs.) The fundamental argument supporting these approaches to building a world order is that national boundaries are inherently limiting to humans. Noted peace researcher Richard Falk has written:

> I think the lesson is slowly being learned, and that world order projects and studies, as a consequence, are increasingly aware, that transformation of the world system presupposes a long ambiguous struggle dependent on the emergence of a robust global social movement. There is no 'quick fix' in the offering, only the slim hope that there will be enough time for a global learning process among elites and masses to evolve in such a way as to be able to encourage a series of political adjustments in the world that gradually shifts behavior in directions that are humane and ecologically sensitive.[26]

Students of peace education need to understand the crucial role of international organizations in resolving world conflict, so that they might appreciate both the strengths and weaknesses of present world structures.

The Role of Nongovernmental and Grass-Roots Organizations in Peace Education

International nongovernmental associations are primarily a phenomenon of the twentieth century. These transnational associations are part of a civilian grass-roots movement which some believe may supplant the work of the United Nations and its agencies in the years to come. NGOs have grown in number from under 200 at the beginning of the century to somewhere in the range of 20,000 at this time. The Union of International

Associations, itself an NGO, publishes a directory of all of these agencies and their functions. NGOs promote peace and justice in several ways. First, by definition, an NGO is a "globe-spanning" organization. To be listed as such, an NGO must have member groups in at least five countries. Examples of international NGOs range from the YWCA to groups working on banning land mines. The Women's International League for Peace and Freedom was one of the first NGOs, an outgrowth of the first wave of feminism in the U.S. Because there are chapters in many countries, NGOs promote civic dialogue across national boundaries. U.N. Secretary-General Kofi Annan has said of NGOs that they are the new "independent partners" of the United Nations. The rise of this civilian "movement" has been so rapid that some fear that NGOs are becoming themselves victims of the bureaucracy which plagues large bodies such as the UN. A newer phenomenon is the rise of grass-roots organizations, whose structures, by their grounding in local work for peace, justice and humanitarian aid, tends to be less bureaucratic and more decentralized.

Many NGOs consult with the UN, through UNESCO or ECOSOC (the Economic and Social Council). A UN committee accredits these organizations and, beginning in 1999, a thorough review of all NGOs was beginning. The feeling among some associated with the UN is that there are too many NGOs that have consultative status, making for unwieldy working relationships. One wonders, however, if this is related to issues of "turf," as it is clear that NGOs signal a rise in "people power" at the grass-roots level, which does not appear to be reducing and will no doubt continue rapid proliferation in the coming century. NGOs now usually hold their own concurrent meetings when world bodies meet, such as at the Earth Summit in Rio de Janeiro, Brazil, in 1992, where enough pressure was placed to push through agreements on the controlling of greenhouse gases. A 1999 article in the *Economist* notes:

> In short, citizens' groups are increasingly powerful at the corporate, national and international level. Are citizens' groups, as their supporters claim, the first steps towards an "international civil society" or do they represent a dangerous shift of power to unelected and unaccountable special interest groups?" Citizens' groups play roles that go far beyond political activism. Many are important deliverers of service, especially in developing countries. As a group, NGOs now deliver more aid than the whole UN system. Intergovernmental institutions such as the World Bank, the IMF, the UN agencies or the WTO have an enormous weakness in an age of NGOs: they lack political leverage.[27]

Elise Boulding credits the incredible growth of NGOs partly to the women's groups which began at the end of the last century in the age of social reform.[28] Essentially, NGOs may be seen as networking systems, promoting social welfare and peace among all the people of the world. Concomitant with the growth of the media and of the Internet, the movement promises to continue to be, in Boulding's words, "new ways of mapping the world."[29]

NGOs are important to peace educators because, among other things, they are examples of peace and social justice work done concomitantly on the local level, nationally and internationally. Educators can, for instance, ask their students to what organizations they or family members belong. If it turns out to be an international NGO, students can undertake to learn more about its structure and functions and what sort of work is done to promote peace and social welfare.[30]

The International Peace Research (IPRA), an NGO, was founded in 1965 by an interdisciplinary group of about seventy scholars interested in collaborating and networking on issues of peace, security and related research. In 1974 the Peace Education Commission (PEC) of IPRA was founded, whose mission involves dissemination of educational materials and the promotion and support of global efforts in educating for peace.

Creative Conflict Resolution and Cross-Cultural Dialogue

If one of the goals of peace education is to bring peace to the world, students of peace education will have to learn how to resolve conflicts nonviolently. Conflict is a daily reality that comes from differing needs, values, goals, resources, scarcity, and competition. Conflict seems to be increasing in our modern world. It is ubiquitous and it is inevitable. The ability to resolve conflict without using force is probably one of the most important skills an individual can learn, yet there are few formal opportunities for such. As before mentioned, one hopeful trend is that there has been in the last decade a rapid growth in the number of programs teaching these skills from nursery school through college. Various organizations are also appearing in both the public and private sectors that offer mediation services and teach the skills of conflict resolution to a wider audience.

Conflict resolution techniques may be taught as a set of skills often referred to as conflict "resolution strategies," which can be classified into three types—avoidance, diffusion, and confrontation.[31] Avoiding conflict can aggravate a particular problem as resentments build up and emotions intensify. Expressing hostile feelings is a good way to avoid withdrawal, but in order to express these feelings constructively people have to be committed to a win-win situation where participants' feelings are expressed and all parties are willing to compromise.

Diffusion is essentially a delaying action that attempts to "cool off a situation," or to keep issues so unclear that confrontation is avoided. Because conflict can often frighten individuals, they often tend to seek ways to defuse it, trying to understate its significance in the hope that it will go away. Conflict can be a necessary and creative dynamic in most relationships, transforming both individuals and the relationship, if approached in a healthy way. Defusing or avoiding conflicts can become destructive if people are afraid to express disagreement or feel put down for their opinions and feelings.

In order to be dealt with constructively, conflict has to be faced. Peace education seeks to avoid power confrontations and rests on compromise and negotiation to resolve conflicts. One way of discussing conflict is to think of it in terms of a continuum going from cooperation to competition and finally to conflict. Cooperation involves people working together to resolve their disagreements. Competition implies that there will be winners and losers. Some forms of competition are mild and friendly while others are intense and destructive. Warfare is the most dangerous and destructive aspect of competition. Peace educators seek to transform conflict by teaching the skills of nonviolence, including good communication. Conflicts can be resolved nonviolently by talking them through, by using votes, compromise, and consensus strategies to clarify information, by creating alternatives, by agreeing to disagree, by seeking mediation or arbitration, and by a firm commitment to solving problems nonviolently.

Conflict resolution involves problem solving between individuals, groups, organizations, and nations. Indeed, the same skills for resolving interpersonal difficulties are used at the international negotiating tables. The Martin Luther King Center for Nonviolent Social Change in Atlanta, Georgia, recommends six steps for resolving conflicts between parties. The first step is to gather information so all parties may become better informed about their areas of disagreement. The second step is to educate people about the problem, and try to provide information that accurately represents both sides of the dispute. The third step is to try to build commitment among parties to participate in a process that will resolve their conflicts. The fourth step is to negotiate a compromise between the parties to which both agree. The fifth step is to put that compromise into place and act on it. The final stage is to attempt to further reconcile differences between parties and evaluate the agreed upon compromise. The success of this process depends upon members who disagree achieving an understanding of both the position and frame of reference of their opponents.[32]

Two Harvard law professors, Roger Fisher and William Ury, recommend that conflict resolution focus on the interests of the people involved in a conflict:

> To sum up, in contrast to positional bargaining, the principled negotiation method focusing on basic interests, mutually satisfying options, and fair standards typically results in a wise agreement. The method permits you to reach a gradual consensus on a joint decision efficiently without all the transactional costs of digging into positions only to have to dig yourself out of them.[33]

A crucial step in this approach to conflict resolution is the generation of options that allow both parties to come away with a sense that they have gained something from the interaction. Digging into positions and holding on to them keeps the parties locked into a competitive win-lose situation, whereas the search for alternatives allows both parties to seek a solution that enables them both to satisfy their needs.

Teaching about conflict resolution can give peace education students skills they may use in their daily lives to express their frustrations in ways that don't physically abuse others. In order for these skills to be successful, all parties must be willing to change their behavior. Conflict resolution optimally works when both parties agree.

There are many groups who teach the skills of conflict resolution, or, to use the newer term, conflict transformation. One of the first to teach these skills to youth was the Children's Creative Response to Conflict Program, in Nyack, New York, an outgrowth of an earlier Quaker program. Their *Friendly Classroom for a Small Planet* is still being used by peace educators, as ways to introduce the concepts associated with peacebuilding: affirmation, communication and cooperative problem-solving. Another program started by Quakers for use in prisons is the Alternatives to Violence Program. AVP uses a model incorporating both "inside" and "outside" trainers, those in prison and community volunteers, and an integral part of the program is the recognition of the power of violence on individual's lives and a personal commitment to a transformation to nonviolence. A youth version of AVP is now widely in use, known as HIPP (Help Increase the Peace Project). The HIPP model rests on empowering students, who cooperate fully in the planning and execution of trainings.

Recent studies have indicated the need to address cultural differences when teaching conflict resolution and peer mediation strategies.[34] Issues around power and differences in communication styles can contribute to the perpetuation of sub-surface conflicts. A deeper, more holistic look at conflict situations is needed, including fostering ongoing relationships with the parties in dispute.[35] Similarly, on an international scale, effective negotiation strategies must take into account social-cultural and political differences of all the parties involved. This requires time and the willingness on the part of those facilitating to be open to new learning.

Truth and Reconciliation and the Movement for Restorative Justice

One of the more hopeful movements beginning in the late twentieth century has been that of restorative justice, one of whose most vivid examples has been the increasing use of truth and reconciliation commissions in countries torn apart by war and internal violence. However, the movement is also rapidly developing interest among criminologists and those who study alternatives to western legal systems. The first well-known of the Truth and Reconciliation commissions was in South Africa, shortly after Nelson Mandela became its first post-apartheid president. Imbedded within the concept of restorative justice is the notion of *reconciliation.* A difficulty is knowing what is contextually meant by this term.[36]

Restorative justice, whose concepts can be seen as a way of intrinsically "humanizing" western-oriented justice systems, is nothing new. Its roots are in the world's indigenous cultures, where traditionally conflicts have been settled by "healing circles," composed of elders of communities listening to the parties involved or the whole community sitting down and hearing one another. As sociologist Elise Boulding describes these healing circles:

> Whatever the peacemaking practice is called, it has a formal, ritual character, and usually involves a gathering of the whole community, not only those involved in the conflict. Not only will stories of the conflict be told, but traditional peacemaking stories may also be told. Often there will be singing, dancing and gift giving as part of the peacemaking ritual. If the conflict is serious it may take a long time to achieve resolution, but no one gives up. And once resolution has been achieved, it is a cause for celebration.[37]

In the restorative justice model, conflict is seen as interactive and "intersocietal."[38] Central to the principles of restorative justice is the notion that crimes involve acts committed *by individuals against individuals and communities* and therefore healing involves necessary repairs to relationships and to the community. Reparations and restitution are the primary goal, not punishment per se. It is the community's responsibility to insure that victims and offenders, as well as others, are part of the restitution process.[39] The "rub" in this process is that what constitutes forgiveness and reconciliation between individuals does not always translate into effective nor ethical political practice on a national or international scale.

The Truth and Reconciliation process in South Africa has been controversial. Critics have felt that many of the perpetrators of unspeakable crimes during the Apartheid era were "let off" too easily and the process of victims listening to theirs and their family's torturers was excruciating. The goal of the South Africa process was one in which pragmatism reigned supreme.[40] Leaders of the newly emerging government were aware that those who had committed past abuses, as well as those who suffered traumas, were all needed for the future of the nation. The goal of justice was seen as secondary to one in which amnesty was granted, in many cases, to abusers who agreed to tell their stories and to listen to the stories of victims. As Tristan Borer points out, "The goal of any search for political justice is to strike a balance between justice and reconciliation."[41] Nevertheless, the issue of shame was central to the hoped for transformations.

In terms of the western judicial system, presently it is preoccupied with "fixing blame" and both victims and offenders have power denied them by the impersonal processes involved.[42] Crimes are not seen as acts committed against individuals as much as they are against the state. As Howard Zehr points out, "Our present justice system represents the power of the state over individuals and communities."[43] Studies have shown that offenders do at times feel guilt.[44] However, there is little opportunity for an offender, in our present legal system, to openly admit to his or her victim the responsibility for harm, precluding healing on both the part of the offender and the victim.

Our present system dichotomizes the process, aided by the media, into "criminals" and victims." There is no room for forgiveness or healing. The abstract nature of the process precludes the offender from taking responsibility for his or her individual actions and for the possibility of healing to take place as an offender hears the impact of his or her act upon a community member. "In a restorative justice model, it is the offender who takes primary responsibility for making things right with the victim and with the community—not the state."[45]

Some differences may be seen between the political-national uses of restorative justice and its use on a more local state or community level. Nevertheless, the principles remain basically the same: acknowledgement-forgiveness-reparations. Forgiveness does not imply that forgetting is necessary. Forgiving means that the life of the victim may proceed, at least partially unencumbered by compulsive thoughts of hate and revenge. And the process may, in turn, have transforming effects upon the perpetrator.

There are many international examples of restorative justice. Toh Swee Hin, Canadian peace educator, cites the example of a group in the Philippines, Kalinaw Mindanao, who actively promote a deep appreciation for traditional ways of nonviolent conflict resolution in that country. Many NGOs, particularly in developing countries, are leading the movement to educate citizens on the vital role these grass-roots and traditional modes can play in promoting a culture of peace.[46]

Nonviolence

> Through our scientific genius we have made of this world a neighborhood; now through our moral and spiritual development we must make of it a brotherhood. In a real sense we must learn to live together as brothers or we will perish as fools.—Martin Luther King

The last concept discussed in this chapter is nonviolence. Nonviolence has been described as a set of skills, as a method for resolving problems and conflicts and as a way of life.[47] The Center for Nonviolence and Peace Studies at the University of Rhode Island describes nonviolence as follows:

> The skills and methods of nonviolence are closely related to those involved in mediation, interest-based negotiation, counseling and process consultation. Nonviolence has a long history, nationally and internationally, of creating positive social change, peacebuilding and elevating the quality of human interaction.[48]

There has not always been agreement among those using nonviolent means of solving problems on exactly which methods are most useful and "successful." Nonviolence may be seen as a continuum of behaviors, from "talking it out" to civil disobedience, that is, the breaking of the law for the sake of conscience. The line below, on a continuum, signifies some of the various behaviors that may be associated with nonviolence.

> Talk (negotiate)…seek mediation…picketing…strike…boycott
> (moving in the direction of more active nonviolence)

Nonviolence is also a philosophy.

Nonviolence has at its roots the essential belief in the possibility of human transformation. Change can occur both on an individual level, as well as societal. Indeed, as one "changes the world," inherent internal changes may inevitably occur. Educators need to see peacebuilding within a holistic paradigm. Increasingly, peace education is being seen as having its essential roots in the work necessary for "inner peace." Inner peace does not mean merely a state of inner being which ignores the reality of human suffering. Rather, holistic peace is seen as encompassing an individual compassion for human need, coupled with a sincere attempt at identifying with and helping to transform the suffering of others, which suffering may be caused by "structural violence"—absence of basic human needs— or actual physical violence—wounds and war. "Woundedness lies at the roots of violence, within ourselves, in others and in our culture. Active nonviolence comes face to face with these wounds."[49] It is no accident that some nonviolent political movements and their leaders have been closely tied with religion (Gandhi in India, Martin Luther King, Jr., in the United States).

This final chapter section will develop a theoretical perspective for nonviolence in education that draws upon the work of Mahatma Gandhi, Martin Luther King, Jr., and Jiddu Krishnamurti.

THEORETICAL PERSPECTIVES ON NONVIOLENCE: GANDHI, KING AND KRISHNAMURTI

The goal of nonviolence in education is to build in the minds of pupils both a desire to live in a nonviolent world, and to give young and old alike the skills so that they might construct that world. Teaching about nonviolence attempts to build a consensus about the best ways to achieve peace. Teachers searching for creative ways to respond to rising levels of violence in schools can turn to Dr. Martin Luther King, Jr., and Mohandas (Mahatma) Gandhi for inspiration. Although neither of these men was a professional educator, both had many insights into the human condition that would be valuable for school personnel concerned about youth crime, rebellion, and antisocial activities. Both Gandhi and King struggled to build a just society. They both believed that without justice there will be no peace. Dr. King devoted his life to righting the wrongs of a racist society. He hoped to transform social institutions to meet the demands of a multiracial society. Gandhi was also committed to multiculturalism:[50]

> I do not want my house to be walled in on all sides and my windows to be stuffed. I want the cultures of all lands to be blown about my house as freely as possible.⁵¹

Gandhi strongly opposed the caste system in India and realized that the best way to reduce class antagonisms, and hence promote peace, was through service that required students to work with people different from them:

> Nothing can be farther from my thought than that we should become exclusive or erect barriers. But I do respectfully contend that an appreciation of other cultures can fitly follow, never precede, an appreciation and assimilation of our own.... An academic grasp without practice behind it is like an embalmed corpse, perhaps lovely to look at but nothing to inspire or ennoble⁵²

Nonviolence promotes empathy and helps students become compassionate towards the suffering of others at a personal level, not just through study. Education can contribute to peacemaking by awakening young people's hearts to the suffering and misery that exists in the world and imbue a sense of compassionate efficacy to work toward changing structures that oppress and impoverish. Gandhi had a holistic view of education that relied upon the hand, heart, mind, and body to arouse in students a sense of common human destiny.

A commitment to nonviolence enables a better appreciation of truth. Rather than there being one source of truth, Gandhi taught that each person can have important insights into the nature of truth. Nonviolence helps people appreciate these insights:

> There is no way to find truth except the way of nonviolence. I do not seek to serve India at the sacrifice of Truth or God. For I know that a man who forsakes Truth can forsake his country, and his nearest and dearest ones.⁵³

Dogma, whether it is taught in schools or through state propaganda, can promote intolerance. For Gandhi, a commitment to seeking truth implied transcending national interests which so often lead to war, refugees, and other problems of violence. He titled his autobiography *An Autobiography: Or the Story of My Experiments with Truth*.⁵⁴ Nonviolence allows a person to be empathic and put him/herself in the shoes of another and see that person's truth. Violence, on the other hand, often depends upon an absolutist approach to truth, where views are dichotomized and translated into enemy images of "the other," sometimes used to rouse citizens into a frenzy of war and hatred, as Hitler used anti–Semitism to gather support for his fascist ideology.

Nonviolence requires a commitment to truth that is profoundly spiritual. In the words of Gandhi: "When you want to find truth as God the only inevitable means is love, i.e. nonviolence."[55] Because truth resides within each person, nonviolence in education encourages respect for all humans, the source of divine inspiration lying within. Educators committed to nonviolence in education encourage students to discover the ways they think about themselves and others, replacing fears, hostilities, negative statements, and prejudices with nonviolent ways of thinking about self and others that respects the truth that can reside within each of us.

Gandhi devoted his life to overthrowing an unjust colonial system with its exploitative economic relationships which destroyed village communities and natural ecosystems. Both King and Gandhi led nonviolent movements to overcome the forms of oppression that cause misery and conflict. The key to nonviolence in education is not just using violence prevention strategies to create peace in schools, but rather teaching young people peacebuilding skills to create a more just world order where the needs of people are met through standards of justice, love, and truth. As King said, "Peace is not just the absence of tension, it is the presence of justice and brotherhood."[56] In order for schools to contribute to the creation of beloved communities, they can prepare students to achieve high standards of justice and teach them to seek reconciliation with adversaries.

King learned from Gandhi that nonviolence is not passivity. Nonviolent methods that can be used to protest and resist evil imply an active commitment to end violence through nonviolent means, by organizing people to achieve common goals, through mediation and conflict resolution, and through education about different forms of oppression. Gandhi and King did not want to polarize the world into warring camps but rather used nonviolence and compassion to help understand an enemy's point of view. At the same time, Gandhi was a realist who saw that it was important to defend oneself, violently only if necessary, if attacked.

Nonviolence as a strategy for change speaks truth to power. As Gene Sharp has pointed out, it implies withholding support from unjust authorities, an active refusal to submit to injustice.[57] Gandhi demonstrated with his life how it takes courage to stand up for nonviolent social principles. Recent history has shown the power of nonviolent movements in places as diverse as the old Soviet Union, the Philippines, South Africa, and recently in Israel and Palestine the very strong nonviolence movement in the Middle East is, unfortunately, not actively covered in the western media).

Nonviolence in classrooms can help heal the pain of violence. Both Gandhi and King understood that violence is the antithesis of creativity and wholeness. It destroys community and makes brotherhood-sisterhood impossible. Martin Luther King, Jr., preached that nonviolence, or a type of love known as *agape*,[58] creates genuine human communities. *Agape*, pure love based on the principles of brotherhood-sisterhood, does not distinguish between worthy and unworthy people. It urges humans to stop their hating and forgive in order to restore community.

King understood that laws can regulate behavior, but morality cannot be legislated. An orientation towards justice and peace can only come through education that changes inner attitudes away from complacency about suffering to anger towards injustice. Education has a key role to play in developing a world perspective, so that children and adults see that they have similarities with people from other cultures, nations, and races. King saw an urgency to teach about nonviolence, since in the era of nuclear arms, the choice is between nonviolence and nonexistence.[59]

Neither King nor Gandhi wrote specifically about the relationship between education and nonviolence. J. Krishnamurti, on the other hand, stated that the responsibility for building a peaceful and enlightened society rests with the educator. Born in South India in 1895, Krishnamurti died in California in 1986. During his lifetime he feared that the present education system made people mechanical and thoughtless and he asked the important question, "What is the good of learning if in the process we are to destroy ourselves?"[60] Krishnamurti's ideas may be said to have been a precursor to postmodern thought when he stated that our modern educational system with its emphasis upon technological knowledge makes us ignorant about ourselves:

> Merely to cultivate the intellect, which is develop capacity or knowledge, does not result in intelligence. There is a distinction between intellect and intelligence. Intellect is thought functioning independently of emotion, whereas, intelligence is the capacity to feel as well as to reason; and until we approach life with intelligence, instead of intellect alone, or with emotion alone, no political or education system in the world can save us from the toils of chaos and destruction.[61]

Postmodern thinkers question the value of the modern world with all its scientific achievements, because it has not solved the more fundamental problems of environmental destruction, social oppression, and human cruelty. More than advanced math, science, and foreign language instruction will be needed if humans are to create a better world. A different kind of education based upon cooperation and caring is required to replace the current system based upon personal gain and competition.

Krishnamurti understood that love was essential for the right kind of education which must promote acceptance of different points of view and stimulate creativity. Love and understanding break down walls of isolation, nationalism, and racism. Students can learn in schools how to resolve their conflicts nonviolently. Compulsion leads to inner strife, which, when projected outward, becomes violence to others. Krishnamurti saw that the key to the right kind of education was self knowledge that leads to love,[62] which alone can create a tranquil mind, capable of resolving tensions in the world which are caused by the wrong kind of relationships.

> One teaches because one wants the child to be rich inwardly, which will result in giving right value to possessions. Without inner richness, worldly things become extravagantly important, leading to various forms of destruction and misery. One teaches to encourage the student to find his true vocation, and to avoid those occupations that foster antagonism between man and man. One teaches to help the young towards self-knowledge, without which there can be no peace, no lasting happiness.[63]

Knowledge based upon the principles of love and nonviolence can lead to the kind of self-awareness that can, in turn, help move individuals toward seeking peaceful relations with others.

Krishnamurti argued that the use of fear or intimidation in education promotes a state of mind that is not conducive to peace. Following authority blindly is denying intelligence. Traditional education based upon authoritarian practices promotes ambition, envy, and enmity. Teachers should encourage the spirit of inquiry and empirical discontent within children. The conditioning of a child's mind to a particular authority breeds enmity. How can there be unity when beliefs divide human beings into isolated communities with restrictive values? According to nonviolent theory, educators should love their students in the way of *agape*, which seeks to draw the best out of them, not in a selfish way to meet their own ego needs.

Nonviolence does not seek to defeat an opponent but rather to "win" through love. A nonviolent strategy is not about humiliation. Young people should understand that the goal of a nonviolent strategy is to defeat the problem, not the persons involved. It is directed against the forces of evil rather than the people who happen to be doing the evil.[64] A person practicing nonviolence avoids imposing not only external physical violence but also internal violence of the spirit. Sometimes this can involve the experience of accepting suffering and punishment rather than striking back, as a way of transforming the aggressor. Nonviolence does not connote passivity. It is an active process, using the "forces" of morality and seeking the highest good in one's so-called enemy. Both Dr. King and Mahatma Gandhi's lives provide excellent examples of how nonviolent strategies can resist injustice. Nonviolent resistance is based on the conviction that the universe is on the side of justice. Those committed to nonviolence have a deep faith in the future.

Nonviolence in education is committed to democratic practices, because a democracy allows for all points of view to be heard in the promotion of the truth. A multicultural approach to education teaches that all cultures have important insights into the "truth." A nonviolent approach to conflict resolution in a diverse world requires that all voices be respected to create a dialogue that will build a consensus about how to create positive peace. In order to appreciate the diversity of life on this planet, students need to be taught global awareness, learning to respect both ecological principles and different human cultures, essential for living together in a "global village."

Students in classes where teachers are promoting nonviolence acquire both theoretical concepts about the dangers of violence and the possibilities of peace, and also the skills to live nonviolently. In addition, through their modeling and their ways of interacting with students, teachers can help students to learn about the power of generative love, care, and justice to build community. These are peacebuilding strategies. Here, nonviolence extends to personal relations and relations with the broader environment.

Do teachers help students find peace within themselves? At one school in Milwaukee, Wisconsin, which has as its motto, "peace works," staff wrote a grant and hired two art therapists to work with children in the inner city who had been traumatized by high levels of violence in their lives. Some of these children had been abandoned by their parents. Others had seen siblings shot. They were placed in a support group called "Peace Bridge" to help students articulate their feelings about violence. Trauma circles, peer counseling, and support groups can help young children manage some of the grief, fear, and anger caused by violent events in their lives. Anger management groups in secondary schools help adolescents deal with some of the deep-seated rage children have who come from abusive or dysfunctional homes. Some urban school districts in the United States have curricula on death and dying to help young people deal with the trauma of losing their friends to suicide, accidental death, or homicide.[65] Such activities can help improve the academic performance of students who are so distracted by violence that they cannot focus on cognitive lessons. Adults who listen and show concern for the problems caused by violence in young people's lives can help heal some of the wounds that often lead to hostile, aggressive behavior.

Nonviolence in education requires more than a theoretical understanding of the problems of violence and knowledge of strategies for peace. Teachers interested in nonviolence in education attempt to stimulate the human heart to be charitable and provide students with skills they can use to demonstrate their feelings of compassion for all forms of life. As Krishnamurti states:

> There must be love in our hearts, not mere learning or knowledge. The greater our love, the deeper will be its influence on society. But we are all brains and no heart; we cultivate the intellect and despise humanity.[66]

A challenge provided by a commitment to nonviolence in education is to figure out how to increase students' abilities to love, peacebuilding in its truest sense. Teachers can instruct youth about alternatives to dysfunctional violent behaviors. They can teach the importance of listening, caring, tolerance, cooperation, impulse control, anger management, perspective taking, and problem solving skills. They could also try to make students aware of their own biases, ways they stereotype others by gender, sexual preference, religious beliefs, or skin color. Children can learn about racial differences and gender identity formation to help them avoid discriminatory behavior. The goal of these instructional activities is to provide students with communication skills and to help them be empathic. But love cannot be taught. It must be "caught" and this comes about through the persistent affection a teacher shows to each student within a particular classroom environment. This in spite of the fact that the teacher (or students) might be having a "bad day" or a particular pupil might be "driving a teacher up a wall." It is love shining through adversity which is the ultimate test of nonviolence.

Other methods are being introduced in schools that contribute both philosophically and practically to learning about nonviolence. Peer mediation techniques are being taught in classrooms throughout the United States to provide students with conflict resolution and problem-solving skills. Providing these helps to educate children beyond hate and hopefully enables them to become more loving. Nonviolent content prepares children to become peacebuilders within their interpersonal relations, their homes, their schools, their physical environments, and in the global village.

Nonviolent Pedagogy

A teacher committed to nonviolence in education uses dialogue. John Dewey argued that classes should be structured in a problem-solving way, so that students could discover their own truths, as opposed to a teacher-centered pedagogy where she or he is the source of all truth. Teachers can borrow both from the Socratic and Deweyian traditions by presenting problems caused by violence and by encouraging students to develop alternative strategies to resolve conflicts nonviolently. Students can learn by questioning assumptions, by examining the implications of conflict resolution mechanisms, and by gathering evidence to support their hunches about nonviolent solutions. In such a classroom students are encouraged to think critically.

Teachers who promote nonviolence in their classes draw upon the principles of cooperative learning.[67] In their classes they set up democratic learning communities where students provide each other feedback and support so that they become proficient in techniques of group process. Such classes, based upon positive interdependence among group members, teach individuals to care for others.[68]

Teachers interested in nonviolence might promote a nontraditional approach to discipline. They can give their students guidelines about how to behave through positive affirmations rather than through punishing. They can use democratic boundary-setting principles which help students to understand the importance of respecting differences. Instead of threatening children, who so often learn from the broader culture that violence is an exciting way to resolve differences, a nonviolent teacher can use positive reinforcement to reinforce agreed-upon rules. Such practices teach that nonviolence can "work." Acting nonviolently neither creates enemies nor invites retribution.

A teacher who is confronted with a student creating a problem in a class might see that as an important learning moment. Rather than humiliating that student, a teacher committed to nonviolence sees a behavior problem as a chance for students to take responsibility for their actions. By encouraging students to mediate their own problems, such teachers do not always have to play the role of judge and jury, meting out punishment in arbitrary ways. They can comfort students who are having difficulty, doing everything possible to care for and affirm those in their charge.

In a nonviolent classrooms, courtesy, care, compassion, and respect help build a "beloved community" where the peace loving instincts of students can flourish. In such a classroom the teacher provides a model of nonviolent behavior, so that students can learn by example that they have free will in making many decisions. Seeing an adult who manages conflicts without using force can teach children they do not have to resort to violence when faced with conflict. Students exposed to peaceful adult role models learn from them nonviolent responses to conflict.

Teachers in nonviolent classrooms study their students carefully. They watch them develop and understand their strengths and weaknesses. To know something is to understand its nature. Teachers have a responsibility to construct a learning environment which responds to the uniqueness of each individual, drawing out each student's inner gifts. In a nonviolent class listening and watching can be seen as at least as important as direct teaching and lecturing.

Administration

A nonviolent school is administered democratically. Children have certain rights, as do faculty, that are respected within such schools. Such schools are like loving families. They provide sanctuaries where children feel good and safe. Bullies are trained in conflict resolution techniques so they can shift their leadership skills toward positive directions. A peaceful school has an inclusive atmosphere where everyone can be seen as a peacemaker. Such schools are run on the principles of site-based management where staff have the authority to make personnel choices and decisions about resources.

Administrators of such schools can have structures in place aside from "ultimate authority" punishments, like suspensions, or expulsions. Structures such as time out rooms for students who are acting aggressively, peer mediation programs, and programs that teach anger management skills, allow students to face the inevitable conflicts in a rational, constructive, and compassionate way. They permit all people on a school staff to search for creative nonviolent solutions to problems that nurture tension, anger, aggression, and violence. Administrators of nonviolent schools do not deal with conflicts coercively. Nonviolence in thought, words, and deeds must be practiced. An equal balance of consequences and empathy replaces punishment wherever possible.

The principal can create school-wide events that might motivate students to seek peace. Pep rallies and school assemblies for peace can inspire youth to seek nonviolent ways to resolve their conflicts. Awards for peacemakers that can help young people understand the importance of nonviolent behavior can be passed out. A school assembly can be held, where each class nominates a student who has excelled at peacemaking. Such recognition helps youth understand the importance of peace.

6. Essential Concepts for the Teaching of Peace

Several schools in the United States have sponsored a week of nonviolence, commemorating the work of Martin Luther King, Jr. During this time children are encouraged to draw pictures of peace, guest speakers urge students to resolve conflicts nonviolently, and students write essays about how to stop the violence in their neighborhoods. Some schools have established "stop the violence" clubs that give students an outlet for expressing their desires to live in a more peaceful world. Principals can also reach out to community groups interested in nonviolence and use those groups to inform students about neighborhood resources to help them deal with problems of violence and find out how to work for peace.

Administrators seeking to create a nonviolent school climate can educate parents about the importance of nonviolent response to discipline at home. Physical means of disciplining children can lower children's self-esteem and make it difficult for children to trust adults, which can be counterproductive to success in school. Many parents teach their children to stand up and fight when challenged. Children often learn violent problem solving behaviors at home. Parents can be told that, even though they want their children to be able to defend themselves, fighting has no place in schools. Principals can sponsor workshops at their schools, teaching "positive parenting," and send home newsletters with tips about the importance of family-school cooperation.

Lasting and sustainable peace schools require the rearrangement of hierarchical relationships into democratic decision-making structures. The ways of peacebuilding must be modeled by administrators if they are to be endorsed by staff and learned by students. The leader of a school where children are to learn about nonviolence must be a good listener and must show deep respect for all people. Respect is the key to influence, insisting on mutual responsibility to solve problems. When there are problems, the administrator can be careful to address the problem and not the person. The goal is to engage in dialogue that does not seek to create winners and losers.

The goal of nonviolence in education is not just to stop the violence and reduce conflict in schools, but rather to get young people to adopt a nonviolent philosophy of life and way of living. Nonviolence provides educators with a set of guidelines by which teachers, students, and school administrators can promote maximum growth for pupils. Nonviolence in education does not just mean a quiet classroom. It suggests a learning environment in which students are acting on problems constructively, managing their conflicts creatively, and taking on challenging tasks.

Conclusion

Peace education is truly a "process in motion." New developments are emerging continually. These topics covered are not meant to be inclusive of the whole of what is taught in peace education, nor are they necessarily totally distinct, one from the other. Optimal peace education is holistic and will include, as much as any didactic sum of knowledge, *attitudes and values* as well. Tony Wagner writes:

> If we listen carefully to students and explore their questions and concerns without trying to impose a particular point of view, students respond with a great deal of openness and depth of feeling. They no longer feel alone and powerless in a solitary world of unshared fears. They are glad for the chance to talk, and they begin to find some basis for hope in the recognition that their concerns about the future are shared by others—adults as well as peers.[69]

Peace education confronts directly the purpose of education. Albert Camus wrote that the nature of human consciousness requires a belief in the future. Peace education is, innately, education for hope.

CHAPTER 7

Foundations for Educating for Peace: Families and Issues in Child and Adult Development

> *If we are to reach real peace in the world, and if we are to carry on a real war against war, we shall have to begin with the children.*
> Mahatma Gandhi

How do children grow up to be peacemakers? What are some factors in their development that help lead them towards working for peace and social change? This chapter examines these issues. It includes the role of the family and discusses pertinent issues in human development, beginning with early childhood and continuing into adulthood. Deeply imbedded in this discussion is the role of morality, the supposition that educating for peace inherently is related to the development of human character. The importance of multi-cultural influences on the development of the child is emphasized. As humans, we find meaning in the multi-faceted opportunities for interacting with the world around us. The extent to which these influences are ethical and caring determine in part the subsequent life choices of children. In this chapter, the contributions of feminist thinkers are included, as the role of women as nurturers contributes to a revision of our traditional notions of education, in its broadest sense.

As humans, our development occurs at different rates and is, for the most part, both orderly and gradual. Some aspects of human development are culturally based. However, each of us has an inherent "biological clock" that dictates, for example, when we reach puberty (though there are factors such as diet that influence this as well).

Some theorists postulate that during critical periods of development it is essential for certain learning to take place in order for an ability to be acquired. Jean Piaget, a Swiss psychologist, constructed complex theories about cognitive, or knowledge-acquiring development, by combining his broad knowledge of biology, philosophy, logic and psychology with observations of his own children.[1] As a result of his observations, he created a theory of cognitive development concentrating on internal processes and actions based upon the manner in which human beings make sense of the world. According to Piaget each person has a set of mental tools, or schemata, which can change either radically or slowly during the time from birth to maturity. As humans adapt to environmental changes, adjustments occur in attitude, values, and knowledge. These changes are determined by maturation, activity, or social experience. Research in the intellectual development of humans indicates that at different stages of growth a person has a characteristic way of viewing the world and explaining it to herself or himself.

Increasingly, psychologists are coming to an understanding of models of human development that are inherently *interactional*. Sheldon Berman, writing in *Children's Social Consciousness and the Development of Social Responsibility*,[2] citing the works of social psychologists such as Bandura, Bronfenbrenner and others, writes:

> Development is fostered by the interaction between a child who is cognitively maturing and actively constructing meaning from his or her experiences and the contextual forces of parents, school, the media and the culture. Development is bidirectional in that the child influences and changes the environment as well.[3]

These interactional models of human development reinforce the notion of the inherent power of children as co-creators of their environment and rest on assumptions of children's ability to influence, not only the course of their own development, but those of the people around them (parents, teachers, community members). Berman writes of social consciousness and social responsibility as "not behaviors that we need to instill in young people but rather they are behaviors that we need to recognize emerging in them."[4] Elise Boulding writes of the task of education being one of "crafting human beings to become who they are."[5] Boulding goes on to note that "the greatest gift our children can give us is the capacity to see the world anew. Parents gain increased awareness if they allow their children to be their teachers."[6]

For peace educators, these views of the partnering that inherently goes on as a child develops are of particular import. Educators have long realized that values such as caring, empathy and compassion come, not from schooling alone, but from the influences of family and community on a child. Indeed, some of these values may be seen to be "set" by the time a child enters the formal school system at around age 5. This is not to say that programs in schools may not influence the course of future development, but rather to say that realistically, peace education will rest on assumptions and values learned early in life in other settings.

The foundations of peace lay in the early years of a person's development. The latest brain research shows that children need consistent nurturing in order to develop prosocial skills. "Capacities for trust, self-esteem, focused learning, and problem-solving skills may be diminished by lack of competent adult attention."[7] Antisocial behavior in children has been shown to come from abusive and neglectful parenting. The development of conscience has been shown to be related to early attachment to a nurturing parent. All children are born with the capacity to become caring, empathetic adults, but this capacity must be developed through appropriate nurturing behavior with adult caretakers. Attachment during the first two years of life is crucial for empathy and healthy social behaviors.

The Family

The influence of the family on a developing child cannot be underestimated. The family is the first educational system of any child. Boulding writes of the family as the "practice ground in making history." Families are "co-creators of society—they form the basis of human interaction."[8] It is in the family where children first learn how humans relate to one another. Boulding notes that most human interactions are themselves peaceful. Assuming that children grow up in "good enough" homes, it is in this setting that they will learn how to negotiate, dialogue, to listen and learn peacemaking skills. Boulding writes of the analogy of children negotiating over toys in the sandbox and how the skills learned here are the same needed for high level treaty talks between nations.[9] It is also true that many families are not "peaceful." Yet even in families where violence might occur, there are still vestiges of the human love necessary to build peaceful societies.

Families provide the child's first education into global citizenship.[10]

Most of this goes on unaware by family members. The types of media with which family members interact, the issues discussed (or not discussed), the newspapers read (or not read), and places visited all influence how a developing child will see the world. Bronfenbrenner believes that the family is an important part of every level of the model of ecology he has developed.[11]

At the same time, families are surrounded by and influenced by all the conditions of violence and war discussed so far in this book. As Peter Somlai and Judith Myers-Walls point out, "globalization is resulting in an increasing number of interactions among highly diverse people at the same time that familiarity and shared values are eroding and traditional linkages among people are being torn down."[12] Some children are taught that there are "undesirable" other young people in their neighborhood with whom they cannot play. They may overhear parents complaining that jobs are hard to come by because "immigrants are taking all the good ones." All such everyday events can have an impact on the attitudes and values of the developing child. The increasing use of civilians as targets for international violence may be seen as one catastrophe of the new kind of war, one in which children are increasingly becoming victims of post-traumatic stress syndrome.

Many parents lack the basic skills necessary to help their children develop healthy attitudes and values, ones in which the wish to serve and care for others and for the world is paramount. It is here that peace educators must invest their energies. Educators For Social Responsibility, a group in Boston promoting the skills and practices of peace and conflict resolution, offers a suggestion to families interested in improving family communication:

> One structure which some families have established to facilitate communication among its members is the family meeting. It is a time set aside regularly each week, or called when necessary, when family members come together to discuss plans, problems and misunderstandings. It is a place for airing differences, for hearing things out. It is also a place to express appreciation and acknowledge jobs done well.[13]

Even for parents who can find the time to construct a cooperative system at home, it becomes difficult to maintain this structure within the social context of life in the early Twenty-First century. Parents who want to raise peaceful children can provide peaceful models by never using personal violence, e.g., spanking, but rather by taking the time to explain the natural consequences of certain actions. Spanking teaches children to use physical violence to resolve disagreements. Some children raised in violent homes suffer from low self-esteem and can develop feelings of paranoia that come from feeling that the adults of the world are "out to get them." Seeing the world as a dangerous place can encourage them to seek peace through strength policies to vanquish perceived and imagined enemies. Furthermore, children raised in severely dysfunctional homes can grow up with large reserves of anger that can form the basis of violent behavior. Because conflict is an inevitable part of life, children need to learn in their families how to take other people's feelings into account in order to deal constructively with conflict.

"Violence is nurtured by excessive competition. Nonviolence, on the other hand, springs from cooperation."[14] By sharing family chores, involving children in adult activities, playing group games and reading to each other, parents can teach important skills about peaceful living, while allowing family members to experience each other as individuals in relation to the family. Parents can show their children that being concerned about others is a natural extension of concern about themselves. Parents and concerned adults hoping to promote a more peaceful world impart to children around them the social considerations of courtesy, generosity, and fairness even to people with whom they disagree. Parents can teach children that they can change their minds without loss of respect or love. Disallowing the viewing of violent images on TV and in home entertainment and on the Internet is important in helping build healthy attitudes.

Children who grow up to become active in nonviolent social change come from homes where there is an emotional closeness. They have successful experiences with problem solving, the ability to cope with stress, feelings of optimism about society, confidence in themselves, and feelings of responsibility for the well-being of others. Warm home relationships, with intellectual stimulation and a knowledge of current events, provide experiences that enable children to face the world with confidence.

The Contributions of Feminist Educators

Feminist educators have emphasized the destructive aspects of competition in western cultures.[15] Peace researchers and educators such as Sara Ruddick, Elise Boulding, Betty Reardon and Birgit Brock-Utne have pointed out the psychological damage caused by male domination in patriarchal societies, creating animosity that reverberates through the social order in many destructive ways.[16] Some have called for a renewal of experiences in classrooms that create caring and nurturing environments. Peace educators have decried the emphasis in peace studies on the narrow view of security as freedom from war, to the exclusion of other "security needs" such as those involved in addressing the basic human condition. Peace means equity and partnership between men and women, according to feminists.[17]

Criticizing the lack of an emphasis upon building caring relationships in modern schooling, feminists have been promoting educational reforms based upon the 3 C's of care, concern, and connection. Jane Roland Martin[18] has argued that a person cannot be considered to be properly educated unless that person's capacity for care has been developed. Nonviolence as a way of acting in the world tries to promote a spirit of caring for other human beings that is the basis for morality. In *Schoolhome*[19] Martin argues that schools should teach domestic skills in order that people learn how better to relate to each other. She models her "Schoolhome" upon Maria Montessori's *casi di bambini*:

> Montessori construed the problem of abolishing war as one of designing the right education for children. She specifically saw it as one of constructing suitable environments for them. When and only when there was a "harmonious interaction" between individual and environment, she said, would the child develop normally and love flourish. The kind of love Montessori had in mind was neither the romantic love of poetry and novels nor the self-sacrificing kind that Western culture attributes to mothers. Permanent and unconnected to either selfishness or a desire to possess, it was directed to all living creatures, to people, and to objects. This "higher form of love" was in her view a prerequisite for the "human harmony" and the "genuine community of mankind" that [we] had to obtain if positive peace was to be achieved.[20]

In order to promote this climate of positive peace, school personnel can teach an ethic of care based on the model used in families.

Nel Noddings has promoted the idea of caring and has criticized traditional educational practices for being solely concerned with rational analysis, critical thinking and self-sufficiency:

> I have argued that education should be organized around themes of care rather than traditional disciplines. All students should be engaged in a general education that guides them in caring for self, intimate others, global others, plants, animals, and the environment, the human-made world, and ideas. Moral life so defined should be frankly embraced as the

main goal of education. Such an aim does not work against intellectual development or academic achievement. On the contrary, it supplies a firm foundation for both.[21]

Feminists challenge educators to take seriously the promise of positive peace by teaching around these themes of care. In traditional classrooms the articulation of feelings and emotions is not encouraged. In nonviolent classrooms care and connection are promoted. Building around a feminist model can help to promote a high level of moral concern and engage young people in concerns for the well-being of plants and animals, including humans. Such a concern will help counteract the callous disregard for life that is at the basis of so much conflict in our postmodern world.

Feminist thinking has also had an influence on how the concepts around caring and compassion are increasingly seen to be important in the development of human character. Sara Ruddick writes of mothers as responsible for the "preservation, growth social acceptability and nurture of children's developing spirit." Ruddick goes on to note the importance in how mothers interpret for their children, especially their female young, what social acceptability means. Whether or not a young person will be able to take a stand in the future, for example against war, depends in part on the messages received at home.[22] (Ruddick does not distinguish between male or females in a role of mother.) The act of mothering itself contains within it the seeds of nonviolence: caring in the midst of a developing child's temper outbursts, for example. A good-enough mother will not retaliate. Mothering, according to Ruddick, is governed by unspoken rules of nonviolence.[23]

Nell Noddings writes that "women's' traditional experience is closely related to the moral approach described in an ethic of care."[24] Women's experiences are grounded in the everyday work of feeding, clothing and caring for young. These experiences, though closely correlated with the marginality of women in some parts of the world, also give women the perspective of basing their life views on the very concrete experiences of intense interactions with those around them. Thus it is increasingly being seen among educators that the skills learned in the home and family are skills inherent to peacemaking. Peace educators can recognize the importance of building on partnerships between the "informal" educational settings of home, family and community and the more formal school settings. The home as well as the school can provide nurturing environments so that children are self-confident and able to take risks to learn important problem-solving skills.

Other Factors Influencing the Development of Social Consciousness

Other factors are also at work to influence whether or not a young person (or an adult) will grow up to be invested in working for the common good and for social change. Building on the recognition of the foundation of a loving home, community psychologists and educators are increasingly recognizing the importance of other role models on a child, these "mentors" seen as part of a community of which the child feels a part. As Elise Boulding writes:

> Probably in the childhood of every activist peacemaker there were one or many experiences of being trusted and attended to by an adult. Such experiences build up a reservoir or competence and inner security that makes it possible to take risks on behalf of what one believes.[25]

It is important that children learn hospitality at a young age, that they be subject to meeting all kinds of different people, gaining a "window to the wider world."[26] Most important to development is a sense of *efficacy*, a "can-do" kind of mentality that rests, not just upon a "me first" attitude but on a healthy sense of self and ego that is also "other-based." One important pattern seen in healthy development is *constructive engagement*, the building of "bridges" with those who are seen as different from oneself. Another important aspect is to nurture time to reflect, time for solitude, for a "Sabbath."[27] In our fast-paced global society, it is important for peace educators to take note of the important need for pause and for spiritual renewal. This is true not only for young people, but for adults as well.

Morals

There is an inherent relationship between the development of social consciousness and responsibility and moral development. Psychologist Lawrence Kohlberg has defined three levels of moral development from childhood to adulthood based empirically on a study of eighty-four boys whose development he followed for a period of over 20 years. Kohlberg's stages of moral judgment trace a progression from an egocentric understanding of fairness based on individual need to a conception of fairness anchored in the shared conventions of societal agreement, and finally to

Stage	Approximate Age	Characteristics
Preconventional	until age 5 or 6	Judgments based on own needs and perceptions and on the physical power of the rule makers
Conventional	until adolescence	Judgment based on social expectations and the belief that one must be loyal to one's family, group, or nation, and maintain the social order
Postconventional	young adulthood (not all people reach this state)	Judgment based on principles that go beyond specific laws or the authority of the people who make the laws

Kohlberg's Stages of Moral Reasoning

a principled understanding of fairness that rests on the free-standing logic of equality and reciprocity. He terms these three views of morality preconventional, conventional and postconventional to reflect the expansion in moral understanding from an individual to a societal to a universal point of view. A key component in moving from one stage to another is the capacity to take the perspective of another person. In the preconventional stage individuals only evaluate their actions in terms of their effects on themselves alone. Children move towards higher levels of moral reasoning when they come to grips with viewpoints which differ from their own. Cognitive dissonance or the challenge to existing cognitive structures regarding right or wrong is essential to growth in moral maturity.

Contemporary psychologists and ethicists have criticized Kohlberg for his seemingly narrow and rather rigid views on human development and his exclusion of girls in his early studies. (Kohlberg in later works has addressed some of these concerns.) In an effort to address the repeated exclusion of women from critical theory-building studies of psychological research, Carol Gilligan conducted research which explored identity and moral development in females. In her book, *In Different Voice*, she challenged Kohlberg by stating that moral judgments of women differ from those of men. Women grow up seeing the world through relationship, seeing a world that coheres through human connections rather than through a system of rules.[28] Men and women may experience attachment and separation in different ways and each may perceive a danger that the other does not see—men in connection, women in separation. Gilligan hypothesized that this difference stems from infancy. Simply stated, since women are usually the primary caregivers, little girls form their identity through attachment to their mother. Little boys form their identity through a separation from mother. Gilligan also postulated that women base their moral decisions on networks of caring and a sense of being responsible to the world, in contrast to men, who often base their moral behavior on abstract principles or laws.

Human Development Through the Life Span: Some "How-To's" for Peace Educators

CHILDHOOD

The years from two to six seem to harbor the greatest number of new fears, such as being lost, bitten or injured. Children are exposed to frightening images on television, in books and in their own lives. Initial experiences with war movies can terrify children. Their wild imaginations worry about being attacked by ferocious animals, being in the dark, losing their parents, being bombed, being abandoned, or going up to high places.[29] Children are most successful when they find practical ways to deal with their own fears. Parents, teachers and siblings can instill fear in young children by modeling negative reactions to frightening situations, or they can provide positive role models dealing with frightening situations by providing accurate information and encouragement, and helping children think through creative responses.

Because young children are particularly vulnerable to the process of identification, the example of peaceful behavior established by teachers, parents, and other significant role models can play an important role in helping them develop as peaceful people. A child will not only imitate the actions of another person but will acquire the person's characteristics.[30] Four interrelated processes establish and then strengthen identification: children believe that they share particular physical or psychological attributes with the model; they experience vicarious emotions similar to those the model is feeling; they want to be like the model; and they behave like the model and adopt the model's opinions and mannerisms. Behaviors indicative of this period include hero-worship.[31]

Teachers and parents can use well-chosen songs, fables, films, and the like to expose a child to peacemakers, real or imagined, in an effort to counterbalance the macho hero-images of TV and history books. Strong men using weapons to kill other people often become the worshipped role models of youth exposed to western culture. Thoughtful consideration of the messages implied in children's books can counterbalance "a hidden curriculum" of competition, aggression, or violence which children get from television, movies, peers, schools, and other influences.

Early childhood educators should be aware of the importance of keeping instructions relatively short. They should also use actions as well as words whenever possible to insure that students do not get confused. Props and visual aids will help children understand lessons. The manipulation of concrete materials helps children express ideas and seek solutions for their concerns. Teachers in child care centers and kindergartens should not expect pupils at this age to see the world from another person's viewpoint and therefore should avoid social studies lessons about worlds far removed. Teachers can offer children choices about what to do in the early childhood classroom. At first, this may be difficult for young children who tend to think of one thing at a time and cannot think ahead about the implications of a choice, but starting with simple choices between two or three options will help children learn to predict the consequences of their actions.

When considering peace studies appropriate to this age group, educators, psychologists and psychiatrists stress the importance of finding out what children already know and making sure they have correct information.[32] Children four to six years of age may be frightened about what they hear on the news or read in comic books or watch on cartoons, while not really comprehending it fully. These young people need to be reassured that adults care about the future and are involved in making the world safe. They should not be misinformed, but at this age they cannot understand the magnitude of such things as the nuclear dilemma or terrorist events. Teachers working with pupils at this age should not emphasize the horrible consequences of war or of terrorism. Children need reassurance from adults and can't cope with visions of a doom-filled world out of control.

The vulnerability of children to social modeling suggests that the most appropriate method to integrate peace education in the elementary school is to create a cooperative, affirmative environment in which children can appreciate who they are and what they are capable of doing. Teachers who display consistent treatment of all children and accept divergent thoughts or styles of life plant seeds of peaceful, cooperative living, the ability to love oneself, and the capacity to accept other people despite their differences. Children in their early school years need to accept diversity by learning about different cultures and figuring out their own backgrounds. They should discuss stereotyping and name-calling. Why are people different? Meeting children from different countries can teach them that people throughout the world have needs similar to theirs, and that it's all right to be different.

An awareness and appreciation of the diversity of individual and collective values the world over can lead to nonviolent resolution of conflict. Children can develop empathy with others by becoming aware of similarities and differences of other people. If they realize that cultures are neither superior nor inferior to one another, they may be inclined to view discussion and dialogue as better means of resolving conflict than the use of force or withdrawal. Developing an understanding of the interdependence of people the world over will help promote the value of cooperation as a means of human welfare. Children need to acquire a value for sharing with others the common resources shared by humans on the planet earth. Knowledge of the manner in which people depend on each other for their basic needs may foster a more humanistic approach to the division of wealth. To have a fair chance for peace, humankind must move towards the development of a sense of community and cooperation on a global basis.

Children entering the concrete operational level of thinking may still have difficulty seeing another person's point of view, but diminishing egocentrism enhances their ability to make moral judgments that take into account the interests of others. At about the age of six, children start to consider more than one aspect of a situation when drawing conclusions. The middle childhood years are characterized by a unilateral respect for authority, which leads, on the part of some children, to feelings of obligation to conform to adult standards and to obey the rules. By the time a child reaches the age of eight or nine, according to Kohlberg, he or she will begin to leave a rather rigid view of morality and enter into a one more inclined toward mutual cooperation. A respect both for authority and for peers allows the child to value his or her own opinions and abilities and to judge people more realistically. Children's view of punishment, both for themselves and for others, also changes. Where once she or he would favor severe, expiatory punishment, the young person will instead prefer milder, reciprocal punishment that leads to restitution of the victim and helps the culprit recognize why an act was wrong. Perceptions of rules also change during this time from a belief that rules must be obeyed because they are sacred or unilateral to the recognition that rules were made by people and can be changed. A belief in their inherent ability to change rules is important for children who may grow up to question authority in ways that promote social change.[33]

Children in their middle childhood years can benefit from values clarification exercises that help analyze the grounding for their beliefs and actions. Certain pedagogical exercises will help them examine values: (1) Seeking alternatives when faced with a choice; (2) looking ahead to probable consequences before choosing; (3) making choices on one's own, without depending on others; (4) being aware of one's own preferences and valuations; (5) being willing to affirm one's choices and preferences publicly; (6) acting in ways that are consistent with choices and preferences; and (7) acting those ways repeatedly, with a pattern to one's life.[34] These skills help children understand the differences between the values people hold and the values they actually live by. Exercises which foster values clarification can be instrumental in helping children aged eight to ten to express their changing attitudes and establish their beliefs about peace and justice issues.

By the age of eleven most children have acquired conceptual tools which enable them to organize their environment meaningfully and to make a distinction between their own culture and that of others. "Children from nine to twelve are often extremely interested in facts. They are collectors of facts, always eager to add to their store."[35] This is the ideal time in life to introduce students to the interdependence of the global community. Research studies done on this age of childhood indicate that children of about ten years of age are receptive to foreign cultures and people but that this open-mindedness declines after this time, so that by fourteen years of age there is a tendency to stereotype people from different cultures.[36] It is therefore helpful for middle school educators to continue to promote cross-cultural experiences and dialoging. Middle school students are sensitive to peer pressure and begin to look more critically at adults. Teachers can build a more sophisticated understanding of the world by bringing in speakers to present different points of view. Adults working with children at this age may think about how to help make them aware of the problems that the world faces. Social psychologist Judith Torney writes:

> Young children need help in understanding the complexity of the world order so that they may have a basis for reacting intelligently to its problems as they grow older.[37]

As students enter their teenage years they don't want to be told what to think, but want to make up their own minds. At this point they also are developing a capacity for a long-term future orientation and a wider world view. This is the beginning of the age of idealism, as young people's capacities for abstract thinking increase, an ideal time to discuss international institutions, world order, cultural differences, civil and human rights. Teachers can stress the contributions of people like Dr. Martin Luther King, Jr., who dedicated his life to peace and justice.

Adolescence

Puberty marks the onset of adolescence. Erik Erikson identified adolescence as a crisis of "identity versus role confusion."[38] The actions of adolescents are sometimes impulsive and not well thought-through. The young person may resort to regression into childishness to avoid resolving conflicts. During this period some adolescents may form cliques or foster an aversion to divergent lifestyles. This may manifest itself as a defense against identity confusion. Adolescents of color and those from poor economic backgrounds often have to deal with issues relating to middle class school cultures, in which obedience to authority is often equated with identification with the mainstream, white and oppressive society.[39]

Development during this time is uneven. The rate of physical growth doubles for about two years as sexual maturation begins. Teenagers are concerned with how they appear to others, as well as being concerned about their identity, as they search for continuity. In spite of all the difficulties during this period in life, Otto and Healy have listed some personality resources and strengths of adolescence, particularly relevant to education for peace. These include (1) considerable energy or drive and vitality; (2) a real concern for the future of this country and the world (idealism); (3) exercising their ability to question contemporary values, philosophies, ideologies and institutions; (4) heightened sensory awareness and perceptibility; (5) courageous; and (6) feelings of independence.[40]

Peace educators can take advantage of these developing concerns about social issues manifesting themselves during adolescence. According to Robert Jay Lifton, author of *The Broken Connection,* by the time that a child today reaches thirteen, his or her appetite for understanding and intuitive grasps of fundamental ethical and moral dilemmas may be at its height. Their realization of the importance in the creation of the future can facilitate an appreciation for educational issues relating to peace. "Many people believe that adolescents' normal growth depends on a social structure which grants young people a place in society."[41]

Teenagers struggle to establish their own identity. Peace educators may suggest that they keep a journal that allows young people to express some of their darkest fears. People at this age are developing complex peer relations and need acceptance. Teachers should set a tone of tolerance for different points of view. Many high school pupils, who may already have well established notions about the world, need information to form enlightened opinions about peace and justice issues and the complicated nature of international relations. As they enter adulthood, teenagers need both a sense of autonomy and of their own authority. This can be provided by letting students plan activities and units. Students can be asked to define their concepts of strength or power. Teachers should assure students that they don't know all the answers, but rather are discussing issues in order to develop a broader understanding of them. This is a period of self-introspection and analysis. Teenagers should be encouraged to think about the way the world is and the way they would like it to be. Adolescents' desires to make the world better will attract some of them to peace education. Peace studies can allow young adults to acquire commitments to adopt careers oriented towards creating a better world.

In school settings peace educators may create an atmosphere of empathy where students are encouraged to place themselves in other people's positions and see themselves through other people's eyes. Students can study the lives of Nobel Peace Prize winners and other nonviolent heroes to develop, through identification, a sense of their own capacity to create a less violent future. In order to do this, parents and teachers of children at all levels have to set up learning environments where responsibility and independence are stimulated, where there is room for experiments with behavior and where cooperation is emphasized rather than competition. Adults in these environments can set an example by their own peaceful behavior.

At the beginning of the new millennium there are approximately two hundred peace studies programs on college and university campuses around the world.[42] Such courses and programs address the effects of political and social violence, the causes of this violence, and what can be done to resolve conflicts peacefully. The rapid growth of these programs in colleges and universities in North America and in Western Europe may be seen as a reflection on the growing alarm about levels of violence (the nuclear threat, terrorism, low intensity conflict, the cost of the arms race, environmental destruction, domestic violence, ethnic violence, etc.). Those concerned about violence are turning to education as a means to heighten awareness about the problems of violence and to stimulate research into alternative methods of dispute resolution, including the promotion of nonviolent alternatives.[43]

Students can now major in peace studies at a variety of universities and colleges, although many choose to take only a course or two. Some programs offer a certificate in peace studies. A peace studies course allows students to study violence, to understand the conditions for positive peace and to learn about efforts to resolve conflicts peacefully. Multidisciplinary peace studies courses capture the dynamic ways that the problems of violence erupt in human communities.

Adulthood

Adulthood is a time of growth, change, and continued development underscored by the realization of one's own mortality. Life experiences form patterns of behavior which affect readiness to learn. Each adult goes through a series of developmental tasks which may include selecting a mate, finding life work, starting a family, managing a home, finding a congenial social group and taking civic responsibility.[44]

Life crises may be caused by periods of disequilibria which signify the onset of a "turning point." A decision must be made to either regress or progress into the next passage of life. The first turning point of adulthood may occur during the stage of the early twenties when individuals move out on their own from their families of origin.

Once an adult has made a commitment to explore a certain facet of existence—college then graduate school or career, employment in hopes of substantial earnings, marriage in hopes of a family—she or he will probably spend the next ten years or so testing out these new options. These are the years in which an individual "finds" him or herself. Women (and increasingly men) come to terms with decisions around childrearing and employment. Some will enter public life, support political candidates of their choice, or may even run for office themselves. Some will find community and world service as their life path, at least temporarily.

The "thirties" may be characterized as a time for developing competence. For example, classroom teachers may now feel secure enough in their daily routines that they are willing to take some risks by branching out from a prescribed curriculum to include peace and justice concepts in their lessons. Teachers who have earned a degree of respect within their schools can start exerting leadership to promote within a school setting awareness of peace issues.

As individuals reach the pinnacle of their middle age, some adults with increasing free time, removed from the demands of early career and small children, may become concerned about the world and threats to the planet. According to Erikson, "generativity" is the central stage of adult development, encompassing "man's relationship to his production as well as to his progeny."[45] Defining generativity as "the concern in establishing and guiding the next generation," Erikson centers adulthood on relationships and devotion to the activity of taking care of others and making sure there will be a secure future.[46] Daniel Levinson sees the ultimate tasks of adulthood as defining a life that brings self-fulfillment and sense of meaning.[47] At this point some individuals make drastic life shifts to work on peace and justice issues. Some may decide that "the rat race" is not worth all the strain and drop out to join a peace group dedicating their lives to bettering humanity.

Adults need information about a constantly changing world. Community education classes held in schools, in churches, and in neighborhood centers can help provide alternative information not provided by mainstream media. Adults need to communicate with others in order to clarify their understanding of public events and of the world at large. The skills of active listening and one-on-one communication can help bridge resistance to new learning. An educator's expertise lies in his or her ability to create an environment in which the *other* will be encouraged to discover and try new skills. One important goal in working with adults in peace education is to encourage them to solve problems themselves and to understand that they can become effective change agents. Peace educators working in adult communities need to develop tangible goals for making the world more peaceful and introduce adult learners to organizations working on peace issues. Since peer acceptance and involvement is an important part of the change process, even among adults, those concerned about war and peace issues need to be introduced to others who share their concerns. Together they may discuss what kind of world they want to live in and to leave to their children.

There are basically four steps to peace studies in adult education: (1) examine the formation of attitudes towards peace, conflict, and justice; (2) envision a peaceful and just world, because society cannot move in a direction until there is a goal; (3) define peace as a process involving all people at the personal, familial, interpersonal, societal and global level; and (4) discuss how we can be peacemakers at home, at work and in the community. Peace educators teaching adults can help citizens relearn patterns of behavior that contribute to violence. Adults need to tell their own stories about their own individual "journeys for justice. "A basis of trust allows people to discuss experiments with nonviolence.

For many adults, retirement means they can concentrate on goals of their own choosing, rather than those imposed upon them by the demands of work and family.[48] This is a period of life when human beings can pursue their lifelong passions. Some may be inclined to do volunteer work. Older people have knowledge and skills to share with others. Retired people have the extra time, and through the concern they show for future generations, can demonstrate their competence by becoming actively involved in peace education endeavors. Many people facing retirement have up to thirty years ahead of them, during which they might work to make the world safe for future generations. In their desire to leave a better world to their progeny, grandmothers and grandfathers can become an important force for peace. Their wisdom about the ways of violence and the struggle for peace can provide important leadership for efforts to make the world less violent.

Conclusion

Peace studies can be introduced by peace educators at the primary level of schooling and can continue in an appropriate fashion throughout the course of an individual's life. At the elementary level young children learn how to respect diversity, resolve conflicts, and acquire an awareness of different cultures. At the middle school level students can study different countries and cultures to gain some understanding of the complexity of the global community. Simulation games can provide an appreciation of the nature of world crisis, and students at this age can start learning the history of the arms race. At the high school level, the nature of human aggression, the causes of war, the challenges of ecological sustainabitlity, and global interrelatedness should constitute peace curricula. Secondary peace education studies should also deal with tensions and controversial issues such as impediments to arms control and reduction of small arms killings and the causes of international terrorism, so that high school graduates will be knowledgeable about contemporary threats. University-level peace studies requires an interdisciplinary structure where students take courses in departments as varied as international relations, political science, communications, philosophy, psychology, sociology, anthropology, history, education, literature, and environmental studies. Adults can explore their own violent behavior and learn new ways to influence decision makers. Perhaps the most important place to address violent behavior is the home, where individuals first learn values and communication skills. The years when children form their ideals of the world and their relationships to other people present an ideal time to begin a humanistic socialization process to promote a consciousness of individual existence in relation to others.

Peace education rests on the assumption that the way to change social systems riddled by violence and committed to war is to change oneself. Until people change one by one they are not going to change by the thousands. Not even the President of the most powerful nation in the world can order profound changes in individual beliefs and behaviors. In considering how to construct peace education programs in families, schools, and adult learning communities, it is crucial to understand the process of individual change so that peace educators can assess the readiness of their pupils to confront the sometimes scary topics that must be addressed in peace education classes. Individuals don't necessarily change in orderly, precise, rational, or direct manners. Often it takes a severe crisis to jolt an adult out of one belief system into another. Understanding the dignity and worth of humankind and feeling good about oneself can facilitate individuals striving for peace on the personal and societal level.

CHAPTER 8

Sensitive Issues in Peace Education

Peace Education, in any realm, involves so much more than imparting facts and information.
Kimberley Huselid Glass

    This chapter discusses some sensitive issues, the nature of which it is helpful for peace educators to be aware. Teaching about the problems of war and human violence raises deep emotions in both teachers and students. Peace education, by confronting commonly held assumptions about the nature of reality, can unsettle students or may at times be frustrating for teachers living in a culture often espousing the values of violence and war. Peace education is often seen as controversial. (Some discussion of the historical nature of this, particularly in the United States, is contained in Chapter 2.) People want to know if peace education works. Is it an effective way to create peace?
    In addition to the need to design age-appropriate curricula (discussed in the previous chapter), peace educators need to be sensitive to the following educational issues: (1) propaganda versus information, (2) the controversial nature of language, (3) the effects of violence in entertainment and the media (4) the long-term nature of peace education, (6) peace education evaluation (5) dealing with emotions, and (7) understanding differing attitudes and values. Each of these topics will be discussed in this chapter. Without an awareness of these issues, peace educators bear the risk of being poorly prepared to deal with the highly controversial and challenging nature of educating for peace. Further discussion on why

peace education is seen as controversial occurs in Chapter 9, "Overcoming Obstacles." Not all of the material covered in this chapter is relevant for every age group. This is particularly true of the last two entries: emotions and attitudes and values, the material of which is most suited to adolescents and adults.

Propaganda vs. Information

Peace educators have at times been accused of indoctrinating their students. An editorial opinion column in *The New York Times* about a student minoring in peace studies at New York University stated:

> The driving interest of "peace" scholars ... is in student activism. Mobilizing student support for the scholars' peace agenda is the unstated but seeming goal in this and other such programs.[1]

Peace educators are sometimes verbally attacked because they challenge mainstream views of security and national defense. Opponents claim that rather than participating in "objective" presentations about the problems of violence that confront humanity, peace educators engage in rhetoric, present only one side, and try to convince students of the correctness of that position. Peace studies has been attacked as being value-laden. Baroness Cox, a sociologist, and Dr. Roger Scruton, a reader in philosophy at Birbeck College, London, note:

> Peace studies should not be taught in schools and universities because it lacks the intellectual rigor to qualify as a serious academic discipline, encourages prejudice and conceals a concerted attempt to manipulate the political thinking of young people.[2]

In contrast to what the above authors state, peace studies itself is seldom a separate discipline, but rather it is interdisciplinary, based in traditional subject matter—political science, history, communications, philosophy, sociology, and other social services. Because peace studies programs typically consist of courses from these academic disciplines, it is not a separate field and is no more subject to lack of intellectual rigor than is its components.

In some peace education classes teachers present a perspective that opposes more traditional points of view that support peace through strength. For example, peace educators might challenge a foreign policy based upon exploitation of the resources of other countries. This might be seen as controversial. Following the events of September 11, 2001, peace activism was decried in the media as being anti-patriotic. The fear around the events seemed to foster polarization. Peace activists, who wished to see an end to *all* violence, including the bombing of innocent civilians in the Afghanistan, who decried the terrorist attacks, were seen as alternately weak and pacifistic, or as enemies of patriotism. Peace education at its best fosters the "inner teacher" within each student. By presenting different points of view about how to respond to violence, educators are hopefully not prejudicing their students, but rather are increasing their ability to understand complex phenomenon. Peter Dale Scott writes: "our task as educators is to open minds, not to close them: We wish our students to acquire not only a viewpoint, but a self-critical perspective on that viewpoint."[3]

Peace education can contribute enormously to students' rational thinking, particularly for older students and adults, by encouraging them to think critically about existing national security policies and to evaluate those policies. The argument that peace studies is somehow value-laden while traditional studies of history and other academic disciplines are not may be seen in part as a polemical argument constructed to discredit a point of view that threatens those with power. Education is neither neutral nor objective in the sense that excludes the teaching of values. Thomas Groome writes:

> By what we teach or fail to teach, and by how we teach it, education has far reaching consequences. Education is never politically neutral. By the very nature of the activity education cannot be a private or 'objective' enterprise that is 'value free.' It is a public and social activity that is always value laden. Education can pretend to be nonpolitical by attempting to take an 'objective' stance toward the present social realities within which it takes place. But then it has the inevitable consequence of fitting people into those social realities as they presently exist.[4]

Education acculturates people to the prevalent beliefs in a society in a way that passes on the traditions and values of that society. An exploration of values seen as non-traditional may be seen as controversial. Peace education curricula are inherently imbued with certain values, e.g. those associated with nonviolence and social justice. These curricula are not, however, uniquely value-laden while other subjects are value-free, and as such should not prejudice students any more than any other subject would.

The claim laid against peace education that it is value-laden, and

8. Sensitive Issues in Peace Education

hence not "objective," is spurious. For example, in 1920 Werner Heisenberg, a physicist, established the uncertainty principle,[5] stating that objectivity cannot be provided in scientific investigations because as soon as an experiment is set up, matter is meddled with, and hence alters its configuration. Extrapolating this, the argument can be made that scientists (and educators) neither present knowledge nor knowledge claims that are truly objective. They may, however, indeed they should, provide many different points of view about a subject. Peace educators themselves may reflect different points of view in relation to the best way to achieve peace. As educators, their role is to present as many different points of view as possible so that students receive as comprehensive an understanding as is possible of the complex role of violence in human society and the path toward peace.

As Heisenberg demonstrated, *all* claims have a value perspective. All courses contain hidden within them the value perspectives of their instructors. The way material is presented, the knowledge that is considered relevant, the textbooks used and the conclusions that are drawn present one value perspective or another. A course or discipline may be balanced or fair when it provides many different points of view, not just one. Scott writes:

> Peace studies has no quarrel with the ideal of 'objectivity.' A sense of striving to overcome the limitations of and to present opposing arguments as fairly as possible [ensures] objectivity is indeed part of our agenda. But we cannot avoid opposition to those ideologists who, by claiming their own social [views] 'scientific,' seek to impose their own ideology of neutrality as a requirement on the rest of the university.[6]

One way of viewing the criticism that peace education indoctrinates students is to see it as an attempt to discredit peace studies because it does not reinforce the existing set of militaristic values that govern most societies. These values condone peace through strength as a means to entrench existing power structures and powerful economic interests. Peace educators set up an open climate in classes where students have the freedom to express their own ideas and hopefully draw their own conclusion about how best to respond to violence in the world. Peace educators should neither prescribe "correct" viewpoints in relation to conflict and war nor tell their students what to do about these problems. They can lay out various options for students, without prescribing how students should respond to these problems. Freedom to disagree is the hallmark of a democratic system. Robin Burns and Robert Aspeslagh write:

> It should be stated that however much our educational aim is to encourage a positive expression of opinion towards equality, justice, disarmament—in other words peace—this does not mean that we deny students the possibility of arriving at other opinions. The freedom to come to one's own decision must always be possible for students.[7]

Helping students analyze the problems of war and peace will increase their analytical skills and help clarify their own values. In this way peace education helps students to develop their own opinions and beliefs.

Language

The use of language can present many thorny problems for peace educators. Language helps to structure reality by delimiting the world with symbols, words, and concepts. Human beings use language to communicate their understanding of what they see, hear, and perceive about the world. As Benjamin Whorf points out, language is both a shaper of ideas and a programmer for mental activity.[8] Through the symbols, words and concepts used in teaching, educators communicate certain norms and expectations about the world.

Peace educators need to be careful about the use of language. Does the use of certain terminology contribute to unhealthy ways of resolving disputes, or does their language challenge the culture of violence by pointing to new and peaceful ways of communicating, thinking, and learning in the classroom? There is an inherent connection between language and values. Jaime C. Diaz writes:

> In a global setting the school, which is asserted to be neutral in society, occupies a privileged position as a communicator of values transmitted to adapt students to the system in force, and as such it tends to be a shaper of conscience.[9]

Many so-called "normal" patterns of language used throughout cultures, and especially in schools, may be seen to condone and support violence. Expressions such as "I will kill you if you lose my book," or "stick to your guns" casually reinforce violent human behavior. Peace educators should, therefore, help unravel the linguistic means by which a culture of violence has been created in modern states. This is by no means an easy task.

Harold Lasswell[10] warned that advanced industrial societies are heading towards becoming "garrison states," whose political leaders are increasingly dominated by specialists in violence. A garrison state depends upon symbols and images to create the metaphor of a frightful world. In the garrison state a frightened citizenry does not question expenditures on military means to eliminate threats from supposed enemies.

Modern political leaders use language and symbols to create a system of political belief that is beyond challenge. Leaders depict their actions as fair and just, while using the mass media to paint pictures of threats that describe the world in such a way that huge outlays for military might and for police forces are seen as necessary to preserve law and order. Dale Spender writes, "men who approve of violence and the military have constructed a violent language and world which provides a language trap which supports their world view."[11]

Thomas Merton described this use of language as the "logic of power"[12] where those with authority are convinced that whatever they say makes sense. For example, in 1947 the name of the United States War Department was changed to the Defense Department to convey the notion of passivity and minimize the national and global perception of aggressive acts carried out by the United States military. Glen D. Hook[13] and others have written extensively about how linguistic metaphors and convoluted statements have been constructed and promoted to advance nuclear weaponry. In the nineteen fifties support for the use of atomic power was promoted through a program adeptly named "Atoms for Peace," whose aim was to convince the American public about the benefits of nuclear power, while avoiding mention of the destructive power of nuclear weapons. With adroit use of language public opinion may be deliberately manipulated to facilitate the acceptance of the use of nuclear weapons. Language used to promote violence is not limited to linguistic symbols.

Linguist Noam Chomsky has written extensively on the role of language as a cultural phenomenon, and of linguistic "laws" whose purpose is to underlie and subvert political discourse.[14] Chomsky's view is that the national media is usually subservient to the dominant political ideology and subsequently both influences and is influenced by future events. What gets into and stays out of the press has deep cultural and political implications. French intellectuals have discussed the notion of *total language*, which includes the mass media, the newspapers, printed materials, symbols and images that appear in the culture:

> In the root of total language is the notion of the totality of human expression as language (conscious or not) and therefore as communication. Today, total language is gaining importance and

acquiring new dimensions with the advent of the electronic age and the attendant multiple messages of different types which are addressed increasingly to our impulses as opposed to our reason.[15]

In general the makers and supporters of weapons of mass destruction have promoted terminology that tries to underplay the horror of modern technological approaches to war in order to make the use of these weapons seem more palatable. Thus, policy makers discuss a "surgical" strike that would wipe out an enemy, only killing thousands of people, as if that many deaths of innocent civilians were acceptable. The strike, by being "surgical," uses a medical metaphor to connote something good, the elimination of a disease or a cancer (the enemy).

The mass media plays an important role in promoting violence by its persistent reporting of its manifestations, to the point of numbness, as well as its often biased reporting of national events. The political influences surrounding the media can prevent reporting of certain events, for fear of loss of advertising revenue. One such example occurred in East Timor in the 1970s, when the Indonesian state massacred over one million East Timorans. Because the Indonesians were seen as a client state and friendly to United States' interests, little attention was given to these atrocities.[16]

The values, and concomitant language, attached to the "good guys" are predominantly masculine values—strength, confidence, commitment, and aggression. The importance of a "macho" perspective on foreign policy has been well documented.[17] In policy debates about national security, values such as caring, nurturing, understanding, flexibility and compassion are seen as not relevant. Labels such as "sensitive" or "tender" make national leaders seem weak and unqualified "to make tough decisions." Once the War on Terrorism began in late 2001 in the United States, overt criticism of President Bush was nonexistent.

The male war system emphasizes winning at any cost; foreign policy becomes a team sport or gambling game, where the "tough get going and the quitters don't win." Such an emphasis on masculine dominance makes alternative approaches unacceptable in the popular imagination. Spender notes, "The idea of masculine superiority is perennial, institutional and rooted at the deepest level of our historical experience."[18] Men make wars, play popular professional sports, and generally establish the parameters of national foreign relations and defense policy. Under this masculine paradigm, gentleness, including promoting alternatives for conducting affairs of state, seems unrealistic:

> Realism is a big word, particularly when it makes claims to "scientific" evidence. It is used widely to discredit those who find something wrong

with the present international system. The kind of realism we are propagating today may result in widespread famine, growing inequalities, and World War III. If we accept the arms race, poverty, racism, and other charming attributes of the present system, we are being "realistic." There is something weird about a human mind capable of producing the contemptuous assertion that those who denounce these phenomena are idealists, ideologues, or dreamers.[19]

In the world of realpolitik, suggestions for how to achieve peace are seen as utopian or unrealistic.

Peace educators should help students reevaluate the language of human culture that embraces violence and the claims inherent in such concepts as security, power, dominance, and peace, claims which are seen to support existing military structures. Writes Mario Borelli:

Peace education as "conscientization," then, is not a factory of dreams, but a school of realism. It is neither sectarian nor prophetic. Neither an ideology nor a religious offering of miracles.[20]

Peace educators take a realistic look at the world as it is constructed by modern language systems and recognize the different forms of violence that dominate human thought and action. Peace education challenges the assumption that social problems have technological and military solutions by teaching students to examine the language claims made by the dominant society. According to Thomas Belmonte:

As educators, we are powerful custodians of our culture's consciousness, and we have a vital role to play in challenging the hegemony of pernicious and outmoded realities. Merely to recite our species' long record of past mistakes is not, however, enough. We must put ourselves and our students in touch with their individual and social potentials as citizens of the world systems only now being born.[21]

Peace educators can construct a new grammar for developing a nonviolent world and challenge current language patterns that support the culture of violence so prevalent in this world. They need to develop new conceptual and linguistic categories that will name a world based on caring and mutual respect rather than the use of traditional masculine categories of dominance and superiority. As Dale Spender has pointed out, language is both a trap and a source of liberation.[22] Language traps us into existing patterns of thought, but also has the potential to liberate our thinking by providing new directions and new concepts. Language, when used carefully and creatively, can help people challenge commonly held assumptions and point to new ways of structuring reality. Peace educators can contribute to the creation of peaceful futures by examining language usage and dialoguing with students about ways to create a new grammar, vocabulary, and conceptual framework for a less violent world.

The Effects of Media and Entertainment Violence

So much slaughter is exhibited daily on television, even in the news, through movies and in newspapers, that citizens throughout the world are becoming inured to violence, guns, and militaristic ways of solving problems. The United States has the highest levels of homicide of any of the advanced industrialized democracies in the world. This has dramatically increased since 1962, when the rate was about equal to the international average.[23] There is strong research connecting the viewing of violence on television and higher rates of aggressive and violent behavior.[24] Aggressive children tend to watch more TV than those who are not overly aggressive. This reinforces their behavior both in the short and in the longer term. A longitudinal study by the American Psychological Association showed a relationship between exposure to TV violence at age eight and later anti-social behavior, violent criminal offenses and spousal abuse some twenty years later.[25] Additional studies have also been performed by the American Medical Association, the Surgeon General's Advisory Committee on Television and Behavior and the National Institutes of Mental Health. All these reports indicate that violence on TV influences violent behavior. This, in spite of the fact that studies also show that violence portrayed does not necessarily have to lead to reinforced violence *if* the violence shown is punished, the perpetrators are not glamorized and the aggression is shown in a negative light.[26]

Americans seem addicted to viewing violence. At least 60 percent of television shows contain violent acts.[27] According to Diane Levin and her colleagues at Wheelock College, since 1984, when the Federal Communications Commission deregulated children's television shows, both the quantity and the realism of violence on TV have increased.[28] This has led to program-length commercial advertising for violent toys, as children are enticed to buy realistic toys shown as characters on TV. Examples include: "GI Joes," "Transformers" and "Teenage Mutant Ninja Turtles," dating from the deregulation in the 1980s. Within one year of deregulation, nine of the ten best-selling toys had TV shows, the most successful shows were the most violent. "Transformers" was shown to have 83 violent acts per hour.[29]

It is clear that, compared to even twenty years ago, American society is more saturated with violent images, fears of violence have increased and there has been an increase in desensitization to its effects, at the same time there is a higher appetite for it. The average child leaving elementary school has witnessed about 8,000 murders and at least 100,000 acts of violence in the media.[30] Three main effects of viewing violence, according to the National Television Violence Study are: learning aggressive attitudes and behaviors, desensitization to violence and an increased fear of becoming victimized by it.[31]

The implications for peace educators are enormous, in terms of media and entertainment violence. Efforts to work with parents and educators of young children should be increased. Children's access to television and violent images in the media, movies and the Internet needs to be curtailed. Students can be challenged on their own attitudes toward media violence. Political action, including editorials and letter-writing, can be encouraged. Students can be taught the connection between their own patterns of consumption and the rise of violent images. Discussions can be held as to why violence "sells."

The Long-Term Nature of Peace Education

Achieving peace takes a long time. A focus on the use of language and the development of a peaceful consciousness raises a further issue for peace educators: the long term nature of their strategies for achieving peace. Understanding the roots of violence is not the same thing as eliminating them. Many peace educators feel a sense of urgency, exemplified by the letterhead used by the Bulletin of Atomic Scientists, containing an image of a clock, indicating the time as three minutes to midnight, illustrating that at midnight an atomic conflagration might destroy the world as we know it. Using educational strategies to prevent ecological catastrophes rests on the assumption that citizens will become alarmed and do something to change political and economic systems that promise environmental destruction. This may or not be the case. Merely focusing on fear is not an effective pedagogical method for working for peace.

People who turn to education as a strategy to help develop a consciousness to prevent violence assume that citizens who become alarmed will do something to change political systems that promise war and environmental destruction, and that those actions will make a difference. Peace education has been practiced for over 100 years by enlightened educators.

In spite of their efforts and activities of millions of people who have joined and actively supported peace movements during this time, the world has grown more violent. (One hundred and twenty "small" wars between 1945 and 1976 accounted for 25 million deaths—more than twice the death rate during the First World War.) Many well-meaning individuals trying to stem the flood of militarism often become burned out and cynical about the prospects for peace.

Even if a peace educator effectively motivates students to work for peace and those students follow through on those commitments, such actions may not produce results for many years. Because any such changes in the world will take years to come about, peace education may not appear to be an effective way to stop the immediate threats. William Ekhardt writes:

> Presumably we want peace studies to contribute toward more peace and less war, but peace educators seldom if ever have any control over world events such as war and peace. The most we can do, as a general rule is to influence the minds of students who attend their classes.[32]

Peace educators can at times, therefore, be engaged in a frustrating enterprise. Living in a violent world, they teach about peace because they want to make the world less violent, but the most they can do is change some students' attitudes or dispositions toward violence.

The prospects for peace education are thus not very encouraging. The patterns of violence in the international system, in individual societies, and in the minds of people are so ingrained that one needs to have a kind of neurotic stubbornness to hold fast to the concept of peace. Sigmund Freud once depicted the weakness of reason in the face of madness, unreasonableness, and the superiority of instincts. Yet, as he indicated, there is something special about this weakness:

> The voice of the intellect is low, but it doesn't rest until it is heard. Finally, after countless repeated impulses, it is heard. This is one of the few points where one may be optimistic for the future of mankind. Education for peace can and must trust this low voice of reason.[33]

Peace educators resemble prophets from a Greek drama, crying out against the madness of violence and human slaughter. As such, they may not always be heard. Seeing threats to the world, they predict the possibility of doom, and teach to the future, but may be denounced as being crazy, utopian, or unrealistic. Peace educators disseminate the findings of peace researchers about how to create a more peaceful world. But research itself does not create a better world. Research is a body of ideas that may or may not become part of public policy. Insights gained from peace research may provide information that might develop important strategies to create alternatives to present policies. However, whether those strategies ever become official policy remains a function of political reality.

In order to avoid frustrations about the lack of their direct ability to make the world more peaceful, peace educators must understand the complex nature of their endeavors. In teaching about peace and violence they take one small step toward creating a less violent world, and they should appreciate the importance of that step. A Buddhist saying is that a journey of a thousand miles starts with the first step. Peace educators may not be changing the social structures that support violence, but they are attempting to build a peace consciousness that is a necessary condition for creating a more peaceful world.

A particular student, for example, stimulated by a peace course, who talks to his or her friends or family, might provoke others to think more carefully about the commitment to militarism that governs political affairs. Often students who take peace education classes become peace educators themselves by organizing forums on war and peace issues. When these forums stimulate others to think through the problems of violence, they create a ripple effect, where people who learn new knowledge and insights share them with others, who share them with others, and the message grows. If that initial educator had not had the courage to denounce the violent state of the world, none of those people subsequently affected by that message may have ever been challenged to think about alternatives to violence.

Peace educators make important contributions to peace by building upon the peaceful instincts of students and creating a space for discussion of the problems of violence. These educational activities are not a sufficient condition for achieving peace, but they are necessary. People's traditional patterns and ways of thinking need to be challenged in order to overcome the culture of violence that dominates this world. Graduates of peace education classes may, in turn, use similar methods to teach others about the problems of war and the hope inherent in peace. (One student in a peace education class taught by Ian Harris was a director of a summer camp who attended meetings with other directors of summer camps throughout the state of Wisconsin. He suggested at one of the meetings that he was going to do a week of peace activities at his camp. Consequently, other directors endorsed this idea and throughout Wisconsin during the summer of 1984 campers were turning their camps into nuclear free zones, writing letters to elected representatives, viewing movies about the problems of war and peace, and discussing ways to live sustainably on Planet Earth.)

These changes may occur as a result of classroom instruction, but no one can predict whether they will last over time. For example, a graduate of a peace education class could be drafted and exposed to a military lifestyle, or as often happens, that student's country could go to war, which could produce a shift where the whole population might become more approving of militaristic values. Such a cultural shift in beliefs about war or peace could negatively influence any nonviolent or nonmilitaristic tendencies students may have acquired in peace education classes.

In this Internet age peace education takes on exciting global dimensions as peace educators link up with others in distant parts of the world. Peace education activities can help create the kind of consciousness described by Teillard de Chardin—where the world is becoming more aware of itself as a limited planet, and where individuals need to trust others to build a safe and healthy planet. Without that consciousness, we are all doomed to wars, pestilence, and struggles for scarce resources:

> The challenge of peace calls for transnational perspectives on disarmament, new forms of international cooperation and exchange, the development of the arts of diplomacy, negotiation, and compromise, the fashioning of the economics of disarmament, and the shaping of policy in congruence with the conditions of global interdependence. If the world is to move away from the brink of terror, then new approaches, new combinations of reality, new risks must occur. Higher education should play a vital role in the evolution of such an imaginative spirit.[34]

Education for peace has to build a belief in the future by creating in students a sense of hope that the world can become better and more safe. People work for peace in a variety of arenas—in the highest reaches of power, in the streets, in clandestine meetings, and in classrooms. Activities of peace educators allow them to use their professional skills to contribute to the dialogue in creating a safer world. They may not see immediate results, but they can appreciate the importance of taking that first step, of doing something about the violent threats that dominate modern life, and using their training to build a consensus for peace. Chris Bartelds writes:

> Peace education does not pretend radically to change the pupils' attitudes in the course of a few lessons. It considers itself as one of the factors in a long-term process of transforming ways of thinking. And it will only produce any real effect if an attitude of international solidarity is

advocated by politics or at any rate by important and influential groups within society.[35]

Political action is necessary to change the nature of social constructs and reduce reliance on violent means to settle disputes. Peace educators may not necessarily all be activists. They may at some time participate in peace movements or support particular causes, but as educators, they focus primarily on teaching activities, appreciating the importance of educating others to help build the consensus that will provide a breeding ground for a peaceful future. The path to peace is a moral road. This world will not become more peaceful until citizens develop a moral revulsion to current violent practices that promote the destruction of the natural habitat, the taking of human life and the maintenance of social structures that perpetuate inequalities. Also needed is the moral will to change reality in more peaceful directions. Human beings have a choice about how to live on this planet. Education, by influencing students' attitudes, information, and ideas about peace, can help create in human consciousness the moral strength that will be necessary to move toward a more peaceful future.

Creating peace is a complex activity that ranges in scope from political leaders negotiating arms agreements to lovers amicably settling disputes. Influencing politics may often seem outside the classroom realm. However it is difficult to separate out the political from other aspects of teaching about peace. Educators will need to ponder how to approach these concepts in their classrooms.

Typically, teachers have certain cognitive goals for their instruction. Teachers may want their students to become aware of the role of violence in their lives, but awareness does not necessarily lead to action. What happens as a result of a particular instructional act is quite outside a teacher's control. Peace educators who hope that their students will become more informed, think critically, learn the skills of conflict management, and use their rights as citizens are not sure what results their peace education activities will have. The activities of educators do not seem so much to be changing political structures as creating both a belief system and a way of life that embraces peace. These beliefs help build a consensus against the use of force. The hope is that peaceful ways of living will influence others, and the effects will spread, slowly transforming violent actions into peaceful behavior.

PEACE EDUCATION EVALUATION

Evaluation of educational programs has two broad goals: (a) to assess the program's impact on desired outcomes, and (b) to provide feedback on various aspects of program operations. In the evaluation literature these goals have been labeled, respectively, *summative* and *formative*. A comprehensive program evaluation plan ideally addresses both the summative and the formative functions, assesses the extent to which desired program effects have been realized and ascertains the degree to which these effects can be credibly attributed to the program. At the same time it is equally important to monitor closely program operations in order to obtain diagnostic feedback on the instruction. Peace education evaluation should assess how well a program has been implemented and its impact upon learners and the broader community. It should establish criteria that will provide a feedback mechanism for program improvement. Such criteria should address such questions as, was the learning ever used, did it have a strong impact upon the learner and hence will last for a long time, were all students affected by the learning, and did it have both implicit and explicit learning? These are challenging evaluation issues, because peace education involves four different dimensions, the cognitive, the affective, the volitional, and the behavioral.

Evaluation of peace education cognitive learning is perhaps the easiest to carry out and answers questions about whether or not students learned the material the teacher intended them to learn. Although, even here, there are issues about the intended learning and other learning that pupils may have acquired that were not intended. The affective dimension concerns feelings and emotions that were aroused as a result of instruction. The volitional aspects of peace education concern whether or not students who received peace education instruction are willing to take some actions to promote peace. The behavioral outcome has to do with whether or not students behave in peaceful ways. Do they demonstrate the learning of pro-social skills? Are they less aggressive? These different aspects of learning about peace make the task of peace education extremely difficult.

Peace education stimulates, at best, a change in consciousness, where students develop peaceful attitudes and skills. In most cases it involves, at its base, the learning of facts and theories—information that may or may not result in a change of consciousness or a desire to work for peace. So peace educators face an important quandary: How effective can they be in bringing peace to the world?

Questions of teacher effectiveness raise the specter of educational evaluation. Teachers do not *cause* students to do anything. They plant seeds in pupils' minds and may not know whether those seeds will grow into plants that ultimately bear fruit. "To bear a fruit" for a peace educator might be to have a student become so concerned about the fate of the earth that that student does something to make the world more peaceful. However, teachers cannot follow their students around to see whether they initiate efforts to bring peace to the world. Therefore, they cannot evaluate the effectiveness of their work by seeing whether their students promote peace. Theoretically, such questions could be answered with detailed longitudinal studies into the peace activities of graduates of peace classes, but in actuality, teachers evaluate themselves according to more immediate criteria. What effect has their teaching had upon their students' minds? Do pupils understand various peace issues and do they have a more sympathetic attitude towards peace?

Peace education hopes to create in students a disposition to promote ecological sustainability, economic well-being, peace, and justice. Peace educators can look to their students to see if these attitudes have been produced as a result of their teaching endeavors. Whether or not these students actually work to change the world is another question. Peace educators cannot control all the complex variables that may contribute to whether a particular student works for peace. But, teachers can control both the information given students and the manner in which it is presented. For example, peace educators can evaluate at the end of peace classes whether students have learned conflict resolution techniques as a result of having been in that class. The effectiveness of peace education, therefore, cannot be judged by whether it brings peace to the world, but rather by the effect it has upon students' thought patterns and knowledge base.

Very little research on the effects of peace education classes has been conducted. A review of the literature on this topic by Baruch Nevo and Iris Brem reported that from articles about 300 peace education intervention programs in the past twenty years, only one-third included elements of effectiveness evaluation. They concluded, "It is quite clear that hundreds of peace education programs are initiated and operated around the globe at any particular period, without being subjected to any act of empirical validation."[36] According to one study by William Ekhardt[37] peace education itself does not produce changes in personality that might result in more peaceful behavior. Such changes in personality might lead to more compassion and less fatalism. However, this study (with a very small population of 12 students) does show attitude changes in the areas of ideology, morality, and philosophy. These are the kind of changes that can occur in a classroom, but it is difficult to predict whether they will last over time. A cultural shift in beliefs about war or peace, for instance activated by a terrorist attack, could negatively influence any pacifist tendencies that student may have acquired in a peace education class. Thus the context in which peace education takes place is an extremely important variable in any study of peace education effectiveness—a variable that is outside the control of the implementer of that program.

There is considerable pressure on peace educators to prove that their educational efforts are effective, pressure that comes from many sides—from the educational research community, from policy makers looking for ways to reduce levels of violence, from taxpayers supporting peace education programs in public schools, and from the larger peace community that looks to education as a potential path to peace.

The educational research community seeks to document the results of instruction. There is solid evidence that teaching younger children conflict resolution and mediation skills can lead to a reduction in acts of physical aggression at schools and an increase in problem-solving and critical thinking skills. The most impact is on those students who are directly trained. However, the whole school can also benefit, particularly when the climate is supportive of conflict resolution processes.[38] Although these studies show a positive impact of peace education instruction upon children's behavior in schools, it is difficult to determine the summative effects of peace education upon pupils' behavior outside the classroom. Let's assume that one student in a peace education class afterwards works for peace. Is that due to what the instructor taught, or was it caused by that student observing the behavior of his or her parents who were peace activists, or was the main reason that person acted peacefully because she was religious and believed in following the tenets of her spiritual beliefs? What about the other students who did nothing that reflected upon their instruction? Does their inactivity negate the worth of the instructor whose one student became an activist?

There are considerable differences between quantitative and qualitative approaches to peace education evaluation. Ideally peace education evaluation will have both quantitative and qualitative aspects. Quantitative studies use control groups and sampling techniques to determine what a group of people have learned as a result of instruction. Qualitative studies typically study in depth a small number of participants and interview them or observe them to see what impact instruction has had upon their behavior. Quantitative studies have for a long time shown the benefits of peace education upon children.[39] In general these studies show positive effects of conflict resolution education programs that decrease aggression among children, reduce bullying in schools, and motivate children's achievement in schools. The most extensive quantitative evaluation of a conflict resolution program in schools conducted with thousands of children in the New York City public schools showed a decrease in discipline problems with children in a Resolving Conflict Creatively Program (R.C.C.P.)

compared to their peers who did not get the conflict resolution instruction.[40] These studies define peace education in a narrow way: Does it have positive effects upon the behavior of children in schools? While it is valuable for teachers to know that conflict resolution education has positive benefits for children, these studies neither evaluate the long term effects of this instruction upon the behavior of students, nor do they assess whether students become active outside the classroom to promote peace and hence reduce levels of war or aggression in the larger society. As Joan Burstyn has pointed out,

> Violence in schools mirrors the violence in society and is exacerbated by the availability of guns, urban and rural poverty, drug and alcohol abuse, suburban anomie, and the media's celebration of violence. Each of these must be addressed if people want to end violence.[41]

In-depth qualitative studies of the effects of peace education are hard to find. One study about an intentional peace community established in a Jewish-Palestinian village in Israel[42] revealed that a comprehensive approach to learning about each other's different language and culture can help to reduce enemy images, but such feelings of empathy are influenced strongly by current events, so that hostilities that erupt in places like the Middle East affect attitudes that are acquired in peace education classes.

Policy makers want to know if peace education is an effective way to address problems of violence. This pressure for tangible results is felt increasingly as levels of ethnic hatred and civil strife rise in a society. Whereas, international peace education might be controversial because it challenges war enhancing policies of states, peace education dealing with civil violence seems attractive to a wide spectrum of school personnel, government officials and civic leaders who want to know that it works before they pour precious resources into educating people about alternatives to violence. Such demands can be an obstacle to peace educators because they do not have hard data to support claims that education reduces violence.

In various cities in the United States community leaders and politicians have launched comprehensive efforts to reduce youth violence and civic crime. These efforts have included hiring more police (a peace through strength strategy) and running violence prevention programs in schools and community centers (a peace education strategy). In many cities where such programs have been effective, politicians have touted the virtues of getting tough with criminals and ignored the benefits of peace education. However, these efforts in combination (peacekeeping, peacemaking, and peacebuilding strategies) have contributed to lower levels of street crime and urban violence in some cities. The problem is in demonstrating that it was the peace education activities that provided these results.

Peace educators pressured from local school officials to show that their approaches work have a hard time developing rigorous studies. Ideally such a study would compare a group of students who had received peace education training with a comparison group that didn't, but such studies are hard to carry out for many reasons: (1) They require pre- and post-tests, access to school records, and to classrooms. Researchers have to get permission from the school, the teacher, and the parents in order to conduct research on minors. (2) In countries where children are mobile, it's hard to find the same subjects to gather follow-up data. (3) Comparison groups are hard to control. Two samples of students may appear similar, but their participation in peace education learning can be influenced by a wide variety of factors, including parents' beliefs, religious upbringing, and previous experiences with conflict resolution education. Subtle and dramatic exposure to violence or experiences with peace inside and outside the classroom would also influence how well students responded to peace instruction. (4) Such studies are expensive and there is little money available for peace education research. These many obstacles to conducting valid evaluations of peace education instruction make it hard for peace educators to satisfy the expectations of policy makers to verify the value of educational approaches to resolving conflict.

The peace research community is also interested in peace education evaluation to see if educational efforts contribute to building a peaceful society. The problem with providing clear answers to these concerns has to do with the level of analysis. Is violence caused by government policies, cultural and community norms, or individual behavior? The answer, of course, is all of the above, and many other factors determine whether or not a person or a group of people pursue violence. In order to provide valid research about the effects of peace education, peace educators have to be clear about what level of problem they are addressing. Michael Van Slyck and Marilyn Stern have demonstrated that it is possible to measure students' attitudes about conflict before and after conflict resolution education activities to see if their attitudes change,[43] but such studies do not demonstrate that the behavior of individuals has actually changed.

The achievement of peace has so many different facets. Peace education is such a complex subject that it is hard to structure evaluation programs to capture its complexity. As mentioned in a chapter 3, "The Practice of Peace Education," there are many different aspects that can influence peace learning that vary from an understanding of international relations to the ability to be compassionate. In conducting evaluations, peace educators need to be clear about their objectives. Even so, there might be all kinds of implicit learning that occurs in a peace education class that was not included in the objectives for that course. For example, one of the authors, Ian Harris, teaches regularly a course on peace education at his university in the school of education (see syllabus in Appendix). This course is designed to highlight the problems of violence that teachers face, review peace strategies, and demonstrate that peace education is a viable strategy for addressing those problems of violence. Many students have had epiphanies in this class not related so much to course content, but rather to reflecting on their experiences of violence. One woman was reminded of abuse she received from a grandfather and went into therapy to resolve some of those issues. Another student in a class devoted to studying the impact of the Vietnam War upon American culture had some very powerful memories of a brother who was damaged psychologically from his participation in that war. Peace education courses stir up all kinds of feelings, but many of the powerful learnings associated with these feelings are not covered in standard paper and pencil course evaluations (see next section for a discussion of how to deal with these emotions in instructional settings).

The creation of peace is also complex. For example, consider the considerable anti-nuclear educational efforts that took place around the world in the 1980s. There were college courses, movies, street demonstrations, and considerable community education efforts designed to educate people about the threat of nuclear weapons and to influence policy makers to reduce their reliance upon deterrence theory. Reductions in nuclear stockpiles, the passing of a comprehensive test ban treaty, and lessened in cold war hostilities seem to indicate that these efforts were successful. However, these changes in policies could be due to the personalities of Ronald Reagan and Mikhail Gorbachev, who were heads of the United States and the Soviet Union at that time. They might also have be caused by economic considerations, where politicians were concerned about the cost of producing nuclear weapons. How could it be proved that changes in nuclear policy were due to peace education activities?

Important questions need to continue to be asked about the outcomes of peace education activities. How might it be determined if the world is less violent because of the efforts described in this book? During the 1930s leading educators and intellectuals, alarmed about the dangers of a growing militarism, turned to peace education to oppose fascism. Maria Montessori lectured extensively throughout Europe about the need to learn how to solve conflicts nonviolently and the need to keep children from being fascinated by war. In her words, "establishing a lasting peace is the work of education; all politics can do is keep us out of war."[44] Thousands of other educators at the same time inveighed against the use of force and promoted democracy. Fifty years later, fascist regimes no longer exist in industrialized democracies in the Western world. Are we to attribute this success in overcoming fascism to the efforts of peace educators? Were they successful in instilling in human minds a respect for human rights and for democratic processes that ultimately triumphed over the forces of fascism? This is a very difficult question to answer and points to the need for complicated research studies to determine the effect of peace education. Clearly, the Second World War, with its peace through strength strategies, played a key role in overthrowing the fascist governments in Japan, Italy, and Germany, but perhaps it could be argued that visions of human rights and democracy inspired the Allied soldiers fighting in those wars. Were the efforts of educators central to producing those visions that motivated forces on the Allied side to produce the tremendous effort necessary to overthrow the Axis powers? It would be nice to think so, but we just don't know.

Similarly, teachers in Japan have played a leading role in promoting awareness about the horrors of the atomic bomb. No nuclear weapons have actually been detonated in acts of aggression since the bombing of Nagasaki in 1945, and forty years later millions of citizens throughout the world opposed any use or production of nuclear weapons. Have these citizens heard the cries of teachers in Japan pleading with humanity to never again resort to such barbarism? What roles have these teachers in Japan played in building the burgeoning consensus that is appearing on this planet opposed to nuclear weapons? It could be stated that these teachers have been supremely successful in their efforts to alert the human community to the dangers of nuclear weapons, but it would be hard to establish a chain of causality from their teaching efforts to the aversion to nuclear weapons that currently exists on this planet.

Dealing with Emotions

Educating for peace involves, as has been discussed, more than the imparting of facts. Traditional concepts of education have not included the affective dimension. Peace educators deal with subjects in their classes that evoke powerful feelings. Fear is one strong emotion that can arise in the discussions of violence. It is important that fears are dealt with in an atmosphere of nurturance and care so that students move beyond their sense of powerlessness. Without confronting such emotions peace educators may contribute to a sense of cynicism on the part of young people about the threatening nature of the world.

Students faced with terrifying images of war and destruction have a natural tendency to deny them. This process of denial has been extensively discussed by Robert Jay Lifton[45] and others who describe it as psychic numbing. The tendency of people faced with such horror is to block it out or displace it in such a way that fear and terror don't constantly dominate their psyches. The challenge for the peace educator, then, is to break through these processes of denial by confronting the horrors of terrorism directly. The study of war and violence in contemporary times means that students and teachers must confront fears of their own deaths, as well as what Jonathan Schell calls the unimaginable concept of planetary extinction.

Researchers such as Elizabeth Kubler-Ross[46] have determined that an individual faced with their own death enters a grieving cycle of five successive stages—denial, anger, bargaining, depression, and acceptance. While there may be disagreement as to whether all people go through all of these in this order, nevertheless, an understanding of these stages may help in transforming fears around personal and social violence.

Often when confronted with the news of their own or a family members' immediate mortality, individuals *deny* it. In this way most people can lead their lives not thinking about nuclear extermination or the imminent threat of terrorism. (since this writing is only several months after the World Trade Center and Pentagon attacks, it is our belief that denial around this was brief at best, since the public was continually bombarded with media pictures of the events. Since September 11 culturally, it can be argued that there is a pervasive sense of anxiety in the United States). Ironically, it can be argued that modern technology demands that people confront the logical implications of going to war, because any war has the possibility of causing severe and irreversible damage to the habitat that nurtures human and natural communities.

Fear can, at times, also be healthy for living organisms. If a child playing on a street sees a truck coming and is afraid, that child will get up and run out of the way of the truck. Fear produces reactions that lead to survival. The feelings of fear and despair experienced by studying different forms of violence can contribute to a life embracing energy, both in the desire to do something to change the state of affairs that causes that fear and by helping students identify with other human beings and life forms that are similarly threatened.

The second stage of grief in death and dying is *anger,* including such thoughts as, "Why must this happen to me? This isn't fair." The anger stage can be a potent mobilizer of energy. People threatened by violence have a natural response to save themselves. At times it is difficult to know with whom to be angry. Following the September 11 attacks, certain people of Arab, Asian or of Middle Eastern descent were harassed and beaten as they became scapegoats for the fear and rage of the American public. It can be argued that President Bush's immediate call for revenge against the terrorists was an quick reaction to cultural fear and rage, directed at Afghanistan, the supposed headquarters of a terrorist network.

The next stage in death and dying is *bargaining.* If I do this, will I be saved? People in this stage attempt to reduce dangers by taking precautions. This is an important phase in the death cycle because individuals at this stage "settle" with their friends and relatives. They come to terms with the hurts they may have caused others and realize that their lives may not have been all they had hoped they might be. In this stage people try to reach compromises that will extend their lives. In relation to previous wounds, this stage may also give rise to attempts of reconciliation with those with whom one has had conflicts. People previously committed to adversarial relationships may work to create a safer future for the next generation. People who go through this stage can feel a great sense of urgency and are very zealous about the need to work for peace. They realize life is short.

The next stage of dealing with death involves true *depression* and *grief.* The anger has been worked through and what is left is a sense of sadness, a mourning for self and loved ones and lost possibilities. Joanna Macy writes:

> Until now, every generation throughout history lived with the tacit certainty that other generations would follow. Each assumed, without questioning, that its children and children's children and those yet unborn would carry on—to walk the same earth, under the same sky. Hardships, failures, and personal death were ever encompassed in that vaster assurance of continuity. That certainty is now lost to us whether we work in the Pentagon or the peace movement. That loss, unmeasured and immeasurable, is the pivotal psychological reality of or time.[47]

Owning and acknowledging these feelings can put peace educators in touch with what Joanna Macy calls the "Web of Life."[48] Humans, in their sorrow, can grow to appreciate the value of life and the horror of anything that threatens this.

The final stage of *acceptance* brings a certain clarity about life and its importance. At this stage people may come to terms with their lives. It is a stage of holism. They appreciate with great sadness that they are (the world is) threatened and resolve to do what they can until the end of their life. Joy returns as an acceptance of life's limitations and the legacy they have left. They have integrated their past and work for the future, given the realist notion that their own life may soon be coming to an end.

Hopefully this discussion of the stages involved with death and dying can provide a useful guide and a metaphorical understanding of some of the emotions involved in discussions of conflict and violence and in educating for peace. It is natural for individuals confronting their own death or the extinction of life on this planet to deny, to be angry, to grieve, to bargain and finally integrate these emotions which can become an important part in building a sense of moral concern for the future of the planet.

Suffering builds compassion. Yet powerful feelings can engender psychological defenses against displays of emotion. Teachers may be afraid to confront emotional issues in classrooms because they are afraid they will "fall apart." But it is these very defenses that must be undone in order for people to transform themselves into effective peacemakers. Feelings of despair, confusion, grief, anger, and helplessness all come up in peace education classes. In reality, when people confront these issues, they rarely come undone. They become healthier. By confronting their deepest fears, the deep seated feelings of despair and sadness that people hold within them may be released into a cathartic sense of compassion about the human condition, particularly if done within a sense of community.

Students need permission in peace education classes to talk about their distress about past experiences with violence that may include emotional and sexual abuse. Peace educators need to give themselves permission to express their own emotions so that they may be examples to their students of loving, caring human beings who are concerned about the fate of the earth. In this way peace education can contribute in important ways to producing future citizens who are neither craven nor silent, but rather are prepared to confront their fears in an attempt to create a safer future.

Discussions about such topics can take the classroom away from a dry, impersonal exchange of facts and ideas to a dynamic environment where students can explore different reactions to forms of violence they have experienced. The emotional nature of these discussions will mean that classes will have deep meaning and significance for students. Such discussions can both free an entrapped citizenry from the defenses they have constructed against talking about important threats to their own existence and contribute to the moral development of students.

Understanding Differing Attitudes and Values

Teaching about peace can be confounding. Everybody wants peace, but differing ideas about how to achieve it make it difficult to come to consensus. Students in a peace education class described their images of peace in the following ways: "Being outdoors, a part of the universe," "meditating," "working with other people to achieve a peaceful world. This image is not exactly peaceful because it involves confronting the power structure"; "living in a world where all people have food, clothing, shelter, and dignity;" "a community working together"; "thinking globally, but acting locally"; "living in a farm community, taking care of one's own needs"; "the family, living together in a caring community. Growing together"; "peace is a dynamic process. Me accepting myself, accepting people around me, and growing together"; "starting internally with myself. Peace is an attitude of accepting other people's points of view"; "a tall tree next to a rippling brook. Thinking of nature as an escape from the immediate"; "peace is each person communicating thought. After something is festering, working it through by communication, and experiencing peace afterwards." These different images may be seen to reflect the life experiences of each of the students in the class.

The following are "wishes for a peaceful world" and come from children in Sheboygan, Wisconsin:

Karen Schmitt (age 12)

I wish all countries would share peace with each other. I want Russia and the U.S. would stop making bombs and start talking over their difficulties. I wish for peace among all people, no matter what color, race, or religion they are. They should learn to become friends. I also want the crime rate to end. I wish for the killing and destruction to stop.

I wish the unemployment to stop so all people will be happy and at peace with each other. I wish the poor and lonely may find happiness where ever they may be. I think that if we want to be able to be peaceful we have to work together and stick up for what we really believe in.

Paul Gartman (age 12)

My hope for peace in the world is that all the nations should get together and stop all the fighting in the world.

I hope for peace so all the killings and injuries will stop.

No one really wants war. Besides, all war gets you is death. I really don't know why there is war. Neither side really wins. They both lose in life and love.

I feel war is useless. It does not get you anywhere but where you started from.

8. Sensitive Issues in Peace Education

Melissa Morton (age 11)

I hope the dreams of war and hunger ending will one day soon come true. Everyone prays day after day and hoping deep down it will. You can look at yourself, see how wealthy you are, as there are people out there starving, dying, and hoping that it would all stop. You hear so much about war and hunger, thinking that one day one of these people could be you. It's all very frightening! Think of young children. They need to know and feel the feel of being able to see the sun set peacefully on the fresh smell of flowers blooming. I know you have dreams and hopes of your own that you would like to see happen one day. We should all get a chance to see a dream happen at one time or another.

This last wish for a peaceful world has been uttered by millions of human beings throughout history—the dream of a world without hunger or war. These peaceful images portray a gentler world than the one most of us inhabit and also form the utopian basis for many religious myths, i.e., the Garden of Eden in the Judeo-Christian tradition.

According to Betty Reardon,[49] individuals hold different notions of what peace is and how to achieve security. For some people security comes only through disarmament, while others believe that the road to it is paved with munitions. "Peace with honor" motivates political leaders, while peace through contemplative withdrawal from the world motivates some who follow the tenets of eastern religions. Peace educators need to begin their classes with a discussion of these different notions so that students may understand the divergent attitudes, values and concepts associated with peace. Burns and Aspeslagh write:

> A discussion which took place at the World Congress on Disarmament Education at UNESCO, Paris, 13–16 June, 1980, provides an illustration of this diversity. The question arose between African and European participants as to what kind of disarmament education each was undertaking. For the European, the main issue was the problem of nuclear armaments and the search for ways to abolish these weapons. The African opposed this view, pointing out that more Africans are killed with conventional arms or die as a result of poverty and starvation than because of nuclear weapons.[50]

Peace education involves helping people evaluate their notions of security, power, dependence, violence, and peace—notions which are formed by everyday realities and impressions they receive from the culture around them. The effectiveness of educational efforts depend, to a large degree, upon discovering the barriers to thinking about peace and national security and helping students to break these down, in themselves and in others. In this way peace education requires a great deal of sensitivity to the different "agendas" that students bring to peace education classes.

Peace education starts with the individual and the right of each person to lead his or her own life, taking destiny into his or her own hands; and therefore according to modern day peace education, it is up to the individual to define what his or her own basic needs are and how to satisfy them. The function of peace education has been to investigate the causes and processes that lead to the non-fulfillment of basic needs.[51] Working with these differences becomes an important part of peace education. Education for peace must begin with our everyday experiences and immediate fears, not with mere models of peaceful world order or of a peaceful social life.[52]

By challenging students' underlying assumptions, peace educators help students understand how their own notions about violence have been formed. Working with individual perceptions and attitudes, within an atmosphere of community learning, helps foster the value of the importance of diversity. Learning how to appreciate different values and points of view constitutes an important part of the peace education process.

CHAPTER 9

Schools as Cultures of War: Overcoming Obstacles

Give Peace a Chance
—John Lennon

This chapter discusses certain barriers educators may face, as they bring their visions of peace and hope into classrooms, schools and community settings. These include: psychological, cultural, political and educational barriers. The presentation of these obstacles will be followed by suggestions to prepare peace educators to teach in our present world, so often seen as filled with conflict and violence.

Critics of our global educational system maintain that often countries use schools to perpetuate nationalistic ideologies, including extolling the valor of war and the promotion of technology that leads to environmental destruction. These critics believe that schools pass on militaristic values emphasizing competition and rituals of patriotism (an example is the almost universal practice of reciting the Pledge of the Allegiance to the American flag, now coming under scrutiny in the face of the recent passage of the U.S. Patriots Act, a response to the events of September 11, 2001). In the face of such traditions, peace educators attempt to teach in ways that will work toward the establishment of the conditions for a less violent world. Cultural barriers and norms may challenge their activities. Teachers may find students resistant to some of the peace concepts and to the use of nonviolent approaches in the classroom. Peace education is often easier "preached than practiced." In 1978 Betty Reardon wrote an article, "Obstacles to Disarmament Education," which presented barriers that need to be overcome in the teaching of the effects of militarism.[1] This chapter will discuss some of the ideas contained in this essay but will also branch out to present new ideas.

At the same time that this material is presented in an advisory way, attempting to warn peace educators about obstacles, it is also meant to provide subject matter for discussions in peace education classes. What are the main barriers that confront peace educators? What obstacles do they have to face in getting students thinking about changing their lifestyles in ways that are more sensitive to the needs of the natural environment and to other humans? Peace educators need to identify the obstacles to the development of peace in their particular settings and to devise ways to deal with them and to share with each other ways that work. Only when these barriers are transformed can peace educators move forward in their attempt to create a less violent world.

Psychological Barriers

At the basis of the pedagogical relationship between teachers and students lies each of their own mental capacities—the various psychological histories that they bring to discussions of how to live more peacefully on this planet. Grounding such relationships is the skill of the teacher to respond to those histories. In working with students to teach them about peace and conflict, educators have many psychological obstacles to face. All human beings desire security, and, as mentioned earlier in this book, different views of security influence how an individual may approach peaceful responses to conflict. There is, among students, widespread ignorance of the devastation caused by the high living standards of advanced, capitalistic countries and resistance to seeing new ways of looking at this phenomenon. Discussions of violence and conflict and living more sustainably on the planet, as previously mentioned, sometimes bring up much fear. This must be overcome if peace educators are to help students commit to changing the ways that humans treat each other and the natural world.

Confronting the human commitment to materialism and violent conflict resolution forces a look at the irrational and aggressive aspects of our personalities which most people don't enjoy viewing and which are often kept hidden from self and others. Classes on these topics can be depressing. Many would prefer to ignore these frightening aspects of human nature and to simply deny that which can threaten daily existence.

Many people feel ignorant of the complex issues surrounding national defense. For example, the United States, by the end of the twentieth century, had twenty-two commissioned level "defense systems." Trident nuclear submarines, which are first strike weapons, constitute one level. Any one of those submarines can launch twenty-four missiles simultaneously. Each of these missiles may contain as many as seventeen independently targeted, maneuverable nuclear warheads. One submarine might obliterate 408 centers of population, hitting each with a nuclear warhead ten times more powerful than the bomb that incinerated Nagasaki.

Faced with such ignorance and fear, taking action against the continuation of national defense policies can seem to be an overwhelming task. Peace education, by providing information about national priorities, environmental costs and foreign policy, can help citizens feel informed enough to engage in debate about these important issues that affect their lives. People who trust leaders often believe that their government has their best interests in mind and do not question a system that "takes care of them." Many people believe that government leaders have moral sensibilities that will keep them from "pushing the nuclear button," and therefore don't believe that a holocaust could happen. (Some might argue that the American public became more aware of their vulnerabilities as a result of the September 11 attacks and, though continuing to trust in their leaders, now realize how much of high level policy is unknown even to the elected officials.) Because of the level of national trust, citizens may be reluctant to challenge the status quo.

Peace education promotes changes in the way human beings think about their commitment to violence and to their sense of security. New ways of thinking of security will involve notions of equity. Moving into a world that is more peaceful will require replacing an economic system based upon domination with one that is more equitable. This may pose challenges to citizens in the United States, whose lifestyles include the consumption of 500 pounds of resources each day (excluding water). Disarmament, and the costs associated with it, must include the transfer of resources out of a world full of arms to one in which security needs for all people include enough to eat, a place to live and clothing to cover. The world is so heavily armed, and militarism has become so deeply ingrained throughout societies, that many people resist moving toward a world that seeks alternative security systems. Betty Reardon writes that "people in general seem to have difficulty in envisioning a disarmed world, and therefore fear what they cannot describe to themselves as a reasonable set of living circumstances.[2]

It is easy to become cynical about the prospects for change and to feel powerless to effect it. Sometimes it is difficult to take a stand. Its easier to let others do it and to take the risks. Government repression of peace movements may contribute to a sense of powerlessness. A basic human desire to be respected by peers keeps many from becoming what they may see as "radicalized." It is difficult to change other people's opinions, to fly in the face of accepted wisdom, and to confront biases about these issues as well as the apathy that exists about doing anything to change the frightening nature of reality. People who feel overwhelmed about these issues will despair that anything can be done to create a more peaceful world. Whole segments of the population feel they cannot get involved in social change efforts because their jobs would be threatened or because they are overwhelmed by the difficulty of confronting the war system. Furthermore, to work for change implies a belief in the future, i.e., "if I learn about alternative security systems I may also work to see them implemented to help secure a future for the world." More and more people in advanced technological nations are living in the present. Seeking immediate gratification, they belong to a "now" generation that doesn't always plan for the future. Living in the present, and feeling overwhelmed by the daily struggles to exist, many modern citizens, though not always conscious of this, have little faith that there will even be a future and can't commit themselves to working for something, which at a deeply subconscious level, they believe will never happen.

Given the difficulties in trying to bring about changes in the social order, people withdraw inside themselves. Some who are concerned about violence try to transform their private lives into a more peaceful way to live. And indeed, this might be seen as working toward peace, albeit on an individual level. Pessimism about changing reality leads to a situation where some feel the only thing they can really change is their own attitudes and behavior.

Further difficulties in learning about peace and war emanate from the nature of western child-rearing practices. Childhood conditioning plays an important part in a person's ability to accept new ideas or work towards a world based on trust rather than fear. In extremely authoritarian households where young people are physically abused, screamed at, or denied respect, children have little or no opportunity to learn responsible, peaceful behavior.[3] In some households parents raise children with psychological patterns that rely on "outside others" to provide answers. These children often aren't willing to accept the ambiguity that goes with trying to change a reliance on rigid, militaristic values. In extreme cases where children are victimized, they may seek scapegoats for the frustration they feel and act out their frustrations destructively. Being raised in a climate of cruelty, they do not readily confide their feelings to others. Since the path to safe, verbal communication, based on a feeling of trust, has been blocked for them, they live in a suspicious world dominated by "enemies" and lack the self-esteem necessary to question military dogma. Children who have been lied to, beaten, humiliated and deceived may grow into angry adults and may harbor deep-seated hatred towards the world that makes it difficult for them to participate in the trusting climate necessary for peace education classes. Fortunately, it is believed that these extreme cases are not the norm. For the most part, children grow up in "good-enough" homes, where, though they may be exposed to violence in some form, they will maintain the resiliency necessary for the conditions to work for social change.

Cultural Barriers

Individuals are influenced by cultures that impose values, attitudes and behaviors that can pose barriers for peace educators. A deeply held value is the efficacy of violence, that it "works." For example, there is wide political support for building prisons in order to "solve" the problems posed by individuals who may commit crimes whose basis lies in conditions of structural violence (poverty, racism). Even though schools may adopt conflict resolution programs, cultural messages may tell children to never back down to a bully, to "always defend yourself." Many homes contain guns. Television glorifies violence and often shields viewers from the reality of the painful effects of violent behavior. Political violence carried out by modern states promotes the notion that brute force and strength are the best ways to settle disputes. Military activities are praised and military values influence many social institutions, including the schools (an example is the increasing military recruiting going on, particularly in large, urban school districts, as a way of encouraging students in their schooling and career path). Likewise, the growth of the Gross National Product (GNP) is seen as a positive development, despite the fact that with increases in capitalistic consumption come corresponding increases in environmental degradation. It can be hard for educators to promote the value of "living with less" in such a materialistic culture.

The constant presence of violence supports a "macho" culture. Respect is thought to be gained by the use of authority and control. In a hierarchical world divided into winners and losers, "being number one" becomes an important cultural consideration. In a world dependent on military systems, being number one is not often defined in terms of social justice or equity, but rather in terms of wealth and of military might. The powerful nations of the world, especially the United States, have the arms to create enormous political, economic and cultural influence over the weaker, less developed countries. This attitude that condones willful exploitation of weaker countries permeates the social fabric of the West. Virgil Elizondo writes:

> Although personal advancement and the enjoyment of the fruit of one's labor is a great and humanizing virtue, advancement at the cost of others and the enjoyment of the fruits of the labor of the exploited other is a dehumanizing and destructive vice. To the degree that this attitude of egocentric individualism becomes ingrained in the culture of a people, authentic personal relationships and cooperation between people becomes impossible. Each one is out for his or her own self! May the best one win![4]

In this system might makes right. Compromise and negotiation are seen as signs of weakness. Competition permeates the natural order of things. Winning is everything, and it is difficult to come up with new ways of thinking to challenge this win-lose mentality. Who wants to be weak? Nationally, a reduction in arms is seen as a sign of capitulation; whereas flexing muscles, threatening, and pushing others around are applauded as signs of strength.

In "macho cultures" young boys are expected to be tough. Cowardice is a sign of weakness, and many men consider that joining the military might prove their manhood. Various institutions support military values. These values in turn become an important part of how men see themselves in modern societies, where the norm is to be cold, domineering, and tough. Tenderness or concern for other human beings are not "masculine traits." Many men at age eighteen actually join the armed forces trained to view an enemy as an "alien other," one without humanity or cultural virtues.

At the end of the Second World War the United States stood in a position of military superiority in the world. Victorious against the Fascist powers and possessing the awesome power of nuclear weapons, the U.S. was seen as the leading and most powerful country in the world. This has continued to be the case, though there are those who believe that the era of U.S. hegemony cannot last indefinitely. Because U.S. citizens enjoy many economic benefits from their country's ability to dominate world affairs, particularly global trade, those in power argue for huge military outlays, even though this results in large numbers of people being confined to low standards of living whose resources are being undercut by the dominance of militarism. There is widespread belief, not just in the United States, that a strong military will increase the stature of a country in the eyes of the world at large. After the Cuban missile crisis, for example, the Soviet Union pulled out all restraints to build a defense capability comparable to that of the United States. Soviet people made tremendous sacrifices in order for the country to reach parity with the U.S. armament industry. Such military build-ups diverted badly needed funds from the domestic sphere and helped to lead to the collapse of a state that failed to provide, and continues to, an adequate standard of living for its citizens. Peacekeeping strategies that don't rely on military might, such as diplomatic negotiation, are seen as signs of weakness. Armaments become a symbol of national strength in a world where states are graded according to their military capacity in international relations. Sustainable practices are not promoted because they may reduce profits. In such cultures, peace can sometimes have a bad image.

The modern arms race is basically a technological race. Rather than building peace through compromise and treaties, countries are committed to "winning" the arms race through technological advances. The "great" nations of the world compete in research and development, where one new weapons system spawns another. People are reluctant to challenge the rationale for such technologies because they are closely bound up in cultural notions of progress. Modern technological advances built upon the most sophisticated scientific principles and discoveries belong to the long list of accomplishments that characterize the advanced nature of modern societies.

This way of thinking began with Descartes and Newton, both of who used the rational science of mathematics to describe the universe in ways that could be manipulated and controlled. It is estimated that over half of the scientists in the world currently work on defense related research, and many U.S. and multi-national corporations lobby hard for defense contracts. One hopeful irony of these developments is that these weapons of mass destruction are so horrible that they are causing some people in advanced countries to question this time honored belief in peace through strength. Joel Kovel writes:

> Each of the Western nations is unique, yet all are easily moved by images of war, and all are united in worshipping technology as the solution to human problems. Undoubtedly, the U.S., the leader in the arms race, leads in this respect, too, just as it leads in the democratic culture of violence, and, by a huge margin, in the homicide rate, a fact that can be ascribed in equal measure to the mythology of the lawless frontier and to the promiscuous prevalence of handguns among the population. It is not

reassuring to have a culture of this kind fermenting beneath 30,000 nuclear warheads and presided over by a President who is the creature of corporate capital and loves the good old Wild West. Nor is it any comfort to behold the grip that technology has over the average mind, despite all the evidence of the menace it presents.[5]

Media coverage, particularly among developed countries, highlights the negative aspects of life in countries that are perceived as being part of an enemy camp. Images may scare citizens into erroneous thinking that changes in the way they live may reduce the quality of their lives. In reality, modern warfare benefits mostly only a relative handful of people "at the top," the wealthy and those who wield political and cultural power, compared to the total population of citizens. About half of the world's citizens subsist on less than two dollars per day.[6] The overwhelming numbers of victims of modern warfare are private citizens, often poor, and most often are women and children.

This mass hysteria about perceived enemies has a profound effect upon educators who may be, by challenging dominant notions of peace through strength, accused of "collaboration with the enemy." For example, during the Cold War, fear of communism in the United States promoted an ethnocentrism that made it difficult for peace educators to create a climate conducive to understanding the complexity of international relations. It has already been noted (Chapter 2) that the name of the American School Peace League was changed earlier in the century to the American School Citizen League, a victim of the need for "political correctness." When one country and its allies are always painted as good, while other countries are seen as evil, students are reluctant to accept suggestions that there may be some value in seeing the good in the enemy. The promotion of peace in the face of such dichotomous thinking can be difficult and may be mocked as an attempt to undermine the dominant strength of a militaristic and capitalist society. Yet peace educators can point out that, for the most part, our everyday interactions are peaceful. Teachers can point to the "human side" of an enemy, placing a "face" on a nameless other.

Demonizing another country provides that "other" as a scapegoat that keeps people from addressing their own individual personal and national domestic problems. Public opinion becomes influenced by the fear of other countries, rather than being formed by an analysis of what may be best for the good of all citizens of the world. Such hysteria has the effect of making any presentation on peace issues suspect in the minds of people saturated with fears of being dominated by evil political systems. Violence is glorified so that young men in wars (and wars are overwhelmingly fought by very young men) are immune to the effects their own actions may have upon innocent civilians of an enemy country.

To counteract these cultural barriers to peace education, teachers need to highlight the terrible effects of violence upon individuals and society, and provide an awareness of the effects of a commitment to militarism and unbridled economic growth. In order to do this successfully they must not ignore the more immediate violence around them. Educators can help by talking about fears that students have in relation to violence on the playground and crime in the neighborhood, and move beyond this to a discussion of national and international violence, while at the same time providing alternative strategies to address conflicts.

Peace educators can confront the dominant macho belief in strength by pointing out how traditional military might and brute force do not provide security in the long-term. For example, it surely is better for Greece and Turkey to negotiate a solution to the crisis on Cyprus than to wage a war in which thousands of their citizens will be killed. Likewise, brute force is not the best way to resolve domestic disagreements.

In terms of enemy threats, peace educators need to challenge students to look closely at their prejudices and examine their cultural biases. Students must learn that distrust of others is a major obstacle to creating a warless world. "All works of love are works of peace."[7]

Political Barriers

Governments and political parties tend to perpetrate many of the cultural values and attitudes mentioned in the previous section. Grounded in these values, citizens are told that the world will be safer with more arms and societies better off with unlimited economic growth. The desire for power and dominance seems so intricately related to national structures, that, as Machiavelli pointed out, political life is itself a sort of war, with competing individuals "at each others' throats." The glorification of war and promulgation of patriotic values creates a climate that makes it hard for peace educators to introduce new ways of thinking about political structures. Nation-states may use internal security forces to maintain their authority over citizens. Modern technology can keep track of "deviant" individuals. Surveillance has become increasingly sophisticated with computers able to store huge amounts of data about groups that engage in "subversive" activities such as promoting disarmament. The swift passage of the Patriots Act in the fall of 2001, following the September 11 attacks, with very little U.S. Congressional dissent, greatly increased the power of the federal government to interfere in the affairs of ordinary citizens, passed in the face of overwhelming fears of subsequent terrorist attacks. To be seen as questioning these tactics can itself be incriminating to an individual who may be subsequently investigated as someone who is "unpatriotic" to the American cause of freedom.

In the developing world, military hardware costs run up huge deficits and postpone the important work that must be done to increase the standard of living of the poorest of the world's citizens. In western societies the defense budgets have become a sort of "industrial policy," a Keynesian flywheel that keeps private investment and public dollars funneled in ways which detract from the more human needs of a society. Throughout the western world, millions of people are making their livelihood by producing instruments of mass destruction (in the United States it is estimated that one out of every ten people works for the Pentagon or for a firm that supplies the Pentagon). A push for disarmament might threaten the economic well-being of millions of people who depend for their living upon this type of state spending. The U.S. Congress has on numerous occasions called for shutting down army bases, but has not been able to find the political will to carry out these closures. As Seymour Melman has pointed out, money spent by the military could be much more productively spent on other sectors of the economy, but powerful forces resist this trend toward economic conversion to peaceful production.[8]

The impact of the war economies upon the potential for peace education may be seen as powerful. In many countries young people can anticipate building lucrative careers working for the military-industrial complex. As engineers or scientists they may work on the "very frontiers of human knowledge" by participating in defense related research. Peace studies and a concern for world social problems and ecological sustainability may be seen as peripheral to the pursuit of a career in business, engineering, or science. Therefore a large number of young people motivated by a desire to succeed in today's world may have no interest in pursuing peace studies. Careers built upon peace education often do not pay well. Peace educators must help to foster attitudes about the benefits of looking at peace, even in careers in business, science and technology, and point out the increasingly interconnective aspects of a growing global economy with concomitant moral and ethical obligations to work toward the elimination of problems associated with structural violence.

National economic policies can effect peace education in other ways. Because of the huge expense of national security systems, many people are driven into poverty. As social service programs are cut to meet defense requirements, more and more people throughout the world may be forced into substandard living conditions, conditions which can be the grounding for future resistance movements. (An example is Palestinian extremist movement, whose stated revolutionary tactics rest upon the oppression felt from the Israeli occupation and oppression.) Victims of extreme poverty struggling from day to day to provide basic necessities have neither time nor energy to concern themselves with issues as abstract as the national security policies. Yet they may find themselves drawn to a charismatic leader or movement that promises them food and shelter and an increase in their standard of living. Such was the case in post World War I Germany, when Fascism arose in the ashes of the poverty and ruin. As opposition movements grow within a given country, national leaders argue for increased guns and a tighter security apparatus to repress dissent. The Colombian military has asked the United States for assistance in suppressing the rebels believed to be fueling the narcotics trade. It may be argued that many of these so-called rebels are poor peasants who are drawn to the movement out of their own poverty and oppression. The U.S. has responded with increased military aid. The effects have been the eradication of the livelihood of many people as U.S. planes destroy rural farm areas, with the concomitant rise of injury and death to innocent civilians and the despoliation of parts of Colombia's tropical forests. With an increase in the supply of arms, the struggle of liberation movements often becomes violent, contributing to a sense of despair that the world will ever be peaceful. In many cases research requests for grants to support the study of nonviolence or alternative international relations are denied by funding sources which place a priority on traditional security studies or on international relations.

Peace educators can work to overcome these obstacles by teaching students that their governments can have different priorities. Students can learn of the important work of the United Nations and its associated agencies. Students can learn the importance of working to realize the goals set forth in the original charter of the United Nations. Noted peace educator Betty Reardon writes:

> It is absolutely essential, as is noted in the 1974 UNESCO recommendation, that member states formulate policies for the improvement of international understanding and for overcoming the misconceptions and cultural ignorance which often permit the toleration of injustice as well as the nurturing of fear of the enemy, which in turn nurtures the arms race. If, according to the guiding principles of the recommendation, education is presented from a global perspective, students will come to understand that the human species has a common

planetary destiny, that we have more in common than differences, and that respect for other people, their cultures, civilizations, values, and ways of life is absolutely essential to the preservation of the species, its cultural diversity and its physical survival.⁹

One way to counteract the perceived nationalistic goals of nation states is to work toward the development of a planetary consciousness. Peace educators can teach that the human race depends for its own survival upon cooperation between people, living in harmony with nature and not on competition between armies or groups of militants. The United Nations represents a vehicle for moving toward a more cooperative world. Students in peace education classes can become familiar with the work of the UN, with its potential and with its limitations, in trying to think through new ways the world can be structured to avoid the tremendous cost of the commitment to militarism.

The most fundamental human right, the right to life, is guaranteed under the Declaration of Human rights. Reardon notes:

> War, the indiscriminate consumer of human lives, is in direct contradiction to the principles of human rights. Disarmament education should illuminate this contradiction and stress the inadmissibility of war.¹⁰

Governments assume that they have a right to kill enemies and repress internal dissent in order to protect sovereignty and ways of living. In challenging this behavior by appealing to human rights, peace educators are risking controversy, but these risks will be essential to the struggle to create a less violent world. Addressing the threats posed by modern commitments to defense and traditional notions of security requires that teachers confront dominant political values. As one student who had taken a peace education course noted:

> The saddest part to me is that the leaders of a country that is supposed to be concerned with human rights should be so obsessed with the production of weapons whose objective is mass violation of the major human right, the right to live.¹¹

Raising such issues in a classroom might pose difficulties for teachers. She or he may be criticized by other colleagues, attacked by angry parents, or perhaps censured by administrators. A person's ability to raise questions about the nature of political reality depends to some extent upon the institutional setting in which he or she works. Tenure and other conditions supporting academic freedom allow individuals to be outspoken in their pursuit of truth. However, for many peace educators, challenging the existing political arrangements may threaten their jobs. Peace educators should understand the nature of the institutions for which they work.

Educational Barriers

Barriers to peace education may vary from one setting to another. Elementary teachers may run into controversy when peace concepts clash with parental values. They can be open about their peace education activities, discussing them with school principals and providing justification to other teachers and school authorities, so that should a challenge or a question arise, those people who often have initial contact with parents are prepared to defend such teaching. At the secondary level peace educators can teach young people eager to learn about their own and other countries. Discussions can center around not just the hegemony of a militaristic paradigm, but on alternative security structures and everyday practices involving peace. Betty Reardon notes:

> Prejudice and ethnocentrism seem more strongly reflected in history and social education texts than in others. Further, history at the secondary level emphasizes wars, and only rarely the story of avoided wars or of events in which there has been peaceful resolution of conflict. Such history reinforces the attitude that war is inevitable, to be expected as a continuous part of human experience, and that there are few if any alternatives to war for playing out international competition in the pursuit of national goals.[12]

An obstacle for teachers of history is to find balanced material. Most history textbooks present in such great detail the accomplishments of war and the progress of technology that they contain little or no information about the peace efforts that have always existed throughout history. For example, emphasis falls upon the dropping of the atomic bomb and not the prior negotiations that were taking place between certain members of the Japanese government and representatives of the United States to end the Second World War. Interesting discussions might take place about why those negotiations failed and the bomb was dropped. Early histories of the United States underscore the war-like nature of Native Americans and neglect the deep peace traditions of certain indigenous tribes. Likewise, historians can study in detail the work of the United Nations in keeping peace and the role of its peacekeeping forces in troubled spots throughout the world. There are many topics that can be presented in history classes that provide understanding of the role of peacemakers in history. Unfortunately few teachers are prepared to teach such material because they have not learned it in school, and the material is not readily available in texts.

Many secondary schools support the Reserve Officer Training Corps (ROTC) and other programs that promote military service. As previously mentioned, military recruiters are an increasing presence in American high schools. For many young men and women, joining the military may be seen as their only option to better themselves. Peace educators can become aware of alternative careers for young people and students can understand that there are other options. Young people can become aware of the process of applying to become a conscientious objector, one who refuses to fight, and of the alternatives inherent in this choice. Since the armed forces recruit strongly at the secondary level, providing students with knowledge about their various options presents a more balanced approach to helping young people in selecting a career path.

Only five percent of the colleges and universities in the United States offer topics on peace and conflict resolution.[13] One explanation for this lack is that professors, steeped in the academic traditions of their respective fields, have their research and teaching agendas set by the established limits of their disciplines. Peace and conflict studies is a new discipline that largely grew out of concern for the nuclear threat, beginning in mid-century. Traditional academics may be reluctant to delve into new areas. International relations as a discipline spends most of its energy studying existing national configurations. History courses focus on the activities of nation states. Security studies present information about current defense arsenals; whereas peace education studies the prospects for a prefigured world to reduce conflict in novel ways. Speculative research in these areas may not receive recognition in traditional academic journals, upon which, in addition to departmental support, professors depend for their livelihood. Therefore, scholars may tend to avoid new areas of research and teaching which can sometimes be perceived as risky.

Henry Nash makes the point that peace and conflict studies require looking into the future and seeing disastrous consequences as a result of current policies.[14] Academics may be uncomfortable gazing into a crystal ball and predicting the future because they can't be sure of the outcome. Consequently, they may focus their efforts on the study of events that can provide a deeper understanding of current states of affairs, but don't point to alternatives for a less violent world. Academics may also be uncomfortable with the subject matter around war and peace, because studying these issues raises concerns that often imply action. College professors are committed to the notion of value free inquiry, and may be concerned that teaching about issues of war and peace may lead "to emotionalism, oversimplification, and even indoctrination.[15] If peace education is seen as engendering a conflict between education and indoctrination, academics might tend to back away from controversial topics to pursue their commitment to what they consider value free inquiry. However, as pointed out in a previous chapter, all academic approaches contain biases and reflect certain values. Peace educators present other sides of the war and peace dilemma not currently included in traditional academic subjects, so that students may have a more balanced presentation about these issues from which to draw their own conclusions.

Professors at institutions of higher education may face obstacles in getting new courses approved on topics relating to war and peace. They need first of all to get approval from their colleagues in their departments, and then course approval moves through channels within the university or college hierarchy. Curriculum committees debate about whether certain courses contain sufficient academic content or if they may overlap existing courses. At each one of these steps, peace educators can expect to be challenged, particularly with content as new or as controversial as some of the material presented in peace studies courses. Preparing for these difficult disputes demands time and psychic energy.

Professors interested in introducing new peace studies courses must make sure that their syllabi have strong academic content. They should discuss these courses with members from other departments who may believe that the subject matter offered overlaps with existing courses. Courses need to be structured so they don't conflict with other offerings on campus. These challenges are demanding, and college teachers need to prepare for them, as it may be that they will not pass easily through the layers of college bureaucracy. This is not to say that an academic need give up trying. Supporters can be lined up and teachers can be prepared to call in experts to defend the academic legitimacy of such pursuits. The good news is that hundreds of such courses do exist on college campuses. Professors throughout the world are taking the risks necessary to establish a new discipline in peace studies. The more people who attempt these efforts, the sooner peace studies will become an accepted discipline in its own right.

College professors are busy people. They have classes to teach, administrative duties, students to advise, and research agendas. Many of these professionals find it hard to drop their existing commitments to develop new courses or sit on committees to promote peace studies. Because there are few research funds in these areas, they may be likely to pursue projects in more traditional areas that have a greater probability of being funded. The irony of focusing narrowly is they may be avoiding preparing their students to take responsible action in the modern world. It can be argued that there are strong ethical reasons for teachers at all levels to make peace and conflict studies a part of their educational practice. Without such a commitment teaching can become a hollow charade that deceives the young about the nature of the world they will inhabit.

At the adult level, in churches and community settings, one main obstacle to introducing peace education is related to the overcoming of what many people perceive as apathy or disinterest about the world, particularly as it relates to global issues. Various programs teaching "how-to's" of community organizing mention that there is no such thing as citizen apathy. Apathy seems to be related to educators "not getting the message across" in ways that will promote concerned study and action. It can also be argued that individuals need to be able to relate issues to their own lives in meaningful ways. If the citizens in a given community are not concerned about an issue, those who have knowledge and awareness of that issue may be negligent in their presentation of the issue to the public and in finding ways to relate it to more individual concerns.

The arms race threatens all people in the world, not only because of the destruction it portends, but also because it robs valuable resources from society in general. Peace educators need to create educational programs that provide the general public with a greater awareness of these problems and to connect them with issues in everyday lives. By gearing peace education classes to a practical level, where students can gain a better understanding of issues that directly affect them, interest and motivation may increase. Lifelong learning can be geared towards helping citizens in all societies reflect constructively on the crucial issues around conflict and what to do about them. Peace educators must use their creativity to construct programs that move through the "conspiracy of silence" surrounding these issues, if the human race is to move beyond war and realize its potential to live peacefully on this planet.

Chapter 10

Moving Forward with Peace Pedagogy: The Basics for Teaching Peace

Education for Peace assumes peace in education.
Magnus Haavelsrud

So far in this book we have discussed the "what" of peace education, including historical and conceptual dimensions. We have also discussed some ways to get peace education started in the various settings and various obstacles and challenges in the teaching of peace. This chapter explores the "how" of peace education. It attempts to answer the question, "What is the optimal pedagogy for peace education?" In addition, we explore some of the dimensions that characterize a peaceful classroom. The discussion is appropriate for educators working with all ages and in various settings. Those who work in community settings might consider substituting the word "organization" for "classroom" or "classroom setting."

As previously noted, peace education is both a philosophy and a process. The philosophy holds values such as trust, caring, empathy, love and a belief in the transformative power of nonviolence. The process involves the skill of problem-solving, and its inherent components of listening, dialoguing, and seeking mutually beneficial solutions. An educator teaching for peace will use conceptual elements of both the philosophy and the process to structure both the formal curricula and also the more informal "hidden curricula" such as the manner in which students relate to one another, the physical space of the classroom and the "teachable moments," those unpredictable occurrences which can transform classrooms. Also important is reaching students "where they are," particularly with regard to their understanding of the elements of the peace process. Not all students will be at the same place in this regard.

In discussing characteristics that help develop peacemakers, Elise Boulding believes there are both internal and external processes at work. Central to the development of those who will "seek to shape their society's future toward peace" are several interlocking sets of inputs, which Boulding developed into a model.[1] Inputs include genetically determined behavioral "blueprints," maturational processes, learning processes including cognition, modeling and reinforcement, accumulated knowledge stock, cultural values and beliefs, the influence of family, peer group, community and the media, and socializing agents such as the family, teachers, peers and other adult role models. Total development is determined, to a large extent, by the cumulative influence of people in that person's environment—family members, friends, neighbors, people in school, peers, fellow workers, figures from the media, and significant others. As a child develops, family has less influence and peers and other adults more. Boulding places great emphasis on the importance of role models on the development of those committed to working toward social change.[2] Thus, the role of the educator can be crucial in terms of both modeling and mentoring. The environment in which a student learns becomes extremely important. Teachers have a key role to play in creating learning spaces conducive to developing the seeds of compassion and nonviolence.

In 1937 Maria Montessori said, "Our hope for peace in the future lies not in the formal knowledge the adult can pass on to the child, but in the normal development of the new man."[3] She believed that educators should establish environments that allow the natural peace-loving instincts of young people to flourish. These instincts might be characterized as concern for other human beings, aversion to violence, desire for freedom, and harmony with others. In classrooms committed to the Montessori model, teachers step aside and allow children to grow. Dr. Montessori believed that each child is a "messiah," capable of saving the human race:

> If at some time the Child were to receive proper consideration and his immense possibilities were to be developed, then a Man might arise for whom there would be no need of encouragement to disarmament and resistance to war because his nature would be such that he could not endure the state of degradation and of extreme moral corruption which makes possible any participation in war.[4]

A Montessori classroom is a carefully structured environment where children learn by freely pursuing their own interests, where they learn to cooperate with other children by working on mutually agreed upon tasks, and where teachers set up classrooms in which the children pursue their own self-development. Because, as Dr. Montessori believed, all children have innate tendencies toward compassion and care for others, such a free environment allows those capacities to develop so that as adults they will have dispositions that abhor violence and express concern for the well-being of others.

Peace educators, therefore, need to take special interest in the learning environments they create. An irony of peace education is that a teacher need not necessarily teach only the topics of peace education in order to conduct a peaceable classroom, which can be a manifestation in any academic discipline.[5] Parents can facilitate peaceful families without formal knowledge of peace curricula. "What is taught" is not nearly as important as "how it is taught" for the development of the skills and philosophical elements inherent in working for peace. Students need to learn the ways of peace. Devi Passad writes:

> A peaceful and warless world cannot be created by providing information and developing intellectual virtues alone, but, first and foremost, by fostering moral self-discipline and by making an aesthetic approach to education, in all its aspects and stages, for the development of men and women to their full humanity, and their capacity to live in creative peace and cooperation with one another and all existence.[6]

Such learning can occur in a variety of places but it needs to be intentional. For example, young children will be pulled in a variety of directions. Their friends will play war games. The media will expose them to killing and violence. Adults concerned about the effects of violence on children need to create environments that will draw out children's natural instincts towards peace and allow them to learn the habits of peacemaking.

What are the characteristics of such an environment? A good way to answer this question is to describe the type of person that environment should produce. Elise Boulding, whose work was previously cited and who is one of the seminal thinkers in peace education and peace research, provides such a description:

> The child who becomes an altruist, and activist, and a nonviolent shaper of the future is then one who feels autonomous, competent, confident about her own future and the future of society, able to cope with stress,

relates warmly to others and feels responsibility for them even when they are not directly dependent on her. She has had many opportunities to solve problems and play out different social roles in the past and her successes have been recognized and rewarded; she has been exposed to a wide variety of events, accumulated a fair amount of knowledge, and has a cognitively complex view of the world. She has been inspired by adult role models, but also nurtured and helped by her own peers. In terms of our model she has had optimal opportunities to develop each of her capacities, cognitive, emotional and intuitive, during her maturing years; her predispositions for bonding, for altruism, for play, for creating alternatives have more than counter-balanced her predispositions for aggression. Her social spaces have been filled with challenges she could meet, role models which have provided rich sources of complex learnings about possible social behavior, and positive reinforcement for her attempts to make constructive changes around her.[7]

Persons disposed toward peace will be saturated with the idea that human beings are born into a world that requires all creatures to live in harmony with others. Plato and Aristotle discussed raising the citizens of Athens with a moral judgment, a sense of right and wrong that meant the learning of something like good manners or good form—a dynamic concept of nobility, of virtue, of wisdom and courage. In order for there to be peace in this world, human beings have to live with each other in communities based on sharing and mutual self-help. The deep-seated urges that propel human behavior have to be directed away from violence and directed towards the peaceful resolution of conflict. People have to be free and courageous enough to choose the path of love and unity with all human beings, instead of the path of hatred, competition and the fragmentation of human society. People need to learn how to vent their frustrations and anger in ways that don't harm others. Peace education has to involve spontaneous creative activity based on respect for other individuals.

As Paulo Friere has pointed out, education can either domesticate or liberate. In order for peace studies to contribute to the creation of a democratic society, it must abandon procedures that are hierarchical and establish democratic classrooms that promote equality, mutual respect, participation, and cooperation. Research supports the conclusion that democratic experiences in schools can contribute to the knowledge, skills, and attitudes essential for democratic citizenship.[8] If a student is to be empowered to bring peace to this world, she or he cannot be a passive recipient of information, but must be an active creator of knowledge. If, as John Dewey said, "we learn the things we do," then students who learn to sit quietly as passive receivers of "truth" from an authority figure will

MEANS	GOALS	
	WAR	PEACE
Politics and Power	direct violence physical strength paternalism wars competition oppression win/lose	safety spiritual-soul strength participation negotiations cooperation justice win/win
Education	selfish behavior authoritarian methods traditional teaching moralistic explanations of behavior coercion structural violence	responsibility open classroom innovation causative or social science explanations of behavior self-motivation freedom to pursue interests

Table 1. A Typology of War and Peace

have learned to function well in an authoritarian society. Some methods of teaching are clearly more empowering than others, and peace education needs to rely on methods that provide by their example ways in which human beings can peacefully coexist on this planet. Peace education points to new ways of educating as indicated by the table shown above.

Using competitive rewards to pit individuals against each other, authoritarian classrooms are divided into winners and losers where students who are accustomed to a routine of losing may acquire a sense of worthlessness, helplessness, and incompetence. In authoritarian classrooms pupils are not able to participate constructively in the development of classroom mores and rules. In such classrooms children are governed by a teacher's sense of right or wrong, and the ethics of adults are seen as superior to the ethics of children.

A peaceful classroom, on the other hand, is an open environment where each student has an equal chance to learn, and the welfare of each individual is maximized. Students and teachers learn to interact with each other in constructive ways. Everybody contributes his or her perspectives on reality, and students and teachers together might set limits for behavior. In order for peace education to be moral, resting on the recognition that students and teachers share something of value with a profound respect for all those engaged in the learning process, peace educators need to establish trusting environments where "people might test their capacity to face truth and enhance their ability to change their minds."[9] This type of teaching differs sharply from indoctrination in which the instructor determines the agenda, and even from advocacy in which the leader rallies others to a cause. Peace educators don't consider themselves the possessors of truth. As advanced learners who may have examined the problems of war, conflict and peace in some detail, they engage their students in a cooperative learning adventure to determine what can be done about profound human problems. Teachers in peace studies classes exhibit humility within a truth-finding process. In peace education the student should not be treated as a passive recipient of knowledge but rather as a cherished human and fellow learner. In various ways this is true no matter the age of the learner.

Two brothers, David and Roger Johnson, associated with the University of Minnesota, have done considerable research into different classroom climates that help determine the way people interact with each other. They have discovered that there are three main goal structures for classrooms, specifying the type of interdependence that exists among students. The three ways that students relate to each other and to the teacher in accomplishing instructional goals are cooperative, competitive and individualistic.[10] A cooperative goal structure exists when students realize they can obtain their learning objectives "if and only if, the other students with whom they are linked can obtain their goals."[11] A competitive goal structure exists if students perceive they can obtain their goal "if and only if, the other students with whom they are linked fail to obtain their goal." And an individualistic goal exists when the achievement of a goal by one student is unrelated to the achievement of the goal by other students. [12] In this latter type of classroom whether or not a student achieves a particular goal has no bearing upon whether other students achieve their goals. In a competitive classroom there are a limited number of rewards; therefore a large proportion of students experience failure, and the environment discourages students from taking on challenges because they fear failure. Those students who are successful in competitive classrooms may learn that winning is the sole goal in life, and that people who don't win have no value. Bertrand Russell noted that a competitive philosophy of life, which views life as a contest in which the winner gains respect, breeds a vicious cycle where intelligence is ignored for strength.[13] Competitive people do not learn for intrinsic reasons. Their learning becomes a means towards the goal of winning. Learning should be rewarding for its own sake; it should not have as its goal getting the "better" of another person.

In a cooperative classroom, students learn to rely on each other. They learn together, and the success of learning activities depends upon the cooperative contributions of all. Everyone in the classroom has different capabilities, but they learn from each other in order to complete tasks. In a cooperative classroom, students learn social skills and democratic values beneficial to society as well as to each individual. Cooperative goal structures, as described by the brothers Johnson, create a democratic classroom where students have the freedom to participate in and influence the decision-making structures that determine their learning environments. Again, this can happen with any age of children.

Democratic classrooms do not imply that individuals are free to do whatever they want. Students may either determine how the class is to be structured or, using a Montessori model, rely on the structured environment created by the teacher, with their own input into what and how they learn. The important element is the classroom "ambiance," the way students and adults relate to one another. Is it with a "winner take all attitude" or is it imbued with love and caring?

Competition is not entirely eliminated in a cooperative classroom. Pupils will still strive for excellence. They will compete to complete tasks within prescribed time limits and to achieve standards agreed-upon by the group. Nor are all projects group oriented in this type of classroom setting. However, cooperative classrooms need have no room for the "zero sum" aspect of competition where when one individual wins, another loses.

Peace education builds upon the traditions of cooperative education to build democratic classrooms and rests on the following five principles of peace pedagogy. Peace Education

1. Builds a democratic community
2. Teaches cooperation
3. Develops moral sensitivity
4. Promotes critical thinking
5. Enhances self-esteem

These five principles provide a framework for setting up a peaceful classroom. Peace educators have numerous opportunities to use these principles to provide democratic learning experiences that allow students to practice and learn behaviors conducive to creating peaceful human societies. These principles, although they are meant to guide a teacher's style of facilitation of learning experiences and the mode of student-teacher interaction, can be used in homes, in school, or in community learning settings. They are not mutually exclusive. Some build upon and reinforce others. Together they provide guidelines for how to establish a peaceful classroom.

1. Building a Democratic Community

In order for there to be peace in the world, individuals will have to learn to live with each other without resorting to destructive violence. In keeping with the vision of Teilhard de Chardin, the world is becoming more close-knit, moving towards an interdependent community where individuals together will learn they have similar goals and will cooperate with each other to achieve those goals. In a global community, human beings depend upon each other. Citizens need raw materials and food produced in other countries. Companies need markets for their products, and we all depend on the planet Earth for food, clothing, and shelter. Human beings rely on each other for collective security and gather together into interdependent communities to satisfy their needs.

People throughout the world are forming intentional base communities to deal with the perverse effects of direct and structural violence. Peace education can help to build unified classroom communities, as model laboratories for learning democratic behavior. Where there is no sense of community and no sense of belonging, people will not develop a sense of responsibility for others. Education that fosters disunity cannot foster a sense of hope. In order to teach those values and behaviors required for living mutually on this planet, peace educators need to create classroom communities based on mutual respect and sharing.

To do this, teachers should, to the extent possible, shape their learning programs with the help and participation of students. This means, on the one hand, building programs based on students' interests and experiences, and on the other, working with students to determine classroom limits and agreed upon accepted behaviors.[14] Peace educators should encourage students to share their own experiences with violence so that members of the class can practice empathy and learn that their own frightening experiences aren't unique. They can also learn from each other strategies for coping with fears and anxieties that come from living in a violent world. Students with different perspectives will actively (and emotionally) disagree with each other, but hearing (and respecting) each other's views and trying to incorporate the views of others while figuring out what to do about conflict and violence becomes an important part of building a democratic learning environment.

For older students, in this democratic process of examining the causes and sources of violence in our lives, the teacher serves as a facilitator who keeps the class moving. He or she asks questions or provides new resources which shed insight into problems. Often opinions need to be clarified and summarized. The teacher does this in a way that helps relate discussions to the goal of that particular lesson. The teacher also checks periodically to see if a discussion is moving in a way agreeable to the group. Another important function of the teacher in peace education classes is to make sure everyone's point of view is listened to in such a way that looking at different perspectives becomes a positive learning experience rather than contending to prove who is right. The peace educator shows a warm concern and interest in the participants, affirming them for their contributions. Thus, the teacher in a democratic classroom becomes a mediator, one who maintains the cohesiveness of the learning group, serving as a powerful role model for peaceful behavior.

A democratic classroom calls for a dialogue among all individuals present. Individual members need to feel comfortable that their contributions will be heard. The teacher asks leading questions and shares his or her own experiences with conflict and ways to search for peace. The teacher encourages sensitively those who are reticent to speak and endeavors in supportive ways to discourage too much talking by those who monopolize time. An open dialogue between learners and educators requires respect and trust which are in turn the key ingredients of a community. A learning community can be shaped by participants sharing experiences from their lives. The instructor can, in turn, share his or her experiences and offer opinions as hypotheses, subject to collective examination. Such interactive pedagogy allows students to get to know teachers in new and exciting ways that enrich the notion of a learning community of intelligent beings exploring complex problems.

Noted Quaker educator Paul Lacey uses the term *Inward Teacher* to describe the process by which teachers help students discover their own joys of learning and the ethos of caring, for self, others and the world.[15] Lacey believes, as did Montessori, that within each student is a spark of the divine. The role of the teacher is to help discover and nurture this. Parker Palmer is unapologetic about using the term "love" for the process of what goes on in good classroom teaching.[16] Teachers must be willing to become vulnerable in taking risks. Palmer notes that no educational reform will succeed "if we fail to cherish—and challenge—the human heart that is the source of good teaching."[17] The essence of good teaching involves the intellect, the emotions and the spirit. The questions asked are equally important as any answers found.

There are many techniques that teachers can use to set up democratic classrooms. One of the most important is to get students to get to know each other at the beginning through a variety of introductory exercises. Students might, for instance, help determine a constitution for a class or at least agree upon mutually acceptable guidelines for appropriate behavior.

At the end of each class period, students and teachers should spend about ten minutes discussing what went on during the class itself. The purpose of such a processing session is not to rehash the ideas brought up in the classroom discussion but rather to explore how people feel about their participation and the participations of others. Such process sessions can help provide a sense of ownership for the class: We are all in this together. How can we make it better? What went wrong? What worked? How can it be improved next time? Processing a session can also provide participants with significant feedback about their own roles in the class interaction.

Becoming a participatory, democratic citizen requires more than an abstract understanding of principles. Behaving democratically is a way of life. Peace educators can prepare their students for this way of life by building classroom communities where individuals pursue their own personal goals, while remaining respectful of the goals of others, tempering their actions through considering the consequences of those actions upon other members of the community. By participating in the establishment of learning communities, teachers and students can acquire an appreciation for the techniques of democratic decision-making.

2. Teaching Cooperation

Part of existing within a democratic learning community is learning how to cooperate with others. In cooperative learning situations, teachers structure small groups to work on projects. Hence, peace studies pupils need to acquire group skills. The Johnson brothers label the collaborative skills essential for learning cooperatively as the following: forming, functioning, formulating, and fermenting.[18] Teachers in peace education classes can teach appropriate skills so that peace education students become proficient in group processes. They do this by determining what skills students need, helping students get a clear understanding of specific group techniques, setting up practice situations, providing feedback and support, and by making sure the techniques are used often enough so they become part of a student's behavior. Depending upon the age of the student, teachers can use this typology in ways that will benefit and enhance their classroom learning.

Forming skills are those skills which insure that group members are present with and working with each other. They help a group coalesce and include communication and group commitment.

Functioning skills involve managing the group's efforts to complete tasks and maintain effective working relationships among members. They include getting a group started, stating the agenda for a particular session in such a way that all participants understand what is expected. At this stage, group members should understand and agree upon a set of operating procedures. They should be able to explain or clarify what is going on to others within the group. Members should be able to paraphrase others' contributions, energize the group with new ideas, and describe their own feelings when appropriate. Functioning skills assist the group in operating smoothly.

Formulation skills include those necessary to build a deeper understanding of the material being studied: summarizing what has been discussed, checking other people's contributions for accuracy, seeking elaboration from others, and making explicit the reasoning processes used to support certain conclusions. Sometimes at this stage a group may have to present its findings to others—in which case the group needs to decide how best to communicate its conclusions. Such reformulation of the material can have important educational benefit to the participants in the group.

Fermenting implies a higher level analysis of what the group has accomplished. At this stage, group members often challenge others' points of view. Academic controversies arise which cause members to re-examine the material, to assemble rationales for their conclusions, or to argue for alternative positions. This involves the ability to criticize ideas and not people, to integrate a variety of different points of view into a single position, to expand upon other findings by group members, to probe for deeper understandings, to generate further answers to difficult questions, and to test reality by checking out the group's conclusions. These skills allow a group to reach high level conclusions that demand considerable intellectual rigor and debate.

Learning these collaborative skills is a lifelong task. Although people may be familiar with one or the other of them, a person's ability to use one or more can always be improved in new situations.

A key component of being able to work cooperatively with others is the ability to manage conflicts. To achieve a more creative resolution of conflict, people need to have the ability to improve their communication skills within group settings. Classrooms provide an ideal environment for testing out skills involved in conflict resolution. Peace educators can help students learn conflict resolution skills by setting up simulations or psychodramas, or role playing different conflict situations. Such structured role playing allows participants to experience conflict directly and learn from others who evaluate their performance. These skills can be used with families, churches, community groups, and at work. Ashley Montague has extolled the value to human communities of cooperation:

> It must never be forgotten that society is fundamentally, essentially, and in all ways a cooperative enterprise, an enterprise designed to keep men in touch with one another. Without the cooperation of its members, society cannot survive, and the society of man has survived because the cooperativeness of its members made survival possible—it was not an advantageous individual here and there who did so, but the group.[19]

Cooperative learning provides tremendous advantages for peace education students. Research shows that cooperative learning environments promote higher achievement levels among students and provide important levels of peer support unavailable in either individualistic or competitive learning environments.[20] Students also can acquire important emotive gains from cooperative classrooms. They tend to know their peers better, and the affection for each other they may generate from working together increases their motivation to learn. In small group settings, students encourage each other to achieve. Cooperative learning situations, based on positive interdependence among group members, teaches individuals to care for other group members and provides them with important survival skills that can foster good working relationships throughout their lives. This type of learning is inherently moral.

3. Developing Moral Sensitivity

The basis of morality is sensitivity and care for other human beings. Democratic classrooms provide good training for developing a moral disposition, because students get to know each other and they rely on each other to complete their tasks. In a cooperative learning situation, it can be difficult for one pupil to ignore another because they depend upon each other to successfully complete group assignments. Working in heterogeneous groups gives students experience with diversity and helps them learn to acknowledge viewpoints different from their own. This type of setting promotes appreciation of ethnic and cultural differences. Through the shared responsibility that takes place in group learning situations, every member's contributions are realized and valued in helping the group reach its goals. When peace educators involve their students in group projects, students can learn to make choices both with a view of what is good for themselves, as well as what is good for the group. Developing feelings of responsibility for others in learning can become the basis of moral thinking. Similarly, in real life, good citizenship involves working with others in setting policy and making decisions.

John Dewey noted that "all education which develops power to share effectively in social life is moral."[21] By confronting the real life situations which cause and perpetuate violence in human communities, peace education allows students to study in-depth social problems and their concomitant values. Peace educators can pose problems around war and peace as moral ones, allowing students to research political decisions such as the dropping of the first atomic bomb, the bombing of Dresden during World War II, or the escalation of the arms race. Examination of such dilemmas promotes moral reasoning precisely because the nature of these issues is so complex that they don't provide easy or pat solutions. To understand fully their complexity requires delving deeply into human nature and the type of social organizations that support militarism.

Carol Gilligan—in her book, *In a Different Voice*—has noted three stages of individual moral development (see Chapter 7 for further discussion of Gilligan's work).[22] The first stage is oriented toward individual survival. At this stage, morality is seen in terms of self-centered responses to sanctions imposed by society. People grow out of this stage as they move from selfishness toward responsibility, with an increased attachment to others. The second stage involves the increased social participation of an individual, toward a morality based more on shared norms and expectations, manifested as an increased capacity for caring. The highest stage in Gilligan's schema is the morality of nonviolence, where care becomes a universal obligation. Nonviolence, involving an injunction against all hurting of others, is elevated to a position governing all moral judgment and action. Peace educators can be prepared to foster this kind of moral development in their classrooms because of their understanding of nonviolence. They can promote nonviolent behaviors by setting up classrooms that are respectful of all members' interests, concerns, and needs. They can use affective group techniques that allow learners to practice nonviolence. It becomes evident that by running a nonviolent classroom, teachers model important moral behaviors for their students.

Peace education has at its core deeply moral considerations. Peace studies serves the cause of life at both physical and spiritual levels, promotes its preservation, and advocates the sacredness of the earth. Students in peace studies classes can think systematically about controversial social issues and rethink their positions on important social, ethical and legal questions, this through identifying key aspects of violent behavior. Students can explore different patterns of argumentation, refining, and qualifying their positions and testing factual assumptions. Peace educators, in a rigorous intellectual climate where all points of view are respected and issues are thoroughly explored, can use a dialectical style to question students' assumptions. Such an approach to the classroom neither teaches that all in the world is wonderful, nor does it gloss over the misfortunes of others. It does not teach selfish individualism where the goal of life is to get ahead, but rather poses a world beset by serious problems that require the cooperative efforts of people working together to find solutions. Paul Goodman at one time complained about the moral indifference of American people:

> It is appalling how few people regard themselves as citizens, as society-makers, in this existential sense. Rather, people seem to take society as a pre-established machinery of institutions and authorities, and they take themselves as I don't know what, some kind of individuals "in" society, whatever that means. Such a view is dangerous because it must result in a few people being society makers and exercising power over the rest.[23]

Peace education attempts to empower people to take some control over their lives by joining with others to reduce violence in the world. Peace educators can instruct students to exert influence in public affairs, whatever their views, by teaching them how to be competent citizens so they can communicate effectively in spoken and written language, collect and interpret information on problems of public concern, describe political-legal decision-making practices, and justify personal decisions on controversial public issues and strategies for action with reference to principles of justice and democracy. Through internships and other community-based activities, students can test out what they learn in the classroom to gain a better understanding of the political processes through which concerned citizens can express their moral impulses.

4. Promoting Critical Thinking

Hannah Arendt once wrote, "Thinking is the urgent work of a species that has responsibility for its survival."[24] It could be argued that the problems of war that threaten human existence have reached their current level precisely because humans, particularly those with political, social and cultural power, are not "thinking straight." What could justify blowing up the whole planet through the massive use of nuclear weapons?

Educators have for a long time supported the development of critical thinking skills in the classroom. Alternatively calling it reflective thinking, divergent thinking, reasoning, inferential skills, or analytic thinking, educators emphasize that students be given problems through which to sift. The important assumption behind this approach is that unless an individual achieves an understanding of the relationship of language to logic, that individual will not develop the ability to analyze, criticize, and advocate ideas. There are differences between the technical problems dealt with in mathematics, science, or engineering, and the human-social problems. "Real-life" problems are rarely settled in a rational manner because of opposing points of view, contradictory lines of reasoning, the realities of power, and value-laden assumptions. Because of the ambiguity that exists within the social and cultural "world," the type of critical thinking promoted in peace education classes must be dialectical where students are encouraged to hear other people's ideas and think through belief systems, moving back and forth between different points of view. The distinguished American anthropologist William Sumner described the kind of developed critical thinking faculty that should be encouraged in peace education classes:

> The critical habit of thought, if usual in a society, will pervade all its mores, because it is a way of taking up the problems of life. People educated in it cannot be stampeded by stump orators and are never deceived by dithyrambic oratory. They are slow to believe. They can hold things as possible or probable in all degrees, without certainty and without pain. They can wait for evidence and weigh evidence, uninfluenced by the emphasis and confidence with which assertions are made on one side or the other. They can resist appeals to their dearest prejudices and all kinds of cajolery. Education in the critical faculty is the only education of which it can be truly said that it makes good citizens.[25]

Participants in peace education classes must be encouraged to evaluate current policies of their governments, their own belief systems, and their action or inaction in relation to justice. The skills for doing this can be taught through social inquiry, a process which involves the following steps: (1) present and clarify a puzzling situation, (2) develop hypotheses from which to explore the problem, (3) define hypotheses, (4) explore assumptions, implications and logical validity of hypotheses, (5) gather facts and evidence to support hypotheses, and (6) form solutions. In this model,[26] the teacher helps move students from stage to stage by sharpening discussion, by focusing student questions and interests, and by providing advice. The students lead this discussion as equals inquiring into social problems and share the responsibility for carrying out the conclusion. The discussion should call upon all to participate. Teachers can provide resources and access to expert opinion when required. When handled successfully, this way of conducting peace education classes helps students negotiate and come to grips with different values that provide the basis for conflicts.

In order to learn critical thinking skills, it is helpful for students to develop their own tentative positions on issues and to defend them before others. In everyday life, peace education students will talk to people who look at events in a variety of ways. Their parents and peers may see situations differently from them, and students can be frustrated at their supposed inability to come to terms with these conflicts and dilemmas. Edward DeBono, a professor from Cambridge, England, who has promoted cognitive thinking skills, says that teachers interested in teaching such skills need to promote two distinct aspects of perception; breadth and change.[27] Breadth implies looking widely and more deeply at a given situation, trying to create a perceptual map that includes all pertinent factors. Change implies trying to see things in a different way to shed light onto some problem. Such an approach broadens a person's ability to see things in more complex ways and increases students' abilities to solve problems creatively.

Students in peace studies classes are, among other things, attempting to understand one of the most vexing problems confronting human beings—the use of force to solve conflict. Teachers in these classes help students understand that problem solving is not a purely cognitive process. Successful problem solving involves feelings, intuitions and hunches. In learning how to be a problem solver, a student needs to recognize his or her own feelings, tune in on his or her intuitions, and follow up on hunches in ways that either confirm or deny them. The affective side of human behavior, therefore, plays an important role in helping people attempting to solve human problems. Furthermore, problem solving should not be a solitary activity. Almost all effective problem solving takes place in groups. Problem solving is an inherently cooperative process in which several individuals get together to accomplish shared goals. Thus, a teacher's attempt to create a democratic classroom can help provide the basis for effective problem solving.

5. Promoting Self-Esteem

Peace education aims to overcome powerlessness so that students can successfully address the problems created by conflicts. Each individual experiences a complex series of events within their family and environment that determines his or her own self-concept, mental health, leadership ability, and interpersonal skills. Research shows that certain skills and attributes contribute to the creation of altruistic individuals who have the capacity to change the world (some of this is discussed earlier in the chapter). The experiences that help individuals realize their own power to create change are successful past experiences with problem solving; the ability to cope with stress; feelings of optimism about society, confidence in self, feelings of responsibility for the well-being of others; experience of emotional warmth, and reward for helping behavior. Peace educator Johan Galtung writes:

> At the heart of peace pedagogy lies the interpretation of our lived experiences: The first point is what everybody would assume will be included in a peace education program: analysis of our present, real world, describing its basic facts to the extent they are relevant for peace problems.[28]

People can experience in their daily lives feelings of fear that make them feel powerless. Sharing these feelings in peace education classes helps validate their perceptions and can build strength as learners realize these problems aren't unique to themselves. Others may feel the same way. This can lead to the perception of the necessity of individual and group action.

In a democratic classroom everyone's opinion is valued. Building class lessons around student experiences of peace can help involve students in the lesson and teaches them to value their experiences. By examining the social reality of people's lives, students can name and understand a world that is desperate for messages of peace. In peace education classes, teachers establish a continuous process of questioning, challenging, acting, and reflecting upon behaviors conducive to peace.

Such examination of daily experiences can help students to articulate an ethical stance in the world. For example, setting up a classroom according to Montessori principles implies letting learners explore at their own pace what they want to learn. Dr. Montessori believed that human beings have a fundamental desire to *work,* that it is instinctual for the human species to produce things (or ideas, or knowledge) and to receive feelings of well-being from productive activity. Accomplishments will help increase students' self-esteem. Therefore, teachers in peace education classes should provide students with concrete tasks which they can accomplish that will reward initiative and creativity. Research on cooperative classrooms indicates that students in democratic environments take greater risks which can help prepare them to be peacemakers.[29] Positive self-esteem comes from action. Peace education students need to try out in practical situations their hunches and ideas about how to bring peace to the world. Margaret Gorman writes:

> Self esteem is derived from significant others and from some kind of achievement. Although the significant others are primarily parents, teachers, and respected others, students who have been engaged in service programs consistently report how much the experience has helped their self esteem.[30]

Ultimately, healthy self-esteem comes from an individual's own sense of accomplishment, based upon their own sense of efficacy and service to the world around them.

Translating their thoughts about peace into action can help students gain a more realistic understanding of the nature of conflict and what to do about it. This is sometimes done through service learning opportunities, field placements and supervised internships where students can experience the daily reality of working to make the world more peaceful. With group support and proper supervision, students can gain insights into their own behavior and learn realistically about their own strengths and weaknesses as peacemakers.

Affirmation is essential to nurturing a sense of competence. So often students live in a "put-down" culture where sarcasm and downgrading are common, even as signs of affection. With so much negative reinforcement, it is easy to give up and accept others' judgment than to struggle both against criticism and against the difficulty of learning new things. Affirmation builds confidence. Though a true sense of self comes from a process of internal molding, hearing that we are doing well encourages us to continue to do so. Teachers should use affirmation activities that will help students feel they are liked and appreciated.[31] Being comfortable with and believing in affirmation and thinking clearly about each individual in the group are key elements in establishing an affirming atmosphere.

Other things that teachers can do to promote self-esteem in their classes include peer tutoring, advising, and counseling. When students help each other learn, their own knowledge of subject matter increases as do their feelings of competence. In some peace studies programs at the university level, students serve as peer counselors helping other students make decisions about what courses to take and helping them search for what type of career might best fit their interests. Faculty are often too busy to spend large amounts of time counseling students full of doubts about their future. Peer counseling can fill an important gap in peace studies programs providing students with important affective support in dealing with a frightening and confusing world. In some schools, such as the Open School in St. Paul, Minnesota, an advisory board of students and faculty determine school governance procedures. Working closely with faculty helps students by giving them actual roles in decision-making with authorities. Student participation in governance can help build democratic classes and schools, while it enables students to acquire a real taste for the problems and challenges of working cooperatively with others.

For many teachers, daily disputes in the classroom are the most pressing challenge to their conflict management skills. Teaching students the techniques of nonviolent problem solving will give them the opportunity to take responsibility for their own conduct. Teachers who have used cooperative skills that involve students in classroom management have discovered a reduction in inappropriate, nonresponsive and obstructive behavior on the part of students.[32] The influence of students upon each other results in more peer encouragement for achievement and greater attention to classroom tasks which students themselves have had a chance to develop.

"Ultimate" democracy in a classroom or a school is an ideal. It should rather be seen on a continuum, as a matter of degree, where on one hand the classroom is totally dominated by the teacher, and on the other hand the teacher and the student share as equals in all aspects of classroom life. Principals and school administrators can contribute to the achievement of democratic behavior in schools by making decisions regarding instruction and appropriate school direction in consultation with other staff members and students, a process known as "site-based management." Principals and administrators can model the democratic behavior they are seeking to foster. Supervisors can also provide opportunities such as in-service sessions on cooperative learning, summer salaries for staff to revise curriculum to include peace and justice activities, praise for teachers' activities to promote cooperative learning, and encouragement for teachers to visit other classrooms. They can also help establish professional support groups for teachers interested in peace education. Principals and school administrators can help establish a school climate that will reinforce the learning of peaceful behavior.

Large schools can tend to be impersonal and alienating environments, where teachers work according to a rigid schedule and students are submitted to impersonal routines. In recent times, some educators have begun alternative schools which foster more of an atmosphere of cooperation and experimentation. The charter school movement may be seen as one manifestation of this trend. Some magnet programs also address this. The Cluster School in Cambridge, Massachusetts, is an example of one such alternative high school. At this school, students and teachers have instituted a community meeting as a governing body where rules and policies are set for the school. No major decisions are made without consulting the whole school community. At first, staff members chaired meetings, but after time, students learned the skills, and they now chair the community meetings. Each meeting's agenda is circulated in advance, and all significant issues are discussed in advance in groups of not more than twelve. In this way students are personally involved in issues and a sense of community is developed. Students learn the empowerment of investiture in their own education.

Approaching peace education by the teaching of the aforementioned skills will not automatically bring about a sudden revolution where the world is instantly transformed into a peaceful kingdom. Rather, this might imply a gradual evolution where citizens who deeply value democratic traditions will work to see that they are maintained in their families, in their workplaces and communities, in their nations and in the world. Adoption of democratic procedures within educational environments may help to bring about a respect for diversity, valuing each individual, and the movement toward a general global well-being.

CHAPTER 11

Conclusion: Visions for a More Hopeful and Interdependent World

It is the skill of learning which is the greatest hope of the human race. It is the will to learn which is the greatest question mark. If the image-maker conceives his role as that of the printer, printing his image upon the plastic minds of mankind, then he betrays his functions as a teacher.
                                                    Kenneth Boulding

Peace educator Betty Reardon, of Columbia University Teachers College, has written:

> Education is that process by which we learn new ways of thinking and behaving, a very significant component of the transition-transformation processes. Education is that process by which we glimpse what might be and what we ourselves can become.[1]

Peace studies includes within it the emerging field of future studies which represents the study of possibilities, as opposed to past and present realities. Draper Kauffman notes that:

> The purpose of future studies is not to predict the future but rather to improve our understanding of the range of alternative futures which might come about and of the role that both chance and deliberate choice might play in either achieving or avoiding any particular future.[2]

In the 1950s Dutch sociologist Fred Polak carried out a study of western images concerning the future of the planet.[3] Polak based his study on historical images as well as those of modern times. He found that positive images of the future are highly correlated with societal ascendancy. That is, those cultures that hold positive visions of the future tend to fare much better than those who do not. In the fifties, Polak was deeply disturbed that there were few such positive images during the mid–twentieth century.[4]

> As long as a society's image of the future is positive and flourishing, the flower of culture is in full blossom. Once the image of the future begins to decay and lose vitality, however, the culture cannot long survive.[5]

Future consciousness represents working toward a goal. Although human beings are goal oriented, there are no crystal balls. Teachers and those who work with youth can't predict the future but they can provide students with skills and concepts needed to understand complex systems. They can help students identify major issues that will shape the future. They can provide an understanding of change and how to cope with it. Exploring the future provides knowledge of what is possible rather than knowledge of what is certain. Future studies attempts to understand large global and international issues, as well as those more local and community-based. Mary Claycomb stated in *People, Law and Future Perspective*:

> In other words, a direct focus on future studies can help insure that the democratic process adapts to the requirements of rapid change and remains the mode by which our country governs itself. What could be more basic to the concerns of the United States than the assurance that we are perpetuating the principles on which our nation was founded? The development of an ability in every student to recognize and provide alternative solutions to future problems should be one of the chief goals of our educational system.[6]

Rather than creating beautiful, optimistic images of the future, western societies too often are filled with hideously deformed images of the future, including environmental poisoning, nuclear destruction and terrorism. Some young people are having nuclear nightmares about their future. The arms races supported in so many lands have become addictive. Countries are borrowing heavily and stealing in order to maintain their habit. They are mortgaging the future of their youth in order to maintain expensive defense budgets that rob valuable resources from social programs. This addiction affects the minds of citizens as they contemplate with terror a civilization that has the power to destroy itself in its own search for dominance. Rap music, heavy metal, drug addiction and rising rates of teenage suicides are just a few indications of the negative effects of such images upon the psyches of individuals living in modern states.

Peace education represents a celebration of life rather than a support for the death-bearing values implied in violent militaristic cultures. Peace education confronts the horrors of these images and presents a vision of a different, nonviolent world. Peace education does not so much tell people what to think about the future but rather how to think about the future. Peace educators help students to vision and then to plan for the future. They can point out to students the already-existing peace loving aspects of human civilization and emphasize the dreams of those trying to create a better future. This type of education does not build upon one vision for the future but rather attempts to create a multiplicity of visions, to restore utopian thinking, and to encourage imagination. In peace education classes students examine how to take control of their own lives to work for a more humanistic society, based on social justice and human rights with equality for all. They ask the question, "What kind of world do we really want and what will it take to get there?"

Peace education allows teachers to use their creative energies to build a better world. The limits to human imagination are what are imposed through cultural beliefs. Reality is a matter of perception. As human beings view the world, they use language to describe it. To a large extent people's expectations determine the nature of their reality. Human beings have always faced scourges of different kinds. They have lived through plagues, suffered through wars, outlasted shortages of food, and existed in periods of drought. In spite of these calamities the power of fantasy and the human will for survival has charted courses for improvement. A proper goal for human existence is to improve the lot of all living things. Peace education helps students see the world in different ways, to examine what it means to be human and to develop a peaceful consciousness.

Many people concerned about nuclear and terrorist threats believe that they can no longer trust governments to make decisions about their future. With the advent of weapons of mass destruction the promotion of national interests has become terrifying. If these weapons are used to protect the sovereignty or to advance the interests of a particular nation, the citizens of that nation and of the world could possibly be threatened with nuclear extinction. As of this writing, President George Bush, as part of his "Nuclear Posture Review" (NPR) is advocating U.S. first-nuclear strike capability for "rogue states," as well as the development of "cute nukes," small weapons capable of massive destruction. This represents a reversal of a decades-old paradigm in which the sentiment was such weapons were to be used only as a last resort. Commentary published in *Sojourners* magazine in 1995 stated:

> To posit nuclear weapons as a response to a terrorist attack is to create both a political disaster and a fundamental moral contradiction. You can't credibly rid the world of weapons of mass destruction while, at the same time, preparing to use them. Nuclear weapons are themselves weapons of terror. Their devastation destroys all distinctions between military and civilian casualties, and that is the essence of terrorism—an attack upon innocent lives.[7]

With this sentiment many concerned citizens feel they can't continue with business as usual. They are feeling the need to plan a future different from what their government represents with its heavy reliance upon weaponry.

Educational means can create new visions of a future that is not so frightening. The destructiveness of modern weaponry has made many feel that war must become outmoded, and people are searching for alternative approaches to national security. This process of raising questions about the existing state of affairs has led to a search for alternatives. The first step in this process is visualization.

A more optimistic scenario for the future has been provided by Herman Kahn and others.[8] This is akin to a "Disneyland" scenario where technology solves many of the problems currently facing human populations. These authors predict that the population growth rate of the world will decline, that technology will provide many new inventions, such as the green revolution, that will help meet the needs of poor and starving people throughout the world, that nuclear power will provide limitless energy, and that the trends indicate a longer and healthier life for most of the world's citizens. These visionaries believe that capital investment will provide economic growth which will benefit the unemployed. They even predict a decrease in the price of oil. Their scenario rests on the success of deterrence theory to avoid nuclear war and suggests successful arms control negotiations. The authors state that the decreasing birth rate, which is already occurring throughout the developing world, will lesson the pressure of population expansion, and they predict that the Earth's "carrying capacity" will absorb the waste and pollution being created. Health care improvements will continue, and new technological inventions will improve common life. These authors discuss real problems that need to be solved, but their dominant tone is optimistic as evidenced by the following quotation:

11. Conclusion

In addition we do not say that a better future happens automatically or without effort. It will happen because men and women—sometimes as individuals, sometimes as voluntary non-profit making groups, and sometimes as governmental agencies—will address problems with muscle and mind and will probably overcome, as has been usual throughout history.[9]

The first step in this process is visualization.

One final future scenario to be presented here may be called the "transformation scenario," where human values are transformed from materialistic and consumer-oriented to generous and considerate of the well-being of others. This scenario has also been called the "Apollo vision" after the first human spaceflights which exhibited the earth as a blue sphere hurtling through space. It assumes that human beings are globally interdependent and that they will work together to change their values and to build a better future for the vast majority of people on this planet. This transformative vision of the future has been discussed by Willis Harman,[10] as he predicts that many people throughout the world are starting to question the traditional industrial thinking based on growth and materialistic progress. Evidence of this transformation comes from the revolution in the 1990s of electronic communications that make connections throughout the world much easier and more accessible. Further evidence for this transformative view was provided during the 1960s with the advent of peace movements, during the 1970s with the growth of the environmental movement, and during the 1980s with an increased concern about the future of the world as evidenced by local groups getting together to plan for the millennium (Y2K). In Europe and also increasingly in the United States, evidence of this transformation comes from the growth of Green parties that are questioning industrial and social policies. At the beginning of the Twenty-First century activists have been protesting the growth of various multi-national corporations and the policies of the World Bank and of the International Monetary Fund.

Evidence that individuals are trying to create new visions to transform their life circumstances comes from a wide variety of liberation movements opposed to tyranny and patriarchy that have been taking place throughout the world. Such a transformation implies a change in thinking and a fundamentally different way of looking at the world. It relies on human beings moving from "compulsion to compassion." It assumes that people can adopt a common goal to live together on this planet. In the transformation vision war is considered outmoded. As Fritjof Capra states:

> If one genuinely wants to reverse the arms buildup, one must make a commitment to fundamental changes that will enable one to break the

> military completely. This means a decision at the outset to work for abolishing both national military arsenals and the war system that brought them into being. Without that commitment for abolition, selected weapons systems may come and go, as arms control agreements rise and fall, but recurring buildups of arms, like the craving for a fix by an addict will always return.[11]

Global peace educator Patricia Mische has argued that nation states need to replace their notions of military security with concepts of "ecological security."[12] Military security is destructive of the environment and wasteful of natural resources. Ecological security emanates from trying to live sustainably in ways that preserve such precious resources as water and clean air, needed to nourish life on the earth.

The transformation scenario notes that in past times civilizations that have not adapted to changing circumstances have become extinct. An essential element in cultural breakdown is lack of flexibility and the use of military might to strengthen a decaying value system. But history also shows that human beings have at times changed their behavior. They have abolished slavery and colonialism. Transformationists hope to probe deeply into the human psyche and instill a belief that violence can be replaced with humane behavior. The transformation approach to the future hopes to create new images of reality which will then provide support for changing social institutions.

Under the paradigm that currently dominates human thought in the advanced industrial countries, the self-interest of people is seen as the most important value. This egocentric view allows the accumulation of fortunes and the conquest of nature at the expense of others less fortunate. The value systems of the wealthy countries exhibit a faith in the logical-mathematical structure of reality and in science and technology as the most effective means to solve human problems. These belief systems also rest on the notion that a state, whether liberal, Fascist, capitalist or Marxist, is the most appropriate institutional framework for solving human problems. This set of beliefs supporting western technology has created a world where, because of nuclear arms and global militarism, humanity faces the very real threat of extinction. Consuming over one billion dollars a day, worldwide military programs stimulate inflation, increase unemployment, deplete scarce resources, slow economic improvement for the poor, and increase environmental pollution. The military priorities of the present international system leave more than half the world's people without adequate shelter and health care, and half of the world's school-age children without teachers and schools. Overpopulation and industrial technology have contributed to the destruction of the environment upon which we depend for life. The deterioration of the natural environment has been accompanied by a corresponding increase in health problems of individuals. These urgent problems are crying for a new solution.

The modern industrial world has been brought about by a commitment to science and technology, to placing the physical universe on a Cartesian axis and describing it mathematically. Objectification contributes to violence while its opposite, empathy, may be seen as the root of nonviolence. Positivistic approaches to science have attempted to quantify reality, while reductionism has broken down the physical world into the smallest possible components in order to measure reality. This approach to knowledge relies on the relational left side of the brain and ignores some of the more holistic intuitions from the right side. Transformation theory seeks a fusion of both types of thinking into a view of an interconnected world in which biological, psychological, social, and environmental phenomena are seen as interdependent. General systems theory, which states that nothing can be understood in isolation but must be seen as part of a whole, forms an alternative to the Cartesian view of the world as consisting of discrete and separate particles.

In order to challenge the existing thought patterns that have created such a violent world, leading "futurists" are calling for a radical change in human belief systems: "What we need, then, is a new 'paradigm'—a new vision of reality; a fundamental change in our thoughts, perceptions, and values."[13] This "aquarian conspiracy"[14] looks for a turnaround of human consciousness in a critical number of individuals to bring about a renewal of society. The new values promoted by these new-age thinkers include nonviolence, economic well-being, social justice, participation in decision making, feminism, spirituality, and ecology. Such a change in consciousness can provide distinctly new ways of thinking about old problems and provide creative solutions to the problems that face human beings on this planet. "A new world, as the mystics have always said, is a new mind."[15] Until there is widespread change in people's attitudes, there will be insufficient political support for changes in major policies and practices that have brought the world to this juncture.

The Role of Peace Education

Peace education can play an important role in helping people clarify their existing values and explore the implications of new values. Michael McIntyre writes:

> Realizing that hope for the future lies in the young people who will soon be decision makers holding the world's destiny in their power, one comes to hope that the value systems they are forming are directed towards peace. How can children and youth learn to become creative, nonviolent social agents in a complex world if they are not forming sound values based on peaceful priorities.[16]

Through an educational process, peace educators can help affirm transformative values, even though those values may contradict the stated policies of their governments. The new values that constitute the transformative vision for the future, and in which peace educators are immersed, include a new approach to defense, the feminist challenge, a spiritual vision, and ecology and sustainability. Australian peace educator Francis Hutchinson believes there are several elements to educating for a peaceful future including actively listening to and engaging young people in creating new visions. We must find new ways of conceptualizing and naming what we think we already know about peace and open ourselves to new possibilities.[17] What is needed is innovative curricula, involving inter- and cross-disciplinary collaboration, continuing to build on a feminist model.[18]

A New Approach to Defense

In modern states citizens have handed responsibility for defense over to their governments and are dependent upon the state to provide security. The transformative vision asks individuals to rethink current defense policies to envision national security not in terms of the maintenance of the privileges of the few but in the equal distribution of wealth and power in society.

Defense itself is not a dirty word. Nobody wants to be defenseless, but citizens must also realize that the term "defense" covers up huge military systems that exploit people. A good example of this double use of "defense" comes from the proposed Star Wars system designed to use laser beams to destroy incoming missiles. If this system were truly defensive it would be placed on the ground. Placing it in space gives it the capacity to "zap" any spot earth and hence introduce a whole new range of offensive weapons into the world's arsenals.

Human societies are approaching a point where individuals are forced to choose between being violent and being victimized. In a world that respects individual freedoms and is concerned with democratic values, citizens would be given some say in their defense policies. Johan Galtung has suggested that citizens should have a right to choose their own defense systems. Do we bolster deterrence or do we look beyond deterrence?

Rather than defense policies being decided behind closed doors, they should be open to public scrutiny. There are many different points of view about defense, and these points of view should be widely debated in peace education classes. Some people believe that modern weaponry is the best response to threats from the perceived enemy. Others look for a way to diffuse existing threats by creating crisis stability, where it would be possible by using sophisticated mediation techniques to back down from threats,[19] thereby avoiding a military confrontation. They cite examples from history that have shown changes in such arch rivals as the British and the French, former President Richard Nixon opening the door for trade and exchanges between the United States and China, and the collapse of the Cold War as a result of the democratization of the former Soviet Union. Peace educators can explore these different options in their classes, challenging students to adopt alternative approaches to defense problems and informing students about the implications of defense policy.

An alternative approach to defense has been suggested by Gene Sharp,[20] who says that nations need to have a system of "transarmament" instead of armaments for self-defense. The notion of transarmament doesn't suggest becoming helpless and vulnerable, but rather it puts the power for defending the country squarely on the shoulders of citizens who are called on to resist tyranny. The idea behind this approach to defense is that the people have to figure out for themselves how to resist an enemy aggressor. This approach suggests that citizens do not have to choose between war and submission. The power of the state comes from citizens who obey laws and pay their allegiance to that state. People can, through training, develop a nonviolent defense where they withdraw their obedience from tyranny. Should a country be invaded and its citizens trained to use civil disobedience to resist the invaders, an invading force would be powerless. Currently the government of Sweden is considering adding transarmament to its defense system by training citizens to resist invasion nonviolently.

The first act of nonviolence in recorded history is in the Book of Exodus in the Bible where Pharaoh ordered that all male babies be killed. The midwives committed civil disobedience by saving some of the male children, most specifically allowing the baby Moses to float down the Nile. He ultimately helped lead the Jewish people to the promised land. Transarmament asks us all to be midwives to a life supporting and loving culture. We are challenged to respond to the genocidal actions threatened by modern states whose commitment to the use of weapons, often of mass destruction, threatens the destruction of untold numbers of innocent civilians.

Military might originates in situations where communication breaks down. Where an opponent feels that he cannot get his own way through negotiation and persuasion, he uses brute force to impose his will. Throughout recorded history humans have struggled to reverse this trend towards brutality, described as "the law of jungle" or "the survival of the fittest." In many countries, military might maintains political systems that otherwise could not survive. Laws and other civilizing institutions such as the United Nations have been introduced to propose alternatives to war for settling grievances between countries. Power brokers often resort to violence when expedient opportunities arise. Against these forces human beings have to introduce and maintain a civilizing process that recognizes the interdependence of all people upon earth. Are human beings forever locked into the "primitive laws of the jungle" or will they be able to build laws and institutions to protect the lives and liberties of citizens and respect the autonomy of people throughout the world?

THE FEMINIST CHALLENGE

Feminists point out that many of the problems associated with violence are also related to male behavior. Their arguments indicate that is primarily males who support wars, that male child-rearing condones violence, and that masculine culture oppresses. Female values are associated with nurturing, cooperation, and nonviolence. Cynthia Adcock writes:

> Militarism is primarily a male phenomenon, and the ultimate power of patriarchy is the organized, legitimized violence of the nation-state. For millennia, part of women's role has been to decry male aggression. We often see ourselves as posing a better way—a more loving, nurturing way of life than the masculine mode poses. Sometimes love and hatred seem polarized along sex lines.[21]

Feminists such as Elise Boulding and Sara Ruddick do point out, however, that women may be seen as, at times, cooperating in acculturating males to violence, through their mothering (glorifying sons going off to war) and that female warriors have always historically existed.[22] Thus not all feminine behavior and norms are associated with nonviolence.

Nevertheless, ten thousand years of history have provided a vivid image of global patriarchy dominated by wars and destruction. While the values of men seem to be heroism, patriotism, toughness, objectification, violence, and competition, female culture most often may be seen as reinforcing empathy and protecting life. The summation of male logic represents nuclear annihilation. The summation of female logic is peace and a world where children will be taken care of by both men and women. The rulers of male-dominated states use their power over others to wage an ever increasing war with life itself. Male violence against women seeps through many levels of the social structure, from intimate relations to the workplace where male bosses may sexually harass female employees. Physical violence against women may culturally be correlated with acts of war. Donna Warnock point out:

> Every three minutes a woman is beaten by her male partner who often claims to love her. Every five minutes a woman is raped, and they call that "making love" too. And every ten minutes a little girl is molested, sometimes by a relative, perhaps her own father. The violence mounts. Every few seconds in America a woman is slapped, slugged, punched, chopped, slashed, choked, kicked, raped, sodomized, mutilated, or murdered.[23]

Patriarchal cultural norms reinforce that men are superior and women inferior. A patriarchal society worships the masculine identity as expressed through power and the rewards it brings. The word "patriarchy" comes from the Latin root "pater" which means "to own." In a patriarchal society men own power. Wars and military systems reinforce patriarchy.

For the past ten thousand years, ever since human societies have been living in cities, patriarchy seems to have become a dominant way of life. Prior to that period, when human groupings were hunters and gatherers, anthropologists tell us that human societies were often matriarchal. What is needed now is to fuse these two identities together into a life enhancing force. The positive sides of the male character—the ability to take risks, the complex knowledge systems, and rationality, the willingness to provide and protect physical and psychological "boundaries"—need to be fused with the positive nurturing and intuitive aspects of female culture to create a new androgynous culture that is based on equality and seeks to affirm rather than destroy life.

The melding of these two opposite cultures represents the bringing together of opposite polarities to create a new value system. Such an approach comes from Taoism and the notion of Yang, which is seen as masculine, and Yin, which is seen as feminine. Yang represents rational knowledge. It is analytical and stands for ego action. The Yin represents responsiveness, the earth, the moon, interior, cooperation, and the self in validation to the environment. For too long the Yang has been rewarded in Western culture. Taoism seeks a unity of the two and the need to move towards a more integrative sense of power based on power over self, rather power over others—power that is expressed through cooperative relations rather than through hierarchies. In order to create a less violent future, individuals need to bring a peace culture into balance with the dominant war culture that seems to control human affairs. Peace education can contribute greatly to this process by legitimizing nonviolence in men and supporting the empowerment of women and children and the partnering relationships between and among them.

THE SPIRITUAL VISION

Spirituality may be considered to have become an important part of a new value system promoting a peaceful future. Here 'spirituality' refers to the strength of the human spirit and the reliance on a power greater than human, to use care and moral concerns to transcend particular oppressive circumstances, unify with others, resist aggression, and struggle against evil. Albert Schweitzer has defined evil as that which threatens life and good as that which affirms it. Human beings have throughout their history resisted evil. An important part of these new values being promoted through ideas of spiritual transformation is the image provided by Teilhard de Chardin of the *planetization* of human beings. As people become related through increased communication, they will also increasingly share the same image of a peaceful planet. Under this image, unbridled nationalism will give way to the love of humanity. Spiritual instincts that allow for the love of other human beings will generate a wider loyalty to a unified world that will abandon national sovereignty in order to adopt a collective security. This spiritual image of the unity of human beings can help promote world citizenship, where all the world's people belong to the same family.

Disunity is seen as a danger that nations and people throughout the earth can no longer endure. With spiritual energy and commitment, human beings can show mercy, compassion, and kindness towards all people. The spiritual mission of human beings seems to be to carry forward an ever-advancing civilization that will oppose warfare and self-aggrandizement. Such spiritual beliefs help people withstand the terror of violence and create alternative belief systems that will create a better future.

Deep within the human psyche lies certain archetypes. One of these is the belief in peace. Such a belief is manifest in all the religions of the world and motivates human behavior to seek to reduce violence. This deep belief in peace forms part of the spirituality behind the transformation scenario. It is a vision of all human beings working together to make the planet a safe place to live. It is a concern for the well being of other human beings. These spiritual beliefs may be lost in a technological world based on material gain, but they are a deep part of the human condition and lie at the heart of the various peace movements. Efforts to bring about peace in the world are a response to these deep seated archetypes and represent the spiritual aspects of human existence. Visioning seeks to capture these archetypes in order that they may serve to move us forward.

Ecology

The new values represented here include a loving respect for all things on the planet. The Earth is a living system. Its different parts relate to each other and maintain a delicate balance that preserves life. Human beings need to become more respectful of the complexity of living environments if we want to survive on this Earth. Such a view of the planet presents a holistic view where the well-being of all life forms on this planet are interrelated. Adding fertilizer and pesticides to the soil may be a good way to promote high yields and hence constitute a profitable form of agriculture for some, but those very same additives can over time kill many of the organisms that provide the richness that make growth possible. Sustainable development means meeting today's economic and social needs without compromising the world's future generations' abilities to meet their needs.[24] We have a choice. We can continue to pursue our own selfish goals and despoil the earth or we can promote ecological balance that will provide a safe home for the future generations that will inhabit this planet.

In some ways this spiritually transformative approach asks us to return to an earlier view of the planet held by Native Americans. Many indigenous people believe that the earth is our mother, and therefore the begged question is "how can we treat our mother cruelly?" To achieve a peaceful future requires an understanding of the natural realm and an attempt to live in harmony with it. Our very existence depends upon a healthy environment. We now have the material resources to co-create our future. It will take knowledge, with transformative vision, based on sound educational practices, in order for the Earth to be sustained in ways which allow equity and justice for all.

A new movement, called "eco-justice," has taken hold at the beginning of the Twenty-First century. This movement involves three key issues: environmental sustainability, equity and justice, and social stability. The developed countries of the "north" are obligated to share their wealth, materially and culturally, with those developing nations of the "south." Our world is increasingly interdependent and computer technology is rapidly increasing the capacity for such sharing.

A paradigm for the eco-justice movement is the Earth Charter, to be presented in September 2002 in Johannesburg, South Africa, at a world gathering on the environment and sustainability. The initiative first began at a similar conference in 1992 in Rio de Janiero, Brazil, in 1992. The Earth Charter Commission in 2000 approved a final draft of the document, including these key points: respect and care for the community of life, ecological integrity, social and economic justice, and democracy, nonviolence and peace. Within each of these key points are many action plans which relate to managing resources, preventing future environmental harm, eradicating poverty worldwide and affirming gender equality. These points are in harmony with the precepts inherent in the Culture of Peace Program adopted by the United Nations for the decade 2000–2010. The Earth Charter is at once an educational tool, an invitation to action by individuals and groups, a catalyst for change, a values framework and inherently a moral document, designed to provide an ethical foundation for the future of the planet. The goal of the movement is to seek United Nations endorsement of the Earth Charter by the end of 2002.[25]

It is estimated that the United States uses 25 percent of the world's oil reserves, most of which is used for transportation. Much of the U.S. foreign policy is based upon the ever increasing need for oil, with paltry sums being donated for research on alternative uses of energy, not dependent upon fossil fuels, such as wind turbines, solar energy, hydrogen generators and fuel cells. According to the Cato Institute, the U.S. spends $30–60 billion per year in securing the roughly $10 billion worth of oil we import from the Middle East, including huge sums for military personnel. We depend upon the Middle East for 56 percent of our oil needs. The United States holds about 5 percent of the world's people, yet controls about 25 percent of the world's wealth, producing 25–30 percent of the world's pollution. The richest nation on earth is the lowest donor of international development assistance on a per capita basis, compared to other industrialized nations.[26] Education seems to hold the key to helping individuals, particularly in developed countries, to understand the interconnections between material consumption, greed and ecological disaster.

Clearly a unilateral usurpation of much of the world's resources portends disaster for all inhabitants of the earth, not just for westerners. A transformative vision holds within it the central concepts of *caring and interconnectedness*, the notion that harming anyone or anything ultimately harms us all. Such a view cannot justify war on any count. War is disastrous to economic, cultural and environmental sustainability. As Peter Raven points out:

Globalization appears to have become an irresistible force, but we must make it participatory and humane to alleviate the suffering of the world's poorest people and the effective disenfranchisement of many of its nations. As many have stated in the context of the current world situation, the best defense against terrorism is an educated people.[27]

The tranformist view of the future depends upon educating for peace. There is no one blueprint for the future. Every visionary will have his or her own images.

Conclusion: Educating for the Future Means Educating for Peace Now

Elise Boulding, futurist and peace educator, has suggested the following exercise, which can be done in a classroom or anywhere with a group of children or adults.[28] Set a two-hundred-year framework (Boulding calls this the "200 year present") by thinking back one hundred years to what life was like and then imagine one hundred years into the future. What changes have taken place in the past one hundred years? What changes can you imagine taking place in the next one hundred years? How successful have peace activities been? Why? In this way peace educators themselves become action researchers, putting theories into practice. Futurists believe that we must *become* the changes we seek.

Peace educators often have an important role to play in helping people create an image of a better future and how to get there. Part of the exercise mentioned above is to imagine yourself some specific time in the future and imagine what the world be like at that time. Then subtract ten years and imagine what the world must be like at that time in order for the world to come into the fruition that was originally imagined. In this way go back every ten years to the present and posit at each ten year interval what changes should take place in order to bring the desired future into existence. This exercise can last for a whole day; workshops on visioning can cover several days, allowing participants to concretize their hopes for a better world by imagining exactly what must be done in order to create a less violent and more just world. This is based on the assumption is that if individuals can realize a desirable and realistically obtainable world, they can devise strategies to achieve it.

Peace education aims to fundamentally change the way that people look at the world and to contribute to a process where individuals agree on what the problems are and what must be done to solve them. Peace education can raise people's levels of expectation about what will happen in the future and the role they can play in determining that future.

Changing lifestyles is a very important part of peacemaking. How can we change the world if we cannot change ourselves? People can learn to have confidence in themselves, be patient, and to maintain a positive attitude. Peacemaking skills can be acquired in the home, on the job, in school, and in social life. Peacemakers need to keep an open mind in order to see many different points of view. They need to learn how to negotiate and compromise. They have to be able to identify their own feelings and the feelings of others. In order to change their lifestyles they need to understand ecology and learn how to live more attuned with nature. They must become good listeners and have the courage to act upon their convictions. If the vast majority of people in this world adopted these skills, the power structures of nations might just change, and for sure the daily lives of individuals would be more peaceful, and the demand on the Earth's resources might equalize to a point where members of the poorer nations would have a chance to share more equitably in the world's bounty.

The achievement of peace on this Earth and the elimination of structural violence is a matter of more than mere wishing. At some point individuals who want peace will have to start participating in affairs of the world in order to bring about desired changes. It begins with individuals defining locally achievable goals and undertaking tasks where they might achieve some success, because such achievements help to provide the confidence necessary to bring about more difficult changes in complex structures and bureaucracies. Peace educators can work toward improving their students' capacities for problem solving and do it in ways that maintain high levels of energy. The goal of participating is to help people gain influence and power in decisions that affect their lives.

It will take an enormous effort to change the problems in society. But it is possible. People working for peace who can achieve their goals create a sense of hope about the future. Peace education can help individuals, communities and societies gear up to wage peace. An important part of this effort will be peace research into the causes of violent behavior as well as into alternative ways of behaving and being. With images of hope, people can develop the courage to create a better world and to become the changes they seek.

Appendix

Syllabus for a Course in Peace Studies
Ian Harris

This is a course offered in a weekend program at the University of Wisconsin–Milwaukee. Participants in the course would most likely be practicing educators in various settings.

COURSE TITLE: Peace Education   COURSE NUMBER: 310-520-101
CREDITS: 3 undergraduate or graduate
INSTRUCTOR: Dr. Ian Harris   E-MAIL: IMH@CSD.UWM.EDU
OFFICE HOURS: Monday, 10:00–12:00, 1:00–4:00 P.M. and by appointment
Wednesday 1:30–4:30
Thursday 1:20–4:30
OFFICE: Enderis 553   OFFICE PHONE: 229-2326
PLACE: Friends Meeting House, 3224 N. Gordon Place
TIME: Friday 6:00–9:30 p.m.
Saturday 9:00–5:00 p.m.
DATES: Sept. 14, 15; Sept. 28–29; Oct. 26, 27; Nov. 16, 17, 2001

DESCRIPTION:

This course will discuss how education and community education can address the threats of violence, and prepares students to teach about peace, nonviolence, and conflict resolution.

This course is offered as part of a certificate in peace studies program at the University of Wisconsin–Milwaukee. If you would like more information about this program, please ask the instructor.

Appendix: Syllabus for a Course in Peace Studies

OBJECTIVES:
- To explore the role of violence in our lives and the lives of others
- To consider the effect of violence upon educational processes
- To examine how peace education can help deal with violence
- To provide examples of peace education activities and curricular ideas

REQUIREMENTS:

Students will be expected to attend all sessions. Because of the concentrated hours of this course, students can only miss one half a day, e.g. a Friday session or a Saturday session. Students who miss more than that are in danger of failing. If some emergency occurs requiring a student to miss more, extra credit work must be done to make up for this time. Students cannot pass this course who miss one whole weekend.

All students taking this course for undergraduate credit will be required to read two books and write three papers.

The books are *Waging Peace in Our Schools* by Landa Lantieri and Janet Patti and *Peace Education* by Ian Harris.

(1) The first paper will be due on October 26, 2001, and will answer the question, "What are the problems of violence that educators are facing in today's world?" For this paper students should refer to class discussions and the book *Waging Peace in our Schools*. Students are also welcome to do research for this paper since this is a popular topic and there are many newspaper and magazine articles on it.

(2) The second paper, due on November 16, 2001, should discuss the question, "What are the advantages and disadvantages of peace education as a strategy to deal with the problems of violence?" For this paper students will be expected to read *Peace Education*. This paper should describe what peace education attempts to do, discuss whether these activities make the world more peaceful, and evaluate the strengths and weaknesses of peace education as a strategy to achieve peace. Students are encouraged to compare peace education, as a strategy, with other strategies—peace through strength, peace through politics, peace through justice, and pacifism.

(3) The third paper, due on December 10, 2001, will be a curriculum on peace studies for the age level that students are working with, e.g., young children, teenagers, or adults. This paper can be a group project.

There will be an extra assignment for students taking this course for graduate credit. They can either (a) do a peace education project during the semester and write up the results of this project in a paper; or (b) do an analysis of Volume 71, Number 3, of the *Peabody Journal of Education* (Peace Education in a Postmodern World); or a report on the book *Peace-*

making for Adolescents: Strategies for Community Leaders and Educators by Ian Harris and Linda Forcey, or choose another book on peace education from the bibliography and do a review of that book, relating the content of the book to major themes in the course.

Participation by Students with Disabilities

If you need special accommodations in order to meet any of the requirements of this course, please contact the instructor as soon as possible.

Accommodation for Religious Observances

Students will be allowed to complete examinations or other requirements that are missed because of a religious observance.

Academic Misconduct

The University has a responsibility to promote academic honesty and integrity and to develop procedures to deal effectively with instances of academic dishonesty. Students are responsible for the honest completion and representation of their work, for the appropriate citation of sources, and for respect of others' academic endeavors.

Grade Appeal Procedures

A student may appeal a grade on the grounds that it based on a capricious or arbitrary decision of the course instructor. Such an appeal shall follow the established procedures adopted by the department, college, or school in which the course resides. These procedures are available in writing from the respective department chairperson or the Academic Dean of the College/School.

Sexual Harassment

Sexual harassment is reprehensible and will not be tolerated by the University, and threatens the careers, educational experience, and well-being of students, faculty, and staff. The University will not tolerate behavior between or among members of the University community which creates an unacceptable working environment.

Incompletes

A notation of "incomplete" may be given in lieu of a final grade to a student who has completed course assignments successfully until the end of a semester but who, because of illness or other unusual and substantiated cause beyond the student's control, has been unable to complete the final paper. An incomplete is not given unless you prove to the instructor that you were prevented from completing course requirements for just cause as indicated above.

Instructional Activities:

Classes will be held in a seminar format with the text providing background information. The instructor will ask leading questions. Students are to come to class with discussion questions and be prepared to share insights into the texts.

GRADES:

Grades for undergraduate students will be 1/4 for each paper, and 1/4 class discussion.

Grades for graduate students will be determined on the following basis: 1/5 for each paper, and 1/5 for class discussion.

Recommended Texts (Not included here due to the inclusion in *Peace Studies* of a bibliography.)

Suggested Course Outline:

PROBLEMS OF VIOLENCE
Weekend of September 14, 15, 2001

FRIDAY, September 14, 2001: 6:00–9:30

6:00–6:30	Introductions. Explanation of Course.
6:30–7:00	Warm up activity
7:00–7:15	Break
7:15–9:00	Problems of Violence in Modern Life

SATURDAY, September 15, 2001: 9:00–5:00

9:00–9:30	Reactions to previous night's activities Identification of interest groups for developing curriculum
8:30–10:00	Video—*There Are No Children Here* Followed by discussion
10:00–10:15	Break
10:15–12:00	Violence in our personal lives
12:00–1:00	Lunch
1:00–2:30	Brainstorming session on violence
2:30–3:00	Break & clean up

3:00–4:00 Brainstorming session on nonviolence
4:00–5:00 Images of Peace

WHAT CAN BE DONE?
Weekend of September 28 and 29, 2001

FRIDAY, September 28, 2001: 6:00–9:30

6:00–7:00 Reaction to Course Content
7:00–8:00 Discussion of book, *Waging Peace in our Schools*
8:00–8:15 Break
8:15–9:00 A brainstorming session on what can be done to bring peace to world.

SATURDAY, September 29, 2001: 9:00–5:00

9:00–10:00 Reactions to previous session
10:00–10:30 Lecture on Different Strategies for Peace
10:30–10:45 Break
10:45–12:00 Video—*From Fury to Forgiveness*
Small group discussion
12:00–1:00 Lunch
1:00–1:30 Video—*Five Desperate Hours*
1:30–3:00 Transforming violence
Small Groups
3:00–3:30 Break & clean up
3:30–5:00 Working in small groups on curriculum

PEACE EDUCATION
Weekend of October 26–October 27, 2001

FRIDAY, October 26, 2001: 6:00–9:30

4:00–4:30 Reactions to previous session
4:30–6:00 Discussion of *Peace Education*
6:00–7:00 Break
7:00–8:30 Varieties of Peace Education
8:30–9:30 Video—*Peace Education in Hawaii*

SATURDAY, October 27, 2001: 9:00–5:00

9:00–10:00 Reactions to previous session
10:00–10:30 Video—*Peacemakers of the Future*
10:30–10:45 Break

10:45–12:00	Discussion of peer mediation/conflict resolution
12:00–1:00	Lunch
1:00–2:00	Discussion of peace pedagogy
	Presentation of different models
2:00–3:15	Video—*Critical Thinking for the Twenty-First Century*
3:15–4:15	Break
4:15–5:00	Small group work on curricula

PEACE EDUCATION STRATEGIES
Weekend of November 16–November 17, 2001

FRIDAY, November 16, 2001: 6:00–9:30

6:00–7:00	Reactions to previous session
7:00–8:00	Violence in schools
8:00–8:30	Break
8:30–9:30	UWM Summer Institute on Nonviolence

SATURDAY, November 17, 2001: 9:00–5:00

9:00–10:00	Reactions to previous session
10:00–12:00	Work in small groups to develop curriculum
12:00–1:00	Lunch
1:00–3:00	Presentations of curricula
3:00–3:30	Break and clean up
3:30–4:00	Video on Costa Rica
4:00–5:00	Ending

During this weekend, the following peace education curricula will be available for review:

Alternatives to Violence (Cleveland, Ohio: Friends Meeting, 1984)

Choosing Nonviolence (Chicago: Rainbow House, 1991)

Conflict Management: A Curriculum for Peacemaking (Denver, CO: Cornerstone, 1983)

Choices: A Unit on Conflict and Nuclear War (Washington: Union of Concerned Scientists, 1983)

Conflict Resolution in the Schools: A Manual for Educators (San Francisco, Jossey-Bass, 1996)

Creative Conflict Resolution Activities for Keeping Peace in the Classroom, K-6 William Kreidler (Cambridge, MA: Educators for Social Responsibility)

Crossroads: Quality of Life in a Nuclear World. (Boston, MA: Jobs with Peace, 1983)

Decision Making in a Nuclear Age (Weston, MA: Halcyon House, 1983)
Developing Nurturing Skills K-12 Curriculum (Family Development Resources, 1992).
Dialogue: A Teaching Guide to Nuclear Issues (Cambridge, Mass: Educators for Social Responsibility, 1983)
Education for Peace and Justice (St. Louis, MO: Institute for Peace & Justice, 1981)
The Friendly Classroom for a Small Planet (Wayne, NJ: Avery Publishing, 1978)
Helping Teens Stop Violence, Oakland Men's Project (Alemeda, CA: Hunter House, 1992)
Keeping the Peace, Suzanne Wichert (Philadelphia, PA: New Society Press, 1993).
Learning Peace, Teaching Peace (Philadelphia, PA: Jane Addams Peace Association, 1974)
Learning the Skills of Peacemaking, Naomi Drew (Jalmer Press, 1994).
Let's Talk About Peace: Let's Talk About Nuclear War (Oakland, CA: Parenting in Nuclear Age, 1983)
Managing Conflict: A Curriculum for Adolescents (New Mexico Center for Dispute Resolution)
A Manual on Nonviolence and Children (Philadelphia: New Society Press, 1984)
Milwaukee Public Schools Curriculum, 1985.
Our Future at Stake (Oakland, CA: Citizens Policy Center, 1984)
PeaceMaker (Dublin, Ireland: Irish Commission for Justice and Peace, 1988)
Peaceworks, Kathleen Miller, Judith Walls, Janet Shank (Elgin, IL: Brethren Press, 1989)
Power to Hurt (Dublin, Ireland: Irish Commission for Justice and Peace, 1988)
So Everybody Fights? (Dublin, Ireland: Irish Commission for Justice and Peace, 1988)
Teaching Students to be Peacemakers, David and Roger Johnson (Minneapolis, MN: International Book, 1995).
Violence Prevention: Curriculum for Adolescents (Newton, MA: Education Development Center, 1987)
Watermelons, Not War! (Philadelphia, Pa: New Society Publishers, 1985).

ALL THESE MATERIALS ARE AVAILABLE FROM THE INSTRUCTOR

Notes

1. What Is Peace Education?

1. Ian Harris. "Editor's introduction." Ian Harris (ed). *Peace Education in a Postmodern World* (special issue): *Peabody Journal of Education*, 71: 3 (1996) pp. 1–11.
2. Betty Reardon. *Comprehensive Peace Education: Educating for Global Responsibility* (New York: Teachers College Press, 1988).
3. Ernest Regehr. *Militarism and the World Military Order* (World Council of Churches, 1980), p. 33.
4. Betty Reardon. *Militarism, Security and Peace Education: A guide for concerned citizens* (Valley Forge, PA: United Ministries in Education, 1982), pp. 16–17.
5. National Institute for Citizen Education in the Law. *Between hope and fear: Teens, crime, and the community* (Washington, D.C., 1995).
6. Statistics often referred to that provide evidence of this epidemic of violence include the following: Homicide has become the third leading cause of death for children 5 to 14 years old and the leading cause of death for young African American men. Counting suicides, a gun takes the life of an American child every two hours. Children's Defense Fund. *Ceasefire in the War Against Children* (Washington, D.C., 1994). Incidents of violence are causing problems in schools. One hundred thousand children carry guns to school each day. Each hour, on average, more than 2,000 students are physically injured upon school grounds. More than 400,000 violent crimes are reported in and around schools each year in the United States with still more going unreported. Chancellor's Working Group in School-Based Violence *Draft report* (New York Board of Education, 1994). Teachers suffer, too. Each hour approximately 900 teachers are threatened. Nearly 40,000 teachers are physically assaulted each year in schools. Louis Harris and Associates, The Metropolitan Life Survey of the American Teacher: Violence in America's Public Schools (New York: Louis Harris and Associates, Inc., 1993).
7. M. Pivoranov. *Towards a culture of peace: International practical guide to the implementation of the recommendations concerning education for international understanding, cooperation and peace education relating to human rights and fundamental freedoms* (Paris: UNESCO, 1994).
8. M. Berlowitz. Urban educational reform: Focusing on peace education. *Education and Urban Society*, 27(1), 82–95 (1994).
9. The October 1994 edition of *Education and Urban Society*, entitled "Conflict Resolution and the Struggle for Justice in Schools," highlighted the latest efforts at school-based conflict resolution. The February 1995 edition of *Educational Leadership* had a special section on mediation in school based responses to conflict, and the August 1995 edition of the *Harvard Educational Review* was dedicated to violence prevention programs in schools. *Phi Delta Kappan* has also produced a special report, "Standing up to Violence," R. C. Sautter, "Standing up to Violence" (Bloomington, IN, 1995).

10. It is interesting to speculate about why nonviolent theory has been not been included in debates about how to make schools safer. Part of the reason may be that the American public knows very little about nonviolence, so that educational leaders have no widespread tradition with a commitment to nonviolent principles to draw upon. A more likely explanation is that people in the U.S. tend to rely upon peace through strength and threats of deterrence to settle disputes. This is seen both in foreign military policy and civil responses to youth crime which emphasize a retributive model of incarcerating people who misbehave, instead of a restorative model of education and training to bring deviants back into the social order.

11. J. Galtung (1976). Peacekeeping, peacemaking, and peacebuilding. In J. Galtung (Ed.), *Peace, war, and defense* (pp. 282–305). Copenhagen: Christian Ejlers.

12. For a more in-depth discussion on the concept of peace, see Johan Galtung, "Violence, Peace and Peace Research," *Journal of Peace Research VI* (1969), pp. 167–191.

13. Michael McIntire, Sister Lake Tobin and Hazel Johns. *Peace World* (Friendship Press, 1976).

14. Paul Smoker and Linda Groff. "Spirituality, Religion, Culture and Peace: Exploring the Foundations of Inner-outer Peace in the Twenty-First Century," *International Journal of Peace Studies*, Vol.1, No. 1 (1996), p. 313.

15. Quoted in *Peace Is Possible* by Elizabeth Jay Hollins (New York: Grossman Publishers, 1966), p. 313.

16. Josezet Halaxz. "Some Thoughts on Peace Research and Peace Education." *Handbook on Peace Education,* Christoph Wulf, ed. (West Germany, Frankfurt/Main: International Peace Research Association, 1974).

17. R. P. Turco, O. B. Toon, J. P. Ackerman, J. B. Pollack, and Carl Sagan. "Nuclear Winter: Global Consequences of Multiple Nuclear Explosions," *Science, 222* (1983), pp. 1283–1292.

18. Walter Wink. *Engaging the Powers: Discernment and Resistance in a World of Domination* (Minneapolis: Fortress Press, 1992).

19. *Ibid.*

20. Ken Butigan and Patricia Bruno O.P. *From Violence to Wholeness* (Las Vegas: Pace e Bene Franciscan Nonviolence Center, 1999). This ten part program has excellent activities to engage students in learning about nonviolence.

21. Peter Ackerman and Jack Duvall. *A Force More Powerful: A Century of Nonviolent Conflict* (New York: St. Martin's Press, 2000).

22. Walter Wink (ed). *Peace is the Way: Writings on Nonviolence from the Fellowship of Reconciliation* (Maryknoll, New York: Orbis Books, 2000), p. 1.

23. J. G. Starke. *An Introduction to the Science of Peace (Irenology)* (Leydn, Netherlands: A. W. Sijthoff, 1968), p. 46.

24. UNESCO. *UNESCO and a Culture of Peace* (Paris: UNESCO Publishing, 1995). This monograph provides a complete description, including a historical overview, of the Culture of Peace Program.

25. Perrin French. "Preventive Medicine for Nuclear War." *Psychology Today*, September 1984, p. 70.

26. Everett M. Rogers. *Diffusion of Innovations* (New York: The Free Press, 1983).

27. Everett M. Rogers and F. Floyd Shoemaker. *Communication of Innovations* (New York: The Free Press, 1971), p. 176.

28. Ronald J. Glossop. *Confronting War* (fourth edition). (Jefferson, NC: McFarland & Co., 2001).

29. Georg Simmel. *Conflict and the Web of Group Affiliation*, trans. K.H. Wolff (Glencoe, IL: Free Press, 1956).

30. Ralf Dahrendorf. *Class Conflict in Industrial Society* (Palo Alto, CA: Stanford University Press, 1959).
31. Gerda vor Staehr. "Education for Peace and Social Justice." *Handbook on Peace Education, op. cit.,* p. 176.
32. Kinhide Mushakoji. "Peace Research and Education in a Global Perspective." *Handbook on Peace Education, op.cit.,* pp. 3–5.
33. Betty Reardon. *Militarism, Security and Peace Education.,* p. 38.
34. Betty Reardon. *op. cit.,* 40.
35. Betty Goezt Lall. Quoted in *Peace is Possible* by Elizabeth Jay Hollins (New York: Grossman Publishers, 1966). p. 287.
36. Thornton B. Munoz. "Working for Peace: Implications for Education." *Education for Peace: Focus on Mankind,* George Henderson, ed. (Washington D.C.: Association for Supervision and Curriculum Development, 1973), p. 13.
37. Adrian Nastase. "Peace Education in Socialist Countries: Problems and Opportunities." *Bulletin of Peace Proposals,* Vol.15, no. 2, 1984, pp. 163–170; "Education for Disarmament: A Topical Necessity," *Teachers College Record,* Vol. 84, no. 1, Fall 1982, pp. 184–191.
38. H.G. Wells. *Outline of History* (New York: Macmillan Press, 1927).
39. Bruce Bonta. *Peaceful Peoples: An Annotated Bibliography* (Metuchen, N.J: Scarecrow Press, 1993).
40. Thomas Gregor. "Introduction," *A Natural History of Peace,* Thomas Gregor (ed.) (Nashville: Vanderbilt University Press, 1996), p. xvi.
41. Sociologist Elise Boulding has done a great deal of work on this concept, also Kenneth Boulding. See E. Boulding, *Cultures of Peace: The Hidden Side of History* (Syracuse University Press, 2000).
42. Frank Hutchinson. *Educating Beyond Violent Futures* (London: Routledge, 1996).
43. Jaime C. Diaz. "Reflections on Education for Justice and Peace." *Bulletin of Peace Proposals,* Vol. 10, no. 4, 1979, p. 375.
44. Thomas Renna. "Peace Education: An Historical Review," *Peace and Change,* vol. VI, nos. 1 and 2, Winter (1980), p. 63.

2. Religious and Historical Concepts of War, Peace and Peace Education

1. National Union of Teachers, *Education for Peace.* London, England, 1984, p. 12.
2. Elise Boulding, *Cultures of Peace: The Hidden Side of History* (Syracuse, NY: Syracuse University Press, 2000).
3. This view is in many of Boulding's writings. This quote is from "Coming Down to Earth in Peace Education," address to 15th conference of Friends Association for Higher Education, William Penn College, June 1994.
4. Erich Fromm, *The Anatomy of Human Destructiveness* (New York: Holt, Rinehart and Winston, 1973).
5. Joel Kovel, *Against the State of Nuclear Terror* (Boston: South End Press, 1983), p. 11C.
6. Simon Weil, "The Iliad, a Poem of Force," in *The Pacifist Conscience,* ed. by Peter Mayer (New York: Holt, Rinehart, and Winston, 1966).

7. John Ferguson, *War and Peace in the World's Religions* (London: Sheldon Press, 1977), pp. 17–18.
8. Margaret Mead et al., *Cooperation and Competition Among Primitive Peoples* (Boston: Beacon Press, 1961).
9. *Book of Jonah*, 27.
10. *Talmud*, Sanhebrin 6:2.
11. Bishop John Wesley Lord, "Inaugural Papers," in *World Religions and World Peace*, ed. by Homer Jack (Boston: Beacon Press, 1968), p. 29.
12. Ferguson, *op. cit.*, p. 48.
13. *Ibid.*, p. 73.
14. Swami Ranganathananda, "Hinduism," *World Religions and World Peace*, p. 46.
15. Hollins, *op. cit.*, p. 167.
16. Ferguson, *op. cit.*, p. 154.
17. Desiderius Erasmus, "Against War," in *Blessed Are the Peacemakers*, ed. by Allen and Linda Kirschner (New York: Popular Library, 1971), p. 121.
18. Desiderius Erasmus, "Letters to Anthony a Bergis," *The Pacifist Conscience*, p. 55.
19. Immanuel Kant, "Perpetual Peace," *The Pacifist Conscience*, p. 74.
20. *Ibid.*, p. 75.
21. J. Pestalozzi. *How Gertrude Teaches Her Children,* L.E. Holland and F.C. Turner, Trans. (Syracuse: W.C. Barden, 1915).
22. W. B. Gallie, *Philosophers of Peace and War* (London: Cambridge University Press, 1978), p. 123.
23. Leo Tolstoy, "Letters to a Hindu," *The Pacifist Conscience*, p. 172.
24. Maria Montessori, *Education and Peace* (Chicago: Henry Regenery Company, 1949), p. viii.
25. *Ibid.*, p. xi
26. Herbert Read, *Education for Peace* (New York: Charles Scribner's Sons, 1949).
27. Teilhard de Chardin, *The Phenomenon of War* (New York: Harper Colophon Books, 1955).
28. Danilo Dolci, "The Maieutic Approach: The Plan of a New Educational Center at Partinico," *UNESCO Prospects*, Vol. 1, No. 3, Summer 1973, p. 138.
29. Marjorie Hope and James Young, in *the Struggle for Humanity* (Maryknoll, New York: Orbis Books, 1979), p. 105.
30. Johan Galtung, *Essays in Peace Research*, Vol. I, *Peace Research, Education, Action*; Vol. II, *Peace, War and Defense*; Vol. IV, *Peace and World Structure*; Vol. V, *Peace Problems: Some Case Studies* (Copenhagen: Christian Eilers, 1975).
31. Johan Galtung, *Peace by Peaceful Means* (Thousand Oaks, CA: Sage, 1996).
32. Johan Galtung and Carl Jacobsen, *Searching for Peace* (London: Pluto Press, 2000)
33. Elise Boulding. "Feminine Inventions in the Art of Peacemaking," *Peace and Change* 20, no. 4, October (1995), 408–438.
34. Gordon, Frank J. "Brief History of WILPF," found in archives, University of Colorado at Boulder in its *Guide to Microfilm Edition* (undated).
35. Birgit Brock-Utne. *Feminine Perspectives on Peace and Peace Education* (New York: Pergamon Press, 1989); Linda Rennie Forcey. "Women as Peacemakers: Contested Terrain For Feminist Peace Studies." *Peace and Change* 16, no. 4 October (1991), pp. 331–354; Betty Reardon. *Comprehensive Peace Education* (New York: Teachers College Press, 1988); Aline Stomfay-Stitz. *Peace Education in America: 1828–1990: Sourcebook for Education and Research* (Metuchen, N.J.: Scarecrow Press, 1993).
36. Merle Curti, *Peace or War: The American Struggle 1636–1936* (Boston: W. W. Norton & Company, 1936), p. 17.

37. *Ibid.*, p. 24.
38. Henry David Thoreau, "Civil Disobedience," in *Civil Disobedience, Theory and Practice*, ed. by Hugo Adam Bedau (New York: Pegasus, 1969), pp. 27–50.
39. Irwin Abrams, *The Nobel Peace Prize and Its Laureates* (Boston: G.K. Hall, 1988).
40. Curti, *op. cit.*, p. 210.
41. David C. Smith and Terrance R. Carson, *Educating for a Peaceful Future* (Toronto: Kagen and Woo, Ltd., 1998) p. 6.
42. At its latest conference in September 2001, 600 delegates from around the world addressed the challenge of "Learning to Live Together."
43. Charles F. Hawlett, "A Dissenting Voice: John Dewey Against Militarism in Education," *Peace and Change*, Vol. III, November 4, 1974.
44. *Ibid.*, p. 50.
45. A. J. Muste, "The Individual Conscience," *The Pacifist Conscience*, p. 348.
46. Stomfay-Stitz, *op. cit.* Much rich historical material is contained in this volume.
47. Stomfay-Stitz, *op. cit.*
48. Martin Luther King Jr. "Pilgrimage to Nonviolence" in *A Testament of Hope: The Essential Writings of Martin Luther King Jr.* James Washington, ed. (San Francisco: Harper & Row, 1986) p. 38.
49. Martin Luther King Jr. "Pilgrimage to Nonviolence," p. 39.
50. M. L. King, Jr. Remaining awake through a great revolution. In J. Washington (Ed.), *A Testament of hope: The essential writings of Martin Luther King, Jr.* (New York: Harper and Row, 1986), p. 276.
51. Priscilla Prutzman, Lee Stern, M. Leonard Burger, Gretchen Bodenhamer. *The Friendly Classroom for a Small Planet* (Philadelphia: New Society Publishers, 1988).
52. Report of the Commission on Proposals for the National Academy of Peace and Conflict Resolution to the President of the United States and the Senate and House of Representatives of the United States Congress. Washington, D.C.: Library of Congress 81-600088, 1981, p. 44.
53. Betty Reardon, *op. cit.*; Elise Boulding. *Building a Global Civic Culture: Education for an Interdependent World* (New York: Teachers College Press, 1990); Ian Harris. *Peace Education* (Jefferson, N.C.: McFarland, 1988).
54. Stomfay-Stitz, *op. cit.*

3. The Practice of Peace Education— What Does It Look Like? Types of Peace Education

1. For a discussion of Human Rights Education, see the special edition of *Bulletin of Peace Proposals* dedicated to this topic, Vol. 14, No. 1, 1983.
2. Elise Boulding, *Cultures of Peace: The Hidden Side of History* (Syracuse, NY: Syracuse University Press, 2000).
3. Adam Curle, *Tools for Transformation: A Personal Study* (Stroud, UK: Hawthorn Press, 1990).
4. Betty Reardon, "Human Rights as Education for Peace," in *Human Rights Education for the Twenty-first Century*, eds. George J. Andreapoulos and Richard Pierre Claude (Philadelphia, PA: University of Pennsylvania Press, 1997, p. 27).

5. C. J. Bowers, *Education, Cultural Myths, and the Ecological Crisis* (New York: SUNY Press, 1993).

6. David Orr, *Ecological Literature: Education and the Transition to a Postmodern World* (Albany, NY: State University of New York Press, 1992).

7. Susan Ahearn, "Educational Planning for an Ecological Future," Betty Reardon and Eva Nordland, eds., *Learning Peace: The Promise of Ecological and Cooperative Education* (Albany, New York: 1994), p. 121.

8. Derek Heater, *Peace Through Education* (London: Falmer Press).

9. Carlos Diaz, Bryon Massialas, and John Xanithopoulos, *Global Perspectives for Educators* (Boston: Allyn and Bacon, 1999).

10. Keith Suter, "Toward a Federal World State," in Michael Salla, Walter Tonetto, and Enrique Martinez (eds.), *Essays on Peace* (Queensland, Australia: Central Queensland Press, 1995), pp. 196–212.

11. Fairborz Moshirian, "The Emerging Economic and Financial Order," Michael Salla, Walter Tonetto, and Enrique Martinez (eds.), *Essays on Peace* (Queensland, Australia: Central Queensland Press, 1995), pp. 213–222.

12. Deutsch UNESCO–Kommission, Recommendations Concerning Education for International Understanding, Cooperation and Peace and Education Related to Human Rights and Fundamental Freedoms. Koln: Keutsche-UNESCO Kommission, 1975, p. 8.

13. Thomas Renna, "Peace Education: An Historical Overview," *Peace and Change*, Vol. VI, Nos. 1 & 2, Winter 1980, p. 63.

14. Bertrand Russell, *Education and the Social Order* (London: Allen and Unwin, 1932, 1972 ed.), p. 90. See also pp. 145 and 152–153.

15. For discussion of disarmament education, see *Bulletin of Peace Proposals*, Vol. 11, No. 3, 1980, which is dedicated to this topic.

16. Quoted in "Concepts of Peace Education: A View of Western Experience," Robin Burns and Robert Aspeslagh, *International Review of Education* XXIXX (1983), p. 330.

17. Tricia Jones and Daniel Kmitta, *Does It Work: The Case for Conflict Resolution Education in Our Nation's Schools* (Washington, D.C.: CREnet, 2000).

18. Richard Bodine and Donna Crawford, *The Handbook of Conflict Resolution: A Guide to Building Quality Programs in Schools* (San Francisco: Jossey-Bass, 1999).

19. Deborah Prothrow-Stith, *Deadly Consequences* (New York: HarperCollins, 1991), p. 176.

20. Janet Patti and Linda Lantieri, *Waging Peace in Our Schools* (Boston, MA: Beacon Press, 1996).

21. Edward Cohen, *Designing Groupwork Strategies for the Heterogeneous Classroom*, 2nd ed. (New York: Teachers College Press, 1994).

22. David Adams, "Toward a Global Movement for a Culture of Peace," *Peace and Conflict: Journal of Peace Psychology*, Vol. 6, No. 3, 2000, pp. 259–266.

23. "Annex II," *Synopsis of the Interregional Experimental Project on the Study of Contemporary World Problems*. Ed-83/Cont. 403/6 Paris, 8 July 1983, p. 1.

24. Recommendation adopted by the UNESCO General Conference, 18th session, Paris, 19 November 1974.

25. *Synopsis of the Interregional Experimental Project on the Study of Contemporary World Problems*, op. cit., p. 2.

26. Quoted in *Militarization, Security, and Peace Education: A Guide for Concerned Citizens*, by Betty Reardon (Valley Forge, PA: United Ministries in Education, 1982), p. 73.

27. Jaime Diaz, "Disarmament Education: A Latin American Perspective," *Bulletin of Peace Proposals*, Vol. 11, No. 3, 1980, p. 273.

28. C. Brunk, "Shaping a Vision: the Nature of Peace Studies." In *Patterns of*

Conflict: Paths to Peace, ed. L. Fisk & J. Schellenberg (Ontario, Canada: Broadview Press), p. 25.

29. The author (MLM) was asked to help consult, following a tremendous rise in requests for school trainings to Community Mediation, a Connecticut based agency teaching and facilitating mediations.

30. Robin Burns, "Continuity and Change in Peace Education," *Bulletin of Peace Proposals*, Vol. 12, No. 2.

31. Betty Reardon. *Comprehensive Peace Education: Educating for Global Responsibility* (New York: Teachers College Press, 1988).

32. Mario Borrelli, "Integration of Peace Research, Peace Education, and Peace Action," *Bulletin of Peace Proposals*, Vol. 10, No. 4, 1979, p. 391.

4. Peace Education as Empowerment Education

1. Theodor Ebwert, "Learning to Work for a Human World," *Gandhi Margg.*, Vol. 6, Nos. 4 and 5, July-August, 1984, p. 294.

2. John Dewey, *The School and Society* (Chicago: University of Chicago Press, 1915), p. 149 (originally published in 1899).

3. John Dewey, *Democracy and Education* (New York: Free Press, 1957), p. 82.

4. George S. Counts, *Dare the School Build a New Social Order?* (New York: Day, 1932).

5. Jurgen Habermas, *Knowledge and Human Interest* (Boston: Beacon Press, 1971).

6. For an interesting discussion of these various educational enterprises, see Ruth Propkin and Arthur Tobier (eds). *Roots of Open Education in America* (New York: City College Workshop Center for Open Education, 1976).

7. Frank Adams, "Highlander Folk School: Getting Information, Going Back and Teaching It," *Harvard Educational Review*, Vol. 42, No. 4, November 1972, p. 505.

8. Corinne Kumor-D'souza, "India: Education for Who and for What?" in Magnas Haavelsrud (ed.), *Education for Peace: Reflection and Action* (Keele, United Kingdom: I.P.C. Science and Technology Press, 1974), p. 110.

9. See Sam Bowles and Herb Gintis, *Schooling in Capitalist America: Educational Reform and the Contradictions of Economic Life* (New York: Basic Books, 1976).

10. This theory has been substantiated for American Schools by Colin Greer, *The Great School Legend* (New York: Penguin Books, 1972), and in England by Paul Willis, *Learning to Labor: How Working Class Kids Get Working Class Jobs* (New York: Columbia University Press, 1981).

11. Jean Anyon, "Ideology and U.S. Textbooks," *Harvard Educational Review*, Vol. 49, 1979, pp. 361–386.

12. See Beatrice Gross and Ronald Gross (eds.), *Radical School Reform* (New York: Simon and Schuster, 1969).

13. Michael W. Apple, *Ideology and Curriculum* (London: Routledge & Kegan Paul, 1972).

14. Fred W. Newmann, *Education for Citizen Action* (Berkeley, CA: McCutchan Publishing Corp., 1975), p. 21.

15. Colin Greer, *op. cit.*, p. 63.

16. For a moving account of one woman's educational experiences and its relation to her growing up poor, see Linda Stout, *Bridging the Class Divide* (Boston: Beacon Press, 1996).

17. Svi Shapiro, "Disempowerment or Emancipation?" *Issues in Education*, Vol. II, No. 1, Summer 1984.
18. Henry A. Giroux, *Theory and Resistance in Education* (Mass.: Bergin & Garvey Publishers, Inc., 1983), p. 69.
19. Gene Sharp, *Power and Struggle: The Politics on Nonviolent Action* (Boston: Porter-Sargeant, 1973).
20. Andrew Czartovyski, *Education for Power* (London: Davis-Poynter, 1974), p. 120.
21. For a good discussion of the struggle to create a nonviolent world, see *The Struggle for Humanity: Agents of Nonviolent Change in a Violent World*, Marjorie Hope and James Young (Mary Knoll, NY: Orbis Books, 1977).
22. Mayumba Wa Nkongola, "Education as a Stabilising Factor on a Less Stable World," *Education for Peace, op. cit.*, p. 290.
23. Magnas Haavelsrud and Robin Richardson, "Peace Education Theory and Praxis," *Bulletin of Peace Proposals*, 1974, Vol. 5, No. 3, p. 197.
24. Christian Bay, *Strategies of Political Emancipation* (Notre Dame, Indiana: University of Notre Dame Press, 1981), p. 81.
25. The original midwife metaphor came from Socrates but has been adapted by Danilo Dolci as the "maieutic" approach. See Otto Klinzberg, "The Maieutic approach: The Plan of a New Education Centre at Partinico," *Prospects*, Vol. III, No. 2, Summer 1973.
26. Barbara Solomon, *Black Empowerment: Social Work in Oppressed Communities* (New York: Columbia University Press, 1976).
27. Richard Remy. *Handbook of Basic Citizenship Competencies* (Washington, D.C.: Association for Supervision and Curriculum Development, 1982).
28. John Dewey, *Handbook of Basic Citizenship Competencies* (Washington, D.C.: Association for Supervision and Curriculum Development).
29. Robert W. White, "Motivation Reconsidered: The Concept of Competence," *Psychological Review*, 66, 1959, pp. 297–333.
30. James S. Coleman, et al. *Equality of Educational Opportunity* (Washington D.C.: Superintendent of Documents, Government Printing Office, 1966).
31. James S. Coleman, et al., *Equality of Educational Opportunity* (Washington: Superintendent of Documents, Government Printing Office, 1966).
32. For a discussion of community development education, see Ian M. Harris, "An Undergraduate Community Education Curriculum for Community Development," *Journal of the Community Development Society*, Vol. 13, No. 1, Spring 1982.
33. For a general discussion of affinity groups, see Murray Bookchin, "Spontaneity and Organization," in *Toward an Ecological Society* (Montreal: Black Rose Books, 1980), pp. 249–274.
34. Ervin Lazlo, *A Strategy for the Future* (New York: George Braziller, 1974).

5. Getting Started

1. For a more complete discussion of how to organize for public peace education activities, see *Organizing Manual: A Guide for Planning Educational Activities on Nuclear War and Arms Control* (Union of Concerned Scientists, 26 Church Street, Cambridge, MA 02238).
2. Betty Reardon, *Militarization, Security, and Peace Education: A Guide for Concerned Citizens* (Valley Forge, PA: United Ministries in Education, 1982), p. 77.

3. For a presentation on how to conduct adult educational programs, see Connie Johnson, *Living Our Visions of Peace* (New York: Friendship Press, 1984).

4. John Dewey, *Democracy and Education* (New York: Macmillan, 1916), p. 10.

5. Alfred North Whitehead, *The Aims of Education* (New York: Macmillan, 1929), pp. 10–11.

6. Derek Heater, *Peace Through Education: The Contribution of the Council for Education in World Citizenship* (London: The Falmer Press, 1984), p. 146.

7. For an example of the wide variety of college courses that can contain justice and peace concerns, see Dick Ringler (ed.), *Nuclear War: A Teaching Guide. Bulletin of the Atomic Scientists*, December 1984.

8. Ralph W. Tyler, *Basic Principles of Curriculum and Instruction* (Chicago: University of Chicago Press, 1979), p. 123.

9. William A. Schubert, *Curriculum: Perspective, Paradigm, and Possibility* (New York: Macmillan Publishing, 1986), p. 379.

10. Kurt Lewin, *Resolving Social Conflicts* (New York: Harper, 1948).

11. Margaret Lindsey, "Decision-Making and the Teacher," in A. Harry Passou (ed.), *Curriculum Crossroads* (New York: Teachers College Press, 1962), p. 39.

12. Ronald Lippert, et al., "The Teacher as Innovator, Seeker and Sharer of New Practices," in Richard I. Miller (ed.), *Perspectives on Educational Change* (New York: Appleton, 1967), Chapter 13.

13. *Ibid.*, p. 308.

14. For a listing of these programs, see Mary E. Finn, "Peace Education and Teacher Education," *Peace and Change*, Vol. 10, No. 2, Summer 1984, pp. 53–70. Though the reference is dated, the authors believe this is still the case.

15. Robin Richardson, "The Process of Reflection Workshops and Seminars in Peace Education," *Bulletin of Peace Proposals*, Vol. 10, No. 2 (1979), pp. 407–413.

16. Finn, *op. cit.*, p. 54.

6. Essential Concepts for the Teaching of Peace

1. Leonard Berkowitz, "The Concept of Aggressive Drive: Some Additional Considerations," *Advances in Experimental Social Psychology*, Vol. 2, ed., L. Berkowitz (New York: Academic Press, 1967), p. 302.

2. Konrad Lorenz, *The Territorial Imperative* (New York: Atheneum, 1961).

3. Laurel Holiday, *The Violent Sex: Male Psychobiology and the Evolution of Consciousness* (Guerneville, California: Bluestocking Books, 1978).

4. Sigmund Freud, *Civilization and Its Discontent* (New York: Norton, 1930).

5. Klaus R. Schever, Ronald P. Abeles, and Claude S. Fischer, *Human Aggression and Conflict* (Englewood Cliffs, New Jersey: Prentice-Hall, 1975).

6. One excellent booklet by David Adams is entitled *Psychology for Peace Activists* (New Haven, CT: The Advocate Press, 1995).

7. Adams, *Psychology for Peace Activists*, p. 78.

8. Adams, *Psychology for Peace Activists*, p. 79.

9. David Barash. "Evolution, Males and Violence." *The Chronicle of Higher Education,* May 24, 2002. See also Barash and Judith Eve Lipton, *Gender Gap: The Biology of Male-Female Differences* (Transaction Books, 2002).

10. *Ibid.*

11. Vamik D. Volkan, *The Need to Have Enemies and Allies: From Clinical Practice to International Relationships* (Northvale, N.J.: Jason Aronson, 1988).

12. William Broyles, Jr., "Why Men Love War," *Esquire*, November 1984, Vol. 102, No. 5, p. 61.

13. Andrew Schmookler, *The Parable of the Tribes* (Albany: State University of New York Press, 1995).

14. Quoted in *Stop Nuclear War! A Handbook*, David P. Barash and Judith Lipton (New York: Grove Press, 1982), p. 326.

15. Helen Caldicott, *Missile Envy: The Arms Peace and Nuclear War* (New York: William Morrow and Company, Inc., 1984).

16. Seymour Melman, *The Permanent War Economy* (New York: Simon and Schuster, 1974).

17. R. D. Turco, O. B. Toon T. P. Ackerman, J. B. Pollock, and Carl Sagan, "Nuclear Winter: Global Consequences of Multiple Nuclear Explosions," *Science*, 222 (1983), pp. 1283–1292.

18. Ronald J. Glossop, *Confronting War: An Examination of Humanity's Most Pressing Problem* (Jefferson, North Carolina: McFarland, 1983), p. 179.

19. Elise Boulding, *Building a Global Civic Culture: Education for an Interdependent World* (Syracuse: Syracuse University Press, 1988).

20. For an excellent in-depth discussion of the role of the UN in peacekeeping, see Victoria Holt, *Briefing Book on Peacekeeping* (Washington D.C.: Council for a Livable World Education Fund, 1994).

21. Elise Boulding, "The United Nations: A Bridge to the Future," *World Outlook*, Winter 1987, p. 110–115.

22. David Adams, "A New Vision of Peace for the 21st Century," *Journal of the Nuclear Age Foundation*, Spring 1999, pp. 4–5.

23. David Adams, p. 5.

24. David Adams, "International Decade for a Culture of Peace and Nonviolence for the Children of the World," UN General Assembly Report, 12 September 2000 (A 55/377).

25. *Ibid.*

26. Richard A. Falk, "Contending Approaches to World Order," *Peace and World Order Studies* (New York: Transnational Academic Program, Institute for World Order, 777 United Nations Plaza, New York, NY, 10017), p. 29.

27. Author unknown, "The Economist: The Non-Governmental Order," *The Economist*, December 11–17, 1999 (obtained via the Internet).

28. Elise Boulding, "Feminist Inventions in the Art of Peacemaking," *Peace and Change*, Vol. 20, No. 4, October 1995, pp. 408–438.

29. Boulding uses this term in several of her writings. For her most complete analysis of NGOs, see *Building a Global Civic Culture* (Syracuse: Syracuse University Press, 1990 (originally published in 1988 by Teachers College Press) and *Cultures of Peace: the hidden side of history*, (Syracuse: Syracuse University Press, 2000).

30. The author (Morrison) first learned about this educational strategy from interviewing Elise Boulding, who did this in all of her university classes.

31. Joah A. Stepis, "Conflict Resolution Strategies," *Annual Handbook for Group Facilitators* (San Diego: University Associates, 1973), p. 139.

32. For further information about this approach to conflict resolution, contact Martin Luther King Center, 449 Auburn Ave., N.E. Atlanta, Georgia, 30312.

33. Roger Fisher and William Ury, *Getting to Yes* (New York: Penguin Books, 1983), p. 14.

34. Candice Carter. "Conflict Resolution at School: Building Compassionate Communities," *Social Alternatives,* Vol. 21, no.1 (January 2002).

35. *Ibid.*

36. Charles Lerch. "Peace Building Through Reconciliation," *International Journal of Peace Studies*, Vol. 5, no. 2, Autumn/Winter (2000), pp. 61–76.

37. This quote is from *Making Peace Where I Live*, a peace education curriculum written and developed by Boulding, the author (Morrison) and three other peace educators: Lyn Haas, Cynthia Cohen and Gail Jacobson. It is a curriculum for 10 to 12 year olds, has been distributed internationally and is designed to teach the skills of oral history so that young people may interview local peacemakers in their communities.

38. Lerche, *op. cit.*, p. 62.

39. "Restorative Justice for Victims, Communities and Offenders," Produced by the Center for Restorative Justice and Mediation, School of Social Work, University of Minnesota in Cooperation with the Minnesota Department of Corrections, Balanced and Restorative Justice Project and the National Organization for Victim Assistance, 1996.

40. Tristan Anne Borer. "Truth, Reconciliation and Justice." *Peace Review*, vol. 11, no.2, June (1999), pp. 303–309.

41. *Ibid.* p. 304.

42. Howard Zehr. *Changing Lenses* (Scottdale, PA: Herald Press, 1990).

43. *Ibid.*, p. 102.

44. Zehr, *op. cit.*

45. "Restorative Justice," University of Minnesota School of Social Work, *op. cit.*

46. Toh Swee Hin, "Education for Peace: Towards a Millennium of Well-Being." Paper for the Working Document of the International Conference on Culture of Peace and Governance (Maputo, Mozambique, 1–4 September 1997). Thanks to David Adams for the gift of this paper.

47. This definition is taken off of the web site of the Center for Nonviolence and Peace Studies at the University of Rhode Island. The director, Dr. Bernard Lafayette, worked closely with Martin Luther King, Jr., during the Freedom Movement (also called the Civil Rights movement).

48. *Ibid.*

49. Ken Butigan, Patricia Bruno O.P., *From Violence to Wholeness*: A Ten Part Program in the Spirituality and Practice of Active nonviolence, (Las Vegas, Nevada: Pace e Bene Franciscon Nonviolence Center, 1999).

50. Quotes from Gandhi used in this paper come from the book *All Men are Brothers*, which is a collection of quotes from Mohandas Gandhi. This book is edited by Krishna Kripilani, hence his name appears under each quote (New York: Continuum, 1992).

51. K. Kripilani, Ed. *Mahatma Gandhi: All Men Are Brothers* (New York: Continuum, 1992), p. 142.

52. *Ibid.*, p. 143.

53. *Ibid.*, p. 73.

54. M. Gandhi. *An Autobiography: Or the Story of My Experiments with Truth* (Ahmadabad: Navijan Publishing House, 1948).

55. M. Gandhi (1937, December 31). *Young India*, p. 3.

56. M. L. King, Jr., "Love, Law, and Civil Disobedience," in *A Testament of Hope: The Essential Writings of Martin Luther King, Jr.*, James Washington, ed. (New York: Harper and Row, 1986), p. 51.

57. G. Sharp, *Civilian-Based Defense: A Post-Military Weapons System* (Princeton, NJ: Princeton University Press, 1989).

58. *Agape* comes from the Greek. It implies an unconditional positive regard for all human beings simply because they are human.

59. M. L. King, Jr. "Remaining awake through a great revolution." In J. Washington

(Ed.), *A Testament of Hope: The Essential Writings of Martin Luther King, Jr.* (New York: Harper and Row, 1986), p. 276.

60. J. Krishnamurti. *Education and the Significance of Life.* New York: Harper and Row, p. 51.

61. *Ibid.*, p. 64.

62. This is similar to Rousseau's concept of *amour propre,* which leads the individual away from selfish concern for self to an understanding of each person's interdependence with other human beings.

63. Krishnamurti, *op. cit.*, p. 113.

64. For an example, see Dr. King's own account of the Montgomery Bus Boycott, *Strive Toward Freedom* (San Francisco, Harper, 1986).

65. See M. L. Ulin, *Death and Dying Education* (Washington, D.C: National Education Association, 1977).

66. Krishnamurti, *op. cit.*, p. 78.

67. See D. W. Johnson, R. T. Johnson, E. J. Holubec, & P. Roy, *Circles of Learning* (Washington, D.C.: Association for Supervision and Curriculum Development, 1984).

68. See a special edition of the *Phi Delta Kappan* (May 1995, Volume 76, Number 9), dedicated to caring in schools.

69. Tony Wagner, "Why Nuclear Education?" *Educational Leadership,* May 1983, p. 41.

7. Foundations for Educating for Peace

1. Jean Piaget, "Intellectual Evolution from Adolescence to Adulthood," *Human Development*, Vol. 15, 1972, pp. 1–12.

2. Sheldon Berman. *Children's Social Consciousness and the Development of Social Responsibility* (Albany: SUNY Press, 1997).

3. Berman, p. 16.

4. Berman, p. 39.

5. Elise Boulding, *One Small Plot of Heaven: Reflections on Family Life by a Quaker Sociologist* (Wallingford, PA: Pendle Hill Press, 1989).

6. *One Small Plot of Heaven,* preface. (Based on an earlier essay, "Friends' Testimonies in the Home.")

7. Robin Carr Morse and Meredith Wiley. *Ghosts from the Nursery: Tracing the Roots of Violence* (New York: Atlantic Monthly Press, 1997), p. 74.

8. *Ibid.*

9. *Ibid.*

10. Judith Myers-Walls and Peter Somlai (eds.). *Families as Educators for Global Citizenship* (Aldershot, UK: Ashgate Publishing, 2001).

11. *Ibid.*

12. *Ibid.*, p. 179.

13. Educators for Social Responsibility, *Perspectives: A Teaching Guide to Concepts of Peace* (Cambridge, Mass.: ERS, 1983), p. 28.

14. James and Kathleen McGinnis, *Parenting for Peace and Justice* (Maryknoll: Orbis Books, 1983), p. 27.

15. Nel Noddings, *The Challenge to Care in Schools: An Alternative Approach to Education* (New York: Teachers College Press, 1993); Jane Roland Martin. *The Schoolhome: Rethinking Schools for Changing Families,* (Cambridge: Harvard University Press, 1992).

16. Elise Boulding has much theoretical work in this area. See, for example *"Feminist Inventions in the Art of Peacemaking," Peace and Change* 20, no. 4, October (1995); Birgit Brock-Utne. *Educating for Peace: A Feminine Perspective* (New York: Pergamon Press, 1985); Sara Ruddick. *Maternal Thinking: Toward a Politics of Peace* (Boston: Beacon Press, 1995).

17. Boulding *op. cit.*

18. J. R. Martin (1985). *Reclaiming a Conversation: The Ideal of the Educated Woman.* New Haven: Yale University Press.

19. *Ibid.*, p. 20.

20. R. Martin. *Schoolhome: Rethinking Schools for Changing Families* (Cambridge, MA: Harvard University Press, 1992).

21. Nel Noddings, *op. cit.*

22. Sara Ruddick, *Maternal Thinking: Toward a Politics of Peace* (Boston: Beacon Press, 1995).

23. *Ibid.*

24. Nell Noddings, *The Challenge to Care in Schools* (New York: Teachers College Press, 1992).

25. Elise Boulding, *The Personhood of Children* (Philadelphia: Religious Education Committee, Friends General Conference, 1975), p. 13.

26. See L. P. Daloz, C. Keen, J. Keen and S. Daloz Parks, *Common Fire: Leading Lives of Commitment in a Complex World* (Boston: Beacon Press, 1996).

27. *Ibid.*

28. Carol Gilligan, *In a Different Voice* (Cambridge, Mass.: Harvard University Press, 1982).

29. A. T. Jersild, "Children's Fears," *Child Development Monographs* (1935).

30. Jerome Kagan, *Personality Development* (New York: Harcourt Brace Jovanovich, 1971).

31. *Ibid.*

32. Marsha Yudkin, "When Kids Think the Unthinkable," *Psychology Today*, April 1984.

33. Kohlberg, Lawrence. *Philosophy of Moral Development* (San Francisco: Harper and Row, 1981).

34. S. W. Olds and D. E. Papalia, *Human Development* (New York: McGraw-Hill, 1981).

35. Educators for Social Responsibility, *Dialogue: A Teaching Guide to Nuclear Issues* (Cambridge, Mass.: ESR, 1983), p. 55.

36. Wallace E. Lambert and O. Klineberg, *Children's Views of Foreign People* (New York: Appleton-Century, Crofts, 1967).

37. Judith V. Torney, "Political Socialization Research in the United States," *Handbook on Peace Education, op. cit.*, p. 272.

38. Eric Erikson, *Identity: Youth and Crisis* (New York: Norton, 1968).

39. See the work of John Ogbu, including "Origins of Human Competence," *Child Development*, Vol. 52, pp. 413–429.

40. H. Otto and S. Healy, "Adolescents' Self-Perceptions of Personality Strengths," *Journal of Human Relations*, 1966.

41. *Decision Making in a Nuclear Age.* ZBR Publications. (Weston, MA: Halycon House Inc., 1983), p. 3.

42. Consortium on Peace, Research, Education and Development. *COPRED Directory of Peace Studies Programs* (Olympia, Washington: COPRED, 2001).

43. Ian Harris, Larry J. Fisk and Carol Rank. "A Portrait of University Peace Studies in North America and Western Europe at the End of the Millennium," *International Journal of Peace Studies*, Vol. 3, no.1, January (1988), p. 93.

44. Daniel Levinson, *The Seasons of a Man's Life* (New York: Alfred A. Knopf, 1978).
45. Erik Erikson, *Insight and Responsibility* (New York: W. W. Norton, 1964), p. 267.
46. Ibid.
47. Levinson, *op. cit.*
48. C. Buhler and F. Massarek, eds., *The Course of Human Life* (New York: Springer).

8. Sensitive Issues in Peace Education

1. Herbert London, "'Peace Studies' Hardly Academic," *The New York Times*, March 5, 1985, p. 27.
2. Nick Word, "'Pie-eyed' Peace Courses Accused of Bias," *The Times Educational Supplement*, January 6, 1984.
3. Peter Dale Scott, "Introductory Essay," *Peace and World Order Studies*, 4th edition (New York: World Policy Institute, 1984), p. 12.
4. Thomas H. Groome, "Religious Education for Justice by Educating Justly," *Education for Peace and Justice*, ed. Padraic O'Hare (San Francisco: Harper & Row, 1983), p. 75.
5. Werner Heisenberg, *The Physicist's Conception of Nature*, trans. from German by Arnold J. Pomerans (Westport, Conn.: Greenwood Press, 1970).
6. Peter Dale Scott, *op. cit.*, p. 13.
7. Robin Burns and Robert Aspeslagh, "'Objectivity,' Values and Opinions in the Transmission of Knowledge for Peace," *Bulletin of Peace Proposals*, Vol. 15, No. 2, 1984, p. 140.
8. John B. Carol, *Language, Thought and Reality: Selected Writings of Benjamin Whorf* (Cambridge, Mass.: MIT Press, 1976).
9. Jaime C. Diaz, "Reflections on Education for Justice and Peace," *Bulletin of Peace Proposals*, Vol. 10, No. 4, 1979, p. 275.
10. Harold Lasswell, "The Garrison State," *American Journal of Sociology*, Vol. 46, No. 1, 1941, pp. 455–468.
11. Dale Spender, *Man Made Language* (London: Routledge & Kegan Paul, 1980), p. 239.
12. Thomas Merton, *The Nonviolent Alternative* (New York: Farrar, Strauss, Liroux, 1977), p. 239.
13. Glen D. Hook, "Making Nuclear Weapons Easier to Live With: The Political Role of Language in Nuclearization," *Bulletin of Peace Proposals*, Vol. 16, No. 1, 1985, pp. 65–77. Glen D. Hook, "The Nuclearization of Language: Nuclear Allargy as Political Metaphor," *Journal of Peace Research*, Vol. 21, No. 3, 1984, pp. 259–275.
14. Noam Chomsky, *On Language* (New York: the New Press, 1998). Thanks also to David Michaels, professor emeritus of linguistics of the University of Connecticut, for a spirited discussion of the work of Chomsky held at a dinner party which the author (Morrison) attended in April 2002. This brief discussion of Chomsky's work cannot do justice to its complexity.
15. Jaime C. Diaz, *op. cit.*, p. 377.
16. Edward S. Herman, *The Real Terror Network: Terrorism in Fact and Propaganda* (Boston: South End Press, 1982).
17. Barnet, *op. cit*, and Marc Feigen Fasteau, *The Male Machine* (New York: Dell Publishing, 1975).

18. Dale Spender, *op. cit.*, p. 146.
19. Roy Preiswerk, "Could We Study International Relations as if People Mattered?" in *Peace and World Order Studies: A Curriculum Guide* (New York: Institute for World Order, 1981), p. 6.
20. Mario Borelli, "Integration of Peace Research, Peace Education, and Peace Action," *Bulletin of Peace Proposals*, Vol. 10, No. 4, 1979, p. 391.
21. Thomas Belmonte, "A Strategy for the Reclamation of Eden," *Bulletin of Peace Proposals*, Vol. 10, No. 4, 1979, p. 343.
22. Dale Spender, *op. cit.*, p. 142.
23. Sissela Bok. *Mayhem: Violence as Public Entertainment* (Reading, MA: Perseus Books, 1998).
24. *Ibid.*
25. *Ibid.*
26. Center for Communication and Social Policy, University of California at Santa Barbara (eds.). *National Television Violence Study 3* (Thousand Oaks, CA: Sage, 1998).
27. Center for Communication and Social Policy, UC Santa Barbara, p. 3.
28. Diane Levin. *Teaching Young Children in Violent Times* (Cambridge, MA: Educators for Social Responsibility, 1994) p. 13. See also Nancy Carlsson Paige and Diane Levin. *Who's Calling the Shots? How to Respond Effectively to Children's Fascination with War Play and War Toys* (Philadelphia: New Society Publishers, 1990).
29. Levin, *op. cit.*
30. Bok, *op. cit.*
31. Center for Communication and Social Policy, UC Santa Barbara, p. 2.
32. William Ekhardt, "Peace Studies and Attitude Change: A Value Theory of Peace Studies," *Peace and Change*, Vol. 10, No. 2, Summer 1984, p. 79.
33. Hans Nicklas and Anne Osterman, "The Psychology of Deterrence and the Chances for Education for Peace," *Bulletin of Peace Proposals*, Vol. 10, No. 4, 1979, p. 372.
34. "The Catholic Bishops' Peace Pastoral and Higher Education," *Harvard Educational Review*, Vol. 54, No. 3, August 1984, p. 319.
35. Chris Bartelds, "Peace Education and Solidarity," *Gandhi Marg*, Vol. 6, Nos. 4 and 5, July–August 1984, p. 308.
36. Baruch Nevo and Iris Brem, "Peace Education Programs and the Evaluation of Their Effectiveness," Gavriel Salomon and Baruch Nevo, eds. *Peace Education: The Concept, Principles, and Practices around the World* (Mahwah, NJ: Lawrence Erlbaum Associates, 2002) p. 275.
37. Eckhardt, *op. cit.* pp. 79–85.
38. Kathy Bickmore. "Good Training is Not Enough: Research on Peer Mediation Implementation," *Social Alternatives*, Vol. 21, no. 1, January (2002).
39. Donald Grossman, John Neckerman, & Ted Koepsell. "The effectiveness of a violence prevention curriculum among children in elementary school: A randomized controlled trial." *Journal of the American Medical Association*, (1997) 277(20), 1605–1611; David Johnson, Roger T. Johnson, & Brian Dudley. "Effects of peer mediation training on elementary students." *Mediation Quarterly*, (1992) 10 (1), 89–87; Metis Associates, Inc. *The Resolving Conflict Creatively Program, 1988–1989: A Summary of Recent Findings.* (New York: Metis and Associates, 1990).
40. Tom Roderick, "Evaluating the Resolving Conflict Creatively Program," *The Fourth R* (1998) 82, 1–9.
41. Joan Burstyn, "The Challenge for Schools: To Prevent Violence while Nurturing Democracy," *Preventing Violence in Schools: A Challenge to American Democracy* eds. J. Burstyn, G. Bender, R. Cassella, H. Gordon, D. Guerra, K. Luschen, R. Stevens, K. Williams (New Jersey: Lawrence Erlbaum, 2001) p. 225.

42. Grace Feuerverger, *Oasis of Dreams: Teaching and Learning in a Jewish-Palestinian Village in Israel* (New York: Routledge Falmer, 2001).
43. Michael Van Slyck and Marilyn Stern. "Conflict Resolution in Educational Settings: Assessing the Impact of Peer Mediation Programs." *Community Mediation: A Handbook for Practitioners and Researchers* (New York: Guilford Press, 1991).
44. Maria Montessori, *Education and Peace* (Chicago: Regenry, 1972) p. viii.
45. Robert Jay Lifton, "Beyond Nuclear Numbing," *Teachers College Record*, Vol. 84, No. 1, Fall 1982, pp. 15–29.
46. Elizabeth Kubler-Ross, *Death: The Final Stage of Growth* (Englewood Cliffs, New Jersey: Prentice-Hall, Inc., 1987).
47. Joanna Rogers Macy, *Despair and Personal Power in the Nuclear Age* (Philadelphia: New Society Publishers, 1983), p. 2.
48. *Ibid.*, chapter 2.
49. Betty Reardon, *Militarization, Security and Peace Education* (Valley Forge, PA: United Ministries in Higher Education, 1982).
50. Robin Burns and Robert Aspeslagh, "Concepts of Peace Education: A View of Western Experience," *International Review of Education*, 1983, p. 312.
51. Robert Aspeslagh, "Basic Needs and Peace Education," *Bulletin of Peace Proposals*, Vol. 10, No. 4, 1979, p. 405.
52. Nicklas and Osterman, *op. cit.*, p. 371.

9. Schools as Cultures of War

1. Betty Reardon, "Obstacles to Disarmament Education," *Bulletin of Peace Proposals*, Vol. 10, No. 4, 1979, pp. 356–367.
2. *Ibid.*, p. 356.
3. For a discussion of the effects of authoritarian child-rearing practices, see Theodore Adorno et al., *The Authoritarian Personality* (New York, 1950).
4. Virgil Elizondo, "By Their Fruits You Will Know Them: The Biblical Roots of Peace and Justice," *Education for Peace and Justice*, Padraic O'Hare, ed. (San Francisco: Harper & Row, 1983), p. 48.
5. Joel Kovel, *Against the State of Nuclear Terror* (Boston: South End Press, 1983), p. 64.
6. John Cassidy. "Helping Hands: How Foreign Aid Could Benefit Everybody," *The New Yorker*, March 18 (2002), p. 61.
7. Author unknown.
8. Seymour Melman, *The Permanent War Economy* (New York: Simon & Schuster, 1974).
9. Betty Reardon, *op. cit.*, p. 358.
10. *Ibid.*
11. *Bulletin of Atomic Scientists*, February 1984, p. 53.
12. Betty Reardon, *op. cit.*, p. 362.
13. *New York Times*, 30 November 1982, p. C3.
14. Henry T. Nash, "Thinking About Thinking About the Unthinkable," *Bulletin of Atomic Scientists*, October 1983, p. 40.
15. *Ibid.*, p. 41.

10. Moving Forward with Peace Pedagogy

1. Elise Boulding. "The Child and Non-violent Social Change." In Christoph Wulf (ed.), *Handbook of Peace Education* (Frankfurt: International Peace Research Association, 1974), pp. 101–132 (Quote is from the preface).
2. *Ibid.*
3. Maria Montessori. *Education for Peace* (Chicago: Henry Regvery Company, 1972).
4. Quoted in Devi Passad, *Peace Education or Education* (New Delhi: Gandhi Peace Foundation, 1984), p. 131.
5. For a discussion of this, see Mary O'Reilly, "The Peaceable Classroom," *College English*, Volume 46, Number 2, February 1984, pp. 103–112.
6. Devi Passad, *op. cit.*, p. 112.
7. Elise Boulding, *op. cit.*, pp. 123–124.
8. Mary A. Hepburn, "Can Schools, Teachers, and Administrators Make a Difference? The Research Evidence," in *Democratic Education in Schools and Classrooms* Mary A. Hepburn (ed.) (Washington, D.C.: National Council for the Social Studies, 1983).
9. Thomas F. Green, *The Activities of Teaching* (New York: McGraw-Hill, 1971), p. 216.
10. David W. Johnson and Roger T. Johnson, *Learning Together and Alone* (Englewood Cliffs, NJ: Prentice-Hall, 1975).
11. *Ibid.*, p. 7.
12. *Ibid.*
13. Bertrand Russell, *The Conquest of Happiness* (New York: Bantam Books, 1958).
14. For a discussion of how to establish rules and guidelines for a democratic classroom, see Ian M. Harris, "Boundaries, Set Theory, and Structure in the Classroom," *Education*, Vol. 93, No. 3.
15. "Education and the Inward Teacher," Pendle Hill Pamphlet 278. (Wallingford, PA: Pendle Hill Press, 1988).
16. *To Know as We Are Known: Education as a Spiritual Journey* (Harper/San Francisco, 1993). See also *The Courage to Teach: Exploring the Inner Landscape of a Teacher's Life* (San Francisco: Jossey-Bass, 1998).
17. *The Courage to Teach*, p. 3.
18. David W. Johnson, Roger T. Johnson, Edythe Johnson Holubec, and Patricia Roy, *Circles of Learning* (Washington, D.C.: Association for the Supervision and Curriculum Development, 1984), p. 45.
19. Ashley Montague, quoted in Johnson and Johnson, *op. cit.*, p. 24.
20. Johnson, Johnson, Holubec, and Roy, *op. cit.*, p. 15.
21. John Dewey, *Democracy in Education* (New York: Macmillan, 1916), p. 418.
22. Carol Gilligan, *In a Different Voice* (Cambridge, Mass.: Harvard University Press, 1982).
23. Quoted in Michael True, *Homemade Social Justice* (Mystic, CT: Twenty-Third Publications, 1982), p. 34.
24. Quoted in *Harvard Educational Review*, Vol. 54, No. 3, August 1984, p. 271.
25. Quoted in Richard Paul, "Critical Thinking: Fundamentals to Educators for a Free Society," *Educational Leadership*, Vol. 42, No. 1, September 1984, p. 10.
26. B. Massailas and B. Cox, *Inquiring in Social Studies* (New York: McGraw-Hill, 1966).
27. *The CORT Thinking Program* (Elmsfor, New York: Pergamon Press, 1984).

28. Johan Galtung, "On Peace Education." In Christoph Wulf (ed.), *Handbook on Peace Education* (Frankfurt: International Peace Research Association, 1974).
29. W. Kegan and M. A. Wallach, "Risk Taking as a Function of the Situation, the Person, and the Group." In G. Mandler, P. Mussen, W. Kegan, and O. A. Wallach, *New Directions in Psychology*, Vol. 3 (New York: Holt, Rinehart, and Winston, 1967), pp. 224–66.
30. Margaret Gorman, "Moral Education, Peace, and Social Justice." In Padraic O'Hare (ed.), *Education for Peace and Justice* (New York: Harper and Row, 1983), p. 166.
31. For a list of affirmation activities, see Stephanie Johnson (ed.), *A Manual on Nonviolence and Children* (Philadelphia, PA: New Society Publishers, 1984).
32. Johnson and Johnson, *op. cit.*, pp. 174–177.

11. Conclusion

1. Betty A. Reardon, *Sexism and the War System* (New York: Teachers College Press, 1985), p. 84.
2. Draper L. Kauffman, Jr., *Futurism and Future Studies* (Washington, D.C.: National Education Association, 1984), p. 11.
3. David Hicks, "Identifying Sources of Hope in Postmodern Times," *Futures Education: World Yearbook of Education 1998*, David Hicks and Richard Slaughter, eds. (unpublished at time of acquisition).
4. See Polak, Fred, *The Image of the Future*, Elise Boulding translation, abridged version (San Francisco: Jossey Bass/Elsevier, 1972).
5. Fred L. Polak, *The Image of the Future* (New York: A. W. Sythoff, Leyden/Oceana Publications, 1961), p. 64.
6. Mary Claycomb, "Foreword," *People, Law, and the Future Perspective* (Washington, D.C.: National Education Association), p. 7.
7. Commentary. *Sojourners*, May-June (1995), p.15.
8. Herman Kahn, *The Coming Boom* (New York: Simon & Schuster, 1982). Julian Simon, *The Ultimate Resource* (Princeton: Princeton University Press, 1981). Julian Simon and Herman Kahn, *The Resourceful Earth* (London: Blackwell, 1984).
9. Julian L. Simon and Herman Kahn, *op. cit.*, p. 3.
10. Willis W. Harman, "The Coming Transformation," *The Futurist*, April 1977, pp. 106–112, and Willis W. Harman, "How I Learned to Love the Future," *World Future Society Bulletin*, November/December 1984, pp. 1–5.
11. Fritjof Capra, *The Turning Point: Science, Society, and the Rising Culture* (New York: Bantam Books, 1982), p. 17.
12. Patricia Mische. "Ecological Security and the Need to Reconceptualize Sovereignty," *Alternatives*, Vol. xiv, no.4, October (1989), pp. 389–428.
13. Fritjof Capra, *op. cit.*, p. 16.
14. See Marilyn Ferguson, *The Aquarian Conspiracy: Personal and Social Transformation in the 1980s* (Los Angeles: J. P. Tarcher, Inc., 1980).
15. *Ibid.* p. 26.
16. Michael McIntyre, Sister Luke Tobin, and Hazel L. Johns, *Peaceworld* (Friendship Press, 1976), p. 17.
17. Francis P. Hutchinson. *Educating Beyond Violent Futures* (London: Routledge, 1996).
18. *Ibid.*

19. See William L. Ury, *Beyond the Hotline: How Crisis Control Can Prevent Nuclear War* (New York: Penguin Books, 1975).

20. Gene Sharp, *Making Europe Unconquerable* (Boston: Ballinger Publishing Co., 1985).

21. Cynthia Adcock, "Fear of Other: The Common Root of Sexism and Militarism," *Reweaving the Web of Life: Feminism and Nonviolence*, ed. Pam McAllister (Philadelphia: New Society Publishers, 1982), p. 210.

22. See Elise Boulding, "Feminist Inventions in the Art of Peacemaking," *Peace and Change* 20, no. 4, October (1995): 408–438 and Sara Ruddick, *Maternal Thinking: Toward A Politics of Peace*. Boston: Beacon Press, 1989, 1995.

23. Donna Warnock, "Patriarchy Is a Killer: What People Concerned about Peace and Justice Should Know," *Reweaving the Web of Life, op. cit.,* p. 20.

24. Thanks to the organizers and speakers of a 4 session course on the Earth Charter and sustainability given by Saint Joseph College, West Hartford, CT, March 2002 for this and other definitions.

25. See the Earth Charter website: www.earthcharter.org. Information based on "The Earth Charter: Values and Principles for a Sustainable Future," pamphlet outlining the basic principles and actions. The Earth Charter International Secretariat, c/o the Earth Council, PO Box 319-6100, San Jose, Costa Rica.

26. Peter Raven, "Science, Sustainability and the Human Prospect," AAAS Presidential Address, Boston, MA, February 14, 2002.

27. *Ibid.*

28. Elise Boulding, in an address to the Peace Education Commission of the International Peace Research Association at the University of Sussex in Brighton, England, on April 14, 1986.

Bibliography and Resource Guide

Educating for peace is best done in a cooperative and collaborative mode. To that end, this bibliography and resource guide owes many thanks to Åke Bjerstedt, of the School of Education in Malmö, Sweden, who graciously gave his permission for us to use his Educating Towards a Culture of Peace: A Select Bibliography Focusing on the Last 25 Years. *Many of the following entries may be found in his book which can be ordered through the School of Education, SE-205 06 Malmö, Sweden; ake.bjerstedt@lut.mah.se. His very complete bibliography has an international focus. In addition, we are grateful to Aline Stomfay-Stitz, editor of the Special Interest Group of the American Educational Research Association newsletter, who shared her resource list with us (www.unf.edu/~astomfay/) and to the Curriculum of Hope project of the Delta Kappa Gamma Society International. Many entries here may also be found on the web site of Ian Harris, who has a link for peace education resources (www.uwm.edu/~imh). In addition, the authors are grateful for a recent publication of the* National Catholic Reporter *(April 26, 2002), "Paths to Peace," including an extensive list of resources. Our listing is by no means complete. There is a vast amount of literature and resources available. Readers are urged to do their own research. Not all of these sources have been personally reviewed by the authors.*

BOOKS AND COLLECTIONS OF PAPERS

Aber, J. L., Brown, J. L. & Henrich, C. C. (1999). *Teaching Conflict Resolution: An Effective School-Based Approach to Violence Prevention.* New York: Columbia University, National Center for Children in Poverty.

Ackerman, P. and Duvall, J. (2000). *A Force More Powerful: A Century of Nonviolent Conflict.* New York: St. Martin's Press.

Adams, D. (Ed.). (1997). *UNESCO and a Culture of Peace: Promoting a Global Movement* (2nd ed.). Paris: UNESCO. (First published in 1995.)

Adams, J.P. (1990). *Peacework: Oral Histories of Women Peace Activists*. Boston: Twayne Publishers.

Alger, C. & Stohl, M. (Eds.). (1988). *A Just Peace Through Transformation* (Proceedings of the International Peace Research Association Eleventh General Conference). Boulder, CO: Westview Press. [With a section on peace education.]

Alonso, H.H., Chatfield, C. and Kriesberg, L. (eds.). (1993). *Peace as a Woman's Issue: A History of the U.S. Movement for World Peace and Women's Rights*. Syracuse, NY: Syracuse University Press.

Alson, S. et al. (1989). *Training Student Mediators in Elementary Schools: A Manual*. New York: Educators for Social Responsibility.

Arnow, J. (1995). *Teaching Peace: How to Raise Children to Live in Harmony Without Fear, Without Prejudice, Without Violence*. New York: The Berkley Publishing Group.

Aronson, E. (2000). *Nobody Left to Hate: Teaching Compassion after Columbine*. New York: Worth Publishers.

Aschliman, K. (Ed.). (1993). *Growing Toward Peace: Stories From Teachers and Parents About Real Children Learning to Live Peacefully*. Scottdale, PA: Herald Press.

Barash, D. and Lipton, J.E. (2002). *Gender Gap: the Biology of Male-Female Differences*. Transaction Publishers.

Baratta, J.P. (1995).*United Nations System Volume 10*. Oxford, England: Clio Press.

Barish, D. (1991). *Introduction to Peace Studies*. Belmont, CA: Wadsworth Publishing Co.

Beer, F.A. et al. (2001). *Meanings of War and Peace*. Texas A and M Press.

Belenky, M.F., Bond, L. and Weinstock, J. (1997). *A Tradition That Has No Name: Nurturing the Development of People, Families and Communities*. NY: Basic Books.

Benson, J. & Poliner, R. A. (1977). *Dialogue: Turning Controversy Into Community*. Cambridge, MA: Educators for Social Responsibility.

Berlowe, B. Janke, R. and Penshorn, J. (photos by Cota, T.). (2002). *The Compassionate Rebel: Energized by Anger, Motivated by Love*. Scandia, MN: Growing Communities for Peace. www.peacemaker.org.

Berman, S. (1997). *Children's Social Consciousness and the Development of Social Responsibility*. Albany, NY: State University of New York Press.

Berman, S. & La Farge, P. (eds.). (1993). *Promising Practices in Teaching Social Responsibility*. Albany, NY: State University of New York Press.

Berry, T. (1988). *The Dream of the Earth*. Sierra Club.

Bey, T. M. & Turner, G. Y. (1996). *Making School a Place of Peace*. Thousand Oaks, CA: Corwin Press.

Bickmore, K. (1991). *Practicing Conflict: Citizenship Education in High School Social Studies*. (Ph.D.) Stanford University, California.

Bickmore, K. (Ed.). (1997). Teaching conflict resolution: Preparation for pluralism [Special issue]. *Theory into Practice*, 36(1).

Biggar, N. (ed.) (2001). *Burying the Past: Making Peace and Doing Justice After Civil Conflict*. Washington, D.C.: Georgetown University Press.

Bjerstedt, Å. (Ed.). (1990–1996). *Peace, Environment and Education* (Peace Education Commission, International Peace Research Association; Malmö: School of Education), 1990, 1 (1–2); 1991, 2 (1–4); 1992, 3 (1–4); 1993, 4 (1–4); 1994, 5 (1–4); 1995, 6 (1); 1996, 7 (1). (Twenty journal issues, available from Malmö School of Education.)

Bjerstedt, Å. (1995). *Controversies Connected with Peace Education: What Do They Mean and How Should They Be Dealt With?* (Peace Education Reports, 15). Malmö: School of Education.

Bjerstedt, Å (2001). *Educating Toward a Culture of Peace: A Select Bibliography Focusing on the Last 25 Years*. Malmö School of Education.

Blakeway, M. S. & Kmitta, D. M. (1998). *Conflict Resolution Education: Research and*

Evaluation. Synopsis and Bibliography. Washington, DC: National Institute for Dispute Resolution.
Bodine, R. J. & Crawford, D. K. (1998). *The Handbook of Conflict Resolution Education: A Guide to Building Quality Programs in Schools.* San Francisco, CA: Jossey-Bass.
Bodine, R. J., Crawford, D. K. & Schrumpf, F. (1994). *Creating the Peaceable School: A Comprehensive Program for Teaching Conflict Resolution. Program guide.* Champaign, IL: Research Press.
Borstelmann, T. (2001). *The Cold War and the Color Line: American Race Relations in the Global Arena.* Cambridge: Harvard University Press.
Boulding, E. (1988). *Building a Global Civic Culture: Education for an Interdependent World.* New York: Teachers College Press.
Boulding, E. (1989). *One Small Plot of Heaven: Reflections on Family Life by a Quaker Sociologist.* Wallingford, PA: Pendle Hill Publications.
Boulding, E. (1991). *Peace, Culture and Society.* Boulder, CO: Westview Press.
Boulding, E. (2000). *Cultures of Peace: The Hidden Side of History.* Syracuse University Press.
Bowers, C.J. (1993). *Education, Cultural Myths, and the Ecological Crisis.* State University of New York Press.
Bowers, C.J. (2001). *Educating for Eco-Justice and Community.* University of Georgia Press.
Brecher, J., Childs, J.B. and Cutler, J. (eds.) (1993). *Global Visions: Beyond the New World Order.* Boston: South End Press.
Brock-Utne, B. (1989). *Feminist Perspectives on Peace and Peace Education.* Oxford, UK: Pergamon Press.
Brown, J.H., D'Emidio-Caston, M. and Benard, B. (2001). *Resilience Education.* Thousand Oaks, CA: Corwin Press.
Brown, L. (1990). *State of the World.* W.W. Norton.
Brownlee, F. and King. J. (2000). *Learning in Safe Schools: Creating Classrooms Where All Students Belong.* Portland, ME: Stenhouse Publishers.
Burns, R.J. and Aspeslaugh, R. (1996). *Three Decades of Peace Education Around the World.* New York: Garland Publishing.
Burstyn, J.N., Bender, G., Casella, R. et al. (2001). *Preventing Violence in Schools: A Challenge to American Democracy.* Mahwah, N.J.: Lawrence Erlbaum Associates.
Cairnes, E. and Dunn, J. (1996). *Children and Political Violence (Understanding Children's Worlds).* Oxford, UK, and New York: Blackwells.
Calleja, J. and Perucca, A. (eds.). (1999). *Peace Education: Contexts and Values.* Leece, Italy: Edizioni Pensa MultiMedia in collaboration with the Division of Democracy, Human Rights and Peace of UNESCO and the Peace Education Commission of the International Peace Research Association.
Canada, G. (1995). *Fist Stick Knife Gun.* Boston: Beacon Press.
Cantor, J. (1998). *"Mommy I'm Scared!" How TV and Movies Frighten Children and What We Can Do To Protect Them.* New York: Harcourt-Brace.
Carlsson-Paige, N. & Levin, D. E. (1990). *Who's Calling the Shots? How to Respond Effectively to Children's Fascination with War Play and War Toys.* Philadelphia, PA: New Society Publishers.
Casella, R. (2001). *"Being Down": Challenging Violence in Urban Schools.* New York: Teachers College Press.
Christie, D.J., Wagner, R.V., and Winter, D.D. (2001). *Peace, Conflict and Violence: Peace Psychology for the 21st Century.* Englewood Cliffs, N.J.: Prentice-Hall.
Clark, W.K. (2001). *Waging Modern War: Bosnia, Kosovo and the Future of Combat.* New York: Public Affairs.
Coles, R. (1998). *The Moral Intelligence of Children.* New York: Penguin Putnam, Inc.

Cook, P.J. and Ludwig, J. (2000). *Gun Violence: The Real Costs.* New York: Oxford University Press.
Crocker, C.A., Hampson, F.O., and Aall, P. (2001). *Turbulent Peace: the Challenges of Managing International Conflict.* Washington, D.C.: United States Institute of Peace.
Daloz, L.A., Keen, C. Keen, J. and Parks, S.D. (1996). *Common Fire: Leading Lives of Commitment in a Complex World.* Boston: Beacon Press.
Dam, K.W. (2001). *The Rules of the Global Game: A New Look at U.S. International Economic Policy-Making.* Chicago: University of Chicago Press.
DiGiulio, R. (2000). *Positive Classroom Management: A Step by Step Guide to Successfully Running the Show Without Destroying Student Dignity* (2nd ed). Thousand Oaks, CA: Corwin Press.
Duke, D.L. (2002). *Creating Safe Schools for All Children.* Boston: Allyn and Bacon.
Felder, R. and Victor, B. (1996) *Getting Away with Murder.* (Domestic Violence). New York: Simon and Schuster.
Feuerverger. G. (2001). *Oasis of Dreams: Teaching and Learning Peace in a Jewish-Palestinian Village in Israel.* New York: Routledge Falmer.
Forcey, L.R. and Harris, I. (1999). *Peacebuilding for Adolescents.* New York: Lang.
Forche, C. (ed.) *Against Forgetting: Twentieth Century Poetry of Witness.* New York: W.W. Norton Co.
Gara, L. and Gara, L.M. (1999). *A Few Small Candles: War Resisters of World War II Tell Their Stories.* Kent, OH: Kent State University Press.
Gleeson, B. and Low, B. (eds.). (2001). *Governing for the Environment: Global Problems, Ethics and Democracy.* New York: Palgrave at St. Martins.
Grant, C.A. and Lei, J.L. (eds.). (2001). *Global Constructions of Multicultural Education.* Muhwah, N.J.: Lawrence Erlbaum Associates.
Groves, B.M. (2002). *Children Who See Too Much: Lessons from the Child Witness to Violence Project.* Boston: Beacon Press.
Hadley, M.L. (2001). *The Spiritual Roots of Restorative Justice.* Albany, NY: State University of New York Press.
Halberstam, D. (2002). *War in a Time of Peace.* New York: Scribners.
Harris, I. M. (1988). *Peace Education.* Jefferson, NC: McFarland.
Harris, I. M. (Ed.). (1996). *Peace Education in a Postmodern World* [Special issue]. *Peabody Journal of Education, 71*(3).
Henderson, M. (1994). *All Her Paths Are Peace: Women Pioneers in Peacemaking.* West Hartford, CT: Kumarian.
Hutchinson. F.(1996). *Educating Beyond Violent Futures.* London: Routledge.
Ikeda, D. (2001). *For the Sake of Peace: Seven Paths to Global Harmony: A Buddhist Perspective.* Santa Monica, CA: Middleway Press.
Janke, R.M., Penshorn, J. and Berlowe, B. (2002). *The Compassionate Rebel.* Scandia, MN: Growing Communities for Peace (P.O. Box 248, Scandia, MN 55073).
Johnson, D. W. & Johnson, R. T. (1989). *Cooperation and Competition: Theory and Research.* Edina, MN: Interaction Books.
Johnson, D. W. & Johnson, R. T. (1995). *Teaching Students to Be Peacemakers* (3rd ed.). Edina, MN: Interaction Books.
Johnson, R. (1993). *Negotiation Basics: Concepts, Skills and Exercises.* Newbury Park, CA: Sage Publishing.
Jones, T. S. & Kmitta, D. (eds.). (2000). *Does It Work? The Case for Conflict Resolution Education in our Nation's Schools.* Washington, DC: Conflict Resolution Education Network.
Juvonen, J. and Graham, S. (eds.). *Peer Harassment in School: the Plight of the Vulnerable and Victimized.* New York: The Guilford Press.

Karr-Morse, R. and Wiley, M. (1997). *Ghosts from the Nursery: Tracing the Roots of Violence.* New York: Atlantic Press.
Katch, J. (2001). *Under Deadman's Skin: Discovering the Meaning of Children's Violent Play.* Boston: Beacon Press.
Klare, M.T. (2001). *Resource Wars: The New Landscape of Global Conflict.* New York: Metropolitan Books.
Klare, M. T. & Chandrani, Y. (Eds.). (1998). *World security: Challenges for a New Century* (3rd ed.). New York: St. Martin's Press.
Koplow, L. (ed.). (1996). *Unsmiling Faces: How Preschools Can Heal.* New York: Teachers College Press.
Kreidler, W. J. (1990). *Elementary Perspectives 1: Teaching Concepts of Peace and Conflict.* Cambridge, MA: Educators for Social Responsibility.
Lantieri, L. and Patti, J. (1996). *Waging Peace in our Schools.* Boston: Beacon Press.
Levin, D. E. (1994). *Teaching Young Children in Violent Times: Building a Peaceable Classroom.* (Gr. K–3.) Cambridge, MA: Educators for Social Responsibility.
Levine, M. (1998). *See No Evil: A Guide to Protecting Our Children from Media Violence.* San Francisco: Jossey-Bass.
Lynd, S. and Lynd, A. (1995). *Nonviolence in America: A Documentary History.* Maryknoll, NY: Orbis Books.
McCarthy, C. (2002). *I'd Rather Teach Peace.* Maryknoll, NY: Orbis Books.
McGinnis, J. (1997). *Educating for peace and justice: K–5.* St. Louis, MO: Institute for Peace and Justice.
McGinnis, J. (2000). *Creating Circles of Peace: Alternatives to Violence Kit for Public Schools: K–5.* St. Louis, MO: Institute for Peace and Justice. (Original publication date 1997.)
Martin, J.R. (1992). *The Schoolhome: Rethinking Schools for Changing Families.* Cambridge, MA: Harvard University Press.
Merryfield, M. and Remy, R. (1995). *Teaching About International Conflict and Peace.* Albany, NY: State University of New York Press.
Miller, M.S. (1995). *No Visible Wounds: Identifying Nonphysical Abuse of Women by Their Men..* New York: Fawcett Columbine.
Moeller, T. G. (2001). *Youth Violence and Aggression: A Psychological Approach.* Mahwah, N.J.: Lawrence Erlbaum Associates.
Myers-Walls, J.A., Somlai, P. and Rapoport, R.N. (2001). *Families as Educators for Global Citizenship.* Ashgate Publishing Co. http:www.ashgate.com.
Nagler, M. (2001). *The Search for a Nonviolent Future.* Berkeley, CA: Berkeley Books.
O'Reilly, M.R. (1993). *The Peaceable Classroom.* Portsmouth, N.H.: Boynton/ Cook Publishers.
Peterson, T.C. (2002). *Linked Arms: A Rural Community Resists Nuclear Waste.* Albany, NY: State University of New York Press.
Porteous, J.D. and Smith, S.E. (2001). *Domicide: The Global Destruction of Home.* Montreal: McGill University.
Powers, R. and Vogel, W. (eds.). *Protest, Power and Change: An Encyclopedia of Nonviolent Action from ACT-UP to Women's Suffrage.*
Prutzman, P. et al. (1988). *The Friendly Classroom for a Small Planet.* Philadelphia, PA: New Society Publishers.
Rapoport, A. (1989; 1995 reprint). *The Origin of Violence: Approaches to the Study of Conflict.* New Brunswick, NJ: Transaction Publishers.
Reardon, B. A. (1986). *Peace Education: A K–12 Curriculum Guide.* (Ed. D.) New York: Columbia University, Teachers College. (87-21192.)
Reardon, B. A. (1988). *Comprehensive Peace Education: Educating for Global Responsibility.* New York: Teachers College Press.

Reardon, B. A. (1993). *Women and Peace: Feminist Visions of Global Education*. Albany, NY: State University of New York Press.

Reardon, B.A. (1997). *Tolerance: the Threshold of Peace* (3 volumes). Paris: UNESCO.

Reardon, B. A. (Ed.). (1988). *Educating for Global Responsibility: Teacher-Designed Curricula for Peace Education, K–12*. New York: Teachers College Press.

Reardon, B. and Nordland, E. (1994). *Learning Peace: the Promise of Ecological and Cooperative Education*. Albany, NY: State University of New York Press.

Reardon, B. A. et al. (2001, In prep.). *Learning to Abolish War: Teaching Toward a Culture of Peace*. New York: The Hague Appeal for Peace Global Campaign for Peace Education; Teachers College University.

Rosenberg, W. (2001). *Legacy of Rage: Jewish Masculinity, Violence and Culture*. Boston: University of Massachusetts Press.

Rucker, P.M. (2002). *This Troubled Land: Voices from Northern Ireland on the Front Lines of Peace*. New York: Random House (Ballantine hardcover).

Schulz, W.F. (2001). *In Our Best Interest: How Defending Human Rights Benefits Us All*. Boston: Beacon Press.

Shannon, W.H. (1996). *Seeds of Peace: Contemplation and Non-Violence*. New York: The Crossroad Publishing Co.

Sharp, G. (1973). *The Dynamics of Nonviolent Action: Part Three*. Boston: Porter Sargent Publishers.

Small, M.F. (2001). *How Biology and Culture Shape the Way We Raise Our Children*. New York: Random House.

Smith, D.C. and Carson, T.R. (1996). *Educating for a Peaceful Future*. Toronto, Canada: Kagan and Woo.

Smoker, P. (1990). *A Reader in Peace Studies*. New York: Pergamon Press.

Stamford, B. H. and Yamamoto, K. (eds.). (2001). *Children and Stress: Understanding and Helping*. Olney, MD: Association for Childhood Education International.

Stomfay-Stitz, A. M. (1993). *Peace Education in America, 1828–1990: Sourcebook for Education and Research*. Metuchen, NJ: The Scarecrow Press.

Thomas, D. C. & Klare, M. T. (Eds.). (1989). *Peace and World Order Studies: A Curriculum Guide* (5th ed.). Boulder, CO: Westview Press.

Thompson, M., Grace, C. with Cohen, L.J. (2001). *Best Friends, Worst Enemies: Understanding the Social Lives of Children (within a climate of school violence)*. New York: Random House.

Touval, S. (2002). *Mediation in the Yugoslav Wars: The Critical Years, 1990–95*. New York: Palgrave at St. Martin's.

True, M. (1991). *Ordinary people: Family Life and Global Values*. Maryknoll, NY: Orbis Books.

True, M. (1995). *An Energy Field More Intense Than War: The Nonviolent Tradition and American Literature*. Syracuse, NY: Syracuse University Press, 1995.

True, M. (1992). *To Construct Peace: 30 More Justice Seekers, Peace Makers*. Mystic, CT: Twenty-Third Publications.

Umbreit, M. (1995). *Mediating Interpersonal Conflicts: A Pathway to Peace*. West Concord, MN: CPI Publishing.

Ury, W. (1999). *Getting to Peace: Transforming Conflict at Home, at Work and in the World*. New York: Viking.

VanAusdale, D. and Feagin, J.R. (2002). *The First R: How Children Learn Race and Racism*. New York: Rowman and Littlefield.

Vanderhaar, G.A. (1990). *Active Nonviolence: A Way of Personal Peace*. Mystic, CT: Twenty-third Publications.

Weeks, D. (1992). *The Eight Essential Steps to Conflict Resolution*. Los Angeles: Jeremy Tarcher, Inc.

Williams, K.P. (2001). *Despite Nationalist Tendencies: Theory and Practice of Maintaining World Peace.* New York: Praeger.

Zinn, H. (1990). *Declarations of Independence: Cross-Examining American Ideology.* New York: HarperCollins Publishers.

ARTICLES AND CHAPTERS ON PEACE AND CONFLICT EDUCATION

Barash, D. (2002). Evolution, Males and Violence. *The Chronicle Review* in *The Chronicle of Higher Education.* May 24, 2002.

Bickmore, K. (1993). Conflict matters: Teaching about peace in the social studies curriculum. *Thresholds in Education, 19* (3), 25–33.

Bing, T. (1993). *Thinking Our Way Into Acting and Acting Our Way Into Thinking in Undergraduate Peace Studies* (Reprint Series, 4:C/CPS/:1). Notre Dame, IN: The Joan B. Kroc Institute for International Peace Studies.

Bjerstedt, Å. (1992). Peace education around the world at the beginning of the 1990s: Some data from questionnaires to ministries of education and members of the Peace Education Commission. *Peace, Environment and Education, 3*(3), 15–36.

Boulding, E. (1988). Image and action in peace building. *Journal of Social Issues, 44*(2), 17–37.

Boulding, E., Cohen, C., Haas, L., Jacobson, G., Morrison, M.L. (2000). Making Peace Where I Live: Proposal for a year 2000 peace education project. *Peacebuilding* (University of Wisconsin – Milwaukee; PEC) (January 2000), 14–15.

Brock-Utne, B. (1984). The relationship of feminism to peace and peace education. *Bulletin of Peace Proposals, 15,* 149–153.

Brock-Utne, B. (1991). The raising of a peaceful boy. *Peace, Environment and Education, 2*(1), 3–12.

Brock-Utne, B. (1996). The challenges for peace educators at the end of a millennium. *International Journal of Peace Studies, 1*(1), 37–55.

Burns, R. & Aspeslagh, R. (1984). 'Objectivity,' values and opinions in the transmission of knowledge for peace. *Bulletin of Peace Proposals, 15,* 139–148.

Butler, F. (1990). The theme of peace in children's literature. *The Lion and the Unicorn, 14,* 128–138.

Crary, D. R. (1992). Community benefits from mediation: A test of the "peace virus" hypothesis. *Mediation Quarterly, 9,* 241–252.

Curle, A., Freire, P. & Galtung, J. (1976). What can education contribute towards peace and social justice? In M. Haavelsrud (Ed.), *Education for peace: Reflection and action* (pp. 64–97). Guildford, Surrey, UK: IPC Science and Technology Press.

Dugan, M. A. & Carey, D. (1996). Toward a definition of peace studies. In *Around the World* (pp. 79–96). New York: Garland.

Eckhardt, W. (1991). Making and breaking enemy images. *Bulletin of Peace Proposals, 22*(1), 87–95.

Forcey, L. R. (1997). Peace studies. In R. S. Powers & W. B. Vogele (Eds.), *Protest, power, and change* (pp. 407–409). New York: Garland.

Forcey, L. R. & Rainforth, B. (1998). Team teaching "Conflict Resolution in Educational and Community Settings": An experiment in collaboration and conflict resolution. *Peace & Change, 23,* 373–385.

Fountain, S. (2001). The impact of conflict resolution education on children in armed conflict: Opportunities and challenges in UNICEF projects. *The Fourth R* (CREnet), (93), 3–6. *Education.* (1993). (27C/90.) Paris: UNESCO.

Groff, L. & Smoker, P. (1996). Creating global/local cultures of peace. In *From a culture of violence to a culture of peace* (pp. 103–128). Paris: UNESCO.

Haavelsrud, M. (1996). Learning democratic global governance. *International Journal of Peace Studies, 1*(2), 67–84.

Haessly, J. (1997). Imaging peace: A pedagogical challenge for youth educators. *Holistic Education Review, 10*(4), 16–25.

Harris, I. M. (1990). The goals of peace education. *Peace Review, 2*(2), 1–4.

Harris, I. M. (1990). Principles of peace pedagogy. *Peace & Change, 15,* 254–271.

Harris, I. M. (1992). Peace studies in the United States at the university and college levels. *Peace, Environment and Education, 3*(1), 3–21.

Harris, I. M. (1993). Teaching love to counteract.... *Thresholds in Education, 19*(3), 12–20.

Harris, I. M., Fisk, L. J. & Rank, C. (1998). A portrait of university peace studies in North America and Western Europe at the end of the millennium. *International Journal of Peace Studies, 3*(1), 91–112.

Hostetler, L. L. (1994). Preparing children for peace. In R. Elias & J. Turpin (Eds.), *Rethinking peace* (pp. 200–204). Boulder, CO: Lynne Rienner.

Howlett, C. (1982). The pragmatist as pacifist: John Dewey's views on peace education. *Teachers College Record, 83,* 435–451.

Hutchinson, F. (1992). Making peace with people and planet: Some important lessons from the Gandhian tradition in educating for the twenty-first century. *Peace, Environment and Education, 3*(3), 3–14.

Hutchinson, F. (1996). Building alternatives to violence: Are there needs and opportunities for teachers and teacher educators to be practical futurists? *Peace, Environment and Education, 7*(1), 3–18.

Hutchinson, F. (1997). Education for future generations: Challenges and opportunities for peace and environmental educators. *Future Generations Journal,* (2), 10–15.

Johnson, D. W. & Johnson, R. T. (1996). Conflict resolution and peer mediation programs in elementary and secondary schools: A review of the research. *Review of Educational Research, 66,* 459–506.

Johnson, D. W. et al. (1995). Impact of peer mediation training on the management of school and home conflicts. *American Educational Research Journal, 32,* 829–844.

Johnson, D. W. et al. (1995). Training of elementary school students to manage conflict. *Journal of Social Psychology, 135,* 673–686.

Johnson, D. W. et al. (1997). The impact of conflict resolution training on middle school students. *Journal of Social Psychology, 137,* 11–21. Johnson, M. L. (1998). *Trends in peace education.* Bloomington, IN: ERIC Clearinghouse for Social Studies / Social Science Education. (ED 417123.)

Kelder, S. H. (1996). The Students for Peace project: A comprehensive violence-prevention program for middle school students. *American Journal of Preventive Medicine, 12*(5, Suppl.), 22–30.

Kessler, R. (1997). Social and emotional learning: An emerging field builds a foundation for peace. *Holistic Education Review, 10*(4), 4–15.

Kmitta, D. (1998). A preliminary meta-analysis of school-based conflict resolution programs. *The Fourth R* (CREnet), (82), 5–24.

Lakey, G. (1994). Why training for nonviolent action? *International Journal of Nonviolence, 2*(1), 41–50.

Lantieri, L. (1995). Waging peace in our schools: Beginning with the children. *Peace, Environment and Education, 6*(1), 3–12.

Lantieri, L., DeJong, W. & Dutrey, J. (1996). Waging peace in our schools: The Resolving Conflict Creatively Program. In A. M. Hoffm (Ed.), *Schools, violence, and society* (pp. 241–251). Westport, CT: Praeger.

Long, J. (1993). Ruffing Montessori school peace curriculum: An informal narrative. *NAMTA Journal, 18*(1), 153–171.

Lopez, G. A. (1989). Conceptual models for peace studies programs. In D. C. Thomas & M. T. Klare (Eds.), *Peace and world order studies* (pp. 73–86). Boulder, CO: Westview Press.

Lopez, G. A. (1994). Challenges to curriculum development in the post-Cold War era. In M. T. Klare (Ed.), *Peace and Word Security Studies: A Curriculum Guide* (pp. 3–13). Boulder, CO: Lynne Rienner.

McCully, A., O'Doherty, M. & Smyth, R. (1999). The Speak Your Piece Project: Exploring controversial issues in Northern Ireland. In L. R. Forcey & I. M. Harris (Eds.), *Peacebuilding for adolescents* (pp. 119–138). New York: Lang.

McGinnis, K. & McGinnis, J. (1990). Parenting for peace and justice. In *Learning to Build a Peaceful World* (pp. 21–33). Independence, MO: Herald Publishing House.

Matsuura, K. (Director-General UNESCO.) (2000). *Address, Award Ceremony of the 2000 UNESCO Prize for Peace Education*; UNESCO, 11 December 2000. (NED/DG/2000/66.) Paris: UNESCO.

Morrison, M.L. (2000). Peace Profile: Elise Boulding. *Peace Review, 12*(2). June, 2000, pp. 337–343.

Morrison, M.L. (2001). The Life of Elise Boulding; educating toward a Culture of Peace. *Vitae Scholasticae: The Journal of Educational Biography, 20* (1), Spring 2001, pp. 7–22.

Morse, P. S. & Andrea, R. (1994). Peer mediation in the schools: Teaching conflict resolution techniques to students. *NASSP Bulletin, 78*(560), 75–82.

Myers-Walls, J. A. (1993). Family-centered contributions to a peaceful future. In K. Altergott (Ed.), *One world, many families* (pp. 72–76). Minneapolis, MN: National Council on Family Relations.

Myers-Walls, J. A., Myers-Bowman, K. S. & Pelo, A. (1993). Parents as educators about war and peace. *Family Relations, 42,*73.

Nelson, L. L., Van Slyck, M. R. & Cardella, L. A. (1999). Peace and conflict curricula for adolescents. In L. R. Forcey & I. M. Harris (Eds.), *Peacebuilding for adolescents* (pp. 91–117). New York: Lang.

Noddings, N. (1992). *The Challenge to Care in Schools.* New York: Teachers College Press.

Nordland, E. (1996). Think and teach globally—act locally. Participants or onlookers: A research program. In R. J. Burns & R. Aspeslagh (Eds.), *Three Decades of Peace Education Around the World* (pp. 291–306). New York: Garland.

Prothrow-Stith, D. (1994). Building violence prevention into the curriculum. *School Administrator, 51*(4), 8–12.

Prutzman, P. (1994). Bias-related incidents, hate crimes, and conflict resolution. *Education and Urban Society, 27*(1), 71–81.

Prutzman, P. & Johnson, J. (1997). Bias awareness and multiple perspectives: Essential aspects of conflict resolution. *Theory into Practice, 36*(1), 26–31.

Raider, E., Coleman, S. & Gerson, J. (2000). Teaching conflict resolution skills in a workshop. In M. Deutsch & P. T. Coleman (Eds.), *The Handbook of Conflict Resolution* (pp. 499–521). San Francisco, CA: Jossey-Bass.

Reardon, B. (1990). Education for peace in religious contexts. In *Learning to Build a Peaceful World* (pp. 51–60). Independence, MO: Herald Publishing House.

Reardon, B. (1994). Learning our way to a human future. In B. Reardon & E. Nordland (Eds.), *Learning Peace* (pp. 21–44). Albany, NY: State University of New York Press.

Reardon, B. (1996). Militarism and sexism: Influences on education for war. In R. J. Burns & R. Aspeslagh (Eds.), *Three Decades of Peace Education Around the World* (pp. 143–160). New York: Garland.

Reardon, B. (1996). Responding to a major problem of adolescent intolerance: Bullying. *Peace, Environment and Education, 7*(1), 19–30.

Roderick, T. (1998). Evaluating the Resolving Conflict Creatively Program. *The Fourth R* (CREnet), (82), 3–21.

Salomon, G. & Nevo, B. (2000). A paucity of peace education research. *Peacebuilding* (University of Wisconsin—Milwaukee; PEC), (January 2000), 9–11.

Sandy, S. V., Bailey, S. & Sloane-Akwara, V. (2000). Impact on students: Conflict resolution education's proven benefits for students. In T. S. Jones & D. Kmitta (Eds.), *Does it work? The Case for Conflict Resolution Education in Our Nation's Schools* (pp. 15–31). Washington, DC: CREnet.

Standing, E. M. (1995). Maria Montessori: World peace through the child [Reprint of a 1962 article]. *The NAMTA Journal* (North American Montessori Teachers' Association), *20*(3), 77–92.

Starkey, H. (1992). Back to basic values: Education for justice and peace in the world. *Journal of Moral Education, 21*(3), 185–192.

Stevahn, L., Johnson, D. W., Johnson, R. T., Laginski, A. M. & O'Coin, I. (1996). Effects on high school students of integrating conflict resolution and peer mediation training into an academic unit. *Mediation Quarterly, 14*, 21–36.

Stevahn, L., Johnson, D. W., Johnson, R. T., Oberle, K. & Wahl, L. (2000). Effects of conflict resolution training integrated into a kindergarten curriculum. *Child Development, 71*, 770–782.

Stomfay-Stitz, A. M. (1992). Fanny Fern Andrews, pioneer American peace educator and international educator. *Peace, Environment and Education, 3*(1), 56–58.

Stomfay-Stitz, A. M. (1993). Heightened awareness of peace education in American educational publications. *Peace, Environment and Education, 4*(2), 3–9.

Stomfay-Stitz, A. M. (1994). Conflict resolution and peer mediation: Pathways to safer schools. *Childhood Education, 70*, 279–282.

Stomfay-Stitz, A. M. (1994). Peace education for children: Historical perspectives. *Peace, Environment and Education, 5*(4), 28–38.

Suter, K. D. (1996). The role of education for a culture of peace. In *From a Culture of Violence to a Culture of Peace* (pp. 209–228). Paris: UNESCO.

Sweeney, B. & Carruthers, W. L. (1996). Conflict resolution: History, philosophy, theory, and education applications. *School Counselor, 43*(5), 326–344.

Toh, S.-H. (1994). Peace education in a postmodern world. In *1994 Viewpoints on War, Peace and Global Cooperation* (pp. 3–16). Milwaukee, WI: The Annual Journal of the Wisconsin Institute.

Toh, S.-H. & Floresca-Cawagas, V. (1995). Weaving a culture of peace. In H. Löfgren (Ed.), *Peace Education and Human Development* (pp. 389–408). Malmö: School of Education.

Toh, S.-H. & Floresca-Cawagas, V. (2000). Educating towards a culture of peace. In T. Goldstein & D. Selby (Eds.), *Weaving Connections* (pp. 365–387). Toronto: Sumach Press.

Torney-Purta, J. (1998). Evaluating programs designed to teach international content and negotiation skills. *International Negotiation, 3*(1), 77–97.

Van Slyck, M. & Stern, M. (1999). A developmental approach to the use of conflict resolution intervention with adolescents. In L. R. Forcey & I. M. Harris (Eds.), *Peacebuilding for adolescents* (pp. 177–193). New York: Lang.

Van Slyck, M., Stern, M. & Zak, J. (1996). Promoting optimal adolescent development through conflict resolution education, training, and practice: An innovative approach for counseling psychologists. *The Counseling Psychologist, 24*, 433–461.

Varis, T. (1995). The role of peace education and the media in the prevention of violence: A global perspective. *Thresholds in Education, 21*(2), 5–10.

Velloso, A. (1998). Peace and human rights education in the Middle East: Comparing Jewish and Palestinian experiences. *International Review of Education, 44,* 357–378.
Verbeck, P. & de Waal, F. B. M. (2001). Peacemaking among preschool children. *Peace and Conflict, 7,* 5–28.
Wahlström, R. (1992). The challenge of peace education: Replacing cultures of militarism. In E. Boulding (Ed.), *New Agendas for Peace Research* (pp. 171–183). Boulder, CO: Lynne Rienner.
Webster, D. W. (1993). The unconvincing case for school-based conflict resolution programs for adolescents. *Health Affairs Journal, 12,* 127–144.
Wegner, G. (1995). Buchenwald Concentration Camp and holocaust education for youth in the new Germany. *Journal of Curriculum and Supervision, 10* (2), 171–188.
Weigert, K. M. (1989). Peace studies as education for nonviolent social change. *The Annals of the American Academy of Political and Social Science, 504,* 37–47.
Will, D. S. (1993). Teaching peace through debunking race. *Peace and Change, 18,* 182–203.
Wulf, C. (1996). The non-deception of violence: A challenge to education. *The International Journal of Humanities and Peace, 12* (1), 69–74.

CURRICULUM MATERIALS

Aaronsohn, E. (1996). *Going Against the Grain: Supporting The Students' Centered Teacher.* Corbin Press. Case study of cooperative and community-building classroom.
Bickmore, K., Goldthwait, P. & Looney, J. (1987). *Alternatives to Violence: A Manual* (Rev. ed.). Akron, OH: Peace Grows.
Bickmore, K., Looney, J. & Goldthwait, P. (1984). *Alternatives to Violence: A Manual for Teaching Peacemaking to Youth and Adults.* Cleveland, OH: Cleveland Friends Meeting. (ED 250254.)
Bodine, R. J., Crawford, D. K. & Schrumpf, F. (1994). *Creating the Peaceable School: A Comprehensive Program for Teaching Conflict Resolution. Program guide.* Champaign, IL: Research Press.
Bodine, R. J., Crawford, D. K. & Schrumpf, F. (1994). *Creating the Peaceable School: A Comprehensive Program for Teaching Conflict Resolution. Student Manual.* Champaign, IL: Research Press.
Boulding, E., Haas, L., Morrison, M.L., Cohen, C., Turpin, L. (2001). *Making Peace Where I Live (MAPWIL).* International curriculum for 10–12 year olds based on interviewing local peacemakers. Student and teacher guide. www.crinfo.org-link to "special projects." PAMOJA-1462 Green Mountain Turnpike, Chester, VT 05143; www.pamoja.net.
Brody, E. et al. (Eds.). (1992). *Spinning Tales, Weaving Hope: Stories of Peace, Justice and the Environment.* Philadelphia, PA: New Society Publishers.
Brooks, E. & Fox, L. (1995). *Making peace: A Reading/Writing/Thinking Text on Global Community.* New York: St. Martin's Press.
Cantor, R. et al. (1997). *Days of Respect: Organizing a School-Wide Violence Prevention Program.* (Gr. 9–12.) Claremont, CA: Hunter House.
Carlebach, D. (1996). *Peace Scholars: Learning Through Literature, Grade 3.* Miami, FL: Peace Education Foundation.
Carlebach, D. & Diekmann, C. (1999). *Peace Scholars: Learning Through Literature, Grade 4.* Miami, FL: Peace Education Foundation.
Classroom Conflict Resolution: Training for Grades 3–6. (1995). San Francisco, CA: The Community Board Program.

Cohen, R. (1995). *Students Resolving Conflict: Peer mediation in schools.* Glenview, IL: Scott, Foresman.
Cohen, R. (1999). *The School Mediators Field Guide.* Watertown, MA: School Mediation Associates.
Cohen, S. (1990). *Secrecy and Democracy.* Cambridge, MA: Educators for Social Responsibility.
Cole, J., Snyder, S. et al. (1997). *Making Peace: Teaching About Conflict and Reconciliation at Key Stage 3 and 4.* Oxford, UK: Oxfam.
Condon, C. & McGinnis, J. (1988). *Helping Kids Care.* (Gr. 2–6.) St. Louis, MO: Institute for Peace and Justice.
Conflict Managers Training Manual for Grades 3–6. (1995). San Francisco, CA: Community Boards.
Conflict Resolution and Peer Mediation for Grades 4 and 5. (1995.) Chapel Hill, NC: Mediation Network of North Carolina.
Conflict Resolution: An Elementary School Curriculum. (1990). San Francisco, CA: The Community Board Program.
Conflict Resolution Education Catalogue. (1998). Washington, DC: National Institute for Dispute Resolution.
Conflict Resolution for Kindergarten Through Grade 3. (1995). Chapel Hill, NC: Mediation Network of North Carolina.
Crawford, D. & Bodine, R. (1996). *Conflict Resolution Education: A Guide to Implementing Programs in Schools, Youth-Serving Organizations, and Community and Juvenile Justice Settings.* Washington, DC: Office of Elementary and Secondary Education. (ED 404426.)
Davis, J. E., Eckenrod, J. S. & United States Institute of Peace. (1994). *Managing World Conflict: A Resource Unit for High Schools.* Washington, DC: United States Institute of Peace.
Deats, R. (2000). *Martin Luther King, Jr., Spirit-led Prophet.* Nyack, NY: Fellowship of Reconciliation.
DeBenedetti, E. (1993). *Conflict Resolution and Diversity.* Washington, DC: NAME/ NIDR.
DeMott, D. W. (1987). *Peacebuilding: A Textbook* (2nd ed.). (Gr. 9–12.) Genesco, NY: High Falls Publications.
Derman-Sparks, L. et al. (1991). *Anti-bias Curriculum: Tools for Empowering Young Children* (2nd ed.). (Preschool–Gr. 3.) Washington, DC: National Association for the Education of Young Children.
Diamond, L. & McDonald, J. (1996). *Multi-track Diplomacy— A System Approach to Peace* (3rd ed.). West Hartford, CT: Kumarian Press.
Diamond, L. (2001). *The Peace Book: 108 Simple Ways to Create a More Peaceful World.* Berkeley, CA: Conari Press.
Drew, N. (1995). *Learning the Skills of Peacemaking: A K–6 Activity Guide on Resolving Conflict, Communicating, Cooperating* (Rev. ed.). Torrance, CA: Jalmar Press.
Edelman, D. et al. (1994). *TRIBE: Conflict Resolution Curriculum for Middle School.* (Gr. 6–8.) Asheville, NC: The Mediation Center.
Elias, M. et al. (1997). *Promoting Social and Emotional Learning: Guidelines for Educators.* Alexandria, VA: Association for Supervision and Curriculum Development. 1250 N. Pitt St. 22314. http:www.ascd.org.
Felice, W.F. (1996). *Taking Suffering Seriously: The Importance of Collective Human Rights.* SUNY Series in Global Conflict and Peace Education. New York: State University of New York.
Fisher, R. & Ertel, D. (1995). *Getting Ready to Negotiate: The Getting to Yes Workbook.* New York: Penguin Books.

Fisher, R., Kopelman, E. & Schneider, A. K. (1994). *Beyond Machiavelli: Tools for Coping with Conflict.* Cambridge, MA: Harvard University Press.
Fisher, R. & Stone, D. (1990). *Working it Out: A Handbook on Negotiation for High School Students.* Cambridge, MA: Harvard Law School.
Fisher, R., Ury, W. & Patton, B. (1991). *Getting to Yes: Negotiating Agreement Without Giving In* (2nd ed.). New York: Penguin Books.
Fitzell, S. (1998). *Free the Children! Conflict Resolution Education for Strong, Peaceful Minds.* Philadelphia: New Society Publishers.
Fletcher, R. (1986). *Teaching Peace: Skills for Living in a Global Society.* (For upper elementary and junior high school students.) San Francisco, CA: Harper & Row.
A Force More Powerful: A Century of Nonviolent Conflict. Study guide. (2000). Washington, DC: Greater Washington Educational Telecommunications Association.
Froschl, M. et al. (1998). *Quit It! A Teacher's Guide on Teasing and Bullying for Use with Students in Grades K–3.* Wellesley, MA: Wellesley College, Center of Research on Women.
Girard, K. & Koch, S. J. (1996). *Conflict Resolution in the Schools: A Manual for Educators.* San Francisco, CA: Jossey-Bass.
Goodman, A. and Smyth, F. (1994). *Nickelodeon's The Big Help Book: 365 Ways You Can Make a Difference by Volunteering!* Tappan, N.J.: Paramount Publishing. 200 Old Tappan Road, Old Tappan, N.J. 07675.
Guerra, N. G., Moore, A. & Slaby, R. G. (1995). *Viewpoints: A Guide to Conflict Resolution and Decision Making for Adolescents.* Champaign, IL: Research Press. (With a separate teacher's guide.)
Halligan, J. (1998). *Conflict Resolution: A Secondary School Curriculum for Grades 7–12* (Rev. ed.). San Francisco, CA: The Community Board Program.
Hedrick, H. K. & The Colorado School Mediation Project. (1997). *Productive Conflict Resolution: A Comprehensive Curriculum and Teacher's Guide for Conflict Resolution Education, Grades 3–5.* Boulder, CO: Colorado School Mediation Project.
Heydenberk, W. & Heydenberk, R. (2000). *A Powerful Peace: The Integrative Thinking Classroom.* Needham Heights, MA: Allyn & Bacon.
High School Mediation Roleplays. (1997). Boulder, CO: Colorado School Mediation Project.
I Dream of Peace: Images of War by Children of Former Yugoslavia. (1994). New York: UNICEF, HarperCollins.
Johnson, D. W. & Johnson, R. T. (1991). *Teaching Children to Be Peacemakers.* Edina, MN: Interaction Book.
Johnson, J. M. & Prutzman, P. (1998). *CCRC's Friendly Classroom Mediation Manual: School Mediation From Planning to Practice.* Nyack, NY: Creative Response to Conflict.
Johnson, J. M. & Prutzman, P. (1998). *CCRC's Student Mediation Resource Guide.* Nyack, NY: Creative Response to Conflict.
Kivel, P. et al. (1997). *Making the Peace: A 15-Session Violence Prevention Curriculum for Young People.* (Gr. 9–12.) Claremont, CA: Hunter House.
Klare, M. T. (Ed.). (1994). *Peace and World Security Studies: A Curriculum Guide* (6th ed.). Boulder, CO: Lynne Rienner.
Kraybill, R. S. with Evans, A. F. & Evans, R. A. (2001). *Peace Skills: A Manual for Community Mediators.* San Francisco, CA: Jossey-Bass.
Kreidler, W. J. (1995). *Teaching Conflict Resolution Through Children's Literature.* (Gr. K–2.) New York: Scholastic.
Kreidler, W. J. (1997). *Conflict Resolution in the Middle School: A Curriculum and Teacher's Guide.* Cambridge, MA: Educators for Social Responsibility.
Kreidler, W. J. (1984). *Creative Conflict Resolution: More Than 200 Activities for Keeping Peace in the Classroom K–6.* Glenview, IL: Scott, Foresman.

Kreidler, W. J. (1990). *Elementary Perspectives 1: Teaching Concepts of Peace and Conflict.* (Gr. K–6.) Cambridge, MA: Educators for Social Responsibility.

Kreidler, W. J. & Poliner, R. A. (1999). *Conflict Resolution in the Middle School: Student Workbook & Journal* (2nd ed.). (Gr. 6–8.) Cambridge, MA: Educators for Social Responsibility.

Kreidler, W. J. et al. (1990). *Peace Studies Curriculum: Handbook/Index.* Millwood, NY: Kraus International Publications.

Kreidler, W. J. et al. (1997). *Adventures in Peacemaking: A Conflict Resolution Activity Guide for Early Childhood Providers.* Cambridge, MA: Educators for Social Responsibility.

Kreidler, W. J., Furlong, L. et al. (1995). *Adventures in Peacemaking: A Conflict Resolution Activity Guide for School-Age Programs.* (Gr. K–6.) Cambridge, MA: Educators for Social Responsibility.

Lamy, S. L. et al. (1990). *Teaching About Global Awareness With Simulations and Games. Grades 6–12.* (Updated.) Denver, CO: Center for Teaching International Relations.

Lantieri, L. & Patti, J. (1996). *Waging Peace in Our Schools.* Boston, MA: Beacon Press.

Lantieri, L. & Roderick, T. (1995). *Peace in the Family: A Training Manual for the Parent Component of the Resolving Conflict Creatively Program.* New York: RCCP National Center.

Lantieri, L., Roderick, T. & Ray, P. (1990). *Resolving Conflict Creatively: A Draft Teaching Guide for Alternative High Schools.* New York: Educators for Social Responsibility.

Lantieri, L., Roderick, T., Ray, P. & Alson, S. (1993). *Resolving Conflict Creatively: A Teaching Guide for Grades Kindergarten Through Six.* New York: Educators for Social Responsibility. (This is a revised version of Lantieri & Roderick, 1988.)

Levin, D. E. (1994). *Teaching Young Children in Violent Times: Building a Peaceable Classroom.* (Gr. K–3.) Cambridge, MA: Educators for Social Responsibility.

Levy, B. (1984). *Skills for Violence-Free Relationships: Curriculum for Young People Ages 13–18.* Santa Monica, CA: Southern California Coalition of Battered Women.

Lewis, B. and Espeland. P (ed.). (1995). *The Kids' Guide to Service Projects: Over 500 Service Ideas for Young People Who Want to Make a Difference.* Minneapolis: Free Spirit Publishing. 612-338-2068.

Lieber, C. M. (1994). *Making Choices About Conflict, Security, and Peacemaking. Part I: Personal Perspectives. A High School Conflict Resolution Curriculum.* Cambridge, MA: Educators for Social Responsibility.

Lieber, C. M. (1996). *Making Choices About Conflict, Security, and Peacemaking. Part II: From Local to Global Perspectives.* Cambridge, MA: Educators for Social Responsibility.

Lieber, C. M. with Lantieri, L. & Roderick, T. (1998). *Conflict Resolution in the High School: 36 Lessons.* (Gr. 9–12.) Cambridge, MA: Educators for Social Responsibility.

Looney, J. (1995). *Workbook for the Course in Peaceful Conflict Resolution: Alternatives to Violence.* Akron, OH: Peace Grows.

Luvmour, S. & J. (1990). *Everyone Wins! Cooperative Games and Activities.* Philadelphia, PA: New Society Publishers.

Macbeth, F. & Fine, N. (1995). *Playing with Fire: Creative Conflict Resolution for Young Adults.* Philadelphia, PA: New Society Publishers.

MacDonald, M. R. (1992). *Peace Tales: World Folktales to Talk About.* Hamden, CT: Linnet Books.

McCarthy, C. (2002). *I'd Rather Teach Peace.* Maryknoll, NY: Orbis Books.

McGinnis, J. (1997). *Educating for Peace and Justice: K–5.* St. Louis, MO: Institute for Peace and Justice.

McGinnis, J. (2000). *Creating Circles of Peace: Alternatives to Violence Kit for Public*

Schools: K–5. St. Louis, MO: Institute for Peace and Justice. (Original publication date 1997.)

Mertz, G. & Lieber, C. M. (2001). *Conflict in Context: Understanding Local to Global Security and Peacemaking.* (Gr. 9–12.) Cambridge, MA: Educators for Social Responsibility.

Minkler, J. (1998). *Active Citizenship: Empowering America's Youth. Social Studies Curriculum for Grades 7–12.* Coarsegold, CA: Center for Multicultural Cooperation.

Moger, S. (1998). *Teaching the Diary of Anne Frank: An In-depth Resource for Learning About the Holocaust Through the Writings of Anne Frank.* New York: Scholastic.

Newman, F. and Weissbrodt, D. (1996). *International Human Rights Law, Policy and Process*, 2nd edition. Cincinnati: Anderson Publishing Co.

Oakland Men's Project. (1992.) *Helping Teens Stop Violence.* Alemeda, CA: Hunter House.

Paley, V. B. (1999). *The Kindness of Children.* Cambridge: Harvard University Press.

People Building Peace: 35 Inspiring Stories from Around the World. (1999). Utrecht, The Netherlands: European Centre for Conflict Prevention.

Pirtle, S. (1998). *Discovery Time for Cooperation and Conflict Resolution* (Includes activities on bias awareness and the expressive arts for Kindergarten through grade 8). Nyack, NY: Children's Creative Response to Conflict Program.

Pirtle, S. (1998). *Linking Up! Using Music, Movement and Language Arts to Promote Caring, Cooperation, and Communication. Pre-K Through Grade 3.* Cambridge, MA: Educators for Social Responsibility.

Poliner, R. A. & Benson, J. (1997). *Dialogue: Turning Controversy Into Community. A Curriculum for Secondary Schools.* Cambridge, MA: Educators for Social Responsibility.

Porro, B. (1996). *Talk It Out: Conflict Resolution in the Elementary Classroom.* Alexandria, VA: Association for Supervision and Curriculum Development.

Prutzman, P., Johnson, J. M. & Fountain, S. (1998). *CCRC's Friendly Classrooms and Communities for Young Children: A Manual of Conflict Resolution Activities and Resources.* Nyack, NY: Creative Response to Conflict.

Reardon, B. A. (1995). *Educating for Human Dignity: Learning About Rights and Responsibilities. A K–12 Teaching Resource.* Philadelphia, PA: University of Pennsylvania Press.

Reardon, B. A. (1997). *Tolerance—The Threshold of Peace.* (3 volumes.) (Also available in French and Spanish.) [Unit 1: Teacher-training resource unit; Unit 2: Primary-school resource unit; Unit 3: Secondary school resource unit.] Paris: UNESCO.

Reardon, B. A. (Ed.). (1988). *Educating for Global Responsibility: Teacher-Designed Curricula for Peace Education, K–12.* New York: Teachers College Press.

Reardon, B. A. & Tierney, J. F. (1990). *Teaching Peace: A Study Guide for The Conquest of War.* Scarsdale, NY: Alternative Defense Project. *Recommended standards for school-based peer mediation programs.* (1996). Washington, DC: NAME/NIDR.

Resolving Conflict: Activities for Grades K–3. (1995). Albuquerque, NM: New Mexico Center for Dispute Resolution.

Respecting Differences: Stepping Stones to Peace. (1992). Miami, FL: Peace Education Foundation.

Rethinking Schools. *Rethinking Our Classrooms: Teaching for Equity and Justice.* Milwaukee, WI: Rethinking Schools, Ltd.

Rigby, K. (2001). *Stop the Bullying: A Handbook for Teachers.* Portland, ME: Stenhouse Publishers.

Schmidt, F. (1997). *Kid Peace Action Network and the Peace Reporters.* (Grades 5–6.) Miami, FL: Peace Education International.

Schmidt, F. (2000).*We Can Work It Out! Creating Peace in the Home.* Miami, FL: Peace Education International.

Schmidt, F. (2001). *Youth Peace Ambassadors: Building Bridges of Peace: A Facilitator's Guide.* Miami, FL: Peace Education International.

Schmidt, F. & Friedman, A. (1991). *Creative Conflict Solving for Kids: Grades 3–4.* Miami, FL: Peace Education Foundation.

Schmidt, F. & Friedman, A. (1993; 1st ed. 1988). *Peacemaking Skills for Little Kids Pre-K–2.* Miami, FL: Peace Education Foundation.

Schmidt, F. & Friedman, A. (1996). *Fighting fair: Dr. Martin Luther King, Jr., for Kids* (3rd ed.). Miami, FL: Peace Education Foundation. (1st ed., 1986.)

Schrumpf, F., Crawford, D. & Bodine, R. J. (1997). *Peer Mediation: Conflict Resolution in Schools. Program Guide. Student Manual* (Rev. ed.). Champaign, IL: Resource Press.

Short, D. et al. (1996). *Conflict in World Cultures: An Integrated Language, Social Studies and Cultural Unit for Middle School World Studies.* Washington, DC: Center for Applied Linguistics.

Silcox, H. (1993). *A How-To Guide to Reflection: Adding Cognitive Learning to Community Service Programs.* Brighton Press. 215-357-5861

Slaby, R. et al. (1995). *Early Violence Prevention Program: Tools for Teachers of Young Children.* Washington D.C.: NAEYC.

Smith, C. A. (1993). *The Peaceful Classroom: 162 Easy Activities to Teach Preschoolers Compassion and Cooperation.* Mt. Rainier, MD: Gryphon House.

Stein, N. & Sjostrom, L. (1996). *Bullyproof—A Teacher's Guide on Teasing and Bullying for Use with Fourth and Fifth Grade.* Wellesley, MA: Wellesley College, Center of Research on Women.

Stephens, L.S. (1995). *The Complete Guide to Learning Through Community Service: Grades K–9.* Allyn and Bacon 800-278-3525.

Stern-LaRosa, C. and Bettman, E.H. (2001). *Hate Hurts.* Washington D.C.: Anti-Defamation League. www.adl.org.

True, M. (1992). *To Construct Peace: 30 More Justice Seekers, Peace Makers.* Mystic, CT: Twenty-Third Publications.

United Nations Association of the United States of America. (1992). *Basic Facts about the United Nations.* New York: United Nations Publications.

Violence Intervention Curriculum for Families. (1996). Albuquerque, NM: New Mexico Center for Dispute Resolution.

Walsh, D. (1994). *Selling Out American's Children: How America Puts Profits Before Values—and What Parents Can Do.* Minneapolis: Fairview Press.

Walter, V. A. (1993). *War and Peace Literature for Children and Young Adults: A Resource Guide to Significant Issues.* Phoenix, AZ: Oryx Press.

Webster-Doyle, T. (1991). *Why is Everybody Always Picking on Me? A Guide to Understanding Bullies for Young People.* Middlebury, VT: Atrium Society.

Webster-Doyle, T. (1993). *Operation Warhawks: How Young People Become Warriors.* Middlebury, VT: Atrium Society.

Webster-Doyle, T. & Russ, A. (1993). *War: What Is It Good For? A School Curriculum.* Middlebury, VT: Atrium Society.

Whalen, Lucille. (1990). *Human Rights: A Reference Handbook.* Santa Barbara, CA: ABC-CLIO, Inc.

PEACE PLACES—SOURCES FOR TRAINING/RESOURCES

ACT—Adults and Children Together
http://www.ActAgainstViolence.org. Washington, D.C. American Psychological Association and National Association for the Education of Young Children. An ongoing project providing community-based training for early childhood violence prevention.

Bibliography and Resource Guide—Peace Places 287

Amnesty International
http://www.hrusa.org. For information on worldwide human rights abuses and what to do about them.

Anti-Bullying Resources
Stenhouse Publishers. PO Box 360, York, ME 03909. 1-888-363-0566.
Wellesley Center for Research on Women. Publications Department. Wellesley College, 106 Central Street, Wellesley, MA 02481. 1-781-283-2510.

The Association for Conflict Resolution
1527 New Hampshire Ave., Washington, D.C., 20036. 202-667-9700. http://www.acresolution.org. A professional organization devoted to enhancing the practice and public understanding of conflict resolution. Merger of the Academy of Family Mediators, the Conflict Resolution Education Network and the Society of Professionals in Dispute Resolution. Provides resources, workshops, seminars and conferences. Has regional chapters.

Center for Conflict Transformation
47 Vine Street, Hartford, CT. 860-246-3369. Margysk@aol.com. Multi-faith, multi-ethnic organization devoted to issues around community conflict transformation. Train police, community leaders, youth and adults.

Center For Defense Information
1779 Massachusetts Avenue NW, Washington, D.C., 202-332-0600. www.cdi.org. Staffed by former military personnel, a clearinghouse for inside information on the Pentagon and on military issues worldwide.

Center on Conscience and War
1830 Connecticut Ave., Washington, D.C., 202-483-2220. www.nisbco.org. Provides information on how to document one's convictions as a conscientious objector to war.

Center for Teaching Peace
4501 Van Ness St. Washington, D.C., 20016. 202-537-1372. Founded by former *Washington Post* columnist Colman McCarthy, works with schools and individuals to begin or expand educational courses on nonviolence at all levels.

Creative Response to Conflict
Children's Creative Response to Conflict, Box 271, 521 North Broadway, Nyack, NY, 10960. 914-353-1796. Fax 914-358-4924. ccrcnyack@aol.com. "Pioneers" in teaching and training materials for conflict resolution. Extensive curricula and trainings.

Curriculum of Hope Project of the Delta Kappa Gamma Society International
C/O Jeanne Morascini and Lisa Young, Storrs, CT, 860-487-1067.
A Connecticut based, grass-roots project; publishes a newsletter packed with resources and information for peace educators worldwide; multi-culturalism, ecology, and peace.

Earth Charter Initiative
http://www.earthcharter.org. Resources and teaching aids for ecology, the Earth Charter initiative and sustainable development.

Educators for Social Responsibility
23 Garden Street, Cambridge, MA 02138. 617-492-1764. http://www.esrnational.org. Originally begun several decades ago for education in a nuclear age, now has evolved to

be a premier organization devoted to conflict resolution and education for social responsibility.

Fellowship of Reconciliation
Box 271, Nyack, NY, 10960. 845-358-4601. FOR@forusa.org. www.forusa.org. An ecumenical faith-based organization addressing issues around peace and social justice. Publishes *Fellowship* magazine.

Free Spirit Publishing
1-800-735-7323. www.freespirit.com. Publications include: *I'm Like You, You're Like Me: A Child's Book About Understanding and Celebrating Each Other; The Bully Classroom: Over 100 Tips and Strategies for Teachers K-8; Classroom Etiquette: 10 Ways to be a Civilized Student* (poster)—designed for middle school and up.

Friends of Peace Pilgrim
7350 Dorado Canyon Road, Somerset, CA, 95684. 530-620-0333. www.peace-pilgrim.org. An American who walked thousands of miles for peace, in sneakers across America, Peace Pilgrim left behind an educational group distributing books and resources on nonviolence and pacifism.

Friendship Through Education
http://www.grindshiptrougheducation.org.

Global Education Associates
http://www.globaleduc.org. Organization devoted to educating for global peace and understanding. Sponsors international exchanges and publishes a newsletter.

Growing Communities for Peace
PO Box 248, Scandia, MN 55073-0248. http://www.peacemaker.org. Peace literature and resources. Oral histories of community peacemakers and activists.

Hague Appeal for Peace
http://www.haguepeace.org. Hague Appeal for Peace and Justice in the 21st Century identifies 50 key action steps related to: root causes of war and a culture of peace; human rights issues; prevention and transformation of violent conflict; disarmament and human security. Lessons for youth of all ages.

Help Increase the Peace Project
4806 York Road, Baltimore, MD, 21212. 410-323-7200. Program of the American Friends Service Committee—Mid Atlantic Region. Aimed at conflict transformation for middle and high school age. Adaptable to younger ages. Based on a Quaker model used in prisons (Alternatives to Violence-AVP).

Human Rights Education Associates
http://www.hrea.org.

Human Rights, Refugees and UNHCR: A Teachers' Guide
cyberschoolbus@un.org. Published by the United Nations High Commission for Refugees, Public Information Section, CP 2500, 1211 Geneva 2 Depot, Switzerland. Teachers' kit designed to help educators prepare lessons which demonstrate the relationship between refugee protection and human rights.

Human Rights Watch
http://www.hrw.org. Nonprofit, nongovernmental organization dedicated to the pro-

tection of human rights worldwide; investigates and exposes human rights violations and holds abusers accountable.

Institute for Defense and Disarmament Studies
675 Massachusetts Avenue, Cambridge, MA 02139. 617-354-1450. www.idds.org. Works with other public interest groups to develop a new approach to preventing war and terrorism.

The Joan B. Kroc Institute for International Peace Studies
100 Hesburgh Center for International Studies, University of Notre Dame, PO Box 639, Notre Dame, IN, 46556-0639. 219-631-6970. www.nd.edu/~krocinst.

Learning to Give: A Project for the Mind
The Council of Michigan Foundations, 630 Harvey Street, Muskegon, MI, 49442-2398. 231-767-8600. www.learningtogive.org. Over 500 lessons involving philanthropy for pre-K through high school. Connects lessons with academic content to meet established standards.

Lion and the Lamb Project
http://www.lionlamb.org. Offers parents and educators resources on nonviolent toy alternatives, information about dealing with violence in children's entertainment and activism opportunities.

Making Peace Where I Live (MAPWIL).
http://www.crinfo.org-link to "special projects" or contact Pamoja at http://www.-pamoja.net. International peace education curriculum utilizing the teaching of oral history skills so that young people might interview peacemakers in their local communities.

Mapping Our World
http://mappingourworld.org/. children worldwide use drawing, writing, photography and video to describe their lives. Education kit features activities on children's rights, art and child labor.

National Peace Foundation
666 Eleventh St. NW, Washington, D.C. 20001, 800-237-3223. www.nationalpeace.org. Among its many activities, includes programs in schools for nonviolence, mediation and conflict resolution.

Nuclear Age Peace Foundation
1187 Coast Village Rd., Santa Barbara, CA, 93108. 805-965-2794. www.wagingpeace.org. Education and advocacy group specializing in nuclear arms reduction and elimination.

Pax Educare— The Connecticut Center for Peace Education
129 Penn Drive, West Hartford, CT, 06119. 860 232-2966. Marylee898@attbi.com. Newly emerging peace library and educational resource center, to link educators, practitioners, academics and activists. Consults on curricula and resources, conducts trainings. Mediation and counseling on conflict and reconciliation issues. Mary Lee Morrison, Founder, Director.

Peace Education Foundation
1900 Biscayne Blvd. Miami, FL, 33132. 800-749-8838. www.peaceeducation.com. Regional and on-site training programs in conflict resolution and mediation for elementary, middle and high schools.

Peace Education International
http://www.peaceeducationintl.com. Florida-based project with materials for educators, parents and children. Director, Fran Schmidt. Includes curricula and manuals for elementary and middle school young people.

Plowshares Institute
PO Box 242, Simsbury, CT, 06070. 860 651-4304. evansrob@hartsem.edu. Faith-based international teaching and training institute devoted to issues around conflict transformation and reconciliation. Local and national trainings as well. Much of their work has been done in South Africa.

Resources for Peace Web Page
http://members.aol.com/rasphila/peace.html. Provides over 175 links to peace and social justice groups and resources.

Rethinking Schools
www.rethinkingschools.org. 1-800-669-4192. Progressive resources and curricula ideas. Publishes a newsletter. Recent publications include: *Reading, Writing and Rising Up: Teaching about Social Justice and the Power of the Written Word* by Linda Christensen (2000), lesson plans and student writing focusing on issues of social justice. Suitable for high school.

Rights Works
joyceapsel@hotmail.com. Teaches about human rights and promotes cooperative and caring learning. Workshops for teachers and students. Director, Joyce Apsel.

Second Nature: Education for Sustainability
http://www.secondnature.org. Resources and teaching aids for educating for a sustainable world.

School of the Americas Watch
PO Box 4566, Washington, D.C., 20017. 202-234-3440. www.soaw.org. An independent organization seeking to close the U.S. Army School of the Americas, recently renamed, where alleged training of Latin American terrorists has historically occurred.

School Mediator Newsletter
http://www.schoolmediation.com. Free on-line newsletter from School Mediation Associates.

Southern Poverty Law Center
http:www.tolerance.org. 400 Washington Ave., Montgomery, AL 36104. Fax 334-264-7310. Headquarters of the Teaching for Tolerance Program. Extensive literature and curricula related to bias, hate crimes, cultural diversity, human and civil rights.

Together, One World: My United Nations, Cut Paste and Play Book
UN Dept. of Public Information 2001. Contact: Public Inquiries Unit GA, 57 United Nations, New York, NY, 10017. Thirty-six page activity book designed to teach elementary children about the United Nations and about the world in which we live. Introduces different cultures, global issues and what can be done to make our world better.

UNESCO
http://www.unesco.org

UNICEF
http://www.unicef.org

United Nations Association—USA
Publications Department, UNA-USA, 801 Second Ave., New York, NY 10017-4706. 212-907-1300. www.unausa.org/publications. Resources for high school Model United Nations programs.

The United Nations International Decade for a Culture of Peace and Nonviolence for the Children of the World
cp@unesco.org. www.unesco.org/iycp.

United Nations High Commissioner for Refugees
Public Information Section, UNHCR, PO Box 2500, 1211 Geneva 2, Switzerland. www.unhcr.ch. Helps students 9 years and up better understand what it is like to be one of the almost 23 million people who live in exile. Includes LEGO people to make the connections with human rights. A section for teachers.

Wilmington College Peace Resource Center
Wilmington College, Pyle Center Box 1183, Wilmington, OH, 45177. 937-382-6661 ext. 371. http://www.wilmington.edu/peaceRC.htm. Resources and educational materials; a lending library for materials and films. Publishes a newsletter with many sources.

FILMS

Folktales of Peace, Mennonite Central Committee, 27 S. 12th St., Akron, PA, 17501. 717-859-1151. www.mcc.org/respub.html. 2 films, 22 and 28 minutes.

A Force More Powerful: A Century of Nonviolence Conflict-Films for the Humanities and Sciences, P.O. Box 2053, Princeton, N.J. 08543. 800-257-5126. www.films.com. 2 films, 90 minutes each.

I and II—Integrating Conflict Resolution into the Elementary School Community. Friends School of Minnesota, 3244 34th Ave., South Minneapolis, MN, 55406. 612-722-2046. www.fsm.pvt.k12.mn.us. 34 minutes.

In Search of Peace Part One: 1948–1967, Museum of Tolerance, 800-553-4474. giftshop@wiesenthal.com. A chronicle of the first two decades of Israel's existence. Insights on the Middle East conflict and events in Israel, an Arab refugee camp, the UN and world capitals.

Mahatma Gandhi: Pilgrim of Peace, A and E Television Network, New Video Group, 126 Fifth Ave., New York, NY, 10011. store.aetv.com. 50 minutes.

Index

Adams, D. 118, 119, 125
Adcock, C. 236
Addams, J. 86
Adult Education 161–162, 206
Affinity Groups 95
Alternatives to Violence Program (AVP) 130
American Association of Educational Research 104
American Federation of Teachers 104
American Peace Society 55, 56
American Psychological Association 172
American School Citizen League 198
American School Peace League 56, 198
Anglo-American Agreement 55
Annan, K. 127
Apeslagh, R. 189
Apple, M. 88
Arendt, H. 220
Associated School Project 77
Association for Supervision and Development 104
Atoms for Peace 169

Bahá'í 1, 44
Bahá'u'lláh 1
Banneke, B. 55
Barash, D. 118
Bartelds, C. 176
Bay, C. 92
Belmonte, T. 171
Berman, S. 146
Bhagavad Gita 42

Bjerstedt, Åke 271
Blue Helmeted Troops 121–122
Borer, T. 132
Boulding, E. 38, 39, 53, 61, 62, 67, 123, 124, 127, 131, 146, 147, 149, 152, 208, 209–210, 236, 241
Boulding, K. 7, 54, 227
Bowers, C.A. 68
Brem, I. 179
Brocke-Utne, B. 53, 149
Bryan, W.J. 56
Buddhism 41–42
Burns, R. 189
Bush, G. 229

Capra, F. 231–232
Carnegie Endowment for International Peace 56
Cato Institute 240
Center for Non Violence and Peace Studies, the University of Rhode Island 133
Center for Research on Conflict Resolution 54
Children's Creative Response to Conflict 130
Chomsky, N. 169
Christianity 43–44
Churches 79
Claycomb, M. 228
Coleman, J. 94
Comenius 45, 46
Compassionate Listening 68
Congress of Racial Equality (CORE) 58

Consortium on Peace, Research, Education and Development (COPRED) 54
Cooperation in the classroom 216–218
Council for Education in World Citizenship 103
Counts, G. 86
Cox, B. 165
Critical Thinking 220–222
Culture of Peace 17, 23, 125, 240
Curle, A. 67
Curriculum of Hope Project of the Delta Kappa Gamma Society 271

Dahrendorf, R. 29
Dalai Lama 13
De Bono, E. 22
de Chardin, T. 45, 50, 176, 238
Democratic classrooms 214–216. 225
Descartes, R. 197
Dewey, J. 57, 85, 86, 94, 97, 102, 141, 210, 218
Diaz, J. 168
Diffusion of conflict 129
Dolci, D. 45, 50, 94

Earth Cbarter 240
Ebwert, T. 84
Eco-Justice 239–241
Economist 127
ECOSOC (United Nations Economic and Social Council) 127
educare 29
Educators for Social Responsibility 103, 114
Einstein, A. 58
Eisenhower, D.D. 28, 120
Ekhardt, W. 174, 179
Elizondo, V. 196
Eramsus, D. 45–46
Erikson, E. 160
Evaluation of peace education 177–184

Falk, R. 126
Fellowship of Reconciliation 53, 58
Feminism 61, 236–238
Fisher, R. 130
Five College Consortium 105
Franklin, B. 55
Freire, P. 51, 210
Freud, S. 118, 174

Friendly Classroom for a Small Planet 60, 130
Futurism 228–231

Gaia 123
Galtung, J. 45, 51–52, 223, 234
Gandhi, M. 15, 21, 29, 38, 115, 134–138, 145
Gartman, P. 188
Gilligan, C. 153, 154
Giroux, H. 90
Global Education Associates 123
Goodman, P. 220
Gorbachev, M. 183
Gorman, M. 223
Greer, C. 89
Gregor, T. 33
Groff, L. 13
Groome, T. 166

Haavelsrud, M. 92, 207
Habermas, J. 86
Harris, I. 62, 95, 114, 175, 183, 271
Healy, S. 158
Heater, D. 69
Hebrew Bible 40–41
Heisenberg, W. 167
Help Increase the Peace Project (HIPP) 130
Highlander School 86–87
Hindu/Hinduism 42–43
Hiroshima Institute for Peace Education 103
Hook, G.D. 169

Institution building (Peace through politics) 17, 22–24
International Peace Research Association (IPRA) 54, 125, 128
Islam 44

James, W. 1
Jaspers, C. 58
Jesus 20, 115
Johnson, D. and R. 212
Jung, C. 66
Just War Theory 43

Kahn, H. 230
Kalinaw Mindanao 133
Kant, I. 45, 46

Kauffman, D. 227
King, M.L., Jr. 15, 21, 38, 59–60, 115, 133, 134–137, 143
Kohlberg, L. 152–153
Kovel, J. 197
Krishnamurti, J. 134, 137–138
Kubler-Ross, E. 185–187
Kumor-D'souza, C. 87

Lacey, P. 215
Lall, B.G. 30
Lasswell, H. 168–169
Lazlo, E. 96
League of Nations 123, 124
Lentz Institute 54
Levin, D. 172
Levinson, D. 160
Lifton, R.J. 158, 185
Lorenz, K. 117

Machiavelli 199
MacMillan, H. 28
Macy, J. 186
Mandela, N. 131
Martin, J.R. 62, 150
Martin Luther King Center 129
McIntyre, M. 233–234
Melman, S. 121
Merton, T. 169
Miles, L. 1
Mische, P. 232
Montessori, M. 45, 48–49, 88, 150, 183, 208–209, 223
Moral Sensitivity 218–220
Morrison, M.L. 104
Morton, M. 189
Munoz, T. 30
Muste, A.J. 58
Myers-Walls, J. 148

Nash, H. 204
Nastase, A. 31
National Catholic Reporter 271
National Defense Education Act 59
National Educational Association (NEA) 104
Nevo, B. 179
New York Peace Society 55
Newman, F. 88–89
Newton, I. 197
Nobel Peace Prize 56

Noddings, N. 62, 150, 151
Nonviolence 20–22
Nuclear Posture Review (NPR) 229

Orr, D. 69
Otto, H. 158

Pacifism 17, 20–2
Passad, D. 209
Patriarchy 237
Peace Education Commission 128
Peace Strategies 16
Peace Studies 80
Peace Through Justice 17, 19–20
Peace Through Strength 17–19
Peace Through Sustainability 17, 24–25
Peacebuilding 11, 17, 25
Peacekeeping 11, 15
Peacemaking 11, 17
Pestalozzi 46–47
Physicians for Social Responsibility 26
Piaget, J. 146
Polak, F. 228
Proverbs, book of 37

Quakers 21, 53, 54–55, 60
Qualitative Research 180–181
Quantitative Research 180

Raven, P. 240
Reagan, T. 2
Read, H. 45, 49–50
Reagan, R. 120, 183
Reardon, B. 30, 53, 62, 67, 149, 189, 191, 201–202, 203, 227
Remy, R. 94
Reproductive Theory 87, 88
Reserve Officers Training Corps (ROTC) 204
Resolving Conflict Creatively Program (RCCP) 74
Richardson, R. 92, 112
Rogers, E. 26
Ruddick, S. 149, 151, 236
Rush, B. 55
Rwanda 29

S-Shaped Cumulative Curve 26–27
Schmitt, K. 188
Schmookler, A. 119
Schubert, W. 110

Schweitzer, A. 238
Scott, P.D. 167
Scruton, R. 165
Shalom 41
Shapiro, S. 90
Sharp, G. 90, 235
Sloan, D. 31
Smoker, P. 13
Somlai, P. 148
Spender, D. 171
Spinoza, B. 1
Spirituality 238
Star Wars 234
Stern, M. 182
Stomfay-Stitz, A. 271
Structural Violence 12
Sumner, W. 21
Swee Hin, T. 133

Taoism 42, 237
Teachers College Peace Education Program 113
Thich Nhat Hanh 13
Thoreau, H. 55–56
Tolstoy, L. 45, 47–48, 56
Total Language 169
Transformation Scenario 231–232
Truth and Reconciliation Commissions 131, 132
Tufts University 115
Typology of War and Peace 211

UNESCO (United Nations Educational, Scientific and Cultural Organization) 9, 22–23, 70, 76–77, 103, 125–126, 127

Union of International Associations 127
United Nations 22–23, 71, 76–78, 123–126
United States Institute of Peace 23–24, 61
United States Patriots Act 191
Universal Declaration of Human Rights 67
Ury, W. 130

Van Slyck, M. 182

Wa Nkongola, M. 91
Wagner, T. 144
War on Terrorism 122
Warnock, D. 237
Weston, B. 65
Whorf, B. 168
Wilson, W. 53
Wink, W. 21
Women's International League for Peace and Freedom (WILPF) 53, 127
Women's Strike for Peace 59
World Council for Curriculum Instruction 103
World Court 126
World Studies 112, 123

Yang 237
Yin 237
Young, N. 84
Young Women's Christian Association (YWCA) 127

Zehr, H. 132